The Time, Place, and Purpose
of the Deuteronomistic History

Program in Judaic Studies
Brown University
Box 1826
Providence, RI 02912

BROWN JUDAIC STUDIES

Edited by

David C. Jacobson
Ross S. Kraemer
Saul M. Olyan
Michael L. Satlow

Number 347

THE TIME, PLACE, AND PURPOSE
OF THE DEUTERONOMISTIC HISTORY
The Evidence of "Until This Day"

by
Jeffrey C. Geoghegan

# The Time, Place, and Purpose of the Deuteronomistic History

## The Evidence of "Until This Day"

Jeffrey C. Geoghegan

Brown Judaic Studies
Providence, Rhode Island

© 2006 Brown University. All rights reserved.

No part of this work may be reproduced or transmitted in any form or by any means, electronic or mechanical, including photocopying and recording, or by means of any information storage or retrieval system, except as may be expressly permitted by the 1976 Copyright Act or in writing from the publisher. Requests for permission should be addressed in writing to the Rights and Permissions Office, Program in Judaic Studies, Brown University, Box 1826, Providence, RI 02912, USA.

*Library of Congress Cataloging-in-Publication Data*

Geoghegan, Jeffrey C.
   The time, place, and purpose of the Deuteronomistic history : the evidence of "until this day" / Jeffrey C. Geoghegan.
     p. cm. — (Brown Judaic studies ; no. 347)
   Includes bibliographical references and index.
   ISBN-13: 978-1-930675-27-8 (cloth binding : alk. paper)
   ISBN-10: 1-930675-27-5 (cloth binding : alk. paper)
   1. Deuteronomistic history (Biblical criticism) 2. Bible. O.T.
—Historiography. 3. Jews—History—To 586 B.C.—Historiography.
I. Title.
BS1286.5.G46 2006
221.6'7—dc22

                                                    2006029495

Printed in the United States of America
on acid-free paper

This book is lovingly dedicated to my parents,
John K. Geoghegan and Faith J. Geoghegan,
whose love toward one another and others has
served as a source of blessing from my earliest
memories "until this day."

יְבָרֶכְךָ יי וְיִשְׁמְרֶךָ
יָאֵר יי פָּנָיו אֵלֶיךָ וִיחֻנֶּךָּ
יִשָּׂא יי פָּנָיו אֵלֶיךָ
וְיָשֵׂם לְךָ שָׁלוֹם

# Contents

*List of Abbreviations* .................................................. xi

*List of Tables and Figures* ............................................. xv

*Acknowledgments* ..................................................... xvii

Introduction: "Until This Day": A Biblical Problem Reexamined ....... 1

1 • "Until This Day" and Biblical Scholarship ...................... 9
    A Survey of Biblical Scholarship on "Until This Day" ........ 10
        1. Early Jewish Scholarship and "Until This Day" ......... 10
        2. Early Christian Scholarship and "Until This Day" ....... 18
        3. Reformation Scholarship and "Until This Day" ......... 23
        4. Enlightenment Scholarship and "Until This Day" ....... 27
        5. Nineteenth-Century Scholarship
            and "Until This Day" ............................. 32
        6. Twentieth-Century Scholarship
            and "Until This Day" ............................. 36
    Summary ................................................. 40

2 • "Until This Day" and the Deuteronomistic History ............. 42
    Uses of "Until This Day" in the Deuteronomistic History ..... 43
        1. Geographical Uses of "Until This Day" ................. 43
        2. Demographic Uses of "Until This Day" ................. 52
        3. Political Uses of "Until This Day" ..................... 57
        4. Cultic Uses of "Until This Day" ....................... 60
    Summary ................................................. 62
    Initial Conclusions ....................................... 64

3 • "Until This Day" and the Deuteronomistic Historian ........... 66
    "Until This Day" and Source Analysis
        in the Deuteronomistic History ....................... 70

viii    Contents

"Until This Day" and Deuteronomistic Language............71
"Until This Day" and Deuteronomistic Interests.............77
   1. Havvoth Jair.......................................77
   2. The Use of Non-Israelite Forced Labor.................80
   3. The Failure to Drive Out the Inhabitants of the Land ....81
   4. The Destruction of Non-Yahwistic Objects
      of Worship ......................................83
   5. The Far North and the Levites.......................84
   6. The Ark of the Covenant of YHWH ..................88
   7. Judahite Landholdings .............................89
   8. Judahite-Edomite Interaction........................91
   9. "Until This Day," Joshua, and the Reforms of Josiah .....93

4 • Deuteronomistic Scholarship in Our Day .....................96
   A Survey of Deuteronomistic Scholarship....................97
   1. Martin Noth's Original Hypothesis ...................97
   2. Early Reactions to Noth's Theory
      of a Deuteronomistic History ......................98
   3. Numerous Exilic Redactions of the
      Deuteronomistic History.........................100
   4. A Josianic Edition of the Deuteronomistic History.......102
   5. A Hezekian Edition of the Deuteronomistic History ....105
   6. The Gradual Formation of the Deuteronomistic
      History in Deuteronomistic "Circles" ...............108
   7. Prophetic Precursors to the Deuteronomistic History ...109
   8. A Singular Exilic or Postexilic Composition............111
   9. A Return to Pre-Nothian Models....................114
   10. So-called "Minimalist" Views of
      Ancient Israelite Historiography ...................116
   Summary................................................118

5 • "Until This Day" and Deuteronomistic Studies ................119
   The Provenance and Scope of
      the Deuteronomistic History......................120
   The Number of Preexilic Redactions of
      the Deuteronomistic History......................132
   The Purpose of the Deuteronomistic History ...............134
   1. The Deuteronomistic History as "Propaganda" ........135
   2. The Deuteronomistic History as "History" ............136
   3. The Deuteronomistic History as "Mediation"..........138

Conclusion: "Until This Day" and
   History Writing in Ancient Israel............................141
   Final Observations and Future Trajectories..................152

Bibliography ................................................. 165

Index of Biblical Passages and Ancient Sources .................... 183

Index of Authors ............................................. 189

Index of Foreign Terms and Phrases ............................ 193

Index of Subjects ............................................ 195

# Abbreviations

| | |
|---|---|
| AASF | Annales Academiae scientiarum fennicae |
| AB | Anchor Bible |
| *ABD* | Anchor Bible Dictionary |
| ACJS | Annual of the College of Jewish Studies |
| *AJS Rev* | *Association for Jewish Studies Review* |
| *Ant* | Josephus, *Jewish Antiquities* |
| ASOR | American Schools of Oriental Research |
| ATANT | Abhandlungen zur Theologie des Alten und Neuen Testaments |
| ATD | Das Alte Testament Deutsch |
| *BA* | *Biblical Archaeologist* |
| *BASOR* | *Bulletin of the American Schools of Oriental Research* |
| BBB | Bonner Biblische Beiträge |
| BETL | Bibliotheca ephemeridum theologicarum lovaniensium |
| *Bib* | *Biblica* |
| BJS | Brown Judaic Studies |
| *BN* | *Biblische Notizen* |
| *BR* | *Bible Review* |
| BTB | *Biblical Theology Bulletin* |
| BTS | Biblisch-Theologische Studien |
| BWANT | Beiträge zur Wissenschaft vom Alten und Neuen Testament |
| *BZ* | *Biblische Zeitschrift* |
| BZAW | Beihefte zur Zeitschrift für die alttestamentliche Wissenschaft |
| CAT | Commentaire de l'Ancien Testament |
| *CBQ* | *Catholic Biblical Quarterly* |
| CBQMS | Catholic Biblical Quarterly Monograph Series |
| *EAEHL* | *Encyclopedia of Archaeological Excavations in the Holy Land.* Edited by M. Avi-Yonah. 4 vols., Jerusalem, 1975 |
| EF | Erträge der Forschung |
| FOTL | Forms of the Old Testament Literature |

| | |
|---|---|
| FRLANT | Forschungen zur Religion und Literatur des Alten und Neuen Testaments |
| *HAR* | *Hebrew Annual Review* |
| HAT | Handbuch zum Alten Testament |
| HBM | Hebrew Bible Monographs |
| HSM | Harvard Semitic Monographs |
| HSS | Harvard Semitic Studies |
| *HTR* | *Harvard Theological Review* |
| HUCA | Hebrew Union College Annual |
| ICC | International Critical Commentary |
| IDB | Interpreters' Dictionary of the Bible |
| *IEJ* | *Israel Exploration Journal* |
| *Int* | *Interpretation* |
| *JBL* | *Journal of Biblical Literature* |
| JHNES | Johns Hopkins Near Eastern Studies |
| *JNES* | *Journal of Near Eastern Studies* |
| *JSOT* | *Journal for the Study of the Old Testament* |
| JSOTSup | Journal for the Study of the Old Testament, Supplement Series |
| KAT | Kommentar zum Alten Testament |
| LD | Lectio divina |
| LXX | The Septuagint |
| MT | Massoretic Text |
| NCBC | New Century Bible Commentary |
| NICOT | New International Commentary on the Old Testament |
| *OBO* | *Orbis biblicus et orientalis* |
| OTL | Old Testament Library |
| OTS | Old Testament Studies |
| *PEQ* | *Palestine Exploration Quarterly* |
| *PJ* | *Palästina-Jahrbuch* |
| *RB* | *Revue Biblique* |
| SBLDS | Society of Biblical Literature Dissertation Series |
| SBLSBL | Society of Biblical Literature Studies in Biblical Literature |
| SBT | Studies in Biblical Theology |
| SFSHJ | South Florida Studies in the History of Judaism |
| SJOT | Scandinavian Journal of the Old Testament |
| SOTS | Society for Old Testament Studies |
| TBAT | Theologische Bücherei Altes Testament |
| *TRE* | *Theologische Realenzyklopädie.* Edited by G. Krause and G. Müller. Berlin, 1977– |
| *VF* | *Verkündigung und Forschung* |
| *VT* | *Vetus Testamentum* |

| | |
|---|---|
| VTSup | Vetus Testamentum, Supplements |
| WMANT | Wissenschaftliche Monographien zum Alten und Neuen Testament |
| ZAR | *Zeitschrift für altorientalische und alttestamentliche Rechtsgeschichte* |
| ZAW | *Zeitschrift für die alttestamentliche Wissenschaft* |
| ZDPV | *Zeitschrift des deutschen Palästina-Vereins* |
| ZTK | *Zeitschrift für Theologie und Kirche* |

# Tables and Figures

Figure 2.1: Place-names existing "until this day" .................. 47
Figure 2.2: Memorials and natural landmarks
existing "until this day" ............................ 51
Figure 2.3: Geographical sites existing "until this day" .............. 53
Figure 2.4: Demographic uses of "until this day" ................... 56
Figure 2.5: Combined data on "until this day" ..................... 63

Table 3.1: "Until this day" by source in the
Deuteronomistic History ........................... 68

# Acknowledgments

The research presented here has benefited significantly from the insights and advice of colleagues at the University of California, San Diego, where this study was initiated as part of the degree requirements for the doctorate in ancient history, and at Boston College, where this book came to fruition, thanks, in part, to a semester-long research leave granted by the Department of Theology.

At the University of California, I want to thank William H. C. Propp, who guided me through the original research and writing of this manuscript and whose careful attention to argumentation and presentation made this a much better work. David Noel Freedman, the editor-in-chief of biblical studies, provided me with invaluable feedback at all stages of writing and, by his own example, taught me what it means to be a gentleman and a scholar. Richard Elliott Friedman, beyond his helpful advice on earlier drafts of this work, instilled in me the importance of evidence, not as a means of supporting one's argument but as a means of deriving it. David Goodblatt assisted me in evaluating postbiblical Jewish sources, an important but often overlooked resource in biblical studies. Thomas Levy ensured that my analysis took into account the relevant archaeological data. Alden Mosshammer demonstrated to me the art of treating ancient sources and personalities critically, yet with humility. Special thanks also go to Michael M. Homan, whose scholarship and friendship have been invaluable to me both in the projects we have done in collaboration and in life. Moreover, I want to acknowledge my indebtedness to the Office of the Dean of Arts and Sciences and to the Department of History at UCSD for providing me with a year-long research grant to write much of the original presentation of this material. The friendship and support of Doug and Nancy Greenwold also deserve special mention.

At Boston College, I wish to express my gratitude to my colleagues in Bible: Pheme Perkins, John Darr, and David Vanderhooft, whose erudition and collegiality have provided the ideal atmosphere for research and teaching. Ruth Langer, another valued colleague at Boston College, provided me with important feedback on my treatment of the Rabbinic evidence. Paul Kolbet and Boyd Taylor Coolman graciously read over my treatment of early Christian commentators and gave me much helpful advice. I have benefited also from colleagues at neighboring institutions, including Richard Clifford, SJ, of Weston Jesuit School of Theology, Mark Leuchter of Hebrew College, and the late Simon Parker of Boston University, whose scholarship and friendship are sorely missed.

Saul Olyan, editor of the Brown Judaic Studies series, deserves special thanks for his careful reading and rereading of this manuscript, which, beyond the insights offered on the substance of the argument, saved me from untold errors in its particulars. Paul J. Kobelski of The HK Scriptorium ensured that the text was expertly and accurately prepared for publication. Gratitude is also due to the anonymous reviewers, whose detailed feedback and suggestions made this a more thorough and well-rounded work. Any errors or deficiencies that remain are, of course, strictly my own.

Lastly, I want to thank my family. To my father and mother, John K. and Faith J. Geoghegan, to whom this book is dedicated, I could hope for no better parents or mentors in life. To my brother, Kevin B. Geoghegan, I owe a debt of friendship that has accrued since childhood. And to my best friend, Jannetta, and our three treasured children, Nathaniel, Brittany, and Abigail, I owe an ever increasing debt of love.

# Introduction

## *"Until This Day":*
## *Reexamining an Ancient Problem*

> The whole field is in a state of flux. It is moving, certainly, but it is not always easy to say in what direction. Sometimes it gives the impression that it is moving in several mutually canceling directions at once. Even upon major points there is often little unanimity to be observed. As a result, scarcely a single statement can be made about the state of the field that would not be subject to qualification.[1]
>
> —John Bright, *The Bible and the Ancient Near East:*
> *Essays in Honor of William Foxwell Albright*

It has become proverbial in many fields: "The 'assured results' of past generations are now in serious doubt." In biblical studies these doubts are nowhere more apparent than in discussions surrounding ancient Israelite historiography.[2] There was a day when most scholars agreed that

---

1. J. Bright, "Modern Study of Old Testament Literature," in *The Bible and the Ancient Near East: Essays in Honor of William Foxwell Albright* (ed. G. E. Wright; New York: Doubleday, 1961) 2.

2. For collected essays and monographs representing the state of the field, see D. V. Edelman, ed., *The Fabric of History: Text, Artifact and Israel's Past* (JSOTSup 127; Sheffield: Sheffield Academic Press, 1991); A. R. Millard, J. K. Hoffmeier, and D. W. Baker, eds., *Faith, Tradition, and History: Old Testament Historiography in Its Near Eastern Context* (Winona Lake, IN: Eisenbrauns, 1994); V. Fritz and P. R. Davies, eds., *The Origins of the Ancient Israelite States* (JSOTSup 228; Sheffield: Sheffield Academic Press, 1996); L. L. Grabbe, ed., *Can a "History of Israel" Be Written?* (JSOTSup 245; Sheffield: Sheffield Academic Press, 1997); L. K. Handy, ed., *The "Age of Solomon": Scholarship at the Turn of the Millennium* (Leiden: Brill, 1997); S. Ahituv and E. D. Oren, eds., *The Origin of Early Israel—Current Debate* (Beer-sheva: Ben-Gurion University of the Negev Press, 1998); V. P. Long, ed., *Israel's Past in Present Research: Essays on Ancient Israelite Historiography* (Winona Lake, IN: Eisenbrauns, 1999); A. Lemaire and M. Saebø, eds., *Congress*

the Bible provided a generally reliable picture of Israel's past, certainly beginning with the united monarchy (eleventh–tenth centuries B.C.E.), and perhaps even earlier. There was little doubt, for example, that David had an affair with Bathsheba. The questions being asked were: "Was Bathsheba complicit?" or even "Did Bathsheba intentionally seduce David by bathing in full view of the palace?" Such questions, in view of the present scholarly climate, appear silly to many, and sexist to most.

As a corrective to the assumptions of past generations, a number of recent studies have argued that the Bible should no longer be looked to as a source for reconstructing Israel's past.[3] In the words of one scholar: "The Israel found on the pages of the Old Testament is an artificial creation which has little more than one thing in common with the Israel that existed once upon a time in Palestine, that is, the name."[4] According to this view, not only are the motives for David and Bathsheba's liaison no longer subjects of serious scholarly inquiry, the event itself never happened, and the very existence of a "David" or "Bathsheba" is in serious doubt.[5]

---

*Volume Oslo 1998* (VTSup 80; Leiden: Brill, 2000); G. Galil and M. Weinfeld, eds., *Studies in Historical Geography and Biblical Historiography* (Leiden: Brill, 2000); L. L. Grabbe, ed., *Did Moses Speak Attic? Jewish Historiography and Scripture in the Hellenistic Period* (JSOTSup 317; Sheffield: Sheffield Academic Press, 2001); A. Malamat, *History of Biblical Israel: Major Problems and Minor Issues* (Leiden: Brill, 2001); V. P. Long, D. W. Baker and G. J. Wenham, eds., *Windows into Old Testament History: Evidence, Argument and the Crisis of Biblical Israel* (Grand Rapids: Eerdmans, 2002); J. Day, ed., *In Search of Pre-Exilic Israel* (JSOTSup 406; Sheffield: JSOT, 2004); J. B. Kofoed, *Text and History: Historiography and the Study of the Biblical Text* (Winona Lake, IN: Eisenbrauns, 2005).

3. G. Ahlström's treatment of Israelite history (*The History of Ancient Palestine* [Sheffield: JSOT Press, 1993]) preserves this transition from general reliance upon the text to general skepticism. Thus, when discussing the Davidic material in Samuel, Ahlström expresses deep reservations about its reliability, describing it as "an artistic novella" written by "a later historiographer," by which he seems to mean a Deuteronomistic writer in the exilic or postexilic period. Yet, when commenting upon David's liaison with Bathsheba, he remarks, "Bathsheba may have intentionally taken her bath that day" (*History*, 486).

4. N. P. Lemche, *The Israelites in History and Tradition* (Louisville, KY: Westminster John Knox, 1998) 165.

5. The disagreements over the historicity of David have been most vividly expressed in the debates over how best to interpret ביתדוד in the Tel Dan inscription. For the early debate, see esp. A. Biran and J. Naveh, "An Aramaic Stele Fragment from Tel Dan," *IEJ* 43 (1993) 81–98; F. H. Cryer, "On the Recently Discovered 'House of David' Inscription," *SJOT* 8 (1994) 1–19; E. Puech, "La stele araméenne de Dan: Bar Hadad II et la coalition des Omrides et de la maison de David," *RB* 101 (1994) 215–41; N. P. Lemche and T. L. Thompson, "Did Biran Kill David? The Bible in the Light of Archaeology," *JSOT* 64 (1994) 3–22; E. Ben Zvi, "On the Reading *bytdwd* in the Aramaic Stele from Tel Dan," *JSOT* 64 (1994) 25–32; E. A. Knauf et al., "Bayt-Dawīd ou BaytDōd? Une relecture de la nouvelle inscription de Tel Dan," *BN* 72 (1994) 60–69; Biran and Naveh, "The Tel Dan Inscription: A New Fragment," *IEJ* 45/1 (1995) 1–18; T. L. Thompson, "Dissonance and Disconnections: Notes on the *bytdwd* and *hmlk.hdd* Fragments from Tel Dan," *SJOT* 9/2 (1995) 236–40; G. Rendsburg, "On the Writing *bytdwd* in the Aramaic Inscription from Tel Dan," *IEJ* 45/1 (1995) 22–25; N. Na'aman, "Beth-David in the Aramaic

Regrettably, the modern exchanges on these issues have, in some cases, devolved into personal attacks and name-calling. Thus, those arguing that the Bible preserves reliable information for the united monarchy might be derided as "biblical maximalists" or "naïve." Conversely, those arguing that Israel's history was largely fabricated in the fifth–fourth centuries B.C.E. might find themselves labeled "biblical minimalists" or "nihilists."[6] Further complicating matters is that these debates about *ancient* history have been brought into discourse with *modern* politics. Thus, those arguing that the biblical texts are an important source for reconstructing Israel's past might be accused of "erasing" Palestinian history. Alternatively, those suggesting that the biblical text contains little reliable information for reconstructing Israel's past might be charged with "revising" Jewish history. Even for the majority of scholars not participating in this banter, knowing who compiled Israel's history, when and for what purpose is integral to rightly understanding that history, as well as for tracing the development of Israelite religion and culture. Even here, however, there is little agreement over what constitutes compelling evidence for locating the writing of Israel's history in one period or another.[7]

To provide just one example: A number of scholars cite God's promise to David of an enduring fiefdom in 2 Samuel 7 as positive evidence for a preexilic edition of Israel's traditions, since it is unlikely that someone living after the destruction of Jerusalem and the demise of the Davidic dynasty would make up such a promise.[8] For others, God's promise to David belongs to the exilic or early postexilic period, where it provided

---

Stela from Tel Dan," *BN* 79 (1995) 17–24; H. M. Barstad and B. Becking, "Does the Stele from Tel-Dan Refer to a Deity Dôd?" *BN* 77 (1995) 5–12; W. M. Schniedewind, "Tel Dan Stela: New Light on Aramaic and Jehu's Revolt," *BASOR* 302 (1996) 75–90.

6. W. G. Dever's recent works chronicle, and in many ways embody, this debate: *What Did the Biblical Writers Know and When Did They Know It? What Archaeology Can Tell Us About the Reality of Ancient Israel* (Grand Rapids, MI: Eerdmans, 2002); idem, *Who Were the Early Israelites and Where Did They Come From?* (Grand Rapids, MI: Eerdmans, 2003).

7. It should be said, however, that the debate over when Israel's history was compiled tends to center around the late preexilic and early postexilic periods. Moreover, the vast majority of scholars are apt to agree that this compilation was accomplished with recourse to at least some preexilic sources, the main disagreements being over the antiquity, quantity and accuracy of these sources, as well as over the methodology governing their use. That is, the view that Israel's history was written in the late-Persian period by those with access to few if any preexilic sources has won over few adherents. See chapters 4 and 5 for further discussion.

8. This view is closely associated with F. M. Cross, *Canaanite Myth and Hebrew Epic: Essays in the History of the Religion of Israel* (Cambridge/London: Harvard University Press, 1973). For the varying interpretations of the Davidic covenant as it relates to the provenance of the Deuteronomistic History, see the survey of scholarship in chapter 4. For the history of interpretation on 2 Sam 7:1–17, see W. M. Schniedewind, *Society and the Promise to David: The Reception History of 2 Samuel 7:1–17* (New York/Oxford: Oxford University Press, 1999).

hope for those wondering if they would ever see the restoration of their religious and political fortunes in their former homeland.[9] And still for others, the Davidic covenant—in fact, the whole of the Davidic history and much of the history that follows—was fabricated in the late postexilic period in order to justify emerging religio-political power structures and territorial claims in Persian-period Yehud or Hellenistic-period Palestine.[10] Other arguments based on thematic evidence or perceived political interests have similarly fallen victim to multiple interpretations.

The present investigation seeks to provide a way around this scholarly impasse, though it was not conceived with this objective in view. On the contrary: this study arose out of an antiquarian interest. I had long been intrigued by an expression that recurs throughout the historical books; namely, the phrase "until this day." For example, following the miraculous crossing of the Jordan River (Joshua 3–4), the biblical text informs us that the Israelites erected a monument of twelve stones, after which Joshua declares:

> Your children will ask in time to come, "What do these stones mean to you?" And you will say to them that the waters of the Jordan were cut off before the Ark of the Covenant of YHWH. When it passed through the Jordan, the waters of the Jordan were cut off! And these stones will be a memorial to the children of Israel forever.
> 
> —Josh 4:6b-7

The text then reports: "And [the stones] are there until this day" (Josh 4:9). Although this represents the only occurrence of "until this day" in connection with the well-known *Kinderfrage* of Israelite tradition, if the biblical record is any indication of the number of memorials scattered throughout ancient Israel "until this day," then the land itself served as a visible narrative of Israel's past.

Not only is Israel's miraculous entrance into Canaan memorialized by a pile of stones "until this day" (Josh 4:9) but so is its defeat of the king of Ai (Josh 8:29) and the destruction of his city (Josh 8:28). In the nearby Valley of Achor, stones mark the grave of Achan and his family, a reminder of the

---

9. This position is often identified with G. von Rad (*Studies in Deuteronomy* [SBT 9; London: SCM, 1953; German original; Göttingen: Vandenhoeck & Ruprecht, 1947] 74–91), who viewed the recurring appeal to the promise to David throughout Kings and the notice of Jehoiachin's release at the end of Kings (2 Kgs 25:27–30) as signaling the future restoration of the Davidic dynasty.

10. See, e.g., P. R. Davies, *In Search of 'Ancient Israel,'* (JSOTSup 148; Sheffield: Sheffield Academic Press, 1992); N. P. Lemche, "The Old Testament—A Hellenistic Book? *SJOT* 7 (1993) 163–93; K. W. Whitelam, *The Invention of Ancient Israel: The Silencing of Palestinian History* (London: Routledge, 1996); T. L. Thompson, *The Mythic Past: Biblical Archaeology and the Myth of Israel* (New York: Basic Books, 1999).

seriousness of violating the ban against collecting spoils in wars of ḥerem (Josh 7:26). In the north, at Ophrah, an altar called "YHWH Shalom" stands where an altar of Baal once stood, a testimony to Gideon's zeal for God (Judg 6:24). And, at Samaria, the remains of the temple of Baal are still used as a latrine "until this day," recalling Jehu's similar zeal (2 Kgs 10:27).

About twenty-five kilometers west of Jerusalem, in a field at Beth-Shemesh, a large stone marks the spot where the Ark of the Covenant came to rest after its return from Philistia, and where some unfortunate villagers made the fatal error of peering into this sacred vessel (1 Sam 6:18). A little closer to the capital, Perez-Uzzah identifies the location where a man named Uzzah steadied the Ark with his bare hand and was similarly struck dead by God (2 Sam 6:8). On the outskirts of Jerusalem, "Absalom's Pillar" stands as a memorial to David's rebellious son "until this day" (2 Sam 18:18).

Within the city proper, the temple's exquisite woodwork, crafted from the rare almug wood not seen in Israel since the time of Solomon, gives testimony to that king's immense wealth and international influence (1 Kgs 10:12). At the temple, numerous resident-aliens work as forced laborers, a policy begun by Joshua (Josh 9:27), renewed by Solomon (1 Kgs 9:21), and continued "until this day." And within the temple itself, the poles of the Ark of the Covenant protrude beyond the Holy of Holies "until this day" (1 Kgs 8:8).

All told, there are over fifty objects and institutions said to exist "until this day," raising the important question: When is "this day"? In truth, this question has perplexed scholars for nearly two millennia. Augustine of Hippo observed 1,600 years ago:

> The meaning of the expression "unto this day," which is frequently used in Scripture, is to be noted... this seems to indicate that these matters are related in Scripture long afterward, and that these books were not written at the time when the events were of recent occurrence.[11]

Although Augustine would go on to defend the traditional authorial ascriptions (e.g., "until this day" in the Torah refers to Moses' day, in the book of Joshua to Joshua's day, etc.), later investigators—such as Don Isaac Abravanel, Thomas Hobbes, Baruch Spinoza, and Julius Wellhausen—set aside these ascriptions in order to determine the actual time indicated by this phrase. At stake, they realized, was the identification of the period and circumstances out of which the biblical text arose. Even if these investigators were ultimately unsuccessful in locating "this day" in Israel's history, their efforts helped give rise to modern critical methods of biblical inquiry.[12]

---

11. Augustine, *Lucutio de Jesu Nave*, 6.25. As cited in E. M. Gray, *Old Testament Criticism: Its Rise and Progress* (New York/London: Harpers, 1923) 36.

12. See chapter 1 for the role of "until this day" in the emergence of critical scholarship.

Advances in the field over the past fifty years have put us in a much better position to determine to whose day "this day" refers. Ironically, it has been during this same period that scholars have largely ignored this phrase, treating it as an artifact of what preoccupied earlier investigations into the Bible's origins. As the present study argues, however, the evidence of "until this day" addresses some of the most pressing questions related to Israelite historiography: When was Israel's history first compiled and by whom? What was the original scope of this history? And, perhaps most important, *why* was this history compiled?

The present investigation proceeds as follows:

Chapter 1 looks at previous attempts to understand the meaning and significance of "until this day." As this survey reveals, earlier investigators were hampered in their pursuit by the state of the field at the time of their inquiry, while more recent studies have suffered from not taking into account the observations of earlier commentators. This neglect has been unfortunate, since these early commentators had uncovered important evidence for identifying to whose day "this day" refers.

Chapter 2 reassesses the use of "until this day" in the biblical text, focusing particularly on Israel's core historical corpus: the Deuteronomistic History (hereafter, the DH). Such a reassessment reveals that, although the phrase is employed to highlight a wide array of objects and institutions in and around ancient Israel, its use reflects a unified temporal and geographical perspective.

Chapter 3 applies to the study of "until this day" literary, historical, and source-critical theories that were largely unavailable to earlier investigators. Specifically, this chapter brings the evidence of "until this day" into dialogue with advances in our understanding of the redactional history of the DH. The outcome of this analysis is no less than the identification of the specific time, place and social location of those responsible for producing this history.

Chapter 4 assesses the current state of Deuteronomistic studies, with particular attention to those issues most relevant to the present study. As this chapter reveals, Noth's theory of a unified DH, once considered an "assured result" of past scholarship, has since undergone significant revision by many scholars, and has been completely rejected by others. Thus, what Bright observed for biblical studies more generally has now come to fruition for Deuteronomistic studies: the field, in the opinion of many, "is in a state of flux."

Chapter 5 applies the findings of "until this day" to this flux. Because the evidence of "until this day" allows us to isolate the specific temporal, geographical and religio-political perspective of those producing Israel's history, we are able to answer many of the questions engaging Deuteronomistic studies with relative precision.

The final chapter considers briefly what factors may have contributed to the emergence of the DH, the author of which, as Van Seters has observed, is "the first known historian in Western civilization truly to deserve this designation."[13] As this chapter suggests, the reasons for this innovation had less to do with large-scale cultural, technological, or even cognitive advances in the ancient Near East (though these played their part), and more to do with the particular life circumstances and convictions of those giving us an account of Israel's past. This chapter concludes by proposing several possible avenues for future inquiry in the DH and related works based on the evidence of "until this day."

---

13. J. Van Seters, *In Search of History: Historiography in the Ancient World and the Origins of Biblical History* (New Haven: Yale University, 1983) 362.

# 1

# "Until This Day" and Biblical Scholarship

Diligenter attendenda et exponenda [est] totius littere series ne et nos qui aliorum errores redarguimus si negligentius actum fuerit merito redarguamur.[1]

—Andrew of Saint Victor

A major shortcoming of recent investigations into the phrase "until this day" has been their failure to take into account the observations of earlier, even "precritical," commentators.[2] The result of this neglect has been that modern scholars often repeat the mistakes of their predecessors or, worse, miss out on their many insights. The following survey seeks to remedy the deficiencies of earlier studies by paying close attention to the observations made by scholars on "until this day" over the past two millennia, whether the explanations of early Jewish and Christian exegetes or the insights of later seventeenth-, eighteenth-, and nineteenth-century "critical" scholars.[3] What becomes apparent from such a survey is that the evidence accumulated by commentators over this period, when viewed

---

1. MS. C.C.C. 30, fo. 61b: "The whole context must be carefully considered and expounded, lest we who rebut the errors of others, if it be done more carelessly, be ourselves rebutted." As cited in B. Smalley, *The Study of the Bible in the Middle Ages* (Notre Dame, IN: Notre Dame Press, 1964) 128.

2. See, e.g., B. S. Childs's article, "A Study of the Formula 'Until This Day,'" *JBL* 82 (1963) 279–92, which represents the only study devoted solely to this phrase in the past century and which engages no scholarship earlier than J. A. Montgomery's "Archival Data in the Book of Kings," *JBL* 53 (1934) 46–52, even though Childs's conclusions on the source of "until this day" go against the findings of several earlier studies, including those of A. Kuenen and W. Vatke (see below).

3. While a survey of this kind cannot be exhaustive in addressing every observation made on our phrase over the past two millennia, it does seek to be exhaustive in presenting the range of ideas expressed.

together, comes a long way in locating "this day" in Israel's past, as well as in answering why the biblical authors employed this phrase in their writing.

## A SURVEY OF BIBLICAL SCHOLARSHIP ON "UNTIL THIS DAY"

### 1. Early Jewish Scholarship and "Until This Day"

Instruct us, our teacher: What does the Torah mean when it says in a number of places "until this day"? What is the exact time intended by this expression?[4]

This question, posed to Abraham ben Moses ben Maimon (1186–1237 C.E.), gets at the heart of the rabbinic debate over the phrase "until this day." And, fittingly for the only son of Maimonides, the great twelfth-century scholar, Abraham's response reflects a keen awareness of this debate: "This hints at the time of the giving of the Torah . . . or it has been written by prophecy." In order to appreciate fully Abraham's answer, it is necessary to trace the history of the rabbinic discussion on "until this day."[5]

### "Until This Day" and the Ark of the Covenant

The main Talmudic discussion surrounding the *meaning* of "until this day" occurs in the context of the debate over what happened to the Ark of the Covenant in the wake of the Babylonian conquest. In tractate *Yoma* 53b–54a,[6] the second-century C.E. *tannaim* Eliezer ben Hyrcanus and Simeon bar Yohai contend that the Ark went into exile. They cite two passages in support of this view: "And at the turn of the year, King Nebuchadnezzar sent for and brought [Jehoiachin] to Babylon with the precious vessels of the house of YHWH" (2 Chr 36:10) and "'Behold, days are coming when every-

---

4. *Responsa of Rabbi Abraham ben Rambam*, sect. 10. Unless otherwise noted, translations are my own.

5. As the rabbinic discussion is guided by several key Talmudic texts, the following survey is ordered by subject matter, not chronology: "Until This Day" and the Ark of the Covenant; "Until This Day" and the Capture of Bethel; and "Until This Day" and the Death of Moses.

6. References are to the Babylonian Talmud. For the formation and interpretation of the Babylonian Talmud, see esp. J. Neusner, *The Formation of the Babylonian Talmud: Studies on the Achievements of Late Nineteenth and Twentieth Century Historical and Literary-Critical Research* (Leiden: E. J. Brill, 1970); D. Goodblatt, "The Babylonian Talmud" in *Aufstieg und Niedergang der Römischen Welt II Principat*, ed. H. Temporini and W. Haase (Berlin/New York: de Gruyter, 1979) 257–336; H. L. Strack and G. Stemberger, *Introduction to Talmud and Midrash* (Minneapolis: Fortress, 1992).

thing that is in your house and that which your fathers have stored up until this day will be carried to Babylon. Nothing will remain,' says YHWH" (Isa 39:6). Certainly the Ark of the Covenant should be reckoned among the "precious vessels" of the temple. Indeed, כלי חמדת בית יהוה should be understood as singular: "*the* precious vessel (i.e., the Ark) of YHWH's Temple" will be carried away into Babylonian exile. Confirming this is Isaiah's comment that "nothing will remain" (לא־יותר דבר), which is interpreted as "not a command will remain." Since the Ark of the Covenant is the repository of the Ten Commandments (דברות; Deut 10:5; 1 Kgs 8:9), this passage likewise predicts the exile of the Ark to Babylon.

R. Judah, however, contends that the Ark of the Covenant remained in Jerusalem following the Babylonian conquest.[7] As evidence, he cites 1 Kgs 8:8: "And the poles [of the Ark] were so long that the heads of the poles could be seen from the Holy Place, but they could not be seen from the outside. And they are there until this day." For R. Judah, as for many rabbinic commentators, "until this day" means "forever"—an interpretation that is informed both by the biblical text and by the conviction that biblical affirmations of this sort had an eternal or prophetic quality.[8] Therefore, since the poles of the Ark still protrude from the Holy of Holies "until this day" (i.e., "forever"), and since the poles are never to be removed from the Ark (Exod 25:15), then the Ark itself must still be located at the temple mount, only it is hidden from view.

The Talmudic discussion then turns to the Babylonian amoraic debate of these same issues. Specifically, Rabbah bar Nahamani (270–330 C.E.) argues against R. Judah's understanding of the phrase:

> But does the phrase "until this day" always mean forever? Is it not written: "And they did not drive out the Jebusites that dwelt in Jerusalem, and the Jebusites dwell with the children of Benjamin in Jerusalem until this day" (Judg 1:21). Would you say here that they did not go into exile as well?[9]

For Rabbah, "until this day" cannot always mean forever, since in certain contexts it has a clear historical endpoint. In the case of the Jebusites living in Jerusalem, that endpoint is the Babylonian conquest of 586 B.C.E.

In defense of R. Judah's view, 'Ulla b. Ishmael notes that 1 Kgs 8:8 contains the word "there" (שם), which, he argues, gives "until this day" a dura-

---

7. The Soncino edition ascribes this interpretation to Judah bar Ilai—the usual identity of R. Judah without patronymic. The Talmud reads R. Judah ben Lakish, as does the Tosefta and all parallels except the Jerusalem Talmud, which reads R. Shimon ben Lakish (likely an error as he is an *amora*). The correct attribution is, in this particular case, not essential to the main argument.

8. For the biblical evidence, see Josh 4:7-9, where "until this day" appears in connection with עד־עולם. For the rabbinic understanding, see *Soṭah* 46b, as well as the comments of 'Ulla and Rashi below.

9. *Yoma* 54a.

tive sense, while in Judg 1:21 "there" is absent, implying something different; namely, that "until this day" is temporally bound.[10] Rabbah, in response, questions the significance of this linguistic distinction, noting that "there" occurs also in 1 Chr 4:43: "And they struck the rest of the Amalekites who had escaped and they settled *there* until this day." Since the Simeonites would have been removed from this region during Sennacherib's campaign, "until this day"—even when accompanied by "there"—can refer to a past condition.

At this juncture the editorial layer of the *gemara* shifts from textual to experiential evidence for the Ark's continuing presence in Jerusalem: Once there was a priest who, having noticed an unusual stone on the temple mount, suspected he had found the hiding place of the Ark. However, when he attempted to relate its exact whereabouts to his fellow priests, he fell over dead, proving he had, in fact, found the Ark's resting place. On another occasion, two priests "with imperfections" were preparing firewood on the temple mount when their axe inadvertently fell on the stone covering the hidden Ark. Fire suddenly burst forth from the stone and consumed them.

The Ark, it would seem, still resides at the temple mount, and "until this day," by implication, means "forever."

## *"Until This Day" and the Capture of Bethel*

The extent to which this understanding of "until this day" would influence biblical interpretation is perhaps best exemplified by the Talmudic discussions surrounding the capture of Bethel. According to Judges 1, Israelite spies ask a man leaving Bethel, then called Luz, to assist them in entering his city. In exchange for his help, the Israelites give the man and his family safe conduct, after which "the man went to the land of the Hittites and built a city and called its name Luz, which is its name until this day" (Judg 1:26). The sages felt that since the city founded by this man is called Luz "until this day"—that is, "forever"—it must still exist, having never experienced destruction or desertion. Yet, the city's uninterrupted occupation would require its survival through a series of conquests known to the rabbis, including those of the Assyrians and Babylonians. To explain this difficulty, *Soṭah* 46b remarks:

> This is the same Luz that Sennacherib entered but did not disturb, and Nebuchadnezzar did not destroy, and also the Angel of Death does not

---

10. The discussion following Rabbah's initial objection lacks specific attribution, and may derive from an editor, otherwise referred to as סתם גמרא (anonymous). However, for clarity, I am placing this interchange in the mouths of the two main figures of the amoraic debate: Rabbah and 'Ulla.

have permission to pass through; rather, when the elderly in it no longer desire to live, they go outside of the walls and die.

As peculiar as this understanding of "until this day" may seem, it had an enduring influence on subsequent commentators. Rashi (ca. 1040–1104 C.E.), for example, when commenting on this same passage, simply states: "Every place it says 'until this day' it means 'forever'." And when commenting on the shortened "today" (הַיּוֹם) of Gen 22:14, Rashi remarks: "'today': the future days, like 'until this day' everywhere it occurs in Scripture, for all the generations to come who recite this verse understand 'until this day' to refer to their own day." Unfortunately, Rashi does not elaborate on this interpretation here or elsewhere.[11] Whether this is because he was aware of the difficulties inherent in interpreting this phrase as forever "everywhere it occurs in Scripture" (difficulties we have already noted in the rabbinic discussions above), or whether this is simply because he had nothing new to add to the traditional interpretation, is unclear. What is clear, however, is that those who did venture to apply the meaning of "forever" universally encountered numerous difficulties that, in the end, required them to revise this understanding.

## *"Until This Day" and the Death of Moses*

The difficulties arising from how to interpret "until this day" resurface in the Talmudic discussions surrounding the account of Moses' death:

> Moses, the servant of YHWH, died there in the land of Moab by the command of YHWH. And he buried him in the valley in the land of Moab opposite Beth-Peor. And no one knows his burial place until this day.

For those accepting Mosaic authorship of the Torah, this passage raises a number of questions. For example, how could Moses recount his own death? Moreover, why would Moses say "until this day" when speaking of his own day?

One opinion among the Talmudic scholars was that Moses learned of his death and the continuing mystery of his burial place through prophetic revelation, which he dutifully wrote down "with tears."[12] R. Simeon defends this view by appealing to Deut 31:24–26, where Moses commands the Levitical priests to put the Torah next to the Ark. R. Simeon asks rhetorically: "Can the scroll of the Law be short one letter?"

---

11. Rashi does comment on the phrase again (see, e.g., Deut 29:3), though not in ways that further the present investigation.
12. *B. Bat.* 15a; *Sifrei* 33:34.

Another opinion among the Talmudic scholars was that Joshua wrote the account of Moses' death, making "this day" Joshua's day.[13] This solution allowed for someone other than Moses to record his death, while at the same time still preserving the traditional authorial ascriptions, as Joshua was held to be the author of the next biblical book. This solution, however, still presented difficulties, since the statement "until this day" seems to imply a considerable lapse of time, and therefore makes little sense even during Joshua's day.[14] This difficulty seems to be the impetus behind the additional conjecture by Abraham Ibn Ezra, the twelfth-century Spanish rabbi, that Joshua wrote this account "at the end of his life."[15] This proposal maximizes the temporal distance between Moses' death and the penning of these words, thereby lessening the difficulties presented by our phrase. As we will see below, this impulse to extend the time between an event and its written account when accompanied by "until this day" is common among commentators who hold to the traditional authorial ascriptions.

Other occurrences of "until this day" are handled in a similar fashion: the phrase was written by the author of the book in question and refers to the author's own day. Thus, Rashbam, the grandson of Rashi, writes regarding Gen 19:37: "'Until this day'—the days of Moses. And so are all uses of 'until this day,' until the days of the scribe who wrote the matter." Similarly, Radak, the late twelfth-, early thirteenth-century exegete, says of Josh 15:63: "Joshua wrote ['until this day'], for he wrote his book, according to tradition, and in his days [the Judahites] had not removed [the Jebusites] from Jerusalem, and we also find them there in the days of David." In relation to the same circumstance, but concerning its account in Judg 1:21, Radak writes, "Samuel the prophet wrote ['until this day'] for he wrote the book of Judges, according to tradition, and in his day there were still Jebusites in Jerusalem and also in the days of David." Similarly, Gersonides, the fourteenth-century scholar, says of the same verse: "Samuel the prophet wrote this book, as our rabbis have said, and it is he who said 'until this day'—this means until the days of his writing this book."

Thus, while the rabbinic commentators would all agree that "until this day" derives from the author of a given book, they would not all agree on its interpretation. "Until this day" could mean: (1) "forever" (R. Judah, 'Ulla, Rashi), (2) anytime before the said entity ceased to exist (Rabbah), or (3) the biblical author's own day (Rashbam, Radak, Gersonides).

---

13. See *B. Bat.* 15a, as well as Rashi's comments on Deut 34:5.
14. That our phrase suggests a considerable lapse of time has been noted by numerous commentators over the centuries. See, e.g., the comments of Augustine, Abravanel, Hobbes, Spinoza, Wesley, de Wette, and Kuenen, below.
15. See Ibn Ezra's comments on Deut 34:6.

Before completing our survey of the rabbinic material, a few additional observations are in order, especially as they relate to Radak's treatment of our phrase, as well as to the observations made by the late-fifteenth, early-sixteenth century scholar, Don Isaac Abravanel—so distinct are his views.

### *Radak (ca. 1160–1235 C.E.)*

We have already noted Radak's opinion, shared by many others, that "until this day" refers to the time of the author and confirms matters persisting to the author's day.[16] Yet, Radak seems to be among the first to observe that several uses of "until this day" are thematically linked. Thus, when commenting upon 2 Sam 24:23, which describes David's purchase of land in Jerusalem from "Araunah the Jebusite," Radak cites several other passages that attest to the continuing presence of Jebusites in Jerusalem, including Josh 15:63, which explains why the Jebusites still dwell in Jerusalem among the Judahites "until this day"; Judg 1:21, which similarly describes why the Jebusites still dwell in Jerusalem, only among the Benjaminites; and 1 Kgs 9:20–21, which notes that the descendants of the non-Israelites (including Jebusites) used by Solomon for his royal building projects still live in Jerusalem. As we will see in chapter 3, these connections among the uses of "until this day" will provide important evidence for identifying the time and place indicated by this phrase.

### *Don Isaac Abravanel (1437–1508 C.E.)*

In addition to serving in the royal courts of Portugal, Spain and Venice, Don Isaac Abravanel wrote extensively on the subjects of philosophy and religion, including commentaries on the Torah, Former Prophets and Daniel.[17] In his introduction to the Former Prophets, Abravanel addresses at length the question of biblical authorship. Unlike his predecessors, however, he does not hesitate to question the traditional authorial ascriptions. Thus, when discussing the authorship of Joshua, Abravanel says that the possibility of Joshua authoring his own book "is very remote." His main

---

16. See, e.g., Radak's comments on Josh 15:63 and Judg 1:21, above.
17. For treatments of Abravanel's life and works, see esp. B. Netanyahu, *Don Isaac Abravanel: Statesman and Philosopher* (Philadelphia: JPSA, 1953); R. Goetschel, *Isaac Abravanel: Conseiller des Princes et Philosophe, 1437–1508* (Paris: Albin Michel, 1996); E. Lawee, *Isaac Abarbanel's Stance toward Tradition: Defense, Dissent, and Dialogue* (Albany: State University of New York Press, 2001); S. Feldman, *Philosophy in a Time of Crisis: Don Isaac Abravanel, Defender of the Faith* (New York: Routledge, 2002).

reason for this determination is not that the book reports Joshua's death, for this could be explained as a postscript, but, as Abravanel puts it, "on account of the things that clearly show Joshua did not write it." Principal among the things that "clearly show" Joshua did not write the book bearing his name is the phrase "until this day":

> It says concerning the erection of stones in the midst of the Jordan, "They are there until this day" (Josh 4:9), and in the matter of the circumcision "He called the name of that place Gilgal until this day" (Josh 5:9), and it says regarding Achan, "Therefore, he called that place the valley of Achor until this day" (Josh 7:26), and it says about the Gibeonites, "Joshua made them in that day hewers of wood and drawers of water for the congregation and for the altar of Hashem until this day" (Josh 9:27), and it says, "Therefore, Hebron belongs to Caleb the son of Jephunneh, the Kenizzite for an inheritance until this day" (Josh 14:14), and regarding the inheritance of the children of Judah it says, "The Jebusites are inhabitants of Jerusalem; the children of Judah were not able to dispossess them, and the Jebusites dwell with the children of Judah in Jerusalem until this day" (Josh 15:63), and thus it says in connection to the inheritance of Ephraim, "The Canaanites dwell in the midst of Ephraim until this day and they serve as forced laborers" (Josh 16:10).

Abravanel concludes, "If Joshua wrote all of this, how can it say 'until this day'? . . . The phrase 'until this day' demonstrates by necessity that the book was written long after the affairs it reports." "And besides," Abravanel continues, "you will not find that it says in the book of Joshua that he wrote it."

Abravanel employs similar argumentation for the book of Samuel, where he observes that "until this day" occurs in contexts that point to a period long after Samuel's life. Citing examples near the beginning of the book, Abravanel writes,

> And thus, in the same way, that which is written demonstrates that Samuel did not write his book, because regarding the matter of the Ark in the land of the Philistines which occurred in his day, it says "therefore the priests of Dagon and all those entering the temple of Dagon do not tread upon the threshold of Dagon in Ashdod until this day" (1 Sam 5:5), and it says when the Philistines returned the Ark "and as far as the great field they made the Ark of Hashem to rest upon it until this day in the field of Joshua of Beth-Shemesh" (1 Sam 6:18), and if these matters were in the days of Samuel how can it say "until this day" which indicates a long duration?

Beyond the evidence of "until this day," Abravanel observes that the reference to the "kings of Judah" in 1 Sam 27:6 also points to a time after Samuel, since "in the days of Samuel the 'kings of Judah' did not exist as a separate entity." Abravanel concludes, "Behold, all I am saying is that Samuel did not write his book either."

Who, then, wrote these books? According to Abravanel, the best candidate for the book of Joshua is Samuel, who, following rabbinic tradition, also wrote the book of Judges.[18] In this way the requirement for temporal distance between the event and the notice "until this day" is met, as "this day" in Joshua and Judges is Samuel's day. Abravanel admits, however, that ascribing Judges to Samuel is not without its problems, since Judg 18:30b states, "And Jonathan the son of Gershom the son of Moses[19] and his sons were priests to the tribe of Dan until the day of the exile of the land." "Until the day of the exile" would seem to suggest that this book was written after the fall of Israel. However, Abravanel responds to this difficulty by arguing that the exile referred to here is not Israel's, but the Ark's, which, during Samuel's life, was captured by the Philistines (1 Samuel 5). Despite the precariousness of this solution (e.g., How does one explain the reference to "the exile *of the land*"?), Abravanel's attempt to determine the time of authorship based on the evidence of "until this day" is well founded and would be picked up again by later exegetes.

Who, then, is responsible for the books of Samuel? In this case, Abravanel's answer is more elaborate, though ultimately informed by the biblical text and rabbinic tradition:

> Samuel wrote about the affairs that took place in his day, and Nathan the prophet wrote in the same way, and Gad the seer wrote also in the same way; each one of them wrote all that happened in his own day.

Here Abravanel is following the notice in 1 Chr 29:29, which states that the events of David's life and rule were recorded by these three prophets. Nevertheless, this explanation still leaves unanswered the question of who brought these various works together. For Abravanel, this could be none other than the one who, according to rabbinic tradition, also compiled the books of Kings:

> The prophet Jeremiah gathered together and combined these writings and set the books in order based on their accounts . . . It is [Jeremiah] who says "until this day" and he was the one who wrote "previously in Israel," "for the prophet of today was previously called a seer," and the rest of the phrases that I have demonstrated indicate a later time—all of them are from the activity of the arranger and compiler.

---

18. *B. Bat.* 14b–15a.

19. The issues surrounding the raised *nun* in Judg 18:30 have been well rehearsed elsewhere. It is generally agreed that "Moses" is the preferred reading, the raised *nun* being understood as an attempt to disassociate Moses' descendants from the shrine at Dan. See, e.g., G. F. Moore, *A Critical and Exegetical Commentary on Judges* (ICC; New York: Charles Scribner's Sons, 1906), 400–402; T. J. Schneider, *Judges* (Berit Olam: Studies in Hebrew Narrative and Poetry; Collegeville, MN: Liturgical Press, 2000) 242–43.

Abravanel, therefore, concludes that "until this day" in the Former Prophets has ultimately two sources: Samuel in Joshua and Judges, and Jeremiah in Samuel and Kings. As we will see later in our study, Abravanel's observations would prove to be among the most insightful of both earlier and later periods.[20]

## 2. Early Christian Scholarship and "Until This Day"

Detailed treatment of the passages that concern us here is rare among the Church Fathers. Still, there is enough information, gleaned from statements throughout their writings, to determine how they understood "until this day." As with the rabbinic material, there exists some diversity of opinion as to what this phrase means and to whose day it refers.

### *Origen of Alexandria (ca. 185–253 C.E.)*

Unfortunately, most of Origen's writings did not survive antiquity. This loss was due not only to the ravages of time but also to the ravages of the emperor Justinian, who in 553 C.E. declared Origen a heretic and commanded that all his works be destroyed.[21] Among the greatest losses was Origen's *Hexapla*, a six-column work containing the Hebrew text of the Old Testament, a Greek transcription, and four Greek translations.[22] Fortunately, enough of Origen's works survived antiquity to give us a glimpse into the life and thought of this prolific third-century Christian scholar.

---

20. Had Abravanel come to the conclusion that the exile spoken of in Judges 18 was Israel's and not the Ark's, and had he consequently assigned the editing of the books of Joshua and Judges to Jeremiah, his analysis of the Former Prophets would have come close to the modern conception of the Deuteronomistic Historian (Dtr). We will pursue this idea further in chapter 3 and in the conclusion.

21. For Origen's life and works, see J. W. Trigg, *Origen: Bible and Philosophy in the 3rd Century* (Atlanta: John Knox, 1983); C. Kannengiesser and H. Crouzel, *Origen: The Life and Thought of the First Great Theologian* (San Francisco: HarperCollins, 1989). For a treatment of Origen's exegetical methods, see R. P. C. Hanson, *Allegory and Event: A Study of the Sources and Significance of Origen's Interpretation of Scripture* (Richmond, VA: John Knox Press, 1959); K. Torjesen, *Hermeneutical Procedure and Theological Method in Origen's Exegesis* (Berlin: de Gruyter, 1985) esp. 1–21; 35–48; 70–87; 108–47; B. E. Daley, "Origen's '*De principiis*': A Guide to the 'Principles' of Christian Scriptural Interpretation," in *Nova et Vetera: Patristic Studies in Honor of Thomas Patrick Halton*, ed. J. F. Petruccione (Washington, DC: Catholic University of America Press, 1998) 3–21.

22. The Greek translations used by Origen are Aquila, Symmachus, the LXX, and Theodotion. Only fragments and partial translations of this massive work have survived. See P. Kahle, "The Greek Bible Manuscripts Used by Origen," *JBL* 79 (1960) 111–18.

We encounter Origen's comments on "until this day" within a treatise directed against Celsus, the second-century Middle Platonist and outspoken critic of Christianity.[23] Celsus, presenting the case of a Jew seeking to persuade his fellow Jews to reject Christianity, asks: "By what, then, were you persuaded? Was it because [Jesus] predicted that after his death he would rise again?" In response, Origen invokes a situation in the Torah he views as similar:

> Now, this question, like the others, can be answered by an appeal to Moses. For we could say to the Jew, "By what, then, were you persuaded? Was it because he recorded the following statement about his own death: 'And Moses, the servant of the LORD died there, in the land of Moab, according to the word of the LORD; and they buried him in Moab, near the house of Phogor. And no one knows his burial place until this day'"? For just as the Jew discredits the statement, that "Jesus foretold that after His death He would rise again," another could make a similar assertion about Moses, saying in reply that Moses also put on record (for the book of Deuteronomy is his composition) the statement, that "no one knows his burial place until this day," in order to magnify and enhance the importance of his burial place, as being unknown to humankind.[24]

Origen's treatment of "until this day," though positioned in an argument against Jewish interpretation, reveals his indebtedness to it. In fact, his comments disclose that he is of the same opinion as those Jewish commentators who argue that Moses wrote of his own death by prophecy. This agreement is not surprising since many of the Church Fathers, Origen included, were familiar with and accepted Jewish tradition concerning the authorship of the biblical books.

## *Jerome (ca. 342–420 C.E.)*

Jerome, writing a century and a half after Origen, was well acquainted with Origen's works, having even translated his homilies on Jeremiah and Ezekiel into Latin.[25] Understandably, then, Jerome concurs with his predecessor that "until this day" likely derives from the presumed author of a particular book and refers to the author's own day. However, Jerome also

---

23. For Celsus's treatment of Jewish sources, see G. T. Burke, "Celsus and the Old Testament," *VT* 36 (1986) 241–45.
24. *Contra Celsum*, II:54.
25. For Jerome's life and works, see esp. J. N. D. Kelly, *Jerome: His Life, Writings, and Controversies* (New York: Harper and Row, 1975; repr. Grand Rapids, MI: Hendrickson, 1998); A. Kamesar, *Jerome, Greek Scholarship, and the Hebrew Bible* (Oxford: Oxford University Press, 1993); S. Rebenich, *Jerome: The Early Church Fathers* (New York: Routledge, 2002).

admits that the phrase might derive from a later period. Thus, when commenting upon "until this day" in the Pentateuch, he writes,

> The word of God says in Genesis, "And they gave to Jacob all the foreign gods that were in their hands, and the rings that were in their ears. And Jacob hid them under the oak that was by Shechem, and lost them until this day." Likewise at the end of Deuteronomy, "And Moses the servant of the LORD died there in the land of Moab according to the word of the LORD, and he buried him in Geth, near the house of Phogor. And no one knows his burial place until this day." We must certainly understand by "this day" the time of the composition of the history, whether you prefer the view that Moses was the author of the Pentateuch or that Ezra restored it. In either case I make no objection.[26]

Jerome's comments reflect a tradition, widely accepted during his day, that the Torah was destroyed during the Babylonian conquest and that Ezra, by divine inspiration, re-created it. As E. M. Gray observes,

> ... the Fathers experienced little or no difficulty in reconciling a belief in the Mosaic authorship of the Pentateuch with an acceptance of a miraculous account of its reproduction by Ezra. Indeed, it seems that this legend of the partial or entire destruction of the Mosaic writings (or even, according to some, of the whole of the sacred volumes) and their later restoration through Ezra, was made use of later to explain any ambiguities or discrepancies encountered in the canonical books.[27]

Jerome's appeal to the Ezra tradition seems similarly motivated: to account for the difficulties arising from the presence of "until this day." As we will see momentarily, later medieval commentators appealed explicitly to this tradition for this purpose.[28]

## *Augustine (354–430 C.E.)*

Augustine expresses his own views on "until this day" in his comments on the book of Joshua, and in so doing he admits to the difficulties caused by this phrase for maintaining the traditional authorial ascriptions:[29]

---

26. *Adversus Helvidium* 1.7.
27. Gray, *Old Testament Criticism*, 27.
28. See the comments of Abelard, below.
29. For Augustine's life and works, see, e.g., H. Chadwick, *Augustine* (Past Masters Series; Oxford: Oxford University Press, 1986); E. Stump and N. Kretzmann, eds., *The Cambridge Companion to Augustine* (Cambridge: Cambridge University Press, 2001); M. T. Clark, *Augustine* (Washington, DC: Georgetown University Press, 1994); J. J. O'Donnell, *Augustine: A New Biography* (New York: HarperCollins, 2005). For Augustine's own expression of his larger interpretive theory, see his *De Doctrina Christiana*.

> The meaning of the expression "unto this day," which is frequently used in Scripture, is to be noted, for the same expression is used concerning those twelve stones which were placed where the Jordan had flowed away downstream and stood still above, while the ark and people were passing over (Josh 4:9); and this seems to indicate that these things are related in Scripture long afterward, and that these books were not written at the time when the events were of recent occurrence.[30]

Augustine argues, however, that this initial impression is in error:

> But what about that harlot, who lived for the space of one man's life and yet it is said "unto this day"? This is said concerning matters which are so appointed that they may not be altered afterward by those who have appointed them; as when it is said that someone has been condemned to perpetual exile; which is not to be taken as meaning that his exile was actually perpetual (the man himself being finite), but that no term was set for it. Thus, no term being set for Rahab's sojourn in Israel, it was written that it endured "unto this day."

As we will see below, later commentators rightly questioned this explanation. However, to Augustine's credit, his comments reveal his awareness that this phrase, "frequently used in Scripture," had implications for locating the biblical authors.

In the period following Augustine, comments upon our phrase largely reflect the opinions of the Church Fathers. G. Fogarty sums up the basic character of scholarship during this period:

> In the early Middle Ages, the "sense of the Fathers" provided the key to understanding the Scripture. Their exegesis became almost synonymous with tradition, whose distinguishing characteristics were antiquity, universality, and consensus. Tradition was static, and the medieval commentator was to hand on what he received or, in the words of Pope Stephen I, *"nihil innovetur nisi quod traditum est"* ("nothing is to be introduced except that which has been received").[31]

One method of exegesis adopted from the Church Fathers and further developed by medieval commentators was that of determining the "spiritual" or, in its most common manifestation, "allegorical" sense of a passage.[32] This approach not only allowed one to derive Christological

---

30. Augustine, *Locutio de Jesu Nave*, VI:25, as cited in Gray, *Old Testament Criticism*, 36.
31. G. Fogarty, "Scriptural Authority: Biblical Authority in Roman Catholicism," *ABD* 5:1024. For a discussion of the influence of the early Fathers on later interpretation, see R. E. McNally, *The Bible in the Early Middle Ages* (Westminster, MD: Newman, 1959); J. S. Preus, *From Shadow to Promise: Old Testament Interpretation from Augustine to the Young Luther* (Cambridge, MA: Belknap Press/Harvard University Press, 1969).
32. For a recent treatment of interpretive methods during this early period, see J. J.

interpretations from the Hebrew Bible but also proved helpful for resolving difficulties such as "until this day." The application of this method for the latter purpose is perhaps best exemplified in the works of the ninth-century Carolingian exegete, Rabanus Maurus.[33]

### *Rabanus Maurus (776?–856 C.E.)*

Rabanus Maurus, like the Jewish scholars of his day, held to the traditional authorial ascriptions. Thus, in his *De Clericorum Institutione*, Maurus writes,

> As for the Old Testament, following the Hebrew tradition, the authors are as follows. First of all, Moses wrote the Pentateuch. Joshua, the son of Nun, composed his book. As for Judges, Ruth and the first part of Samuel, Samuel wrote them. The remainder of Samuel to the end, David wrote. Jeremiah composed all of Kings: for previously the royal histories were separate.[34]

When discussing Josh 6:25, therefore, Maurus, like Augustine before him, feels compelled to explain the meaning of "this day" in light of the tradition that Joshua wrote this book. For Maurus, this phrase has at least two interpretations—one literal, the other spiritual. The literal meaning of the notice, "Rahab dwelt among Israel until this day" is Joshua's day, a view corresponding to, and no doubt informed by, Augustine's earlier treatment of this passage. The spiritual meaning of Rahab's continued presence among Israel, however, is "forever." In what sense is Rahab still dwelling among Israel "until this day"? Rabanus explains that just as Rahab, a non-Israelite, was made part of Israel through her faith in God, so Gentile Christians have been made part of Israel, and will remain so forever, through their faith in God's Son.

### *Peter Abelard (ca. 1079–1142 C.E.)*

Another example of following the "sense of the Fathers" comes from the work of the late eleventh-, early twelfth-century Benedictine monk, Peter Abelard. Contrary to Rabanus, however, Abelard does not appeal to an

---

O'Keefe and R. R. Reno, *Sanctified Vision: An Introduction to Early Christian Interpretation of the Bible* (Baltimore: Johns Hopkins University Press, 2005).

33. For a discussion of Rabanus Maurus and the Carolingian revival, see Smalley, *The Bible in the Middle Ages*, 37–46.

34. R. Maurus, *De Clericorum Institutione*, II:54. The main difference between R. Maurus's view and the traditional Jewish opinion is that Maurus maintains that David wrote the second half of Samuel, whereas Jewish tradition ascribed this material to Nathan and Gad based on 1 Chr 29:29.

allegorical or typological interpretation to alleviate the difficulties posed by "until this day." Rather he interprets the phrase literally and attempts to understand its meaning historically. Thus, when discussing Moses' death in Deuteronomy 34, Abelard makes explicit what was implicit in Jerome's comments; namely, that the tradition about Ezra's re-creating the Bible after the exile explains this seemingly non-Mosaic passage. Abelard writes,

> Ezra himself, who not only rewrote the Law, but also, according to the common report of the ancients, the whole series of the sacred Scriptures, which had also been burned, in such a way as seemed to him suitable for his readers, made this and several other additions to the writings of the Old Testament.[35]

For early Christian commentators, then, both the Ezra tradition and the spiritual sense of scripture proved useful for overcoming the interpretational difficulties caused by "until this day."

## 3. Reformation Scholarship and "Until This Day"

The Reformation, with its emphasis on *sola scriptura*, witnessed a renewed emphasis on the literal meaning of scripture and, with it, a renewed interest in the historical interpretation of "until this day."

### *Martin Luther (1483–1546 C.E.)*

Martin Luther, the father of the Reformation, was well versed in both early Jewish and Christian scholarship. Luther's knowledge of the Jewish commentators, especially Rashi, Ibn Ezra and Radak, came largely from the Latin translations of their works by the Franciscan, Nicholas of Lyra.[36] Nicholas's influence upon Luther was so marked that it became a point of ridicule among his detractors:

> Si Lyra non lyrasset,
> Lutherus non saltasset.
>
> If Lyra had not played the lyre,
> Luther would not have danced.

---

35. Abelard, *Heloissae Problemata*, Problema XLI, de Deut. XXXIII and XXXIV, as cited in Gray, *Old Testament Criticism*, 32.

36. H. M. Orlinsky, "Jewish Influences on Christian Translations of the Bible," in *Essays in Biblical Culture and Bible Translation* (New York: Ktav, 1974) 423–40. For a biography of Luther, including the influence of Nicholas on his life and writings, see M. Brecht, *Martin Luther* (3 vols.; trans. J. L. Schaaf; Philadelphia: Fortress Press, 1985–1993).

It is understandable, then, why Luther's comments on "until this day" reflect the views of these earlier Jewish commentators. In his remarks on Gen 47:26, for example, Luther writes, "Moses reports that this law endured 'until this day,' that is, to the time when he wrote this account." And concerning the report of Moses' death, Luther remarks,

> Moses did not write this chapter, but Joshua or Eleazar, unless you want to say that his death, as if foreseen, was self-described in this way.

Luther's remarks, then, are well within the traditional approaches to our phrase, even reflecting both sides of the rabbinic debate over who wrote the account of Moses' death: Moses' immediate successors or Moses by prophecy.

### *John Calvin (1509–1564 C.E.)*

John Calvin, the French reformer and author of the influential *Institutes of Christian Religion*, similarly ascribes "until this day" to the authors of the books in which it appears. Thus, in an attempt to explain how Moses could confirm the existence of Rachel's tomb in Canaan (Gen 35:20), Calvin remarks, "This memorial remained standing until the people came out of Egypt." This explanation, of course, does not solve the problem, since Moses never entered Canaan to see Rachel's tomb. Calvin himself seemed unaware of this difficulty, but later commentators within the reformist tradition noted it and proposed alternate explanations for how Moses could confirm the presence of Rachel's Tomb, including that he visited Canaan during the forty years he tended his father-in-law's flocks, or that, upon the spies' return from scouting out the land, they informed Moses of the tomb's continued existence.[37]

When it comes to the biblical books outside of the Torah, Calvin is much more at ease in dismissing the traditional authorial ascriptions. Accordingly, in his introduction to Joshua Calvin writes, "As for the author of this book, it is better to suspend judgment than to make random assertions. Those who think it was Joshua because his name stands on the title page base their arguments on weak and inadequate grounds." What role, if any, "until this day" played in Calvin's determination is unclear, as he does not comment upon its use in this book—a peculiar silence given its prevalence there.[38]

---

37. *The Holy Bible According to the Authorized Version (A.D. 1611) with an Explanatory and Critical Commentary and a Revision of the Translation*, by Bishops and Other Clergy of the Anglican Church, (I/I Genesis–Exodus; London: John Murray, 1877) 17, 188.

38. "Until this day" appears eleven times in Joshua when employed etiologically: Josh

## *John Wesley (1703–1791 C.E.)*

John Wesley, though writing two centuries after Luther and Calvin, is best treated with them, as their influence is everywhere visible in his writings.[39] Despite this influence, Wesley's comments on "until this day" mark a significant departure from theirs. In fact, Wesley's analysis reflects a critical stance toward the sacred text that is unique within the tradition he represents, coming closest to the views expressed by Abravanel two centuries earlier and by Wesley's own contemporaries within the emerging field of critical scholarship. Wesley's remarks on Deut 3:14, for example, demonstrate his comfort with the notion that others contributed to the books of Moses:

> 'Unto this day'—This must be put among those passages which were not written by Moses, but added by those holy men, who digested the books of Moses into this order, and inserted some few passages to accommodate things to their own time and people.

Wesley sees this editorial process of inserting "some few passages" as occurring across traditional authorial boundaries. Thus, concerning Josh 4:9, Wesley writes,

> 'Unto this day'—This might be written either 1) by Joshua who probably wrote this book near twenty years after this was done; or, 2) by some other holy man divinely inspired, who inserted this and some such passages both in this book *and in the writings of Moses* (emphasis mine).

Wesley's first proposal reflects Ibn Ezra's similar desire to extend the time between the event described and the penning of the words "until this day." We see this same impulse in Wesley's comments on Josh 15:63 (Jebusites in Jerusalem), where he reasons that since Joshua lived "many years after the taking of Jerusalem," he could have written these words. And again, when commenting on 1 Sam 5:5, Wesley writes, "'This day'—When this history was written, which if written by Samuel towards the end of his life was a sufficient ground for this expression."

Yet, Wesley seems to have preferred the explanation that later editors inserted "until this day" to an already existing text. Thus, in an additional comment on Josh 15:63, Wesley suggests that "until this day" was inserted after Joshua's day "by some other man of God." "But," he adds, "this must

---

4:9; 5:9; 6:25; 7:26 (2x); 8:28, 29; 9:27; 10:27; 13:13; 14:14; 15:63; 16:10. For a complete list of its etiological use throughout the Bible, see chapter 2, n. 3.

39. For discussions of Wesley's life and works, see R. G. Tuttle, Jr., *John Wesley: His Life and Theology* (Grand Rapids: Zondervan, 1978); S. E. Ayling, *John Wesley* (London: Collins, 1979).

be done before David's time, when the Jebusites were quite expelled, and their fort taken." Admittedly, the rabbis had already observed that the Jebusites continued to live in Jerusalem even after David's conquest of the city (e.g., 2 Sam 24:16). Therefore, Wesley's determination of the latest time allowed by the phrase in Joshua is based on a faulty premise. Nevertheless, his contention that "until this day" may have been added secondarily by the same hand in both the Torah *and* the Former Prophets, without an explicit appeal to the Ezra tradition, is unique among the commentators treated thus far, as even Abravanel was hesitant to ascribe material in the Torah to a hand other than Moses'.

### *Andreas Masius (1516–1573 C.E.)*

We conclude our survey of biblical commentators before the Enlightenment with the sixteenth-century Flemish scholar Andreas Masius. In his comments on the book of Joshua, Masius unabashedly criticizes Augustine's handling of our phrase:

> 'Divus Augustinus' interprets the words "and they have been there unto this day" (Josh 4:9) as if they merely signified that these stones had been placed in the river by Joshua with the intent that they should remain there forever. But since he thinks that these are the words of Joshua himself, writing the account of his own deeds, he is very far from correct. For who could understand that a man, when he put up a monument and at the same time made a record of it in writing, would say that it remained in its place unto the day on which he had set it up?[40]

Masius's comments make explicit what Augustine had already anticipated: "until this day" suggests an interval long after the events being recorded. Masius, in his analysis of Josh 6:25, gives his own view of how to understand the phrase:

> Of course, the phrase "Rahab remained in Israel unto this day" is to be so understood—according to my certain opinion—that the posterity of Rahab was living even at that time among the Israelites, in the enjoyment of their laws and their religion, at the time when this history was being compiled from the sacred annals, either by Ezra or some other, several ages after the time at which the events took place.[41]

Masius's argument is similar to that of Abelard's: those compiling Israel's history (likely Ezra) employed "until this day" to testify to the persistence

---

40. Andreas Masius, *Josuae imperatoris historia illustrata et explicata* (1574), as cited in Gray, *Old Testament Criticism*, 37.

41. Masius, *Joshuae*, as cited in Gray, *Old Testament Criticism*, 37.

of objects and institutions during their own day. Had Masius and his predecessors applied this interpretive approach to other occurrences of our phrase, then they would have realized its shortcomings.[42] Nonetheless, Masius's insights, as well as his critical engagement of earlier, well-established interpretations (e.g., Augustine's), were a harbinger of the critical approach about to ensue.[43]

## 4. Enlightenment Scholarship and "Until This Day"

> But about the midst of this Age, a certain Author that shall be nameless started up, whose Opinion afterwards found some Disciples, and these have been so hardy, as to deny that Moses was the Writer of the Pentateuch, and pretend to shew several Passages in him, which were manifestly writ since his time.[44]

These comments, written by the French priest Jean le Clerc, refer to the seventeenth-century British philosopher, Thomas Hobbes, who, in his political opus *Leviathan*,[45] discusses at length the origins of the biblical books—and, in the process, comments extensively on "until this day."[46]

### *Thomas Hobbes (1588–1679 c.e.)*

Hobbes sets forth the following proposition in his attempt to determine the biblical authors:

> It is not argument enough that they were written by Moses, because they are called the five Books of Moses; no more than these titles, the Book of Joshua, the Book of Judges, the Book of Ruth, and the Books of the Kings are arguments sufficient to prove, that they were written by Joshua, by

---

42. For example, the notice that the poles of the Ark still protrude from the Holy of Holies (1 Kgs 8:8) or that the kingdoms of Edom and Israel are still in rebellion against Judah (1 Kgs 12:19; 2 Kgs 8:22) suggest a period prior to the fall of Jerusalem and the Davidic state. For the general preexilic provenance indicated by "until this day," see chapters 2 and 3.

43. For the contributions of Masius to the development of critical scholarship, see esp. H.-J. Kraus, *Geschichte der historisch-kritischen Erforschung des Alten Testaments* (3rd ed.; Neukirchen-Vluyn: Neukirchener Verlag, 1982).

44. *Twelve Dissertations out of Monsieur Le Clerc's Genesis* (London: Baldwin, 1696) 113–14.

45. First published in 1651, the full title is *Leviathan, or The Matter, Form, and Power of a Commonwealth Ecclesiastical and Civil*. Citations are from the Oxford University edition (Oxford and New York: Oxford University Press, 1996).

46. For a discussion of Hobbes's political and religious views, see F. C. Hood, *The Divine Politics of Thomas Hobbes* (Oxford: Clarendon Press, 1964).

the Judges, by Ruth, and by the Kings. For in titles of books, the subject is marked as often as the writer. The history of Livy denotes the writer; but the history of Alexander is denominated from the subject.[47]

Having established this, Hobbes argues that those traditionally credited with writing the biblical books did not. To defend his claim, Hobbes relies almost exclusively on the evidence of "until this day":

> We read in the last chapter of Deuteronomy, verse 6, concerning the sepulchre of Moses that no man knoweth of his sepulchre to this day, that is, to the day wherein those words were written. It is therefore manifest, that those words were written after his interment. For it were a strange interpretation to say Moses spake of his own sepulchre (though by prophecy), that it was not found to that day, wherein he was yet living.[48]

Regarding the book of Joshua, Hobbes argues:

> That the book of Joshua was also written long after the time of Joshua, may be gathered out of many places of the book itself. Joshua had set up twelve stones in the midst of the Jordan, for a monument of their passage; of which the writer saith thus, 'They are there unto this day' (Josh 4:9); for 'unto this day,' is a phrase that signifieth a time past, beyond the memory of man. In like manner, upon the saying of the LORD, that he had rolled off from the people the reproach of Egypt, the writer saith, 'The place is called Gilgal unto this day' (Josh 5:9); which to have said in the time of Joshua had been improper. So also the name of the valley of Achor, from the trouble that Achan raised in the camp, the writer saith, 'remaineth unto this day' (Josh 7:26); which must needs be therefore long after the time of Joshua. Arguments of this kind there be many others; as Josh 8:29, 13:13, 14:14, 15:63.[49]

Hobbes applies this same approach to the books of Judges, Samuel, Kings and Chronicles—the last two works dating to after the exile since "the history of them is continued till that time."[50] While Hobbes, like Masius, fails to account for the use of "until this day" in connection with objects no longer existing after the exile (e.g., the Ark of the Covenant; 1 Kgs 8:8), his overall observations about the potential of this phrase for dating the biblical books became quite influential.[51] Despite this influence, in 1683, thirty-two years after its publication, the University of Oxford ordered all copies

---

47. *Leviathan*, III, 33.4. Cf. the comments of Calvin, discussed above.
48. *Leviathan*, III, 33.4.
49. *Leviathan*, III, 33.6.
50. *Leviathan*, III, 33.9.
51. For Hobbes's contributions to the nascent field of critical scholarship, see Kraus, *Geschichte*, 57–58.

of *Leviathan* destroyed, along with other writings deemed "Heretical and Blasphemous, infamous to Christian Religion, and destructive of all Government in Church and State."⁵²

### *Isaac de la Peyrère (1594–1676 C.E.)*

In a work devoted to arguing that humans existed prior to Adam and Eve, Isaac de la Peyrère, a French Millenarian and influential writer of the seventeenth century, attempts first to establish that Moses was not responsible for everything attributed to him in the so-called "Books of Moses." Like Hobbes, La Peyrère appeals primarily to the evidence of "until this day" to defend this claim:

> That which we read in the third Chapter of Deuteronomy does manifest that they are written long after Moses; "Jair the son of Manasseh possessed all the Country of Argob, and it is called after his name, Basan Hanock Jair, to this day." Moses could never had said "to this day"; For Jair scarcely had possession of his own Villages at that time, when Moses is brought in so speaking. And hence it manifestly appears, that the author intended to show whence, according to the most ancient and first original, that City was called Jair, deriving the cause from Moses to his own time: and therefore, as was fit, called it Jair from the ancient Jair, until this day.⁵³

Although La Peyrère believes "Moses made a diary of all those wonderful things which God did for the people of Israel," the final compilation and redaction of the Pentateuch did not occur until much later. Based on his analysis of "until this day" in Deuteronomy, La Peyrère concludes, ". . . these essayes of Deuteronomy were written long after David's time, a great while after Moses."⁵⁴ La Peyrère's primary reason for dating Deuteronomy after David is found in Deut 2:22, which he interprets to mean that just as the Edomites took possession of Mount Seir from the Horites, so the Israelites later took possession of it from the Edomites, and remained there "until this day." Because Israel did not conquer Edom until the time of David, and because "until this day" signifies a considerable lapse of time since this event, La Peyrère comes to the conclusion that Deuteronomy was composed long after David. Although La Peyrère's analysis is based on an incorrect reading of Deut 2:22 (the passage makes no reference to Israel's

---

52. From *The Judgement and Decree of the University of Oxford Past in their Convocation* (1683), as cited in Gaskin's introduction to *Leviathan*, xi.
53. I. de la Peyrère, *The Theological Systeme upon that Presupposition, that Men were before Adam* (London, 1655) 205–6.
54. *Theological Systeme*, 207–8.

conquest of Edom, only Edom's conquest of this region[55]), his marks one of the first detailed attempts at using internal evidence to identify the time indicated by "until this day."

### Baruch de Spinoza (1632–1677 C.E.)

Spinoza, the seventeenth-century Jewish philosopher, like his English counterpart, felt that a correct understanding of the Bible was essential for the proper governing of a people—the desired result being that religion and politics mix only as topics of discussion at social gatherings, not in public policy. Therefore, in his *Tractatus Theologico-Politicus*,[56] in the chapter entitled "Of the authorship of the Pentateuch, and the other historical books of the Old Testament," Spinoza goes to great lengths to scrutinize the traditional authorial ascriptions, and in so doing he, like Hobbes, depends heavily upon the evidence provided by "until this day."

When discussing the Pentateuch, for example, Spinoza argues that the presence of "until this day" demonstrates that "such testimony cannot have been given of Moses by himself, nor by any who immediately succeeded him, but it must come from someone who lived centuries afterwards, especially as the historian speaks of past times."[57] He comes to the same determination for the book of Joshua, saying "the phrase 'unto this day' shows that the writer was speaking of ancient times."[58] Spinoza concludes that all the historical books, from Genesis to Kings, "are compilations, and that the events therein are recorded as having happened in old time."[59] Spinoza suggests that this compilation was the work of one person:

> When we put these three considerations together, namely, the unity of the subject of all the books, the connection between them, and the fact that they are compilations made many generations after the events they relate had taken place, we come to the conclusion, as I have just stated, that they are all the work of a single historian.[60]

For Spinoza, as for several others already discussed, this historian was Ezra. Although this identification had been proposed by others, Spinoza's

---

55. For the textual problems that may have given rise to this reading, see M. Weinfeld, *Deuteronomy 1–11* (AB 5; Garden City, New York: Doubleday, 1991) 158.
56. Spinoza's *Tractatus Theologico-Politicus* was published in 1670 anonymously and with the fictitious name of a printer from Hamburg. Citations are taken from *The Chief Works of Benedict de Spinoza* (trans. R. H. M. Elwes; New York: Dover, 1951).
57. *Tractatus Theologico-Politicus*, VIII:II.
58. *Tractatus Theologico-Politicus*, VIII:IV.
59. *Tractatus Theologico-Politicus*, VIII:IV.
60. *Tractatus Theologico-Politicus*, VIII:IV.

arguments for the compositional unity of the historical books based upon diverse bodies of evidence (e.g., redactional, literary, historical) became a model for subsequent scholarship.

## *Richard Simon (1638–1712 C.E.)*

Shortly after the publication of Spinoza's *Tractatus*, Richard Simon, a French Oratorian priest, wrote what he intended to be a rebuttal.[61] In his *Histoire Critique du Vieux Testament*, Simon argues that, while certain parts of the Torah are not from Moses—such as those containing our phrase and other material indicating a later time—the core of these books belongs to him. The same cannot be said, however, for the supposed authors of the other biblical books. Regarding the book of Joshua, Simon writes,

> Don Isaac Abravanel wholly rejects the opinion of his ancient Doctours, who have in the Talmud attributed to Joshua the Book that bears his name, and he proves the contrary by many actions and ways of speech which could not proceed from him. As when it is said in the 4th Chapter and 9th Verse that "the twelve stones that Joshua set up in the midst of the Jordan remain to this day." And in the 5th Chapter and 9th Verse, "This place is called Gilgal to this day," from whence it is easie to conclude that one part of this Book was writ some time after these things happened.[62]

And again, for the books of Samuel:

> The Books which we have under the name of Samuel cannot likewise be wholly his, by reason of certain ways of speaking which were not in his time, besides they contain Histories which happened not till after his death. When he speaks of the Ark which was taken by the Philistines, he says that "the high Priests of Dagon, and those who enter into his temple, tread not upon the threshold of the temple to this day." And in another place he adds that "the Ark is to this day in the field of Joshua the Bethshemite." Samuel could not report after this manner deeds which he was not witness of.[63]

Simon also reiterates Abravanel's observation that the reference to the "kings of Judah" in 1 Sam 27:6 is anachronistic and therefore must be assigned to a time after Samuel.

Although Simon intended his work to be a defense of the Bible against the attacks of Hobbes, Spinoza and others, Simon's own book—"a mass of

---

61. R. Simon, *A Critical History of the Old Testament* (London, 1682. French: Paris, 1678).
62. Simon, *A Critical History*, I:VIII.
63. Simon, *A Critical History*, I:VIII.

impiety," as one critic labeled it—was banned by the Church, and all copies were ordered burned. Only six of the original thirteen hundred copies are known to have survived.[64] Two more editions of Simon's work were subsequently published in the Netherlands: one in 1680 (Amsterdam) and another, with a new preface by Simon, in 1685 (Rotterdam). A century later, Johann Salomo Semler translated Simon's work into German, where it had a significant influence on the development of critical scholarship then emerging in Germany.[65]

## 5. Nineteenth-Century Scholarship and "Until This Day"

The advent of the nineteenth century brought with it unprecedented advances in biblical scholarship. With these advances came further developments in the analysis of "until this day."[66]

### *Wilhelm M. L. de Wette (1780–1849 C.E.)*

The contributions of de Wette to the critical study of the Bible, especially his determination that the book of Deuteronomy should be connected with the reforms of Josiah, are well known.[67] In truth, de Wette felt that not only Deuteronomy but most of the historical books were written long after the events they recorded. De Wette, like his predecessors, based this conclusion largely upon the evidence of "until this day."[68] However, his attempts to

---

64. Gray, *Old Testament Criticism*, 104.
65. Simon's emphasis on the role of scribes in compiling and editing Israel's historical books has led some to consider him the founder of modern historical criticism of the Bible. See, esp., Kraus, *Geschichte*, 70; and P. Gilbert, *Petite histoire de l'exégèse biblique* (Lire la Bible 94; Paris: Cerf, 1992) 211–22.
66. For accounts of this period, see J. W. Rogerson, *Old Testament Criticism in the Nineteenth Century* (Philadelphia: Fortress, 1985); R. M. Grant and D. Tracy, *A Short History of the Interpretation of the Bible* (New York: Macmillan, 1963); T. K. Cheyne, *Founders of Old Testament Criticism* (London: Methuen, 1893); R. Smend, *Deutsche Alttestamentler in drei Jahrhunderten* (Göttingen: Vandenhoeck & Ruprecht, 1989); and Kraus, *Geschichte*.
67. De Wette, *Dissertatio critica exegetica qua Deuteronomium a prioribus Pentateuchi libris diversum, alius cujusdam recentioris actoris opus esse monstratur* (Halle, 1805). Wellhausen, in his introduction to the *Prolegomena*, called de Wette "the epoch-making pioneer of historical criticism in this field." See also R. Smend, *Deutsche Alttestamentler in drei Jahrhunderten*, 38–52; J. W. Rogerson, *W. M. L. de Wette, Founder of Modern Biblical Criticism: An Intellectual Biography* (JSOTSup 126; Sheffield: JSOT Press, 1992).
68. De Wette, *Lehrbuch der historisch kritischen Einleitung in die kanonischen und apokryphischen Bücher des Alten Testaments* (5th ed.; Berlin: Reimer, 1840) § 147.

determine the time of authorship based on this phrase often led him in differing, even contradictory, directions.

For example, de Wette noted that the reference to the Canaanites fleeing Gezer and settling at Beeroth "until this day" (Josh 16:10) points to a period of composition for the book no earlier than the time of Solomon, since 1 Kgs 9:16 informs us that Pharaoh had conquered Gezer from the Canaanites and gave it as a dowry to his daughter.[69] Yet, de Wette had already assigned Josh 16:10 to the document "Elohim," the authorship of which he placed during the time of Saul.[70] In agreement with this determination, de Wette argues that the presence of Jebusites in Jerusalem "until this day" (Josh 15:63) points to a time before David's conquest of Jerusalem (although he admits it could refer to a time after David in light of 2 Sam 24:16). However, Joshua's curse upon the one who would rebuild Jericho (Josh 6:26) suggests that this passage was written after the reign of Ahab, during whose reign Jericho was rebuilt and this curse fulfilled (1 Kgs 16:34).[71] De Wette encounters similar problems when attempting to determine the date of other biblical books. In Kings, for example, de Wette suggests that "until this day" must have already been present in the compiler's sources, since its use points to the preexilic period (e.g., 2 Kgs 8:22; 14:7; 16:6), yet the book itself was not compiled until the exile, based on the last notice of that book.[72] De Wette's conclusions for Kings, in fact, aptly summarize his findings for the whole of the Former Prophets: "the common references to a later time, such as 'until this day' . . . do not indicate the same time."[73]

One shortcoming of de Wette's analysis, particularly in Kings, is that he does not allow for more than one stage of development for these books. Before the century's end, however, another scholar would argue for two stages of development for Kings, throwing new light on the analysis of our phrase.

### Abraham Kuenen (1828–1891 C.E.)

That scholar was Abraham Kuenen, who in his *Historisch-critisch Onderzoek* set forth the theory of a dual redaction of the books of Kings.[74] In fact, it was

---

69. De Wette, *Einleitung*, § 169.
70. De Wette, *Einleitung*, § 158, 168, 169.
71. De Wette, *Einleitung*, § 169.
72. De Wette, *Einleitung*, § 185–86. De Wette notes the allusions to the exile in Kings (1 Kgs 8:47; 9:7-8; 14:15; 2 Kgs 20:17) as well as the explicit descriptions of this exile at the end of the book (2 Kings 25).
73. De Wette, *Einleitung*, § 185.
74. The complete title is *Historisch-critisch Onderzoek naar het onstaan en de verzameling*

the preexilic provenance of "until this day" in these books that provided important evidence for his theory. Before evaluating Kuenen's analysis of Kings, however, brief attention must be paid to his treatment of our phrase in its other contexts.

While Kuenen admits that there is nothing to preclude a Mosaic date for "until this day" in the Pentateuch, he believes its use in Genesis, and certainly in Deuteronomy (particularly Deut 3:14 and 34:6), derives from a period long after Moses.[75] As a result, Kuenen attributes "until this day" to the authors believed responsible for these books, which, during his day, meant the recently identified J, E, P, and D sources.[76] Because Kuenen, like most of his contemporaries, treated Genesis through Joshua (the so-called "Hexateuch") as a literary unit, his approach to "until this day" in Joshua is the same: the phrase belongs to the sources making up this book. When attempting to date Joshua, Kuenen, like de Wette, concludes that "the majority of the passages where one encounters this formula leaves us uncertain as to the precise date of the book."[77] Nevertheless, Kuenen's analysis allows him to make some approximations. For example, Kuenen argues that "until this day" in Josh 15:63 points to a time "after David, for until then Jerusalem was still completely in the power of the Jebusites (Judg 19:12), and after its capture by David they remained there along with the Israelites." Similarly, Kuenen observes that Josh 9:27 (the Gibeonites' service at the "altar of YHWH") ascribes to Joshua a policy actually begun by Solomon in connection with the temple.[78] Kuenen finds confirmation for this in the observation that the Gibeonites are still independent during the reign of Saul (2 Sam 21:2). Although Kuenen is unable to pinpoint when this policy was attributed to Joshua, he believes that it had to be a long time after Solomon, since those living nearest his reign would know that he, and not Joshua, established it.[79] The same can be said of Josh 16:10 (the subjugation of the Gezerites), which also ascribes to Joshua a state of affairs actually begun by Solomon.[80] For Kuenen, therefore, although "this day" cannot be located precisely, it suggests a time

---

*van den Boeken des Ouden Verbonds* (3 vols.; Leiden: Akademische Boekhandel van P. Engels, 1861–1865). This survey makes use of both the German and French translations. While the German is closer to the Dutch original, Kuenen oversaw the French translation and incorporated many new insights on biblical criticism, in general, and "until this day," in particular.

75. Kuenen, *Historisch-kritische Einleitung in die Bücher des Alten Testaments*, trans. T. Weber (Leipzig: Otto Schulze, 1887) I:34.

76. Kuenen, *Histoire Critique des Livres de L'Ancien Testament*, trans. M. Pierson; 2 vols. (Paris: Michel Levy, 1866) 40.

77. Kuenen, *Einleitung* I:34.

78. Kuenen, *Einleitung* I:35–36, n. 8.

79. Kuenen, *Einleitung* I:227, n. 15.

80. Kuenen, *Histoire Critique*, 306.

long enough after Solomon's reign that policies instituted by him could be ascribed to someone else.

In the book of Judges, Kuenen similarly observes that "until this day" points to a period long after the events it describes. Yet, here again he concludes that its use does not yield a precise date for the book.[81] The same is true for the books of Samuel, where the phrase likewise indicates that "a considerable lapse of time exists between the events themselves and the time of those who relate them to us," but in answer to the question, "Are we able to determine this period?" Kuenen simply says "No."[82]

Yet, when Kuenen turns to Kings, he comes to a very different conclusion regarding the purpose and provenance of our phrase. Here he observes that "until this day" both confirms realities no longer true after the exile and in many cases appears in passages bound to the very structure of Kings (e.g., 2 Kgs 8:16-24; 14:1-7; 16:1-9).[83] As this structure derives from someone with a Deuteronomistic perspective, Kuenen concludes that "until this day" refers to the time of the preexilic Deuteronomistic redactor (his Rd[1])—a view subsequently embraced by J. Wellhausen, S. R. Driver, and others.[84]

Despite its subsequent influence, Kuenen's conclusion for "until this day" in Kings is somewhat perplexing, especially in view of his earlier analysis of the phrase in Joshua. For example, Kuenen notes that "until this day" in Joshua mirrors its use in Kings, particularly in its reference to non-Israelite forced labor (e.g., Josh 9:27; 16:10; 1 Kgs 9:21). Yet, he assigns "until this day" in Joshua to the various authors of this book, while in Kings he attributes the phrase to a preexilic Deuteronomistic redactor. This is all the more puzzling when we consider that elsewhere Kuenen concludes that the book of Joshua underwent a "Deuteronomistic recension," which includes a number of passages where our phrase appears (Josh 8:29b-30; 9:27b; 10:27; 14:14).[85] These connections seem to have escaped Kuenen's notice, but will prove significant when attempting to locate the provenance of "this day."

---

81. For Kuenen, Judg 2:6–3:6 is the work of a Deuteronomistic author as a preface to the judge cycles, which span from Judg 3:7 to 16:31. Judg 1:1-2:5 and 17-21 also contain very old material, but were added secondarily. Chapters 19–21, although consisting of some older material, show signs of postexilic editing.

82. Kuenen, *Histoire Critique*, 389.

83. Kuenen, *Einleitung*, I:90–91. Based on his analysis of the content and structure of Kings, Kuenen identifies two distinct strata running through these books: one preexilic, the other exilic. His analysis laid the foundation for the theory of a dual redaction of the DH.

84. J. Wellhausen, *Die Composition des Hexateuchs und der historischen Bücher des Alten Testaments* (Berlin: Reimer, 1889) 298–99. S. R. Driver, *Introduction to the Literature of the Old Testament* (New York: Charles Scribner's Sons, 1892) 188.

85. Kuenen, *Einleitung*, I:126.

## Wilhelm Vatke (1806–1882 C.E.)

We close our survey of nineteenth-century scholarship with another individual whose influence on the field of biblical studies has been sizeable. Wilhelm Vatke's determination that D predated P,[86] when combined with de Wette's association of D with the Josianic reforms, set the stage for Wellhausen's landmark study.

Concerning "until this day," Vatke, like de Wette before him, observes that in most cases the source of this phrase is too difficult to isolate. He points out, for example, that although the phrase in Kings indicates a time prior to the exile, the book itself was not completed until exilic or postexilic times.[87] He suggests, therefore, that "until this day" belonged to the compiler's sources, and not to the compiler himself. Unfortunately, Vatke does not engage Kuenen's analysis of Kings, which is regrettable since Vatke comes to the same conclusion Kuenen did regarding the source of our phrase, only for a different book.

In his analysis of Joshua, Vatke observes that "until this day" frequently appears adjacent to Deuteronomistic redactional material. For example, he notes that "until this day" in Josh 7:26 is immediately followed by the Deuteronomic command, "Do not fear nor be dismayed" (Josh 8:1; cf. Deut 1:21). Likewise, in Josh 8:28 "until this day" is used in connection with the Deuteronomic description of the destruction of cities (Deut 13:17). And again, in Josh 8:29 "until this day" is immediately followed by Joshua's reading of the Law as commanded by Moses in Deut 27:1-8. These and other examples lead Vatke to conclude: "'until this day' (in Joshua) is the usual formula of the Deuteronomist."[88] Vatke's insights, although coming at the end of a long and prestigious career, seem to have gone largely unnoticed by later commentators.

## 6. Twentieth-Century Scholarship and "Until This Day"

While the above survey might leave one with the impression that a thorough evaluation of "until this day" had already been accomplished by the

---

86. W. Vatke, *Die biblische Theologie wissenschaftlich dargestellt. Teil 1: Die Religion des Alten Testamentes nach den kanonischen Büchern entwickelt* (Berlin: G. Bethge, 1835). Vatke's relative dating of D and P has since been called into question, though it remains the scholarly consensus. For the current state of the question, see E. W. Nicholson, *The Pentateuch in the Twentieth Century: The Legacy of Julius Wellhausen* (Oxford: Oxford University Press, 1998) esp. 3–28, 196–221.

87. Vatke, *Historisch-kritische Einleitung* (Bonn: E. Strauss, 1886) 468–69. Vatke's views on "until this day" in Kings, in fact, seem informed by de Wette's.

88. Vatke, *Historisch-kritische Einleitung*, 422.

twentieth century, in fact, it was not until B. S. Childs's 1963 *JBL* article, "A Study of the Formula 'Until This Day,'" that a work devoted exclusively to this phrase appeared.[89]

## Brevard S. Childs

After providing a brief statistical sketch of "until this day" in the biblical text, Childs turns to its grammatical use.[90] He observes that the phrase appears primarily in two grammatical constructions. The first Childs calls the "pure, unbroken" form; namely, עַל־כֵּן + perfect verb + object + עַד הַיּוֹם הַזֶּה. For example, Josh 7:26b reads:

עַל־כֵּן קָרָא שֵׁם הַמָּקוֹם הַהוּא עֵמֶק עָכוֹר עַד הַיּוֹם הַזֶּה

> Therefore the name of that place is called 'the Valley of Trouble' until this day.

In these cases, which only account for eight of its over eighty appearances, the subject is "general or impersonal," the verb is "frequentative," and "until this day" modifies the verb.[91]

In contrast to this "pure" form is the use of "until this day" with the converted imperfect. For example, Josh 6:25 reads:

וַתֵּשֶׁב (רָחָב) בְּקֶרֶב יִשְׂרָאֵל עַד הַיּוֹם הַזֶּה

> And (Rahab) settled in the midst of Israel until this day.

In these cases the verb is no longer impersonal but specific, and "until this day" no longer modifies the verb but a noun. The reason for these changes, Childs argues, is that "until this day" in these latter cases "has been added secondarily as a redactional commentary on existing traditions."[92] Childs notes that the same is true for all uses of "until this day" with the converted imperfect, whether transitive or intransitive, since in the absence of this phrase these same grammatical structures are always "historical past, specifically aorist." In Childs's estimation, then, "עַד הַיּוֹם הַזֶּה . . . in the great majority of cases is a formula of personal testimony added to, and confirming, a received tradition."[93]

In light of its redactional nature, Childs argues that the biblical histo-

---

89. Cf. I. L. Seeligmann's study ("Etiological Elements in Biblical Historiography," *Zion* 26 [1961] 141–69 [Hebrew]), which, while including a discussion of "until this day," is concerned with etiological tales more generally.
90. For the statistics related to "until this day," see chapter 2.
91. Childs, "Until This Day," 281.
92. Childs, "Until This Day," 283.
93. Childs, "Until This Day," 292.

rian employed "until this day" much like his Greek and Roman counterparts used similar formulae: "to validate some aspect of the tradition which can still be verified in his own time." Childs writes:

> In our opinion, the use of the formula in the OT is closely parallel to this latter usage, namely, to the historian's personal witness . . . the writers are recording independent tradition to which they add the formula secondarily.

Childs concludes his study by considering who might be responsible for this "formula of personal testimony." He begins by noting that "until this day" in Josh 15:63 (Jebusites in Jerusalem) and 16:10 (Canaanites in Gezer) "points to a period not later than the tenth century"—presumably because, in the former case, David conquered Jerusalem and displaced the Jebusites in this century and, in the latter case, Pharaoh conquered Gezer and gave it to his daughter as a dowry during this same century (1 Kgs 9:16).[94] Then, skipping to the books of Kings, Childs observes:

> The formula appears in material most likely from the source styled the 'Book of the Acts of Solomon' (1 Kgs 11:41; cf. 8:8; 9:21), from material in the 'Book of the Chronicles of the Kings of Judah' (2 Kgs 8:23; cf. 2 Kgs 8:22; 10:27, etc.), from a collection of prophetic narratives (2 Kgs 2:2), and only infrequently from the Deuteronomistic Historian (2 Kgs 17:23, 34).

Based upon the variety of sources where "until this day" appears in Kings, as well as the temporal distance between its use in Joshua and Kings, Childs concludes, "the formula reflects the age of many different redactors."

Childs's determination that "until this day" is redactional has been widely accepted, and even further elucidated, by subsequent scholarship.[95] A number of scholars, however, although not engaging Childs's study directly, continue to embrace Kuenen's conclusion that "until this day" in Kings reflects the perspective of a preexilic Deuteronomistic redactor.

## *Frank Moore Cross*

F. M. Cross, in his influential *Canaanite Myth and Hebrew Epic*, argues that "until this day" constitutes important evidence for establishing the existence of a preexilic edition of the DH. He writes,

---

94. Childs, "Until This Day," 292.
95. See, e.g., B. Long, *The Problem of Etiological Narrative in the Old Testament* (BZAW 108; Berlin: de Gruyter, 1968); R. G. Boling, *Judges: A New Translation with Notes and Commentary* (AB 6A; Garden City, New York: Doubleday, 1975); idem, *Joshua: A New Translation with Notes and Commentary* (AB 6; Garden City, New York: Doubleday, 1982); S. L. McKenzie, *The Trouble With Kings: The Composition of the Books of Kings in the Deuteronomistic History* (Leiden: E. J. Brill, 1991); A. Caquot and P. de Robert, *Les Livres de Samuel* (CAT 6; Geneva: Labor et Fides, 1994); R. D. Nelson, *Joshua: A Commentary* (OTL; Louisville: Westminster John Knox, 1997).

Older literary critics, as well as their more recent followers, argued for two editions of the Deuteronomistic complex of traditions, one pre-Exilic, the basic promulgation of the Deuteronomistic history, and one Exilic, retouching the earlier edition to bring it up to date ... Some of their arguments are very strong, for example, the use of the expression "to this day," not merely in the sources but also in portions by the Deuteronomistic author, which presumes the existence of the Judean state, notably 2 Kgs 8:22 and 16:6.[96]

Similarly, R. E. Friedman, in his *The Exile and Biblical Narrative*, cites "until this day" as positive evidence for a preexilic layer within the DH.[97] And, more recently, M. Cogan and H. Tadmor have connected "until this day" in 2 Kings specifically to Cross's preexilic Deuteronomistic redactor (Dtr¹).[98] While these scholars ultimately base their arguments for the existence of a preexilic edition of the DH on evidence other than "until this day," they all agree that this phrase provides additional support for this thesis.[99]

However, not all scholars who hold to Cross's theory of a dual redaction of the DH have agreed with his estimation of the value of "until this day" for identifying a preexilic stratum in this history. Rather, they agree with Childs's contention that the exact provenance of "until this day" is too difficult to ascertain.

## *Richard D. Nelson*

R. Nelson, for example, in his *The Double Redaction of the Deuteronomistic History*, argues that "until this day" should be placed among those "arguments of little value" for establishing a preexilic redaction of the DH.[100] As Nelson observes, Childs's insight that this phrase is redactional "does not

---

96. F. M. Cross, *Canaanite Myth and Hebrew Epic* (Cambridge: Harvard University Press, 1973), 275. Cross's analysis originally appeared in "The Structure of the Deuteronomic History," in *Perspectives in Jewish Learning* (ACJS 3; Chicago: College of Jewish Studies, 1968) 9–24.

97. R. E. Friedman, *The Exile and Biblical Narrative* (HSM 22; Decatur, GA: Scholars Press, 1981) 5.

98. M. Cogan and H. Tadmor, *2 Kings* (AB 11; Garden City, New York: Doubleday, 1988) 96, 214. Their reasons for assigning "until this day" to a preexilic Deuteronomistic redactor will be addressed in chapter 3 when considering the use of "until this day" across the DH.

99. A. Campbell ("Martin Noth and the Deuteronomistic History" in *The History of Israel's Traditions: The Heritage of Martin Noth*, ed. S. L. McKenzie and M. P. Graham [JSOTSup 182; Sheffield: JSOT, 1994] 31–62) overstates Cross's dependence on "until this day," though he is right to insist upon the presence of Deuteronomistic ideology in connection with Deuteronomistic language–subjects taken up in chapter 3.

100. R. Nelson, *The Double Redaction of the Deuteronomistic History* (JSOTSup 18; Sheffield, 1981) 24.

automatically determine whether this commentary was added by the historian or by his literary predecessors." He continues,

> In fact, in most cases, the phrase belongs without question to the historian's narrative sources: the *Sammler* of Joshua (Josh 4:9; 5:9; 7:26; 8:28-29; 10:27), the judges narratives (Judg 6:24; 10:4; 15:19), the Ark Story (1 Sam 5:5; 6:18; 2 Sam 6:8), the Rise of David (1 Sam 27:6; 30:25; 2 Sam 4:3), the Succession History (2 Sam 18:18), and the Elisha cycle (2 Kgs 2:22).[101]

Thus, similar to Childs, Nelson argues that the presence of "until this day" in so many sources indicates that it derives from many different hands.

## SUMMARY

Early Jewish and Christian commentators, although attempting to grapple with the evidence as best they could, were at a disadvantage when analyzing "until this day" due to the constraints imposed upon them by the traditional authorial ascriptions. For these commentators (e.g., Rashbam, Radak, Gersonides, Origen), "until this day" belonged to the reputed author of a given book, despite the phrase's seemingly late provenance. The exception to this rule was the notice of Moses' death, which, although possibly deriving from Moses himself (R. Simeon, Luther), was likely written by Joshua or Eleazer (Rashi, Ibn Ezra). Another possibility is that these seemingly late notices derive from Ezra, who, according to tradition, re-created by divine inspiration the biblical books after they had been destroyed during the Babylonian conquest of Jerusalem (Jerome, Abelard).

It was not until the fifteenth and sixteenth centuries that the evidence of "until this day" resulted in the serious questioning of the traditional authorial ascriptions (Abravanel), and by the seventeenth and eighteenth centuries, discussions of "until this day" became the hallmark of the emerging field of biblical criticism (Hobbes, Spinoza). Most scholars, however, were content to point out the inadequacies of the earlier authorial ascriptions without locating the time and place indicated by "until this day." If a time was suggested, it was usually based on the last datable event within a particular book, which for Kings meant the exile and for Chronicles the reign of Cyrus.

By the beginning of the nineteenth century, more attention was paid to determining to whose day "this day" referred, with the hope of tracing the development of the biblical text (de Wette, Kuenen, Vatke). Although some scholars felt they could isolate the source of the phrase for individual books

---

101. Nelson, *Double Redaction*, 24.

(e.g., Kuenen for Kings; Vatke for Joshua), in most cases they felt stymied by what they perceived as conflicting evidence.

The twentieth century saw unprecedented advances in biblical scholarship, yet it was during this same period that scholars largely ignored "until this day." The phrase had served its purpose by demonstrating the inaccuracy of the traditional authorial ascriptions, but further study seemed fruitless for generating new information for tracing the origins of the biblical books. Childs's study is a notable exception. However, his analysis left many questions unanswered. For example, how does his conclusion that "until this day" is redactional fit into recent models for understanding the development of the biblical text? To what redactors do we ascribe these notices of "personal testimony" and what information, if any, does the phrase itself provide for determining when and where they lived? And what of Vatke's and Kuenen's conclusion that "until this day" in Joshua and Kings, respectively, derives from a single Deuteronomistic redactor? Is this an accurate appraisal of the evidence? What about the other books making up the DH—a hypothetical work that, at the time of Vatke's and Kuenen's writing, had not yet been identified? Are there indications in these other books that "until this day" belongs to a Deuteronomistic redactor, or is Childs's and Nelson's observations correct that the use of this phrase is too varied to belong to a single hand? Finally, what about Radak's observation that several uses of "until this day" are thematically linked? Are there other such connections among the objects and institutions said to persist "until this day"? Are there reasons why some objects and institutions are thus highlighted and others are not? Does the location or character of these objects and institutions give us any indication of who may be pointing them out to us, when, and why?

Scholars have long sensed that "until this day" held the key for understanding the origins and development of the biblical text. By combining the insights gained from the above survey with recent advances in our understanding of the redactional history of the biblical text, the identification of whose day is "this day"—which has engaged scholars for nearly two millennia—may now be possible.

## 2

# "Until This Day" and the Deuteronomistic History

καὶ νῦν οὗτος ὁ βασιλεὺς ἕστηκε ἐν τῷ ἱρῷ τοῦ Ἡφαίστου λίθινος, ἔχων ἐπὶ τῆς χειρὸς μῦν, λέγων διὰ γραμμάτων τάδε· ἐς ἐμέ τις ὁρέων εὐσεβὴς ἔστω.[1]

—Herodotus, *Histories* 2.141.6

The impulse to substantiate received traditions by appealing to extant objects is common among ancient historians.[2] In the biblical text, this historical impulse is expressed most often by the phrase "until this day." In the DH alone "until this day" appears over forty times to highlight some aspect of Israelite culture or history.[3] This chapter surveys these various

---

1. "And even now a stone statue of the king stands in the temple of Hephaestus, with a mouse in his hand, and an inscription that reads: 'Look at me, and learn reverence.'" Herodotus appeals to this statue and its inscription as evidence of Sennacherib's failed invasion of Egypt. According to Herodotus's sources ("the priests of Hephaestus"), mice swept through the Assyrian camp and ate its weaponry, forcing Sennacherib and his army to return home. This statue, erected by the Egyptian king "Sethos," commemorates this event and warns other would-be invaders against such actions. Some have seen in Herodotus's account an echo of the biblical story of Sennacherib's sudden retreat due to the devastation of his army by the angel of YHWH (2 Kgs 19:35–36). Herodotus's account of the mice, by this view, is a distorted account of a plague that devastated the Assyrian army, a circumstance that the Bible ascribes to angelic agency. For further discussion, see Cogan and Tadmor, *2 Kings*, 249–51.

2. See, e.g., Herodotus, *Histories* 1.181; 2.135.4; 4.10.3; 4.12.1; 7.178.2, etc.; Thucydides, *Peloponnesian War* 1.93.2, 5; 2.15.2, 5; 6.54.7, etc.; Pausanias, *Description of Greece* 3.22.12; 8.15.4; 8.44.1, etc.

3. When used etiologically (the focus of this study), "until this day" appears six times in Genesis (19:37, 38; 26:33; 32:33; 35:20, 47:26); forty-three times in the DH (see chapter 3, figure 3.1, for a complete list); ten times in Chronicles, five of which repeat material from Samuel-Kings (1 Chr 4:41, 43; 5:26; 10:19 = 1 Kgs 12:19; 13:11 = 2 Sam 6:8; 2 Chr 5:9 = 1 Kgs 8:8; 8:8 = 1 Kgs 9:21; 20:26; 21:10 = 2 Kgs 8:22; 35:25); and once in Ezekiel (20:29). Only twice in the DH

uses in order to determine more specifically how this phrase is used, why it is so used, and, if possible, to begin to isolate to whose day or days "this day" refers.

## USES OF "UNTIL THIS DAY" IN THE DEUTERONOMISTIC HISTORY

The phrase "until this day" is employed in the DH to highlight four principle aspects of Israelite society: (1) its geography, (2) its demography, (3) its political policies, and (4) its cultic practices.

### 1. Geographical Uses of "Until This Day"

"Until this day" appears most frequently in narratives recounting the etiology of an aspect of Israel's geography.[4] In particular, our phrase testifies to the persistence of (a) place-names, (b) memorials, and (c) natural landmarks.

#### a. Place-Names

The geographical locations said to persist "until this day" include: (i) two regions and (ii) six individual sites or settlements.[5]

*i. Regions*
**(1) Origin of the name Havvoth Jair (Deut 3:14; Judg 10:4).**
In the context of describing the settlement of various peoples, Deut 3:14 reports, "Jair the son of Manasseh took all of the region of Argob as far

---

do we find a variant formula: Josh 10:27 has the longer עַד־עֶצֶם הַיּוֹם הַזֶּה, which in the context has the same meaning as עַד הַיּוֹם הַזֶּה (cf. Josh 4:9; 7:26; and 8:29); 2 Kgs 10:27 has the shorter עַד הַיּוֹם, again with the same meaning as עַד הַיּוֹם הַזֶּה and with textual evidence for the fuller phrase (LXX, Targumim, Vulgate, and two Hebrew manuscripts). The remaining uses of "until this day" are in direct speech (see conclusion). Phrases bearing some similarity to עַד הַיּוֹם הַזֶּה, but not included in the present study (as they appear in direct speech), include: כַּיּוֹם הַזֶּה (though, see conclusion, n. 42); עַד־עָתָּה (though, see chapter 5, n. 35) and עַד־הֵנָּה. The related phrases עַד־הַיּוֹם הַהוּא (Judg 18:1) and עַד הַיָּמִים הָהֵם (1 Kgs 3:2; 2 Kgs 18:4) are discussed in chapter 3.

    4. The phrase itself is not etiological in the strict sense. See Childs, "Until This Day" and B. O. Long, "Etymological Etiology in the Dt Historian," *CBQ* 31 (1969) 35–41.

    5. The importance of distinguishing between large geographical areas (e.g., regions) and individual sites (e.g., cities, camps, etc.) becomes apparent below (see, "Summary").

as the border of the Geshurites and the Maacathites." As a result, this region is called Havvoth Jair "until this day."[6]

Judges seems to offer an alternative explanation for the naming of Havvoth Jair. According to Judg 10:4, "Jair the Gileadite," a judge who ruled over Israel twenty-two years, had "thirty sons who rode on thirty donkeys and had thirty cities in Gilead." They called these cities Havvoth Jair, which remains their name "until this day."[7]

Despite the seeming discrepancies between these two accounts (which will be taken up in chapter 3), both passages attest to the persistence of the place-name "Havvoth Jair" to describe a region in northern Transjordan consisting of numerous cities.[8]

## (2) Origin of the name Cabul (1 Kgs 9:13).

Solomon, in exchange for materials needed to build his palace and temple in Jerusalem, gives Hiram of Tyre twenty cities in the far north of Israel. Upon seeing his newly acquired territory, Hiram is disappointed and declares, "What are these cities you have given to me, my brother?" The name "Eretz Cabul" (אֶרֶץ כָּבוּל), which is said to derive from this event, is still used for this region "until this day."[9]

---

6. The meaning of "Havvoth" (חַוֹּת), which appears only in connection with this region (see Num 32:41; Deut 3:14; Josh 13:30; Judg 10:4; 1 Kgs 4:13; 1 Chr 2:23), is uncertain, though cf. Arabic ḥiwā, "a circle of tents" or "an encampment" (hence, the "settlements" or "villages" of Jair). On the awkward syntax of this verse, see S. R. Driver, *A Critical and Exegetical Commentary on Deuteronomy* (3rd ed.; ICC; Edinburgh: T & T Clark, 1902; repr. 1951) 54–57; M. Weinfeld, *Deuteronomy 1–11*, 182–85. Otherwise, there are no text critical issues affecting the interpretation of this verse.

7. Reading the second occurrence of עֲיָרִים ("donkeys") in MT as עָרִים ("cities"). Cf. LXX (πόλεις), Vulgate (*civitatum*).

8. According to Num 32:41, Havvoth Jair is located just east of the Sea of Galilee in a region granted to the Transjordanian tribe of Manasseh. The reasons for the discrepancies between Deut 3:14 and Judg 10:4, where Deuteronomy extends the geographical area of this region and increases its habitations from thirty to sixty, are discussed in chapter 3.

9. The connection between Hiram's disappointment and the naming of this region is unclear. LXX renders כָּבוּל as ὅριον ("boundary"), presumably for Hebrew גְּבוּל ("border"), but this does not clarify matters. Josephus (*Ant.* 8.5.3 §142) proposes Phoenician *ke bal* "good for nothing," which, though appealing, remains speculative. Alternatively, *b. Šabb.* 54a relates the name to *kbl* ("to bind or tie"), understanding אֶרֶץ כָּבוּל as "a land of binding" (i.e., a land where one's feet get bound in the marshy clay). In short, the matter remains unresolved. The town of Cabul is usually identified with the modern-day village of Kabul, situated about 8 km southeast of Acco. The lack of evidence for Iron Age occupation, however, has led Z. Gal ("Cabul, Jiphtah-El and the Boundary between Asher and Zebulun in the Light of Archaeological Evidence," *ZDPV* 101 [1985] 114–27) to identify biblical Cabul with Khirbet Ras ez-Zeitun (Horvat Rosh-Zayit), about 2 km northeast of Kabul, where there is evidence of a fortified town as early as the tenth century B.C.E. The relationship between the village of Cabul and the larger "land of Cabul" remains uncertain.

## ii. Individual Sites or Settlements

**(1) Origin of the name Gilgal (Josh 5:9).**

Prior to conquering Canaan, the Israelites are circumcised—a deed that was neglected by the wilderness generation. In response, YHWH announces, "Today I have rolled away the reproach of Egypt from upon you" (הַיּוֹם גַּלּוֹתִי אֶת־חֶרְפַּת מִצְרַיִם מֵעֲלֵיכֶם).[10] The location of this event is called Gilgal "until this day."[11]

**(2) Origin of the name Emek Achor (Josh 7:26b).**

As a result of Achan's violation of the ban in the battle of Jericho, he and his family are executed. Because Achan "troubled" (עכר) Israel by his actions, the place of his judgment is referred to as the "Valley of Trouble" (עֵמֶק עָכוֹר) "until this day."[12]

**(3) Origin of the name Luz (Judg 1:26).**

During the period of the judges, a man from Luz (Bethel) assists the Israelites in capturing his city. In exchange, the Israelites spare the man, who then relocates to "the land of the Hittites," where he founds a city and names it Luz, which is its name "until this day."[13]

**(4) Origin of the name Mahaneh Dan (Judg 18:12).**

Judges 18 traces the migration of the Danites from the central coast of Israel to their new tribal territory in the far north. On their way, six hundred

---

10. The Old Greek lacks the end of v. 9 and the first half of v. 10, most likely due to haplography (גלגל > גלגל). See R. Nelson, *Joshua*, 93.

11. The exact location of Gilgal is unknown. The notice in Josh 4:19—that it is "on the eastern border of Jericho" (בִּקְצֵה מִזְרַח יְרִיחוֹ)—provides only a general locale. Among the proposed sites are Tell en-Nitla, 3.5 km east of Jericho, and two sites near Khirbet el-Mefjir, about 3 km northeast of Jericho. See J. Muilenburg, "The Site of Ancient Gilgal," *BASOR* 140 (1955) 11–27; and B. M. Bennett, Jr., "The Search for Israelite Gilgal," *PEQ* 104 (1972) 111–22.

12. Emek Achor is located on Judah's northern border (Josh 15:7) and has been identified with modern-day El Buqê'ah ("the little valley"), bordered by Wâdī Dabr on the north and Wâdī en-Nár on the south. See, e.g., F. M. Cross and J. T. Milik, "Explorations in the Judaean Buqê'ah," *BASOR* 142 (1956) 5–17. Alternatively, H. W. Wolff ("Die Ebene Achor," *ZDPV* 70 [1954] 76–81) has identified Emek Achor with Wâdī en-Nuwê'ime north of Jericho. This location, however, seems too far north in light of Josh 15:7. Again, its approximate location is what concerns us here. For textual analysis, see the discussion of Josh 6:26a below.

13. The location of this new Luz is unknown. The "land of the Hittites" has traditionally been identified with the region just north of ancient Israel (Syria and Lebanon, both of which were under Hittite control in the Late Bronze Age). However, N. K. Gottwald (*The Tribes of YHWH: A Sociology of the Religion of Liberated Israel, 1250–1050 B.C.E.* [Maryknoll, NY: Orbis, 1979] 559–60) has proposed that the Luz referred to here was west of Bethel (cf. Josh 16:2). The tradition that Bethel was once called Luz is mentioned in a number of passages (Gen 28:19; 35:6; 48:3; Judg 1:23). There are no textual variants in this verse bearing on the use of "until this day" or the meaning of the passage.

Danites set up camp near Kiriath Jearim, northwest of Jerusalem, which is called Mahaneh Dan "until this day."[14]

### (5) Origin of the name Perez-Uzzah (2 Sam 6:8).

Second Samuel 6 records David's first attempt at bringing the Ark to Jerusalem. During its transfer, Uzzah places his hand upon the Ark to steady it and is struck dead by God. Because God "burst forth" (פָּרִץ) upon Uzzah, the location of this event is called Perez-Uzzah "until this day."[15]

### (6) Origin of the name Joktheel (2 Kgs 14:7).

Amaziah, king of Judah, defeats the Edomites in the Valley of Salt, whereupon he captures Sela and renames it Joktheel, a name that persists "until this day."[16]

## b. Memorials

We are given the locations of eight memorials that remain "until this day." These fall into two general categories: (i) individual memorials or burial mounds and (ii) national memorials or commemorative stones.

### i. Individual memorials or burial mounds
### (1) Moses' Tomb (Deut 34:6).

After YHWH shows Moses the land of Canaan from atop Mount Nebo, Moses dies and is buried in the valley opposite Beth-Peor.[17] While the

---

14. The statement that Mahaneh Dan is "in Kiriath-jearim (modern-day Deir el-'Azar) in Judah" (בְּקִרְיַת יְעָרִים בִּיהוּדָה) places it about 14 km northwest of Jerusalem. However, the statement following "until this day" ("behold it is west of Kiriath-Jearim," הִנֵּה אַחֲרֵי קִרְיַת יְעָרִים) places it even further west. As with Judg 1:16, there are no significant textual issues bearing on the translation of "until this day" or the passage as a whole.

15. While the exact location of Perez-Uzzah is unknown, the narrative in 2 Samuel 6 places it somewhere between Baale-Judah (i.e., Kiriath-Jearim; cf. Josh 15:9 and 1 Chr 13:6) and Jerusalem. Perhaps, following McCarter (2 Samuel, 170), this location marked a breach in the fortifications of Jerusalem, though it may also have denoted a noteworthy topographical feature or geological phenomenon (e.g., a fissure or spring). Two Hebrew manuscripts read "the name of" (שֵׁם ה...) before "that place" (הַמָּקוֹם הַהוּא). Otherwise, there are no textual variants affecting the interpretation of the passage or "until this day."

16. The traditional identification of Sela with Petra (LXX; Eusebius) is unlikely. The best candidate is modern-day es-Sela', just north-west of Buseira (biblical Bozrah). In support of the latter identification, excavations have revealed the remains of a fortified city dating from the ninth to seventh centuries B.C.E. See B. Mazar, "Sela," EncMiqr 5.1050–51; Y. Aharoni, The Land of the Bible: A Historical Geography (2nd ed.; Philadelphia: Westminster, 1979) 441. Such remains are absent at Umm el-Bayyârah (the region surrounding Petra) until the seventh century B.C.E. See W. M. Fanwar, "Sela," ABD 5.1073–74.

17. The valley opposite Beth-Peor places Moses' tomb in northwest Moab (note the addi-

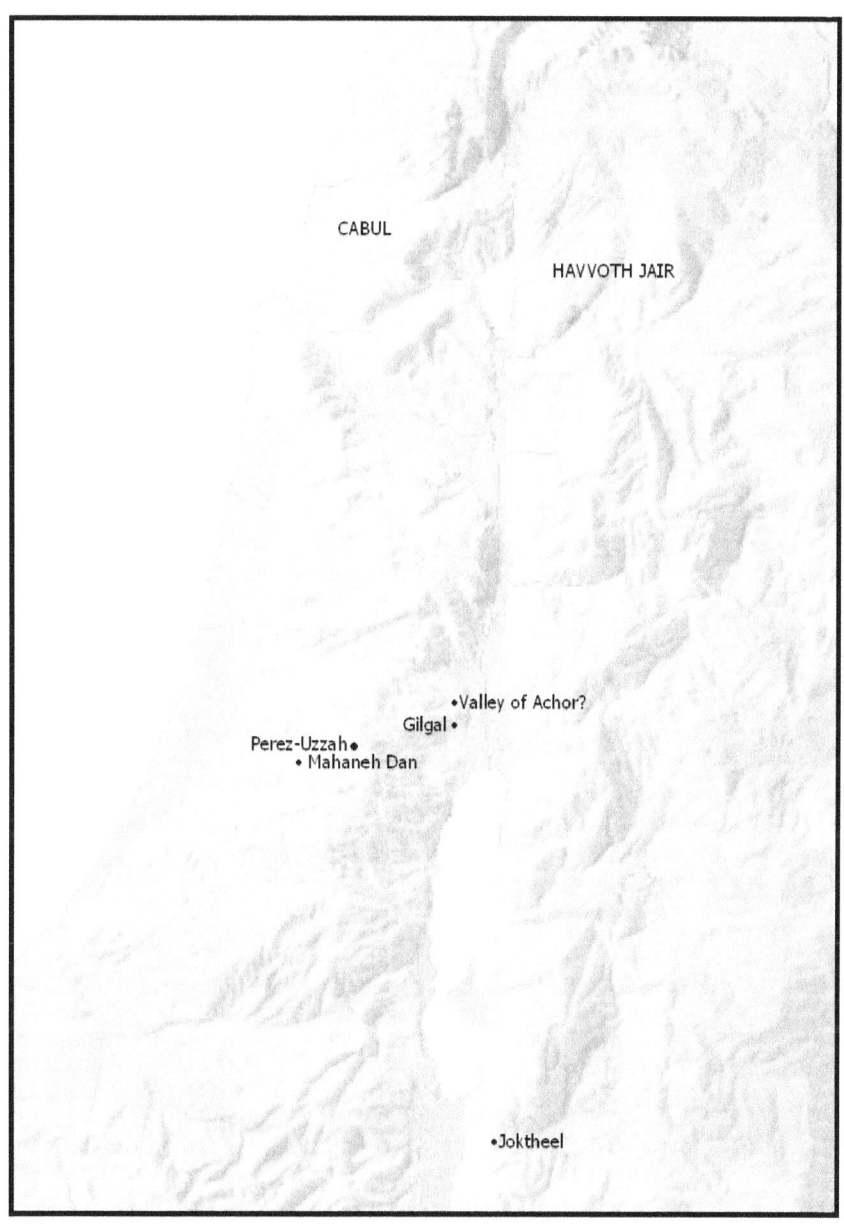

Figure 2.1: Place-names existing "until this day."

approximate location of his burial is known (the valley), its exact location remains unknown "until this day."

### (2) Achan's Burial Mound in the Valley of Achor (Josh 7:26a).

After confessing his violation of the ban during the conquest of Jericho, Achan and his family are executed and "a large pile of stones" (גַּל־אֲבָנִים גָּדוֹל) is erected over their bodies. These stones stand in the Valley of Achor "until this day."[18]

### (3) Burial Mound at Ai (Josh 8:29).

After hanging the king of Ai on a tree, the Israelites take his body down and cast it into the city's gate, after which they cover it with a "large pile of stones" (גַּל־אֲבָנִים גָּדוֹל) that can be seen "until this day."[19]

### (4) Burial Cave at Makkedah (Josh 10:27).

Upon executing the five kings of the failed Amorite confederacy, the Israelites throw their bodies into a cave at Makkedah and cover the entrance with "large stones" (אֲבָנִים גְּדֹלוֹת[20]), which remain there "until this day."[21]

### (5) Absalom's Pillar (2 Sam 18:18).

Concerned that his name will be forgotten after death, Absalom erects

---

tion of "in the land of Moab" in MT, which is lacking in several important Greek manuscripts). Although the exact location of Beth-Peor is unknown, the possibilities include Khirbet 'Ayun Musa, about .5 km north of Mt. Nebo, Khirbet el-Meḥaṭṭa on the Mushaqqar ridge; and Khirbet esh-Sheikh Jayil. Actually, it is not Moses' tomb that is said to persist (although this is implied); rather, the ignorance of its exact location continues "until this day." Whether this is mentioned to discourage attempts at locating and/or venerating Moses' tomb (cf. Moses' bronze serpent; 2 Kgs 18:4) or for some other reason, is unclear. On the use of "until this day" in connection with possible sites of cultic activity, see the discussion in the conclusion.

18. LXX lacks the initial "until this day" in Josh 7:26a, likely due to its perceived redundancy with its use at the end of the verse. For a similar use of the phrase to attest to both a place name and a memorial, see Josh 8:28–29, below. For the identification of this valley, see the earlier discussion of this verse.

19. LXX lacks "large" (μέγαν; see Josh 7:26) in the phrase "a large pile of stones" and describes the location of the casting of the corpse as "into the pit" (εἰς τὸν βόθρον), seemingly reading Hebrew פחת for פתח in the phrase פתח שער העיר. The general location of the burial is all that concerns us here. See n. 25.

20. As noted above (n. 3), this verse marks the only occurrence of the fuller phrase (עַד־עֶצֶם הַיּוֹם הַזֶּה) in the Hebrew Bible. For similar notices of stone memorials, see Josh 4:9; 7:26; and 8:29.

21. Joshua 15 places Makkedah near Lachish (15:41) and Azekah (15:10) in the Shephelah. Its exact location is unknown. Noth ("Die fünf Könige in der Höhle von Makkeda," *PJ* 33 [1937] 22–36) suggested a location further southeast based on the descriptions by Eusebius. Cf. G. E. Wright ("The Literary and Historical Problem of Joshua 10 and Judges 1," *JNES* 5 [1946] 105–14), who prefers the biblical description over Eusebius.

a standing stone (מַצֶּבֶת) in the King's Valley,[22] which is still called "the Pillar of Absalom" (יַד אַבְשָׁלֹם) "until this day."[23]

*ii. National memorials or commemorative stones*
**(1) Memorial of Twelve Stones near the Jordan River (Josh 4:9).**
Upon crossing the Jordan River, Joshua commands that twelve stones (שְׁתֵּים עֶשְׂרֵה אֲבָנִים), representing the twelve tribes of Israel, be erected as a memorial to this event. These stones "are there until this day."[24]

**(2) Ruins at Ai (Josh 8:28).**
After defeating Ai, the Israelites burn the city, which explains why it is "a tel of perpetual/ancient desolation (תֵּל־עוֹלָם שְׁמָמָה) until this day."[25]

### c. Natural Landmarks

Three natural landmarks remain "until this day": (i) two springs and (ii) one rock.

*i. Springs*
**(1) Origin of the Spring at Lehi (Judg 15:19).**
Following his slaying of a thousand Philistines with a donkey's jawbone (לְחִי), Samson becomes thirsty and calls out to YHWH (וַיִּקְרָא אֶל־יְהוָה).

---

22. Determining the location of Absalom's pillar is dependent upon a proper identification of the "King's Valley." From Gen 14:17–18, it would seem that the King's Valley is somewhere near Jerusalem. According to Josephus (*Ant* 7.10.3 §243), Absalom's pillar was located about two stadia (ca. 400 m) outside of Jerusalem. While Josephus does not specify in what direction from the city, it seems he has in mind the Kidron Valley to the east (the location of the present-day "Absalom's Pillar," which dates to about the time of Josephus). For the identification of the King's Valley, see M. C. Astour, "Shaveh, Valley of," *ABD* 5.1168.

23. The use of the Niphal of קרא (וַיִּקָּרֵא) with "until this day" is unique in the DH, where the Qal predominates. The consonantal text allows for the Qal, which may be original (cf. LXX: ἐκάλεσεν).

24. The location of these stones—whether on the bank of the river or in its midst (or both), or even at Gilgal—is unclear. See, e.g., the comments of Boling, *Joshua*, 168–75. Perhaps, as with other uses of "until this day," we have two accounts of a stone memorial, one of which is confirmed by our phrase. See, e.g., Absalom's grave versus his pillar (2 Sam 18:17–18) and the two altars built by Gideon (Judg 6:24, 26–27). LXX and Vulgate describe the memorial of v. 9 as consisting of "twelve other stones" (Greek: ἄλλους δώδεκα λίθους; Latin: *alios quoque duodecim lapides*) in order to clarify the relationship between this altar (at the Jordan) and the other described in the preceding and following verses (at Gilgal).

25. Ai ("the Ruin") is usually identified with Et-Tell ("the heap"), a large site just east of modern Beitin (biblical Bethel; cf. Gen 12:8). See J. A. Callaway, *The Early Bronze Age Citadel and Lower City at Ai (et-Tell)* (Cambridge, MA: ASOR, 1980).

In response, God causes a spring to issue forth from the ground. This spring, which is called "Spring of the Caller" (עֵין הַקּוֹרֵא[26]), remains at Lehi (לְחִי) "until this day."[27]

**(2) Origin of a Fresh Spring at Jericho (2 Kgs 2:22).**
As one of his first acts as Elijah's successor, Elisha miraculously purifies a poisoned spring at Jericho, a condition that persists "until this day."[28]

*ii. A Rock*
**(1) Rock of the Ark at Beth-Shemesh (1 Sam 6:18).**
"The large rock" (אֶבֶן הַגְּדוֹלָה[29]), upon which the Ark rests after its return from Philistia, still stands in the field of Joshua of Beth Shemesh "until this day" (1 Sam 6:18).

## Observations on the Geographical Use of "Until this Day"

Combining the above data we discover that there is a significant concentration of geographical sites in the southern part of the country. The most notable exceptions are the Cabul (1 Kgs 8:8) and Havvoth Jair (Deut 3:14; Judg 10:4), which are not merely individual sites, but large geographical areas consisting of twenty and upwards to sixty cities, respectively. Conversely, the sites in the southern part of the country are individual settlements, such as Mahaneh Dan (Judg 18:12), Gilgal (Josh 5:9), Joktheel (2 Kgs 14:7), individual sites, such as Emek Achor (Josh 7:26), Perez-Uzzah (2 Sam 6:8), detailed topographical features, such as the springs at Lehi (Judg 15:19) and Jericho (2 Kgs 2:22), or individual monuments and memorials, such as the twelve stones near the Jordan River (Josh 4:9), the ruins at Ai (Josh 8:28), the burial mound at Ai (Josh 8:29) and in the Valley of Achor (Josh 7:26), the burial cave at Makkedah (Josh 10:27), the large stone in the field at Beth-Shemesh (1 Sam 6:18), and Absalom's pillar in the King's Valley (2 Sam 18:18).

---

26. Perhaps originally "Spring of the Partridge" (see 1 Sam 26:20 and Jer 17:11 for קֹרֵא as "partridge").

27. Lehi is customarily associated with Khirbet eṣ-Ṣiyyāgh at the mouth of Wadi en-Najil (about 7 km east of Timnah), an identification based upon both the biblical data and the assumed relationship between Arabic eṣ-Ṣiyyāgh and Greek *siagōn* ("jaw"; so Aquila and Symmachus; cf. Josephus *Ant* 5.8.9 §300).

28. The identification of Jericho (Tell es-Sultan) poses no difficulties. The extent of occupation prior to the seventh c. B.C.E., however, remains a disputed matter. See T. A. Holland and E. Netzer, "Jericho," *ABD* 3.723–40.

29. Reading אֶבֶן (LXX: λίθου) for MT's אָבֵל. See McCarter, *1 Samuel*, 130.

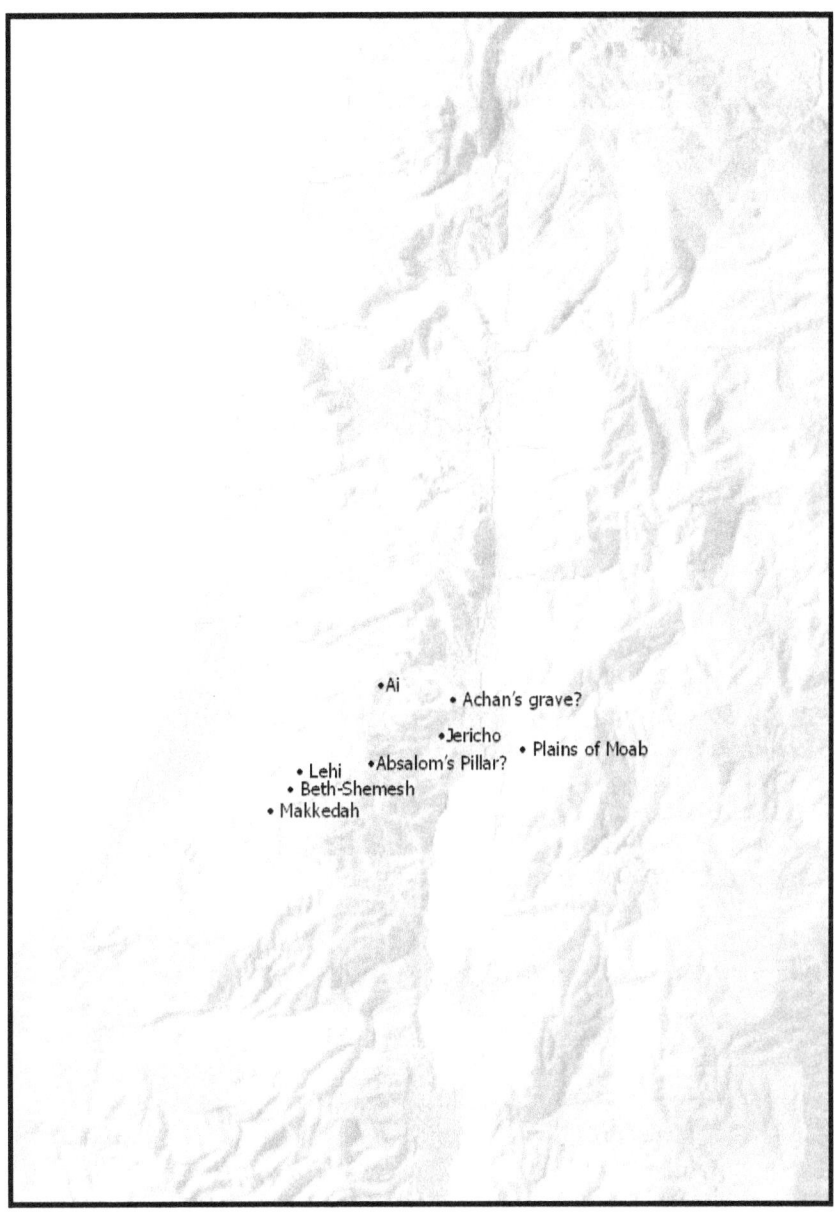

Figure 2.2: Memorials and natural landmarks existing "until this day."

Related to this point, there are a number of memorials intended to remind Israel of its past, whether the mighty acts of God on its behalf (e.g., the memorial of twelve stones near the Jordan River, the ruins of Ai, the king of Ai's grave, the burial cave at Makkedah), or the consequences of disobeying God's commands (e.g., Achan's grave). The large stone at Beth-Shemesh actually commemorates both, as it recalls God's power in returning the Ark from Philistine control and marks the spot where numerous villagers were struck dead for looking into this sacred object (1 Sam 6:18–19). Chapter 3 explores the significance of these connections when discussing "until this day" in relation to the Ark of the Covenant.

## 2. Demographic Uses of "Until This Day"

Demographically, "until this day" appears in a number of passages that seek to explain why people live where they do.

### a. Migrations and Settlements

The migration and settlement patterns highlighted by "until this day" fall into four general categories: (i) dispossession, (ii) cohabitation, (iii) acquisition, and (iv) deportation/importation.

*i. Dispossession*
**(1) Why the "descendants of Esau" live in Seir (Deut 2:22).**
Deut 2:20–23 represents a rather lengthy historical note giving an account of the previous inhabitants of Ammon and Edom. Deut 2:22 explains that YHWH removed the Horites from Seir in order that the descendants of Esau could settle in their place "until this day."[30]

**(2) Why the Beerothites live in Gittaim (2 Sam 4:3).**
In the context of describing the waning days of Ishbosheth's failed reign, the author of 2 Samuel 4 explains how those dwelling in Beeroth, a Gibeonite city, could be considered Benjaminites. According to 2 Sam 4:3, the original inhabitants of Beeroth fled to Gittaim and live there as aliens "until this day."[31] Therefore, those who now live in Beeroth are Benjaminites.

---

30. LXX of Deut 2:21 also includes the phrase "until this day" (ἕως τῆς ἡμέρας ταύτης), which may be influenced by v. 22. Haplography in MT, though lacking any clear mechanical explanation, is also possible.

31. Although we are not given the reason why the Beerothites fled to Gittaim, J. Blenkinsopp (*Gibeon and Israel: The Role of Gibeon and the Gibeonites in the Political and Religious History*

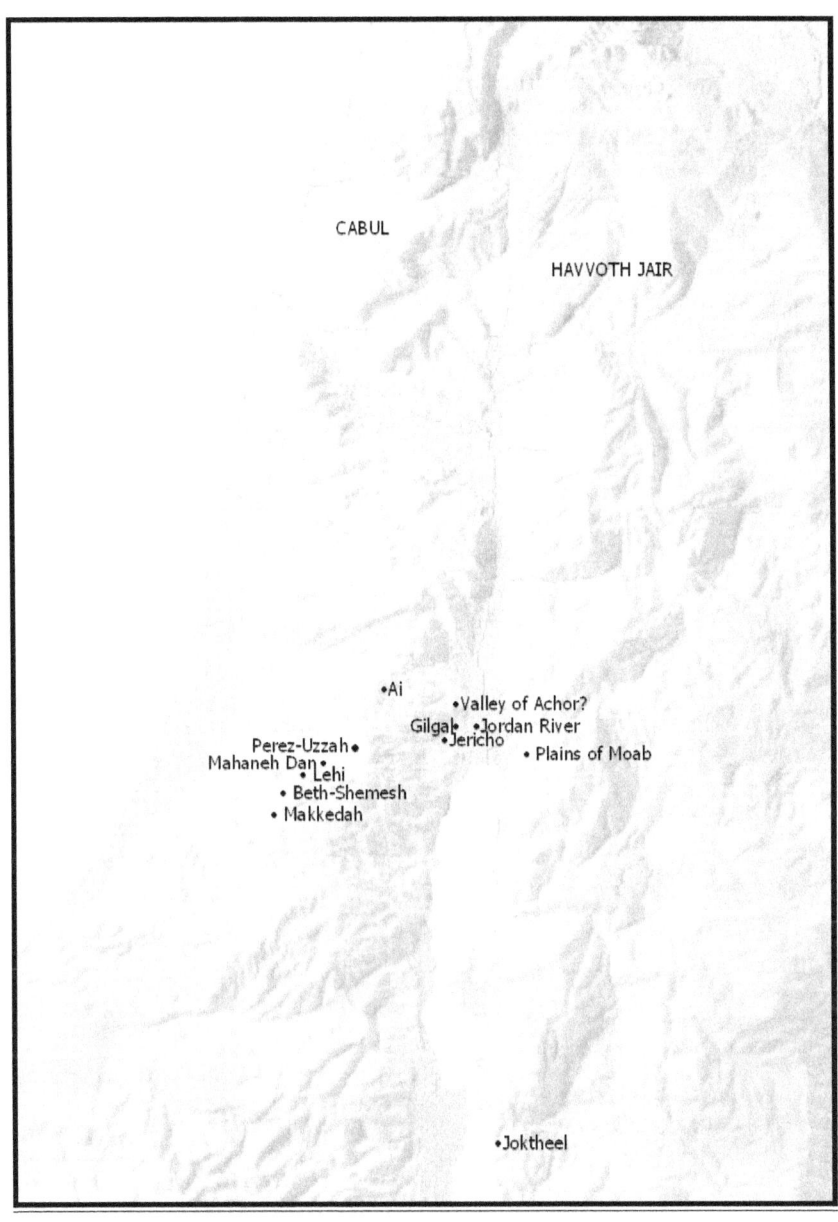

Figure 2.3: Geographical sites existing "until this day."

### (3) Why the Edomites live in Elath (2 Kgs 16:6).

During the reign of Ahaz, Jerusalem is besieged by an Aramean-Israelite coalition. Although Jerusalem withstands the assault, Rezin takes advantage of Ahaz's weakened position and drives the Judahites from Elath. Subsequently, Edomites[32] settle in Elath, where they dwell "until this day."

*ii. Cohabitation*

On a number of occasions the Israelites fail to dispossess a people or willingly allow them to remain in their midst. Consequently, these people still live in the midst of Israel "until this day."

### (1) Why Rahabites still live in the midst of Israel (Josh 6:25).

As repayment for her role in protecting the Israelite spies sent to Jericho by Joshua, Rahab and her family are spared during the city's destruction and are allowed to settle among Israel, where they remain "until this day."

### (2) Why Geshurites and Maacathites still live in Israel (Josh 13:13).

The two-and-a-half tribes east of the Jordan fail to dispossess the Geshurites and Maacathites during the conquest of the land.[33] As a result, the Geshurites and Maacathites live in Israelite territory "until this day."[34]

### (3) and (4) Why Jebusites still dwell in Jerusalem (Josh 15:63; Judg 1:21).

In Josh 15:63 we are informed that the Judahites fail to remove the Jebusites from Jerusalem, while in Judg 1:21 the Benjaminites are blamed. Despite this discrepancy, both narratives affirm that Jebusites still reside in Jerusalem "until this day."[35]

---

*of Early Israel* [SOTS 2; Cambridge: Cambridge University Press, 1972] 100) has suggested that their association with the Gibeonites made them a target of Saul's wrath. Gittaim is placed within Benjaminite territory (2 Sam 4:3; Neh 11:33), and may be an alternate designation for Israelite Gath (1 Chr 7:21; 8:13), but beyond this its location is unknown.

32. The Ketib of MT is אֲרַמִּים while the Qere is אֲדוֹמִים. The Qere finds support from LXX, the Targumim and Vulgate. The Syriac, along with more minor manuscripts of the Targumim and Vulgate, reflects the Ketib. Following Cogan and Tadmor (2 *Kings*, 186–87) one would expect Edomites in the far south. *Daleth/resh* confusion is well attested throughout the development of the Hebrew script. See E. Tov, *Textual Criticism of the Hebrew Bible* (Minneapolis: Fortress Press, 1992) 245–46.

33. The territory of Geshur and Maacah is located within northern Transjordan in the tribal allotment of Manasseh (Josh 13:11).

34. LXX adds καὶ τὸν Χαναναῖον ("and the Canaanite") after "Maacathite." Cf. Josh 16:10, where Canaanites are said to dwell among Israel (specifically, among Ephraim) "until this day."

35. LXX lacks "with the children of Judah" in the phrase "and the Jebusites dwell with

**(5) Why Canaanites still dwell in Gezer (Josh 16:10).**
Because the Ephraimites fail to dispossess the Canaanites who live in Gezer,[36] the Canaanities still dwell among Ephraim "until this day," only they now serve as forced laborers (מַס־עֹבֵד).[37]

*iii. Acquisition of Land*
**(1) Why the Calebites have possession of Hebron (Josh 14:14).**
Caleb is granted Hebron as an inheritance because he "followed fully after YHWH the God of Israel" (יַעַן אֲשֶׁר מִלֵּא אַחֲרֵי יְהוָה אֱלֹהֵי יִשְׂרָאֵל). As a result, Hebron belongs to the Calebite clan "until this day."

**(2) Why the kings of Judah have possession of Ziklag (1 Sam 27:6).**
After going over to the Philistines, David requests a city for himself, his men and their families. Achish of Gath agrees, giving him Ziklag, which belongs to the kings of Judah "until this day."[38]

*iv. Deportation/Importation*
**(1) The Deportation of the Northern Kingdom (2 Kgs 17:23).**
Despite God's warnings through the prophets, the northern kingdom persists in its rebellion against the house of David and continues in its wor-

---

the children of Judah in Jerusalem until this day" in Josh 15:63, perhaps because it was thought to be repetitive with the reference to "the children of Judah" earlier in this verse. The omission may also intend to alleviate the tension between this verse and its parallel in Judg 1:21, where the Jebusites are said to dwell "with the children of Benjamin in Jerusalem until this day."

36. Gezer has been identified with Tell el-Jazari, in the foothills of the Judean range in the northern Shephelah. See W. G. Dever, H. D. Lance and G. E. Wright, *Gezer I: Preliminary Report of the 1964–66 Seasons* (HUC/Nelson Glueck School of Biblical Archaeology Annual 1; Jerusalem: HUC Biblical and Archaeological School, 1970).

37. LXX lacks the notice regarding the Canaanites forced labor (וַיְהִי לְמַס־עֹבֵד), perhaps due to the addition of an extended notice concerning the capture of Gezer by the king of Egypt during the time of Solomon: ἕως τῆς ἡμέρας ταύτης ἕως ἀνέβη Φαραω βασιλεὺς Αἰγύπτου καὶ ἔλαβεν αὐτὴν καὶ ἐνέπρησεν αὐτὴν ἐν πυρί καὶ τοὺς Χαναναίους καὶ τοὺς Φερεζαίους καὶ τοὺς κατοικοῦντά ἐν Γαζερ ἐξεκέντησαν καὶ ἔδωκεν αὐτὴν Φαραω ἐν φερνῇ τῇ θυγατρὶ αὐτοῦ ("until this day until Pharaoh the king of Egypt went up and took it and burnt it with fire; and the Canaanites and the Perezites and those living in Gezer they destroyed. And Pharaoh gave it as a dowry to his daughter"). This addition is best explained as an attempt to bring Josh 16:10 into conformity with 1 Kgs 9:16 (note the repetition of ἕως to introduce the additional clause). On the relationship between Josh 16:10 and 1 Kings 9, see chapter 3.

38. Ziklag has traditionally been identified with Tell el-Khuweilfeh about 15 km northeast of Beer-Sheba, although there is a growing consensus that Tell esh-Shari'a, midway between Beer-Sheba and Gaza, is biblical Ziklag. See E. D. Oren, "Esh-Shari'a, Tell (Tel Sera')," *EAEHL* 4 (1978) 1059–69; idem, "Ziklag: A Biblical City on the Edge of the Negev," *BA* 45 (1982) 155–66; J. D. Seger, "The Location of Biblical Ziklag according to Tel Halif Excavations," in *Man and Environment in the Southern Shephelah*, ed. E. Stern and D. Urman (Jerusalem: Masadah, 1988) 139–50. Some mss read עַל־כֵּן instead of לְכֵן.

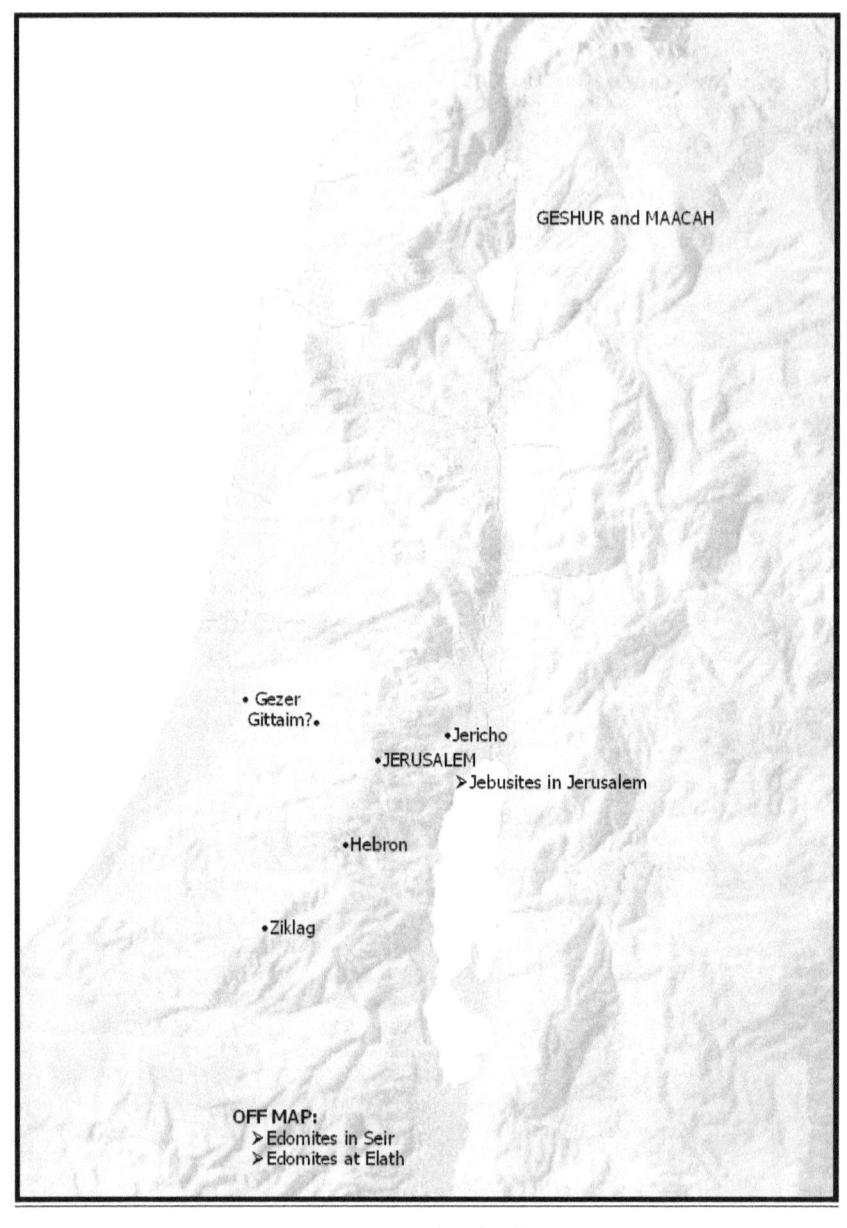

Figure 2.4: Demographic uses of "until this day."

ship at the alternate cultic sites established by Jeroboam. As a result, God sends them into exile, where they remain "until this day."[39]

**(2) The Importation of Foreigners into Israel (2 Kgs 17:34 and 41).**
After exiling the northern kingdom, the king of Assyria resettles Israel with people from Mesopotamia and Syria, who, though "fearing YHWH" (vv. 32, 33, 41), still serve other gods "until this day."[40]

*Observations on the Demographic Use of "Until This Day"*

As with the geographical data, the demographic use of "until this day" is predominantly southern (Judahite ownership of Ziklag; Calebite ownership of Hebron; Edomites in Seir and Elath; etc.). The only clear exception is the reference to Geshur and Maacah (Josh 13:13), which, like Havvoth Jair and Cabul, is a large geographical region in the far north consisting of numerous settlements. The notices mentioning the deportation of the northern tribes (2 Kgs 17:23), the importation of foreigners in their place (2 Kgs 17:34), and the idolatry of these new northerners (2 Kgs 17:41), although describing activities occurring in the north, are being related by someone living in the south or, if written in exile, by someone with strong southern sympathies. The importance of these findings are discussed in greater detail below.

## 3. Political Uses of "Until This Day"

"Until this day" is employed several times to indicate the ongoing existence of political realities relating to ancient Israel. For clarity, these will be discussed under (a) Domestic Affairs and (b) Foreign Affairs.

---

39. LXX, Syriac and a Hebrew manuscript add יהוה following כַּאֲשֶׁר דִּבֶּר in 2 Kgs 17:23. For the use of "until this day" with the formula כַּאֲשֶׁר דִּבֶּר + PN, see chapter 3.

40. The redactional history of 2 Kings 17 is complicated and, as a result, has generated conflicting interpretations. See the summary and bibliography in M. Z. Brettler, *The Creation of History in Ancient Israel* (London/New York: Routledge, 1995) 112–34. The synopsis presented here attempts to make sense of the text as it stands, though many scholars (see, e.g., Cogan and Tadmor, *2 Kings*) understand vv. 24–41 to refer to two distinct groups: vv. 24–33 describe the syncretistic tendencies of the new northerners in the land and vv. 34–40 speak of the continuing disobedience of the old northerners in exile. We will return to this passage in chapter 3.

## Domestic Affairs

Israel's domestic policies fall under two general categories: (i) the subjugation of non-Israelite populations, and (ii) the establishment of laws.

*Subjugation of Non-Israelite Populations*
**(1) Subjugation of the Hivites (Josh 9:27).**
Because the Hivites of Gibeon trick Israel into making a covenant with them, Joshua allows them to live, but subjects them to servitude. Specifically, they are forced to become "hewers of wood and drawers of water for the congregation and the altar of YHWH"—services they render "until this day."[41]

**(2) Subjugation of the Amorites, Hittites, Perizzites, Hivites and Jebusites (1 Kgs 9:21).**
Solomon reduces to "forced labor" (מַס־עֹבֵד) those whom the Israelites failed to dispossess from the land—a policy that continues "until this day."[42]

*ii. The Establishment of Laws*
**(1) The Distribution of War Spoils to Non-Combatants (1 Sam 30:25).**
David establishes a law that whether a man goes to battle or guards the camp, he will share equally in the war spoils—a law still in effect "until this day."[43]

## b. Foreign Affairs

The foreign affairs highlighted by "until this day" relate to the rebellion of nations formerly subject to the kingdom of Judah.

---

41. LXX adds διὰ τοῦτο ἐγένοντο οἱ κατοικοῦντες Γαβαων ξυλοκόποι καὶ ὑδροφόροι τοῦ θυσιαστηρίου τοῦ θεοῦ ("therefore those living in Gabaon became hewers of wood and drawers of water for the altar of God") following "the altar of God," which may be an attempt to expand and clarify the rather compact Hebrew or, alternatively, which may have fallen out of MT due to haplography (from "altar of YHWH" to "altar of YHWH"). In any case, the institution being described is the same.

42. LXX adds "Canaanites" and "Girgashites" to the list, after "Perizzites" and "Jebusites," respectively. This plus brings the total nation count to the symbolically significant seven. Although haplography in MT is possible, the principles of *lectio dificilior* and *lectior brevior*, along with the absence of these two nations in the Vulgate, weigh in favor of MT's shortened list as the preferred reading. The connections between 1 Kgs 9:21 and Josh 16:10, which mark the only occurrences of מַס־עֹבֵד in the DH, are discussed in chapter 3.

43. For legislation related to war spoils, see Deut 13:16–18; 20:14.

*i. The Rebellion of Nations*
**(1) The Rebellion of the North (1 Kgs 12:19).**
Rehoboam's failed "negotiations" with the north after the death of Solomon result in Israel's breaking away from the House of David, a state of affairs that persists "until this day" (וַיִּפְשְׁעוּ יִשְׂרָאֵל בְּבֵית דָּוִד עַד הַיּוֹם הַזֶּה).

**(2) The Rebellion of Edom (2 Kgs 8:22).**
During the reign of Jehoram, Edom rebels against Judah, a condition that continues "until this day" (וַיִּפְשַׁע אֱדוֹם מִתַּחַת יַד־יְהוּדָה עַד הַיּוֹם הַזֶּה).

## *Observations on the Political Use of "Until This Day"*

As with the geographical and demographic data, the political data of "until this day" reflect a southern orientation. For example, while Solomon acquires non-Israelite forced labor from all over Israel, very few of his actual building projects are in the north (e.g., Megiddo and Hazor).[44] Further establishing the southern perspective reflected in the use of "until this day" is that both Joshua 9 and 1 Kings 9 connect the use of non-Israelite forced labor with the temple: "at the place he will choose" (Josh 9:27) and at "the temple of YHWH" (1 Kgs 9:15).

This raises another point of interest first hinted at by Radak and explicitly set forth by Kuenen: the references to non-Israelite forced labor seem to ascribe the same policy to Joshua and Solomon (cf. also Josh 16:10, which, like 1 Kgs 9:15–21, mentions מַס־עֹבֵד). If this observation is correct, it marks the third time when "until this day" verifies the existence of a single matter, but in different books and with conflicting details (cf. the naming of Havvoth Jair [Deut 3:14; Judg 10:4] and the reason for Jebusites in Jerusalem [Josh 15:63; Judg 1:21], discussed above). We will return to this phenomenon of "multiple attestation" in chapter 3.

Also establishing the southern orientation of "until this day" is its use to describe the ongoing rebellions of Israel and Edom against Judah (1 Kgs

---

44. B. Halpern ("Sectionalism and the Schism," *JBL* 93 [1974] 519–32) has even argued that it was Solomon's exploitation of northern resources for southern building projects that resulted in the north's dissatisfaction with the Davidic monarchy and the eventual secession from the union. The question of whether the monumental gates at Hazor, Gezer and Megiddo are Solomonic does not affect our observations regarding the southern orientation of "until this day." For a discussion of the relevant archaeological data in reconstructing the political and economic development of Israel and Judah at this time, see J. S. Holladay, Jr. "The Kingdoms of Israel and Judah: Political and Economic Centralization in the Iron IIA-B (ca. 1000–750 B.C.E.)" in *The Archaeology of Society in the Holy Land*, ed. T. E. Levy (New York: Facts on File, 1995) 368–98.

12:19; 2 Kgs 8:22). In fact, when we combine the political and demographic data, it becomes apparent that our phrase reflects a marked interest in Edom: (1) Edomites dispossess the Horites from Seir and live in their place "until this day" (Deut 2:22), (2) Judah's forces defeat ten thousand Edomites in the Valley of Salt, capture Sela, and rename it Joktheel "until this day" (2 Kgs 14:7), (3) Edom rebels against Judah during the reign of Jehoram and remains independent "until this day" (2 Kgs 8:22) and (4) Edom settles in Elath, where they continue to live "until this day" (2 Kgs 16:6). This interest in Edom will become important for understanding to whose day or days "this day" refers (see chapter 3).

## 4. Cultic Uses of "Until This Day"

"Until this day" is employed in connection with a number of cultic matters, which are addressed here under the headings: (a) Cultic Institutions and (b) Cultic Objects.

### *a. Cultic Institutions*

The cultic institutions said to persist "until this day" most naturally divide into two categories: (i) Israelite and (ii) Non-Israelite.

*i. Israelite Cultic Practices*
**(1) Why the Levites carry the Ark of the Covenant, minister before YHWH, and pronounce blessings in his name (Deut 10:8).**
    YHWH, via Moses, sets the Levites apart for the above distinctions, which they fulfill "until this day."

*ii. Non-Israelite Cultic Practices*
**(1) Why the priests of Dagon do not step on the threshhold of Dagon's temple (1 Sam 5:5).**
    The dismembered parts of Dagon's image come to rest on the threshold of Dagon's temple when it falls before the Ark of YHWH. As a result, all those entering Dagon's temple do not step on the threshold "until this day."[45]

---

45. For the practice of jumping over thresholds in connection with the Jerusalem cult, see Zeph 1:9. For the position "keeper of the threshold" in Israelite contexts, see, e.g., 2 Kgs 22:4; 23:4; 25:18; Jer 35:4. For the significance of entryways, sacral or otherwise, see W. H. C. Propp, *Exodus 1–18: A New Translation with Introduction and Commentary* (AB 2; New York: Doubleday, 1999) 441.

## b. Cultic Objects

As with cultic institutions, the cultic objects said to exist "until this day" can be classified under two categories: (i) Israelite and (ii) Non-Israelite.

### i. Israelite Cultic Objects
**(1) The construction of an altar to YHWH (Judg 6:24).**
Following his encounter with the angel of YHWH, Gideon builds an altar, naming it "YHWH Shalom." This altar is in Ophrah of the Abiezerites "until this day."[46]

**(2) The protruding poles of the Ark (1 Kgs 8:8).**
When the Ark is brought into the temple at its dedication, the poles are of such a length that they protrude from the Holy of Holies, a situation that persists "until this day."[47]

**(3) The presence of almug wood in Israel (1 Kgs 10:12).**
Almug[48] wood imported from Ophir[49] and used to build the temple, the royal palace, and several musical instruments has not been imported nor has it appeared in Israel from the time of Solomon "until this day."[50]

### ii. Non-Israelite Cultic Objects
**(1) The destruction of Baal's temple and pillar (2 Kgs 10:27).**
Jehu invites the priests of Baal for a sacrifice where, unknown to them, they are the sacrificial victims. After slaughtering the priests, Jehu's armed men destroy the pillar and temple of Baal,[51] the ruins of which serve as a latrine "until this day."[52]

---

46. The book of Judges places Ophrah in the Valley of Jezreel (Judg 6:35). Y. Aharoni (*The Land of the Bible. A Historical Geography* [2nd ed.; Philadelphia: Westminster, 1979] 263) identifies Ophrah with modern 'Affuleh, which lies in the Jezreel. There are no textual phenomena in this verse bearing on the use of "until this day" or the interpretation of the passage.

47. LXX lacks "until this day" in 1 Kgs 8:8 (though, cf. Origen), but attests the phrase in 2 Chr 5:9.

48. Chronicles reads אלגומים (2 Chr 9:10; see also 2 Chr 2:7). Ugaritic (*almg*) and Akkadian (*elammukku*) support the reading of 1 Kgs 10:11, 12 (אלמגים). The exact identification of this wood remains unknown. For discussion, see Cogan, *1 Kings*, 313.

49. The location of Ophir is unknown, though southern Arabia seems the most likely location. See D. W. Baker, "Ophir (Place)," *ABD* 5.26–27. Whatever Ophir's location, the destination (i.e., Jerusalem) of its goods is what concerns us here.

50. The phrase לֹא בָא־כֵן עֲצֵי אַלְמֻגִּים וְלֹא נִרְאָה ("Such almug wood has not come nor appeared") intends to underscore the uniqueness of the wood and Solomon's ability to procure it. Cogan, *1 Kings*, 314.

51. LXX and some Hebrew manuscripts read "pillars" (מצבות) and lack the phrase "and they tore down the temple of Baal," likely due to haplography (הבעל ... הבעל).

52. Second Kings 10:27 marks the only occurrence of the shorter phrase (עַד הַיּוֹם) in the

## Observations on the Cultic Use of "Until This Day"

As with the other uses of "until this day," there are a number of cultic institutions and objects located in the south, including: (1) the Ark of the Covenant, (2) the Levites' role in connection with the Ark and the sanctuary, and (3) the wood used in constructing the temple, royal palace and various temple instruments. In light of this predominantly southern perspective, it is interesting that two cultic objects identified as persisting "until this day" are in the north: (1) the altar of YHWH at Ophrah, and (2) the destroyed temple of Baal in Samaria. Importantly, both of these cultic sites mark defunct places of Baal worship: the altar at Ophrah stands where an altar of Baal once stood, and the latrine in Samaria was once an active place of Baal worship.[53]

Also significant is the recurrence of "until this day" in connection with the Ark of the Covenant. Not only do the poles of the Ark still protrude from the Holy of Holies (1 Kgs 8:8) and the Levites still have responsibility for bearing the Ark (Deut 10:8), but several items commemorate the Ark's activity, including: (1) the memorial near the Jordan River (Josh 4:9), recalling the Ark's role in providing dry passage for the Israelites, (2) the Philistine practice of jumping over the threshold of Dagon's temple (1 Sam 5:5), testifying to the Ark's "humbling" of Dagon's image, (3) the rock at Beth-Shemesh (1 Sam 6:18), where the Ark was placed after its return from Philistia, and (4) the ominous naming of Perez-Uzzah (2 Sam 6:8), where Uzzah was struck dead after touching the Ark. The significance of these connections for determining the time, place and purpose of "until this day" will be explored in chapter 3.

## SUMMARY

Most apparent among the various occurrences of "until this day" is its use in connection with southern entities or in contexts that reflect southern concerns. In fact, its use reflects a *detailed* knowledge of the south that is virtually lacking for the north. For example, "until this day" confirms the persistence of: (1) a pile of stones near the Jordan River (Josh 4:9), (2) a pile of stones in the Valley of Achor (Josh 7:26), (3) the scattered remains of the city of Ai (Josh 8:28), (4) a pile of stones over the king of Ai (Josh 8:29), (5) a pile of stones covering the mouth of a cave at Makkedah (Josh 10:27), (6) a

---

DH, though there is strong textual support (LXX, Targumim, Vulgate, two Hebrew manuscripts) for the fuller phrase.

53. The only cultic entity not found in Israel is the practice of not stepping upon the threshold of the temple of Dagon (1 Sam 5:5), though it is connected with other uses involving the Ark of the Covenant.

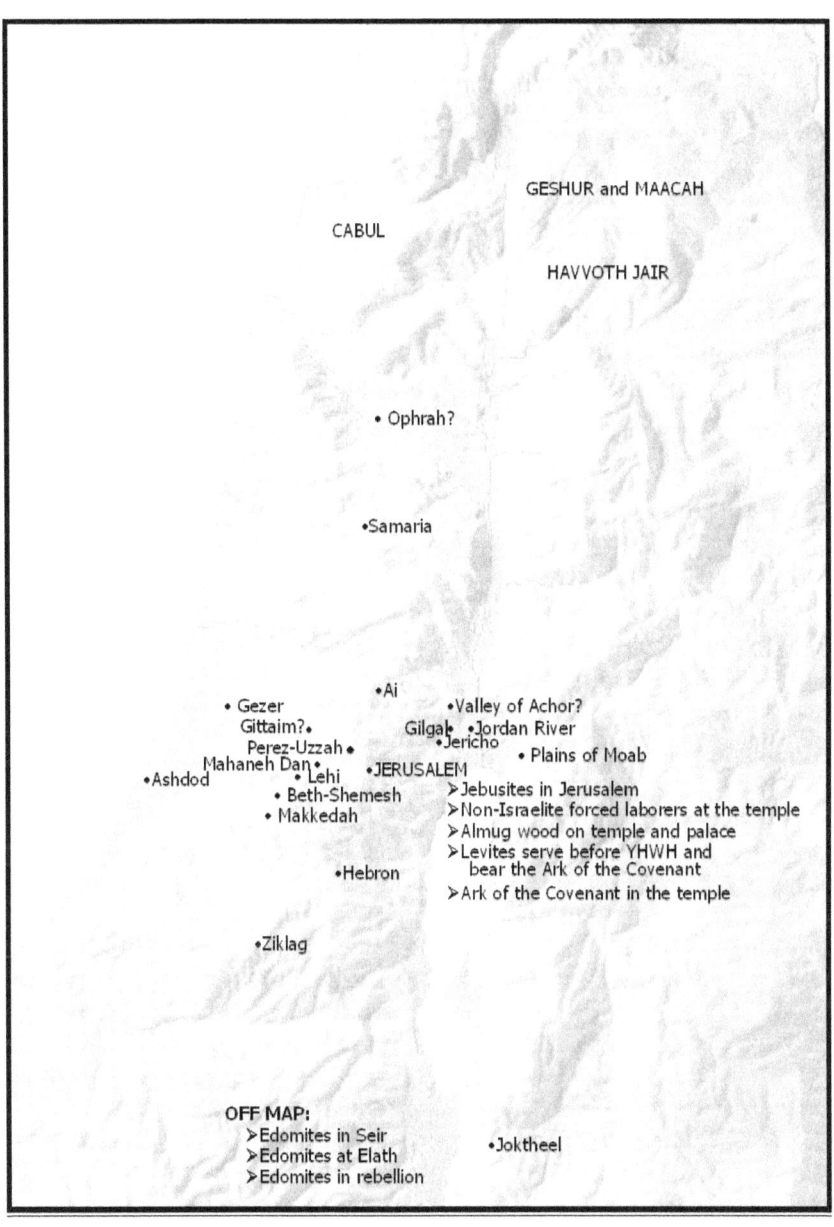

Figure 2.5: Combined data on "until this day."

single rock in a field at Beth-Shemesh (1 Sam 6:18), (7) a spring at Lehi called "Spring of the Caller" (Judg 15:19), and (8) a monument in the King's Valley called "Absalom's Pillar" (2 Sam 18:18). In contrast, three of the five northern locations said to exist "until this day" are large geographical areas consisting of numerous cities (Deut 3:14; Josh 13:13; Judg 10:4), not individual objects or sites. The only *individual* objects in the north said to persist "until this day" are the altar to YHWH at Ophrah (Judg 6:24) and the destroyed pillar and temple of Baal in Samaria (2 Kgs 10:27), both of which, as noted above, share the distinction of being former sites of Baal worship.

In addition to the overall southern orientation reflected in the use of "until this day," whenever there is any indication of when our phrase is being used it is preexilic: (1) Israel and Edom are still "in rebellion" against the kingdom of Judah (1 Kgs 12:19; 2 Kgs 8:22), (2) the "kings of Judah" still have ownership over Ziklag (1 Sam 27:6), (3) non-Israelite forced labor is still used in connection with the temple (Josh 9:27; cf. 1 Kgs 9:21), (4) the Levites still have responsibility for bearing the Ark of the Covenant (Deut 10:8), (5) the poles of the Ark still protrude from the Holy of Holies in the temple (1 Kgs 8:8), and (6) almug wood is still visible on the temple edifice, royal palace, and certain temple instruments (1 Kgs 10:12). Most, if not all, of these items cannot properly be said to exist after Jerusalem's destruction by the Babylonians in 586 B.C.E. Moreover, it should be pointed out that these preexilic notices further confirm the southern perspective of the one(s) employing "until this day."

## INITIAL CONCLUSIONS

The survey in chapter 1 revealed that a number of scholars (Kuenen, Wellhausen, Cogan and Tadmor, etc.) had noted the preexilic provenance of "until this day" in Kings. However, no one had observed that the same could be said about "until this day" across the DH. While some of its uses are more or less atemporal (e.g., toponyms) and therefore could also derive from exilic or postexilic times, there is no instance where this is required. On the contrary, there only exist examples where a preexilic date is required.

Chapter 1 also revealed that a number of scholars had noted that "until this day" in Kings reflects southern interests. However, no one had observed the clearly southern perspective reflected in its use across the DH. While we might expect to find a southern perspective in Kings, since its compilation is usually ascribed to those with southern sympathies (see the survey of Deuteronomistic scholarship in chapter 4), to find this same perspective across the DH is somewhat surprising, especially since a number of scholars credit northern priestly or prophetic circles with preserving many of the traditions making up this corpus.[54]

---

54. For the sources making up the DH and their possible provenance, see chapter 4.

This last observation raises the question of source identification. If "until this day" is found primarily in southern sources, then we will have accounted for the southern perspective reflected in its use. However, if "until this day" is found in both northern and southern sources, then another explanation for its southern orientation is required. Indeed, such a finding would suggest that at least some of its uses were incorporated into the DH after the fall of the north, when northern traditions had occasion to be merged with southern sources. Therefore, identifying the sources where "until this day" appears, which will be taken up in the next chapter, is essential for further establishing to whose day "this day" refers, as well as for determining when the DH may have been compiled and by whom.

Finally, the survey in chapter 1 revealed that at least as early as the thirteenth century, Radak observed a thematic connection among some of the uses of "until this day." Specifically, he noted that several passages refer to the continuing presence of non-Israelites in Jerusalem, where they serve as forced laborers "until this day" (see esp. Josh 9:27; Josh 15:63; Judg 1:21; 1 Kgs 9:21). At present no one has followed up on Radak's observations. Childs comes closest, sorting the various uses of "until this day" by categories.[55] However, he utilizes these categories as a means of organizing his material, not as a means of generating new data for analysis. For example, Childs rightly classifies Josh 9:27 and 1 Kgs 9:21 together, labeling them "sociological etiologies." But his analysis ends there, noting only that: "The redactor of earlier tradition affirms that a condition associated with a past event in Israel's history continued to exist also in his day."[56] The repeated use of "until this day" to highlight the same socio-political reality across sources raises several important questions. For example, why is the particular institution of "forced labor" important to those employing "until this day"? Does the repetition of such a notice tell us anything about when "this day" is or who may be pointing out this institution and why? And what of the other realities that similarly receive multiple attestation by use of "until this day" (e.g., the Ark of the Covenant, Edom, etc.)? Do these notices shed light on the ones employing this phrase (i.e., their *Sitz im Leben*, their purpose for writing, etc.)? The following chapter seeks to answer these and related questions, the outcome of which is the identification of the specific temporal, geographical, and social location of those compiling Israel's history.

---

55. Childs's categories, which bear some similarities to the above, include: Etymological, Ethnic and Geographic, Cultic, Nature, Political, Legal, and Sociological etiologies. Childs, "Until This Day," 284–89.

56. Childs, "Until This Day," 289. In Childs's defense, his main concern is to demonstrate that the etiological element of the narratives where "until this day" appears is secondary to the tradition itself. As a result, he often misses the significance of the categories he creates.

# 3

# "Until This Day" and the Deuteronomistic Historian

Der Deuteronomiker ist der letzte Verfasser des ganzen Buches [Josua]. Er hat in demselben zwei grössere Stücke geschrieben, cap. I und cap. XXIII, ausserdem aber viele Glossen, Erläuterungen und Zusätze, Berichtigungen nach seiner Weise . . . "bis auf diesen Tag" ist gewöhnliche Formel des Deuteronomikers.[1]

—Wihelm Vatke, *Historisch-kritische Einleitung*

Dass die wesentliche Formung des Buches der Könige noch während des Bestehens des jüdischen Reichs erfolgt ist, wird man ferner aus עד היום הזה II 8, 22. 14, 7. 16,6 (Kuenen a. O. p. 263), was hier ohne Zweifel vom Epitomator und nicht aus seiner Quelle stammt, schliessen.[2]

—Julius Wellhausen, *Die Composition des Hexateuchs und der historischen Bücher des Alten Testaments*

Abraham Kuenen concluded over a century ago that "until this day" in Kings derived from a preexilic Deuteronomistic redactor (his Rd[1]).[3] His reasons for this identification were two-fold: (1) "until this day" reflects a unified temporal perspective throughout Kings (i.e., preexilic),

---

1. "The Deuteronomist is the final editor of the entire book [of Joshua]. He wrote therein two large sections, ch. 1 and ch. 23, in addition to many remarks, comments, additions and corrections in his own style . . . 'until this day' is the usual formula of the Deuteronomist." *Historisch-kritische Einleitung*, 422.

2. "That the essential formation of the book of Kings took place during the existence of the Judean kingdom, one can further conclude from "until this day" 2 [Kgs] 8:22; 14:7; 16:6 (Kuenen, a. O. p. 263), which here undoubtedly comes from the compiler and not from his sources." *Die Composition des Hexateuchs*, 299.

3. A. Kuenen, *Einleitung* I:90–91. For a summary of Kuenen's analysis, see chapter 1.

and (2) the phrase is integrally bound to the Deuteronomistic structure of these books.

Shortly after Kuenen's study, Wihelm Vatke came to the same conclusion, only for the book of Joshua.[4] His reasons were likewise two-fold: (1) "until this day" repeatedly appears in connection with other Deuteronomistic redactional material, and (2) the phrase consistently highlights matters of Deuteronomistic concern.

Regrettably, Kuenen's and Vatke's insights were never united, partly due to an accident of history, as Vatke's study appeared shortly before Kuenen's death and Vatke died shortly after the appearance of Kuenen's work in German, and partly due to the state of the field, as the redactional histories of Joshua and Kings were treated as separate phenomena.

Over a half century later, Brevard S. Childs, in the only study devoted solely to "until this day," similarly observed that this phrase was redactional.[5] However, unlike Vatke and Kuenen, Childs concluded that the phrase derived from "many different redactors." In defense of his position, Childs appealed, ironically, to the books of Joshua and Kings, where he noted that the phrase appeared in too many sources to belong to one person. Childs, unfortunately, did not engage Vatke's and Kuenen's arguments for assigning this phrase in these works to a Deuteronomistic redactor, nor did he explain how the presence of "until this day" in so many sources necessitated a multiplicity of redactors. His findings could very well indicate the opposite: a single redactor with access to all of these sources employed "until this day" whenever encountering something that still existed at the time of his editorial enterprise. As further evidence for this proposal, we observed in chapter 2 that "until this day" often attests to the same matters (the Ark of the Covenant, Edomite-Judahite relations, the rights and responsibilities of the Levitical priests, etc.), even when appearing in different sources or literary units. Moreover, the use of the phrase throughout the DH reflects a unified temporal (preexilic) and geographical (southern/Judahite) perspective.

In light of these observations, the present chapter is devoted to two related tasks: (1) an analysis of "until this day" by source in the DH, and (2) an evaluation of the language, themes, and interests reflected in its use across this corpus. What we discover is that Vatke's and Kuenen's conclusions for the books of Joshua and Kings individually actually apply to the whole of the DH: "until this day" is Dtr's own witness to geographical, political, demographic, and cultic realities mentioned in his sources that continued to exist at the time of his historical activity.

---

4. W. Vatke, *Einleitung*, 422.
5. B. S. Childs, "Until This Day," 292.

| Deut | Joshua | Judges | Samuel | | |
|---|---|---|---|---|---|
| | | | AN | HDR | SN |
| Deut 2:22 | | | | | |
| Deut 3:14 | | | | | |
| Deut 10:8 | | | | | |
| Deut 34:6 | | | | | |
| | Josh 4:9 | | | | |
| | Josh 5:9 | | | | |
| | Josh 6:25 | | | | |
| | Josh 7:26 | | | | |
| | Josh 7:26 | | | | |
| | Josh 8:28 | | | | |
| | Josh 8:29 | | | | |
| | Josh 9:27 | | | | |
| | Josh 10:27 | | | | |
| | Josh 13:13 | | | | |
| | Josh 14:14 | | | | |
| | Josh 15:63 | | | | |
| | Josh 16:10 | | | | |
| | | Judg 1:21 | | | |
| | | Judg 1:26 | | | |
| | | Judg 6:24 | | | |
| | | Judg 10:4 | | | |
| | | Judg 15:19 | | | |
| | | Judg 18:12 | | | |
| | | | 1 Sam 5:5 | | |
| | | | 1 Sam 6:18 | | |
| | | | | 1 Sam 27:6 | |
| | | | | 1 Sam 30:25 | |
| | | | | 2 Sam 4:3 | |
| | | | 2 Sam 6:8 | | |
| | | | | | 2 Sam 18:18 |

**AN** = Ark Narrative   **HDR** = History of David's Rise   **SN** = Succession Narrative

**Figure 3.1: "Until This Day"**

| Kings | | | | | |
|---|---|---|---|---|---|
| AS | PC | EC | CKJ | CKI | DTR |
| 1 Kgs 8:8<br>1 Kgs 9:13<br>1 Kgs 9:21<br>1 Kgs 10:12 | | | | | |
| | 1 Kgs 12:19 | | | | |
| | | 2 Kgs 2:22 | | | |
| | | | 2 Kgs 8:22 | | |
| | | | | 2 Kgs 10:27 | |
| | | | 2 Kgs 14:7<br>2 Kgs 16:6 | | |
| | | | | | 2 Kgs 17:23<br>2 Kgs 17:34<br>2 Kgs 17:41 |

**CKJ** = Chronicles of the Kings of Judah  
**AS** = Acts of Solomon  
**EC** = Elijah-Elisha Cycle  
**Dtr** = Deuteronomistic Historian  
**PC** = Prophetic Cycle  
**CKI** = Chronicles of the Kings of Israel  

**by source in the Deuteronomistic History**

## "UNTIL THIS DAY" AND SOURCE ANALYSIS IN THE DEUTERONOMISTIC HISTORY

Childs's observation that "until this day" appears in every major source of the books of Kings raises the question of where else in the DH this phrase appears. The findings are fascinating, yet somewhat predictable, once the redactional nature of "until this day" has been determined and Dtr has been identified as one of its sources (see Figure 3.1).

Most significantly, "until this day" occurs in every source believed to make up the DH—whether northern or southern, annalistic or literary.[6] While we might call into question the exact parameters of some of these sources, even their independent existence, the conclusion remains the same: "until this day" cuts across the whole of the DH, regardless of the source type or provenance. It may be, of course, that this phrase was of such common stock that multiple redactors employed it. Yet, it is difficult to reconstruct the circumstances under which *every* redactor (for the phrase is, in nearly every case, redactional) would choose to confirm the persistence of geographical, political, demographic or cultic realities by means of the exact same phrase and with the same grammatical peculiarities identified by Childs.[7] Although this proposal is possible, when we combine the

---

6. The "Acts of Solomon" (1 Kgs 11:41), "Chronicles of the Kings of Judah" (1 Kgs 14:29; 15:7, 23; 22:46; 2 Kgs 8:23; 12:20; 14:18; 15:6, etc.) and "Chronicles of the Kings of Israel" (1 Kgs 14:19; 15:31; 16:5, 14, 20, 27; 22:39; 2 Kgs 1:18; 10:34; 13:8, etc.) are biblical terms for what seem to be royal annals. For the identification of the "Ark Narrative," see L. Rost, *The Succession to the Throne of David* (HTIBS 1; Sheffield: Almond Press, 1982; German; Stuttgart: W. Kohlhammer, 1926); A. Campbell, *The Ark Narrative (1 Sam 4–6; 2 Sam 6): A Form-Critical and Traditio-Historical Study* (SBLDS 16; Missoula, MT: Scholars Press, 1975); P. D. Miller and J. J. M. Roberts, *The Hand of the Lord: A Reassessment of the "Ark Narrative" of 1 Samuel* (JHNES; Baltimore: Johns Hopkins, 1977); McCarter, *1 Samuel*, 23–26; G. Ahlström, "The Travels of the Ark: A Religio-Political Composition" *JNES* 43 (1984) 141–49. For the "History of David's Rise," see Rost, *Throne of David*; N. P. Lemche, "David's Rise," *JSOT* 10 (1978) 2–25; McCarter, "The Apology of David," *JBL* 99 (1980) 489–504; idem, *1 Samuel*, 27–30; W. Dietrich and T. Naumann, *Die Samuelbücher* (Erträge der Forschung 281; Darmstadt: Wissenschaftliche Buchgesellschaft, 1995) 47–86. For the "Succession Narrative," see Rost, *Throne of David*; R. N. Whybray, *The Succession Narrative: A Study of 2 Samuel 9–20, [and] 1 Kings 1 and 2* (SBT 2/9; Naperville, IL: Allenson, 1968); McCarter, *2 Samuel*, 9–16. For the "Prophetic Cycle" and "Elijah-Elisha Cycle" see S. L. McKenzie, "The Prophetic History in Kings," *HAR* 9 (1985) 203–23. The exact parameters, even the independent existence, of these sources are matters of on-going debate and do not affect the overall observation that "until this day" is present in every major literary unit making up the DH. For a recent argument against the independent existence of the Succession Narrative, see S. Frolov, "Succession Narrative: A 'Document' or a Phantom?" *JBL* 121/1 (2002) 81–104. See, too, the general skepticism of Van Seters (*In Search of History*, 322–53) regarding Dtr's recourse to narrative sources.

7. For the grammatical incongruities resulting from the addition of "until this day," see Childs, "Until This Day," 281–84. Of its forty-three occurrences in the DH, only twice do we find a variant formula (Josh 10:27; 2 Kgs 10:27).

phrase's distribution with its unified geographical (southern) and temporal (preexilic) orientation, then more lines of evidence begin to converge on Dtr.

In the end, however, this evidence is only suggestive. It shows that "until this day" derives from a limited geographical and, perhaps, temporal provenance, but it is not enough to show that the phrase derives from a single source, let alone from the hand of Dtr. What is required is the identification of specific Deuteronomistic language and interests in connection with "until this day" similar to those observed by Vatke and Kuenen in Joshua and Kings, respectively. That is, if "until this day" is redactional and derives from Dtr, then we would expect to find other Deuteronomistic material in its proximity.[8] And, in fact, we do.

## "UNTIL THIS DAY" AND DEUTERONOMISTIC LANGUAGE

In Josh 9:27, for example, "until this day" is immediately followed by the phrase "at the place he will choose"—an addition invariably ascribed to Dtr:[9]

וַיִּתְּנֵם יְהוֹשֻׁעַ בַּיּוֹם הַהוּא חֹטְבֵי עֵצִים וְשֹׁאֲבֵי מַיִם לָעֵדָה
וּלְמִזְבַּח יְהוָה עַד־הַיּוֹם הַזֶּה אֶל־הַמָּקוֹם אֲשֶׁר יִבְחָר

> And Joshua made them on that day hewers of wood and drawers of water for the congregation and for the altar of YHWH *until this day at the place he will choose*.

Both "until this day" and "at the place he will choose" are redactional, fitting uncomfortably into the grammatical structure of the sentence. Specifically, Joshua's past action is awkwardly extended to the historian's present by the addition of "until this day" and is localized at the temple by the addition of "at the place he will choose." As we will see below, "until this day" is Dtr's witness to the use of non-Israelite forced labor in connection

---

8. For the purposes of this study, the identification of "Deuteronomistic" material will be based primarily upon the studies of S. R. Driver (*Introduction*, 91–96), M. Noth (*The Deuteronomistic History*, 36, 93, 98), and M. Weinfeld (*Deuteronomic School*, 142, 167 n. 3, 324, 337).

9. Driver, *Introduction*, 100; Noth, *The Deuteronomistic History*, 38; Weinfeld, *Deuteronomic School*, 324. See, more recently, J. Briend, "The Sources of the Deuteronomistic History," in *Israel Constructs Its History: Deuteronomistic Historiography in Recent Research*, ed. A. de Pury, T. Römer, and J-D Macchi (JSOTSup 306; Sheffield: Sheffield Academic Press, 2000; French; Geneva: Labor et Fides, 1996) 360–86, esp. 363.

with the temple during his own day, while "at the place he will choose" reflects his concern for centralized worship.[10] As we will also see below, the addition of Deuteronomistic material after "until this day" is an editorial technique repeated by Dtr throughout his history.

In Josh 14:14 "until this day" is followed by another telltale sign of Dtr's editorial activity:

עַל־כֵּן הָיְתָה־חֶבְרוֹן לְכָלֵב בֶּן־יְפֻנֶּה הַקְּנִזִּי לְנַחֲלָה עַד־הַיּוֹם הַזֶּה
יַעַן אֲשֶׁר מִלֵּא אַחֲרֵי יְהוָה אֱלֹהֵי יִשְׂרָאֵל

Therefore Hebron belongs to Caleb the son of Jephunneh the Kenizzite as an inheritance *until this day because he followed fully after YHWH the God of Israel*.

While Weinfeld traces the expression "to follow fully after YHWH" to the Pentateuchal traditions surrounding Caleb (Num 14:24, 32:11, 12), he affirms that its presence here and elsewhere in the DH (Josh 14:8, 9; 1 Kgs 11:6) derives from a Deuteronomistic redactor.[11] Even Childs, who, as we have seen, ascribes "until this day" to many different redactors, admits this passage reflects "a theological doctrine of the deuteronomist."[12]

Given the presence of "trademark" Deuteronomistic phrases, these two examples of Dtr's editorial use of "until this day" are fairly straightforward. Other cases, though less obvious at first glance, are no less important for establishing Dtr's editorial technique of inserting material reflecting his own particular interests following his use of "until this day."

In Joshua 6, for example, "until this day" is followed by the curse on anyone who would rebuild Jericho (Josh 6:25–26):

²⁵וַתֵּשֶׁב בְּקֶרֶב יִשְׂרָאֵל עַד הַיּוֹם הַזֶּה . . .
²⁶וַיַּשְׁבַּע יְהוֹשֻׁעַ בָּעֵת הַהִיא לֵאמֹר אָרוּר הָאִישׁ לִפְנֵי יְהוָה
אֲשֶׁר יָקוּם וּבָנָה אֶת־הָעִיר הַזֹּאת אֶת־יְרִיחוֹ בִּבְכֹרוֹ יְיַסְּדֶנָּה
וּבִצְעִירוֹ יַצִּיב דְּלָתֶיהָ

And [Rahab] settled in the midst of Israel *until this day* . . . *And Joshua swore at that time: "Cursed be the man before YHWH who determines to rebuild this city Jericho. With his firstborn he will lay its foundations and with his youngest he will establish its doors.*

That "until this day" is redactional is apparent by the way it extends Rahab's past action (וַתֵּשֶׁב; "and she settled") to the historian's present. That "until this day" and the material following belong to Dtr is indicated by his appeal to this same curse later in his history (1 Kgs 16:34):[13]

---

10. Cf. Deut 12:5–26; 14:23–25; 15:20; 16:2–16; 17:8–10; 18:6; 23:17; 26:2; 31:11.
11. Weinfeld, *Deuteronomic School*, 78, 337. See also Deut 1:36.
12. Childs, "Until This Day," 287.
13. For the attribution of 1 Kgs 16:34 to Dtr, see J. Gray, *I & II Kings*, 334–35; Cogan, *1 Kings*, 421–23. For the text critical issues involved with 1 Kgs 16:34, in particular its absence

בְּיָמָיו בָּנָה חִיאֵל בֵּית הָאֱלִי אֶת־יְרִיחֹה בַּאֲבִירָם בְּכֹרוֹ
יִסְּדָהּ וּבִשְׂגוּב צְעִירוֹ הִצִּיב דְּלָתֶיהָ כִּדְבַר יְהוָה אֲשֶׁר
דִּבֶּר בְּיַד יְהוֹשֻׁעַ בִּן־נוּן

In [Ahab's] days, Hiel of Bethel rebuilt Jericho. He laid its foundations with Abiram his firstborn and he established its doors with Segub his youngest, according to the word of YHWH, which he spoke by the hand of Joshua the son of Nun.

The phrase כִּדְבַר יְהוָה אֲשֶׁר דִּבֶּר בְּיַד, "according to the word of YHWH which he spoke by the hand of [PN]," is Dtr's characteristic way of highlighting a fulfilled prophecy (e.g., 1 Kgs 13:26; 14:18; 15:29; 16:12; 17:16; etc.), and reflects his concern for the efficacy of the prophetic word (see esp. Deut 18:20–21). Significantly, this concern shows up again in connection with "until this day" in 2 Kgs 2:22, following Elisha's purification of the spring at Jericho—the same city, it should be noted, that is the object of Joshua's curse:

וַיֵּרָפוּ הַמַּיִם עַד הַיּוֹם הַזֶּה כִּדְבַר אֱלִישָׁע אֲשֶׁר דִּבֵּר

And the water has been healed *until this day according to the word which Elisha spoke.*

Thus, not only does Joshua's curse anticipate its actualization in 1 Kgs 16:34 as part of Dtr's prophecy-fulfillment pattern manifest throughout the DH,[14] it also helps account for the conditions requiring Elisha's miracle, which similarly participates in this pattern by means of parallel phraseology (כִּדְבַר יְהוָה אֲשֶׁר דִּבֶּר / / כִּדְבַר אֱלִישָׁע אֲשֶׁר דִּבֵּר).[15]

---

from the Lucianic recension, see L. Mazor, "The Origin and Evolution of the Curse upon the Rebuilder of Jericho: A Contribution of Textual Criticism to Biblical Historiography," *Textus* 14 (1988) 1–26.

14. For the theme of prophecy-fulfillment in the DH, see esp. G. von Rad, "Die deuteronomistische Geschichtstheologie in den Königsbüchern" in *Gesammelte Studien zum Alten Testament* (TB AT 8; Munich: Kaiser, 1958) 189–204; I. L. Seeligmann, "Die Auffassung der Prophetie in der deuteronomistischen und chronistischen Geschichtsschreibung," *Congress Volume: Göttingen, 1977* (VTSup 29; Leiden: Brill, 1978) 254–84; E. Würthwein, "Prophetisches Wort und Geschichte in den Königsbüchern: Zu einer These Gerhard von Rads," in *Altes Testament und christliche Verkündigung: Festschrift für A. H. J. Gunneweg zum 65. Geburtstag*, ed. M. Oeming and A. Graupner (Stuttgart: W. Kohlhammer, 1987) 399–411; H. Weippert, "Geschichten und Geschichte: Verheissung und Erfüllung im deuteronomistischen Geschichtswerk," in *Congress Volume: Leuven, 1989*, ed. J. A. Emerton (VTSup 43; Leiden: Brill, 1991) 116–31.

15. For similar observations concerning the significance of this curse and its fulfillment for establishing the authority of the prophetic word, see M. A. Sweeney, "On the Literary Function of the Notice Concerning Hiel's Re-Establishment of Jericho in 1 Kings 16.34," in *Seing Signals, Reading Signs: The Art of Exegesis. Studies in Honor of Anthony F. Campbell, SJ for his Seventieth Birthday*, ed. M. A. O'Brien and H. N. Wallace (JSOTSup 415; London/New York: T&T Clark, 2004) 104–15.

Related to Dtr's use of "until this day" in Joshua 6 is his use of the time notice "at that time": וַתֵּשֶׁב בְּקֶרֶב יִשְׂרָאֵל עַד הַיּוֹם הַזֶּה . . . וַיַּשְׁבַּע יְהוֹשֻׁעַ בָּעֵת הַהִיא, "And [Rahab] settled in the midst of Israel *until this day* . . . and Joshua swore *at that time*" (Josh 6:25b-26a). This redactional procedure serves to bring the action of the narrative back to Joshua's time, having been offset by Dtr's addition of "until this day." A similar redactional technique is attested in 2 Kgs 8:22:

וַיִּפְשַׁע אֱדוֹם מִתַּחַת יַד־יְהוּדָה עַד הַיּוֹם הַזֶּה
אָז תִּפְשַׁע לִבְנָה בָּעֵת הַהִיא

And Edom rebelled from under the hand of Judah *until this day*. Then Libnah rebelled *at that time*.

Cogan and Tadmor, building on the work of J. A. Montgomery, have argued that the historian's use of these various time notices attests to his recourse to written sources.[16] Concerning the time notices בָּעֵת הַהִיא ("at that time") and אָז ("then") in particular, they observe:

> These words are opening formulae which introduce quotations from earlier, perhaps archival, sources. Assyrian and Babylonian historical literature display a similar phenomenon, in which the phrases *ina tarṣi PN*, 'in the days of PN' and *ina umišuma*, 'at that time' (lit. 'in his days') signal verbatim quotations from chronicles.[17]

Based on Cogan and Tadmor's assessment, we might reconstruct the historian's editorial procedure as follows: his source, which he informs us is "the Chronicles of the Kings of Judah" (2 Kgs 2:23), contained the notice concerning Edom's and Libnah's revolt during the reign of Jehoram (851–843 B.C.E.). As Edom remained independent of Judahite control during the historian's day, he adds his standard formula of continuation ("until this day") and then resumes citing his source by means of the historical notice אָז ("then"). He then concludes his citation with the notice בָּעֵת הַהִיא ("at that time") to emphasize the past aspect of Libnah's revolt. In fact, the historian's precision in contrasting Edom's rebellion ("until this day") with Libnah's ("then . . . at that time") suggests that Libnah has since come back under Judahite control, which occurred at least by the reign of Hezekiah and seems to have continued until the Babylonian conquest.[18] As we will see below, "until this day" consistently points to this same period.

---

16. J. A. Montgomery, "Archival Data," 46–52.
17. Cogan and Tadmor, *2 Kings*, 186.
18. See 2 Kgs 19:8. Note, too, that Josiah's wife, Hamutal, who is the mother of both Jehoahaz (2 Kgs 23:31) and Zedekiah (2 Kgs 24:18), comes from Libnah, suggesting that the city was part of Judah during Josiah's day as well.

Returning to the book of Joshua: in Josh 8:28, Ai is described as a "tel of perpetual ruin until this day" (תֵּל־עוֹלָם שְׁמָמָה עַד הַיּוֹם הַזֶּה), a phrase that Weinfeld rightly notes reflects the "deuteronomic descriptions of the destruction of cities" (see Deut 13:17, the only other occurrence of תֵּל עוֹלָם in the Bible).[19] Similarly, in Josh 10:27 "until this day" is followed by a description of the ban (vv. 28–43), which again, as Weinfeld observes, is "based on the law of the ban in Deut 20:10ff" and which is "formulated in distinct Deuteronomic phraseology."[20] Indeed, Dtr employs a similar redactional technique here as he does in Joshua 6; namely, the use of "until this day" followed by a time notice that brings the action back to the past. This notice, in turn, is followed by material reflecting Dtr's own particular interests; in this case, the proper implementation of the ban as commanded in Deuteronomy:

וְאֶת־מַקֵּדָה לָכַד יְהוֹשֻׁעַ בַּיּוֹם הַהוּא וַיַּכֶּהָ לְפִי־חֶרֶב וְאֶת־מַלְכָּהּ
הֶחֱרִם אוֹתָם וְאֶת־כָּל־הַנֶּפֶשׁ אֲשֶׁר־בָּהּ לֹא הִשְׁאִיר שָׂרִיד

And Joshua took Makkedah on that day, and he struck it and its king with the edge of the sword, proscribing them and every living being in it, leaving no survivors.

Josh 10:28a

This association between the ban and "until this day" would also explain why Dtr earlier points to the persistence of Achan's grave (Josh 7:26), as this pile of rubble would provide a sobering example of what happens to those who violate this prohibition. Indeed, the Deuteronomic law governing Achan's violation of the ban is the same one informing the description of Makkedah's (and Jericho's and Ai's) destructions:

[16]הַכֵּה תַכֶּה אֶת־יֹשְׁבֵי הָעִיר הַהִיא לְפִי־חָרֶב הַחֲרֵם אֹתָהּ
וְאֶת־כָּל־אֲשֶׁר־בָּהּ וְאֶת־בְּהֶמְתָּהּ לְפִי־חָרֶב:
[17]וְאֶת־כָּל־שְׁלָלָהּ תִּקְבֹּץ אֶל־תּוֹךְ רְחֹבָהּ וְשָׂרַפְתָּ בָאֵשׁ אֶת־הָעִיר
וְאֶת־כָּל־שְׁלָלָהּ כָּלִיל לַיהוָה אֱלֹהֶיךָ וְהָיְתָה תֵּל עוֹלָם לֹא תִבָּנֶה עוֹד:
[18]וְלֹא־יִדְבַּק בְּיָדְךָ מְאוּמָה מִן־הַחֵרֶם לְמַעַן יָשׁוּב יְהוָה מֵחֲרוֹן אַפּוֹ
וְנָתַן־לְךָ רַחֲמִים וְרִחַמְךָ וְהִרְבֶּךָ כַּאֲשֶׁר נִשְׁבַּע לַאֲבֹתֶיךָ:

And you will strike the inhabitants of that city with the edge of the sword, proscribing it and all those in it, and its livestock with the edge of the sword. And all of its spoil you will gather into the midst of its square, and you will burn with fire the city and all its spoil as a whole burnt offering to YHWH your God, and it will be a tel of perpetual ruin and it will not

---

19. Weinfeld, *Deuteronomic School*, 142.
20. Weinfeld, *Deuteronomic School*, 167, n. 3. Cf. Deut 2:34–35; 3:6–7; 7:2; 13:16–17; 20:14–17.

be built again. Do not let anything that is devoted cleave to your hand in order that YHWH might turn from his fierce anger and show you compassion, and he will have compassion on you and he will increase you as he swore to your fathers.

Deut 13:16–18[21]

Another connection between "until this day" in Josh 7:26 and 10:27 is its use to testify to the persistence of stone memorials, which would suggest that similar uses of the phrase in Joshua would also derive from Dtr. Beyond the monument of twelve stones commemorating Israel's crossing of the Jordan (Josh 4:9, which will be discussed below), the only other memorial said to persist "until this day" in Joshua is the grave of the king of Ai (Josh 8:29), a passage with clear affinities to the notice concerning Achan's grave:

וַיָּקִימוּ עָלָיו גַּל־אֲבָנִים גָּדוֹל עַד הַיּוֹם הַזֶּה

And they erected over him (Achan) a large pile of stones until this day.

Josh 7:26a

וַיָּקִימוּ עָלָיו גַּל־אֲבָנִים גָּדוֹל עַד הַיּוֹם הַזֶּה

And they erected over him (the king of Ai) a large pile of stones until this day.

Josh 8:29b

Aside from the obvious grammatical parallels between these two passages, there is good reason to ascribe "until this day" in both passages to the same redactional hand, in general, and to Dtr, in particular. In Josh 7:26, "until this day" is followed by YHWH's admonition אַל־תִּירָא וְאַל־תֵּחָת, "Do not fear or be dismayed" (Josh 8:1), which in the DH appears only in material belonging to Dtr: the prologue (Deut 1:21) and epilogue (Deut 31:8) of Deuteronomy and in Josh 10:25.[22] In Josh 8:29, "until this day" is followed

---

21. See also Deut 7:2 and 20:17. Significantly, the law of the ban in Deut 13:16–18 relates to cities within Israel that promote the worship of other gods or that, in other ways, lead Israel astray from proper worship of YHWH. While this law would certainly have relevance for the events recounted in the book of Joshua, it has additional significance for the period indicated by "this day"; namely, the reign of Josiah, when these laws inform the king's actions against alternate sites of worship and their priesthoods, specifically Bethel. See, e.g., 2 Kgs 23:15–20. For similar observations about the provenance and purpose of the laws of ḥerem, see M. G. Brett, "Genocide in Deuteronomy: Postcolonial Variations on Mimetic Desire," in *Seeing Signals, Reading Signs*, 75–89. For other parallels between Joshua and Josiah, see below.

22. Weinfeld, *Deuteronomic School*, 344. Cf. אַל־תַּעַרְץ וְאַל־תֵּחָת (Josh 1:9; cf. Deut 7:21) and the positive חֲזַק וֶאֱמָץ (Deut 31:7, 23; Josh 1:6, 7, 9, 18), both of which derive from Dtr. For the ascription of Josh 8:1 and 8:29 to Dtr in particular, see most recently Briend, "The Sources of the Deuteronomistic History," 367.

by six verses describing Joshua's building of the altar on Mount Ebal and the reading of the law, which specifically fulfills Moses' words in Deut 27:1–8 and which Noth rightly identified as material Dtr "added himself."[23]

These initial observations strongly suggest that "until this day" belongs to Dtr in Joshua (so far we have accounted for eight of its eleven appearances in this book, and will account for the remaining three below) and selected passages in 2 Kings (we have accounted for two of its eight appearances in this book, and will account for the remaining six below). However, it is the use of "until this day" across the DH to refer to the same or similar matters—matters of central interest to Dtr, no less—that establishes that "this day" is Dtr's day.

## "UNTIL THIS DAY" AND DEUTERONOMISTIC INTERESTS

### 1. Havvoth Jair

As observed in chapter 2, "until this day" is employed in both Deut 3:14 and Judg 10:4 to verify the persistence of the name Havvoth Jair, even though these narratives differ on the exact parameters of this region and how this area received its name. Deuteronomy places the region of Havvoth Jair in the Bashan and traces its name to "Jair the son of Manasseh," while Judges locates Havvoth Jair in Gilead and attributes the name to "Jair the Gileadite":

יָאִיר בֶּן־מְנַשֶּׁה לָקַח אֶת־כָּל־חֶבֶל אַרְגֹּב עַד־גְּבוּל הַגְּשׁוּרִי
וְהַמַּעֲכָתִי וַיִּקְרָא אֹתָם עַל־שְׁמוֹ אֶת־הַבָּשָׁן חַוֹּת יָאִיר
עַד הַיּוֹם הַזֶּה

---

23. Noth, *The Deuteronomistic History*, 93. See also Driver (*Introduction*, 94, 100) and Weinfeld (*Deuteronomic School*, 171, 339) regarding the Deuteronomistic language in these verses. Based on the pattern observed above—namely, Dtr's practice of inserting his own material immediately following "until this day"—the placement of vv. 30–35 in the DH (as opposed to LXX, which places these verses after 9:2, and 4QJosh[a], which places them before 5:1) seems to be preferred. It may even be that Dtr introduced this material as a marginal note or interlinear gloss that was subsequently inserted at different points in the text. Although this reconstruction is admittedly conjectural, that Dtr intended "until this day" to be understood as secondary to his source is suggested by the manner in which, except in rare cases (see, e.g., Josh 4:9; 1 Sam 5:5), he makes little effort to integrate it into the larger syntax of the sentence.

Jair the son of Manasseh took the whole region of Argob as far as the border of the Geshurites and the Maacathites, and he named them—that is the Bashan—according to his name, Havvoth Jair, until this day.

Deut 3:14

וַיְהִי־לוֹ (וְיָאִיר הַגִּלְעָדִ) שְׁלֹשִׁים בָּנִים רֹכְבִים עַל־שְׁלֹשִׁים עֲיָרִים
וּשְׁלֹשִׁים עֲיָרִים לָהֶם לָהֶם יִקְרְאוּ חַוֺּת יָאִיר עַד הַיּוֹם הַזֶּה
אֲשֶׁר בְּאֶרֶץ הַגִּלְעָד:

And he (Jair the Gileadite) had thirty children who rode upon thirty donkeys, and they had thirty towns. These they named Havvoth Jair until this day which are in the land of Gilead.

Judg 10:4

Weinfeld has argued that Judges 10 reflects the older tradition and that the Deuteronom(ist)ic tendency to extend this territory to the Bashan and to increase its number of settlements from thirty to sixty indicates that Havvoth Jair was important to Deuteronomistic circles.[24] For similar reasons, Weinfeld ascribes the addition "and all of Havvoth Jair in Bashan, sixty cities" in Josh 13:30 to a Deuteronomistic scribe.[25] Weinfeld's observations are important to our study because they explain why "until this day," which is used almost exclusively for southern entities, would be employed by Dtr in connection with a region in the far north. Yet, Weinfeld's observations are also confirmed by our study, since not only is "until this day" used in connection with Havvoth Jair in these two passages, but it appears again in relation to this same region in Josh 13:13, which, like Deut 3:14, mentions the Geshurites and Maacathites:

וְלֹא הוֹרִישׁוּ בְּנֵי יִשְׂרָאֵל אֶת־הַגְּשׁוּרִי וְאֶת־הַמַּעֲכָתִי
וַיֵּשֶׁב גְּשׁוּר וּמַעֲכָת בְּקֶרֶב יִשְׂרָאֵל עַד הַיּוֹם הַזֶּה

And the Israelites did not dispossess the Geshurites and the Maacathites. And Geshur and Maacah live in the midst of Israel until this day.

That "until this day" in Josh 13:13 belongs to Dtr is suggested not only by its affinities to similar notices already ascribed to him in the book of Joshua (e.g., Josh 6:25: וַיֵּשֶׁב [רָחָב] בְּקֶרֶב יִשְׂרָאֵל עַד הַיּוֹם הַזֶּה: "And [Rahab] lives in the midst of Israel until this day"), but also because it is followed by a notice regarding the inheritance of the Levites, a group that, as we will see momentarily, is of central concern to Dtr:

---

24. Weinfeld, *Deuteronomy 1–11*, 185.
25. Weinfeld, *Deuteronomy 1–11*, 185; See also Boling (*Joshua*, 340), who ascribes Josh 13:13b-14 to Dtr. Moore (*Judges*, 274–75) similarly gives the Judges tradition chronological priority, attributing Deut 3:14 and Josh 13:30 "to the latest redaction of the history."

רַק לְשֵׁבֶט הַלֵּוִי לֹא נָתַן נַחֲלָה אִשֵּׁי יְהוָה אֱלֹהֵי יִשְׂרָאֵל
הוּא נַחֲלָתוֹ כַּאֲשֶׁר דִּבֶּר־לוֹ

Only to the tribe of Levi he did not give an inheritance. The offerings of
YHWH the God of Israel are his inheritance, as he said to him.

Josh 13:14

While אִשֵּׁי יְהוָה is usually understood to be a mark of the Priestly source (see Lev 2:3, 10; 4:35; 5:12; 6:11; 7:30, 35; 10:12–13; 21:6, 21; 24:9), there are several pieces of evidence that argue against assigning this particular notice to the Priestly source. In fact, this evidence further establishes that Dtr is its source. First, יְהוָה אֱלֹהֵי יִשְׂרָאֵל never occurs in material traditionally ascribed to P.[26] Second, we have already encountered the phrase יְהוָה אֱלֹהֵי יִשְׂרָאֵל twice in connection with our phrase: Josh 8:30, where Joshua fulfills Moses' command to build the altar on Mount Ebal; and Josh 14:14, which, like Josh 13:14, relates to inheritance rights and which, like Josh 8:30, manifests Dtr's redactional activity: עַד הַיּוֹם הַזֶּה יַעַן אֲשֶׁר מִלֵּא אַחֲרֵי יְהוָה אֱלֹהֵי יִשְׂרָאֵל ("until this day because he followed fully after YHWH the God of Israel"). Third, the closest parallel to Josh 13:14 is Deut 18:1–2, which seems the impetus behind the notice in Josh 13:14:

לֹא־יִהְיֶה לַכֹּהֲנִים הַלְוִיִּם כָּל־שֵׁבֶט לֵוִי חֵלֶק וְנַחֲלָה
עִם־יִשְׂרָאֵל אִשֵּׁי יְהוָה וְנַחֲלָתוֹ יֹאכֵלוּן וְנַחֲלָה
לֹא־יִהְיֶה־לּוֹ בְּקֶרֶב אֶחָיו יְהוָה הוּא נַחֲלָתוֹ כַּאֲשֶׁר דִּבֶּר־לוֹ

The Levitical priests, the whole tribe of Levi, will have no portion or inheritance with Israel. They may eat the offerings of YHWH and his inheritance, but they will have no inheritance in the midst of their kindred. YHWH, he is their inheritance, as he said to them.

A final indication that the notice concerning the Levites' inheritance in Josh 13:14 belongs to Dtr is that a similar notice appears in Deuteronomy, where it again follows "until this day":

בָּעֵת הַהִוא הִבְדִּיל יְהוָה אֶת־שֵׁבֶט הַלֵּוִי לָשֵׂאת אֶת־אֲרוֹן בְּרִית־
יְהוָה לַעֲמֹד לִפְנֵי יְהוָה לְשָׁרְתוֹ וּלְבָרֵךְ בִּשְׁמוֹ עַד הַיּוֹם הַזֶּה׃
עַל־כֵּן לֹא־הָיָה לְלֵוִי חֵלֶק וְנַחֲלָה עִם־אֶחָיו יְהוָה הוּא
נַחֲלָתוֹ כַּאֲשֶׁר דִּבֶּר יְהוָה אֱלֹהֶיךָ לוֹ

At that time YHWH set apart the tribe of Levi to carry the Ark of the Covenant of YHWH, to stand before YHWH, to minister to him and to

---

26. For source identifications, see S. R. Driver, *Introduction*; M. Noth, *A History of Pentateuchal Traditions* (Chico, CA: Scholars Press, 1981. German; Stuttgart, 1948); and R. E. Friedman, *The Bible with Sources Revealed: A New View into the Five Books of Moses* (San Francisco: HarperSanFrancisco, 2003).

bless his name *until this day. Therefore, Levi does not have a portion and an inheritance with his brothers. YHWH is his inheritance, as YHWH your God said to him.*

Deut 10:8–9

Why the Levites, their inheritance, and the far northern region of Havvoth Jair are important to Dtr will be explored below.

## 2. The Use of Non-Israelite Forced Labor (מַס־עֹבֵד)

Although the Hebrew word for forced labor (מַס) occurs fifteen times in the DH,[27] the phrase מַס־עֹבֵד occurs only twice, and, importantly, both times it appears with "until this day." In Josh 16:10 we are informed that those whom the Israelites did not remove from the land were subjected to forced labor (מַס־עֹבֵד) "until this day," while in 1 Kgs 9:21 we are told that the descendants of those whom the children of Israel were unable to destroy, "Solomon brought up for forced labor (מַס־עֹבֵד) until this day." The closest linguistic parallel to the phrase מַס־עֹבֵד in the DH occurs in Deuteronomy itself when describing how to treat those who surrender peaceably:

כִּי־תִקְרַב אֶל־עִיר לְהִלָּחֵם עָלֶיהָ וְקָרָאתָ אֵלֶיהָ לְשָׁלוֹם׃
וְהָיָה אִם־שָׁלוֹם תַּעַנְךָ וּפָתְחָה לָךְ וְהָיָה כָּל־הָעָם הַנִּמְצָא־בָהּ
יִהְיוּ לְךָ לָמַס וַעֲבָדוּךָ׃

When you draw near to a city to wage war against it, offer it peace. And if it accepts your offer of peace and opens itself to you, then all the people who are found in it will become forced labor for you and will serve you.

Deut 20:10–11

That "until this day" in Josh 16:10 and 1 Kgs 9:21 are related to Deuteronomy 20 is indicated not only by similarities in vocabulary (מַס־עֹבֵד and מַס וַעֲבָדוּךָ) but also because the only other reference to the subjection of non-Israelites "until this day" is in a narrative related to Deuteronomy 20, where non-Israelites (i.e., Gibeonites) surrender peaceably (albeit, deceitfully) and are made forced laborers, and where Dtr's hand is clearly at work:

וַיִּתְּנֵם יְהוֹשֻׁעַ בַּיּוֹם הַהוּא חֹטְבֵי עֵצִים וְשֹׁאֲבֵי מַיִם
לָעֵדָה וּלְמִזְבַּח יְהוָה עַד־הַיּוֹם הַזֶּה אֶל־הַמָּקוֹם אֲשֶׁר יִבְחָר

---

27. Deut 20:11; Josh 16:10; 17:13; Judg 1:28, 30, 33, 35; 2 Sam 20:24; 1 Kgs 4:6; 5:27 (2x), 28; 9:15, 21; 12:18.

> And Joshua made [the Gibeonites] on that day hewers of wood and drawers of water for the congregation and for the altar of YHWH *until this day at the place he will choose*.
>
> Josh 9:27

In these cases, Dtr employs "until this day" to account for the presence of forced laborers at the temple ("at the place he will choose") during his own day.[28] Why Dtr has an interest in the activities and policies related to the temple will, again, be addressed below.

## 3. The Failure to Drive Out the Inhabitants of the Land

Related to the Deuteronomistic interest in non-Israelite forced labor are the notices of Israel's failure to dispossess the original inhabitants of the land "until this day." While some of these notices have been discussed earlier, here is the complete list:

> 1) וְלֹא הוֹרִישׁוּ בְּנֵי יִשְׂרָאֵל אֶת־הַגְּשׁוּרִי וְאֶת־הַמַּעֲכָתִי
> וַיֵּשֶׁב גְּשׁוּר וּמַעֲכָת בְּקֶרֶב יִשְׂרָאֵל עַד הַיּוֹם הַזֶּה׃
>
> And the Israelites did not dispossess the Geshurites and Maacathites. And Geshur and Maacah live in the midst of Israel until this day.
>
> Josh 13:13

> 2) וְאֶת־הַיְבוּסִי יוֹשְׁבֵי יְרוּשָׁלַם לֹא־יָכְלוּ בְנֵי־יְהוּדָה לְהוֹרִישָׁם
> וַיֵּשֶׁב הַיְבוּסִי אֶת־בְּנֵי יְהוּדָה בִּירוּשָׁלַם עַד הַיּוֹם הַזֶּה׃
>
> And the children of Judah were unable to dispossess the Jebusites living in Jerusalem. And the Jebusites live with the children of Judah in Jerusalem until this day
>
> Josh 15:63

> 3) וְלֹא הוֹרִישׁוּ אֶת־הַכְּנַעֲנִי הַיּוֹשֵׁב בְּגָזֶר
> וַיֵּשֶׁב הַכְּנַעֲנִי בְּקֶרֶב אֶפְרַיִם עַד־הַיּוֹם הַזֶּה וַיְהִי לְמַס־עֹבֵד
>
> And they did not dispossess the Canaanites living in Gezer. And the Canaanites live in the midst of Ephraim until this day, and they have become forced laborers.
>
> Josh 16:10

---

28. Beyond the phrase "at the place he will choose," the phrase "hewers of wood and drawers of water" appears only in Joshua 9 and Deuteronomy 29, the latter of which is in the context of Moses' covenant renewal (v. 10).

(4) וְאֶת־הַיְבוּסִי יֹשֵׁב יְרוּשָׁלַ͏ִם לֹא הוֹרִישׁוּ בְּנֵי בִנְיָמִן
וַיֵּשֶׁב הַיְבוּסִי אֶת־בְּנֵי בִנְיָמִן בִּירוּשָׁלַ͏ִם עַד הַיּוֹם הַזֶּה:

And the children of Benjamin did not dispossess the Jebusites living in Jerusalem. And the Jebusites live with the children of Benjamin in Jerusalem until this day.

Judg 1:21

(5) בְּנֵיהֶם אֲשֶׁר נֹתְרוּ אַחֲרֵיהֶם בָּאָרֶץ אֲשֶׁר לֹא־יָכְלוּ בְּנֵי יִשְׂרָאֵל
לְהַחֲרִימָם וַיַּעֲלֵם שְׁלֹמֹה לְמַס־עֹבֵד עַד הַיּוֹם הַזֶּה:

Their children who remained after them in the land, whom the children of Israel were unable to destroy, these Solomon brought up for forced labor until this day.

1 Kgs 9:21

We have already observed that in nos. 1 (Josh 13:13, which is followed by the inheritance of the Levites; cf. Deut 10:8–9; Deut 18:1), 3 (Josh 16:10, which refers to מַס־עֹבֵד; cf. Deut 20:11) and 5 (1 Kgs 9:21, which also refers to מַס־עֹבֵד) there are compelling reasons for assigning "until this day" to Dtr. Therefore, explaining why this phrase in nos. 2 and 4 does not belong to Dtr seems the greater challenge, especially since nos. 2, 3, and 4 represent consecutive uses of the phrase, and since no. 1 is separated from no. 2 only by Josh 14:14, where Dtr's editorial activity is patent ("until this day because he followed fully after YHWH"). Yet, the proximity and similarities of these notices are not the only reasons for assigning "until this day" in nos. 2 and 4 to the same hand in general, and to Dtr in particular.

Both Josh 15:63 and Judg 1:21 testify to the same thing: the presence of Jebusites in Jerusalem. Yet, as with the notices regarding Havvoth Jair, the details differ. In Josh 15:63 Judah is said to be responsible, while in Judg 1:21 Benjamin is faulted. As in the case of Havvoth Jair, the historian adds his notice of continuity to each tradition because his main concern is verifying what persists "until this day," not reconciling the discrepancies among the accounts describing their origins. (We will return to the subject of the historian's methodology below.) Another indication that "until this day" in Josh 16:53 and Judg 1:21 belongs to Dtr is that these are not the only times "until this day" is employed to testify to the continuing presence of Jebusites in Jerusalem. So does no. 5, which we have already ascribed to Dtr. The full passage reads:

²⁰כָּל־הָעָם הַנּוֹתָר מִן־הָאֱמֹרִי הַחִתִּי הַפְּרִזִּי הַחִוִּי וְהַיְבוּסִי אֲשֶׁר
לֹא־מִבְּנֵי יִשְׂרָאֵל הֵמָּה: ²¹בְּנֵיהֶם אֲשֶׁר נֹתְרוּ אַחֲרֵיהֶם בָּאָרֶץ
אֲשֶׁר לֹא־יָכְלוּ בְּנֵי יִשְׂרָאֵל לְהַחֲרִימָם וַיַּעֲלֵם שְׁלֹמֹה לְמַס־עֹבֵד
עַד הַיּוֹם הַזֶּה

All those people remaining of the Amorites, the Hittites, the Perizzites, the Hivites and the *Jebusites*, who were not of the children of Israel, their children remaining after them in the land, whom the children of Israel were unable to destroy, these Solomon brought up for forced labor until this day.

1 Kgs 9:20–21

That the notices concerning the continuing presence of Jebusites in Jerusalem in Josh 15:63 and Judg 1:21 refer to the same institution of non-Israelite forced labor as described in Kings is confirmed by the reference to the Hivites in this same list of laborers. Dtr has already told us of their presence in Jerusalem, and their work at the temple, only he did so back in the book of Joshua, in a passage previously seen to have connections with several other uses of "until this day" and which bears obvious signs of Dtr's editorial activity:

And Joshua made them (the Gibeonites, *who are Hivites*; cf. Josh 9:7) on that day hewers of wood and drawers of water for the congregation and the altar of YHWH *until this day at the place he will choose*.

Josh 9:27

Dtr's interest in the centralization of worship and the administration of the Jerusalem cult is further emphasized by the next use of our phrase.

## 4. The Destruction of Non-Yahwistic Objects of Worship

The same Deuteronomic passages that command Israel to dispossess the original inhabitants of the land (Deut 7:1–4), also command Israel to destroy their objects of worship:

כִּי־אִם־כֹּה תַעֲשׂוּ לָהֶם מִזְבְּחֹתֵיהֶם תִּתֹּצוּ וּמַצֵּבֹתָם תְּשַׁבֵּרוּ
וַאֲשִׁירֵהֶם תְּגַדֵּעוּן וּפְסִילֵיהֶם תִּשְׂרְפוּן בָּאֵשׁ

Rather, this is what you will do to them: you will tear down their altars and shatter their pillars and chop down their *asherim* and burn their engraved images with fire.

Deut 7:5

Israel, nonetheless, fails to carry out this charge, as YHWH (via Dtr) reminds them:

¹וַיֹּאמֶר אַעֲלֶה אֶתְכֶם מִמִּצְרַיִם וָאָבִיא אֶתְכֶם אֶל־הָאָרֶץ אֲשֶׁר
נִשְׁבַּעְתִּי לַאֲבֹתֵיכֶם וָאֹמַר לֹא־אָפֵר בְּרִיתִי אִתְּכֶם לְעוֹלָם׃
²וְאַתֶּם לֹא־תִכְרְתוּ בְרִית לְיוֹשְׁבֵי הָאָרֶץ הַזֹּאת מִזְבְּחוֹתֵיהֶם תִּתֹּצוּן
וְלֹא־שְׁמַעְתֶּם בְּקֹלִי מַה־זֹּאת עֲשִׂיתֶם׃

And he said, "I made you to go up out of Egypt and I brought you to the land that I swore to your fathers and I said that I would never break my covenant with you. And you were not to make a covenant with the inhabitants of this land. Their altars you were to tear down, but you have not listened to my voice. What is this you have done?"

Judg 2:1b-2

Yet, there are a few examples in Israel's history where the command to tear down (נָתַץ) such altars *is* fulfilled. In fact, the only individual objects said to exist "until this day" in the north testify to the tearing down of places of Baal worship.[29]

In Judges 6, Gideon "tears down" (נָתַץ: vv 28, 30, 31, 32) his father's altar to Baal at Ophrah and builds an altar to YHWH that stands "until this day."[30] Similarly, in 2 Kings 10, Jehu "tears down" (וַיִּתֹּץ; 2 Kgs 10:27) the temple and altar of Baal in Samaria, which is used as a latrine "until this day." As in a number of cases already discussed, our phrase is then followed by Dtr's own redactional material; in this case, his appraisal of Jehu's reign:

27וַיִּתְּצוּ אֵת מַצְּבַת הַבַּעַל וַיִּתְּצוּ אֶת־בֵּית הַבַּעַל וַיְשִׂמֻהוּ לְמַחֲרָאוֹת עַד־הַיּוֹם: 28וַיַּשְׁמֵד יֵהוּא אֶת־הַבַּעַל מִיִּשְׂרָאֵל: 29רַק חֲטָאֵי יָרָבְעָם בֶּן־נְבָט אֲשֶׁר הֶחֱטִיא אֶת־יִשְׂרָאֵל לֹא־סָר יֵהוּא מֵאַחֲרֵיהֶם עֶגְלֵי הַזָּהָב אֲשֶׁר בֵּית־אֵל וַאֲשֶׁר בְּדָן:

And [Jehu's men] tore down the pillar of Baal and the temple of Baal and made it a latrine *until this day. Thus, Jehu eradicated Baal from Israel. Only Jehu did not depart from the sins of Jeroboam son of Nebath by which he made Israel to sin; namely, the calves of gold at Bethel and Dan.*

2 Kgs 10:27–29

That the only individual objects said to persist "until this day" in the north are defunct sites of Baal worship seems beyond coincidence, especially in light of the Deuteronomistic interest in their removal and the Deuteronomistic language used to describe their destruction. Moreover, the presence of Deuteronomistic material following the second of these notices strongly suggests that "until this day" in both cases derives from Dtr.[31]

## 5. The Far North and the Levites

Thus, four of the five northern sites said to exist "until this day" have clear Deuteronomistic associations: Havvoth Jair (Deut 3:14; Judg 10:4), Geshur

---

29. The tearing down (נָתַץ) of places of non-Yahwistic worship occurs only two other times in the Bible: the Beth-Baal during Jehoash's reign (2 Kgs 11:17–18) and various altars during Josiah's religious reforms (2 Kgs 23:12–15).

30. Although the passage as it stands seems to describe the construction of two altars to YHWH in the same location, presumably a single altar is intended. See Moore, *Judges*, 190.

31. We will see more evidence for identifying these notices regarding the destruction of non-Yahwistic places of worship to Dtr below when discussing to whose day in particular "this day" refers. See "Judahite-Edomite Interaction" and "'Until This Day,' Joshua, and the Reforms of Josiah," below.

and Maacah (Josh 13:13; cf. Deut 3:14), the altar at Ophrah (Judg 6:24) and the (destroyed) temple of Baal at Samaria (2 Kgs 10:27). The only remaining northern entity said to persist "until this day" is the Cabul (1 Kgs 9:13), which, like Havvoth Jair, is a large geographical region consisting of numerous cities and situated in the far north. As "until this day" in the chapter that precedes the Cabul passage (1 Kgs 8:8) and in the same chapter just eight verses later (1 Kgs 9:21) belong to Dtr, it seems reasonable that "until this day" in 1 Kgs 9:13 belongs to Dtr as well.[32] Yet, as in the case of non-Israelite forced laborers, there is more evidence to suggest "until this day" in 1 Kgs 9:13 derives from Dtr than merely its similarities with and proximity to these other uses.

B. Halpern has argued that the Cabul was of considerable interest to northern Levitical priests (specifically, Gershonite priests), and that Solomon's sale of this territory to Hiram of Tyre was a particular offense to this group.[33] Halpern notes:

> The Cabul, which comprised much of the older tribal allotment of Asher, contained at least three Mushite Levitical cities, Abdon, Rehob, and Mishal. Possibly Helkath was also included. Their loss meant the loss of one third of the Gershonite cities, a blow of no small proportions to the clan prestige.[34]

This Levitical interest in the far north would also seem to explain the use of "until this day" in connection with Havvoth Jair and the Bashan. As Halpern observes:

> From the outset, the Aramean recovery of Syria constituted a threat to the northern tribes. The Gershonite Levites were, of course, first among those threatened, and in the ninth century they lost city after city as Damascene forces ranged into the area of the old tribal allotments.[35]

The relationship between these two northern regions and "until this day" is not mere coincidence. As noted earlier, Dtr places the notice of the Levites' inheritance in the context of this same region (Josh 13:13b-14a): "And Geshur and Maacah (which is in the region of the Bashan; see Deut 3:14) live in the midst of Israel *until this day. Only to the tribe of Levi he did not give an inheritance.*" This notice concerning the Levites' lack of an inheritance would fit more naturally at the beginning or end of the inheritance lists,[36] yet it appears here, exactly where we would expect it if Halpern's

---

32. First Kgs 8:8 reflects Dtr's interest in the Ark of the Covenant (see the discussion on "The Ark of the Covenant of YHWH," below). First Kgs 9:21 describes the use of non-Israelite forced labor (see "The Use of Non-Israelite Forced Labor," above).
33. B. Halpern, "Sectionalism and the Schism," *JBL* 93 (1974) 519–32.
34. Halpern, "Sectionalism," 523.
35. Halpern, "Sectionalism," 522.
36. Cf. Joshua 21, where the Levitical cities do end the tribal lists.

analysis is correct—in the context of the allotment of the far north—in particular, the Bashan (Josh 13:8–12). That is, Dtr inserts a notice about the Levites' lack of an inheritance in the context of the description of the territory they once occupied but have since lost.[37]

That three of the five items persisting "until this day" would involve this far northern region (the other two items being the defunct sites of Baal worship) suggests that Dtr, at minimum, has an interest in these northern Gershonites, and it may even indicate his affiliation with them. While we will return to this subject later, Dtr's interest in the Gershonites would also seem to account for a historical notice similar to "until this day," which also appears in the context of Levitical priests in the far north, who are themselves probably Gershonites:[38]

וִיהוֹנָתָן בֶּן־גֵּרְשֹׁם בֶּן־מְנַשֶּׁה הוּא וּבָנָיו הָיוּ כֹהֲנִים
לְשֵׁבֶט הַדָּנִי עַד־יוֹם גְּלוֹת הָאָרֶץ

And Jonathan, the son of Gershom, the son of Moses[39], he and his sons were priests to the tribe of Dan *until the day of the exile of the land*.

Judg 18:30

Apart from the phrase "until this day" (עַד הַיּוֹם הַזֶּה), the phrase "until the day of the exile of the land" (עַד־יוֹם גְּלוֹת הָאָרֶץ) marks the only other occurrence of the formula עַד (הַ)יוֹם in the DH to express a longstanding condition, except one—and it too belongs to Dtr, even appearing in this same narrative:[40]

בַּיָּמִים הָהֵם אֵין מֶלֶךְ בְּיִשְׂרָאֵל וּבַיָּמִים הָהֵם שֵׁבֶט הַדָּנִי מְבַקֶּשׁ־
לוֹ נַחֲלָה לָשֶׁבֶת כִּי לֹא־נָפְלָה לּוֹ עַד־הַיּוֹם הַהוּא בְּתוֹךְ־שִׁבְטֵי
יִשְׂרָאֵל בְּנַחֲלָה

---

37. In view of this connection between "until this day," the Levites and the Bashan, it is noteworthy that the Gershonites' inheritance begins with this same region (Josh 21:27). One is struck, in fact, by the number of Levitical cities that are elsewhere the subject of "until this day," either by name—Hebron (Josh 14:14), Beth-Shemesh (1 Sam 6:18), Gibeon (Josh 9:27), Gezer (Josh 16:10) and, in a manner, Libnah (2 Kgs 8:22)—or by association with the larger regions of Cabul (Mishal, Abdon, Rehob and perhaps Helkath and Jokneam) and Havvoth Jair (Golan, Ramoth-Gilead and perhaps Kedesh)

38. For the relationship between the Gershonites and the priests of Dan, see W. H. C. Propp, "Gershon," *ABD* 2:994–95. See, also, Halpern, "Levitic Participation in the Reform Cult of Jeroboam I," *JBL* 95 (1976) 33–40.

39. On the raised *nun* of Judg 18:30, see the notes on this passage in chapter 2.

40. The only other uses of the phrase refer to the end of an individual's life (1 Sam 15:35 [Samuel's]; 2 Sam 6:23 [Michal's]; 2 Sam 20:3 [David's concubines]; 2 Kgs 15:5 [Azariah's]) or a period beginning and ending within an individual's life "until the day of his peaceful return" (2 Sam 19:25 [David's]).

In those days there was no king in Israel, and in those days the tribe of Dan was seeking an inheritance in which to settle, for an inheritance in the midst of the tribes of Israel had not fallen to it *until that day*.

Judg 18:1

That "until that day" should be traced to Dtr is suggested not only by its similarities to "until this day" in structure ( . . . עַד־הַיּוֹם ה) and purpose (inheritance rights) but also because the two uses of the plural of "until that day" ("until those days") in the DH also belong to Dtr. In 1 Kgs 3:2 "until those days" appears in connection with Dtr's name theology, in a passage that describes the absence of centralized worship prior to the temple—a concern already reflected in the use of "until this day" (see Josh 9:27; Judg 6:24; 2 Kgs 10:27):

רַק הָעָם מְזַבְּחִים בַּבָּמוֹת כִּי לֹא־נִבְנָה בַיִת לְשֵׁם יְהוָה
עַד הַיָּמִים הָהֵם

Only the people were sacrificing at the high places because *until those days* the house for the name of YHWH had not been built.

In 2 Kgs 18:4 "until those days" appears again, only this time in Dtr's appraisal of King Hezekiah's reign, which also has to do with alternate places and objects of worship:

הוּא הֵסִיר אֶת־הַבָּמוֹת וְשִׁבַּר אֶת־הַמַּצֵּבֹת וְכָרַת אֶת־הָאֲשֵׁרָה
וְכִתַּת נְחַשׁ הַנְּחֹשֶׁת אֲשֶׁר־עָשָׂה מֹשֶׁה כִּי עַד־הַיָּמִים הָהֵמָּה הָיוּ
בְנֵי־יִשְׂרָאֵל מְקַטְּרִים לוֹ וַיִּקְרָא־לוֹ נְחֻשְׁתָּן

He removed the high places and shattered the pillars and chopped down the *asherah* and broke into pieces the bronze serpent which Moses made because *until those days* the children of Israel were burning incense to it. And it was called Nehushtan.

Importantly, 2 Kgs 18:4, with its notice about the destruction of the bronze serpent during Hezekiah's reign, reflects the same *terminus a quo* as Judg 18:30, with its notice of "until the day of the land's exile"—namely, after the fall of the north. Recall, too, that Dtr's description of Libnah's past rebellion against the Judahite throne, in contrast to Edom's continuing rebellion, also pointed toward this same general time period.

In light of the connections among these various time notices—connections that point to Dtr as their source—it is significant that in Judges 18, in addition to "until that day" and "until the day of the exile of the land," our phrase also appears:[41]

---

41. In fact, it seems a reasonable hypothesis that most of the time notices, not just within Judges 18, but throughout the DH, belong to Dtr. This makes sense given Dtr's task of compiling disparate sources into a more-or-less chronological order. See, e.g., B. Peckham, "His-

וַיַּעֲלוּ וַיַּחֲנוּ בְּקִרְיַת יְעָרִים בִּיהוּדָה עַל־כֵּן קָרְאוּ לַמָּקוֹם הַהוּא
מַחֲנֵה־דָן עַד הַיּוֹם הַזֶּה הִנֵּה אַחֲרֵי קִרְיַת יְעָרִים:

And [the Danites] went up and camped at Kiriath-jearim in Judah. Therefore they named that place Mahaneh Dan *until this day*—it lies west of Kiriath-jearim.

Judg 18:12

The historian, who has already demonstrated his interest in tribal inheritance (נַחֲלָה; see, e.g., Deut 10:8–9; 18:1–2; Josh 13:13–14; 14:14) points to a site in the south that recalls Dan's migration toward its tribal allotment in the north—a migration that also accounted for the presence of Gershonite-Levites in the north.

## 6. The Ark of the Covenant of YHWH

The relationship between Dtr, the Levites, and "until this day" is further established by the use of this phrase in connection with "the Ark of the Covenant of YHWH"—a designation that many consider to be Dtr's characteristic name for this vessel.[42] Indeed, "until this day" is used more times with the Ark of the Covenant than with any other object or institution in ancient Israel.

In Deut 10:8, the Levites are appointed, among other things, to bear the "Ark of the Covenant of YHWH," a task they fulfill "until this day." This activity is then described in Joshua 3–4, where the "Levitical priests" (Josh 3:3)—another characteristically Deuteronom(ist)ic phrase (see Deut 17:9; 18; 18:1; 24:8; etc.) cross the Jordan River bearing the "Ark of the Covenant of YHWH" (Josh 3:3; 4:7), after which stones are erected to mark the place of this miracle "until this day" (Josh 4:9). In Josh 8:30–35, which is a Deuteronomistic insertion immediately following "until this day" (Josh 8:29), the "Levitical priests" (Josh 8:33) are found once again bearing the "Ark of the Covenant of YHWH" (Josh 8:33) while Joshua reads the law.[43]

Then, as if to emphasize the ramifications of not handling the Ark properly, "until this day" highlights several places where its sanctity is

---

tory and Time" in *Ki Baruch Hu: Ancient Near Eastern, Biblical, and Judaic Studies in Honor of Baruch A. Levine*, ed. R. Chazan, W. W. Hallo, and L. H. Schiffman (Winona Lake, IN: Eisenbrauns, 1999) 295–314. See also M. Leuchter ("A King Like All the Nations: The Composition of 1 Sam 8,11–18," *ZAW* 117 [2005] 543–58), who makes a similar case for the time notice ביום ההוא in prophetic speech in the DH.

42. See, e.g., C. L. Seow, "Ark of the Covenant," *ABD* 1:387.

43. Josh 8:30–35 is discussed in more detail below (see "'Until This Day,' Joshua, and the Reforms of Josiah").

compromised, including: (1) Ashdod, where the Ark is brought into the temple of Dagon with disastrous consequences for Dagon's image, and resulting in a cultic practice that persists "until this day" (1 Sam 5:5); (2) Beth-Shemesh, where a stone standing "until this day" marks the location where some unfortunate villagers looked into the Ark and were struck dead by YHWH (1 Sam 6:18), and (3) Perez-Uzzah, a place-name persisting "until this day," where Uzzah steadied the Ark on its way to Jerusalem and was similarly struck dead (2 Sam 6:8).

With the Ark's last appearance with "until this day," all ends well as the "Ark of the Covenant of YHWH" (1 Kgs 8:1, 6) is brought to rest in the temple, where its poles protrude from the Holy of Holies "until this day" (1 Kgs 8:8). All told, there are seven occurrences of "until this day" in connection with the Ark of the Covenant. Nelson has rightly stated that Dtr is "very much interested in the ark."[44]

## 7. Judahite Landholdings

Although the interests highlighted by "until this day" are predominantly theological and cultic, the one employing this phrase is interested also in the Judahite throne and its policies. For example, "until this day" is twice used to refer to cities important to the Davidic throne: Hebron, David's first capital, and Ziklag, which "belongs to the kings of Judah until this day."

עַל־כֵּן הָיְתָה־חֶבְרוֹן לְכָלֵב בֶּן־יְפֻנֶּה הַקְּנִזִּי לְנַחֲלָה עַד הַיּוֹם הַזֶּה

Therefore, Hebron belongs to Caleb the son of Jephunneh the Kenizzite as an inheritance until this day.

Josh 14:14

לָכֵן הָיְתָה צִקְלַג לְמַלְכֵי יְהוּדָה עַד הַיּוֹם הַזֶּה

Therefore, Ziklag belongs to the kings of Judah until this day.

1 Sam 27:6

---

44. Nelson, *The Double Redaction*, 123–24. Nelson adds: "Deut 10:1–5, with its emphasis upon the ark as container for the law tablets, expresses the exact same view as the historian in Deut 31:24–26 and 1 Kgs 8:9, 21." For similar remarks, see Noth, *The Deuteronomistic History*, 90. The Chronicler's repetition of 1 Kgs 8:8 (2 Chr 5:9) would seem, at first glance, to mitigate the conclusion that this notice in the DH points to the preexilic period. However, the use of "until this day" across the DH to emphasize the proper handling of the Ark, along with the other preexilic uses of the phrase noted above and in what follows (see, "Judahite-Edomite Relations" and "'Until This Day,' Joshua, and the Reforms of Josiah"), indicates that these notices were originally part of a unified, preexilic redaction of the DH and that the Chronicler's maintenance of the phrase in 2 Chr 5:9 (and elsewhere; see chapter 2, n. 3) is just that: his preservation of a notice in his preexilic source.

In the case of Hebron, "until this day" is immediately followed by the comment "because he followed fully after YHWH," which, as we noted above, derives from Dtr. In the case of Ziklag, the anachronistic reference to "the kings of Judah" in the book of 1 Samuel, in combination with the thematic and linguistic parallels with the Hebron passage, suggests that it too derives from Dtr.[45] Thematically, these two notices reflect the historian's general concern for inheritance rights already noted above. Linguistically, these passages mark the only occurrences of the formula לָכֵן/עַל־כֵּן הָיְתָה ... עַד הַיּוֹם הַזֶּה in the Hebrew Bible.[46] The closest parallel (עַל־כֵּן ... הָיָה), though expressed in the negative, also appears in the context of "until this day," and has already been discussed above in connection with this historian's interest in the Levites' role in bearing the Ark of the Covenant, as well as in their inheritance rights:[47]

עַל־כֵּן לֹא־הָיָה לְלֵוִי חֵלֶק וְנַחֲלָה עִם־אֶחָיו יְהוָה הוּא נַחֲלָתוֹ
כַּאֲשֶׁר דִּבֶּר יְהוָה אֱלֹהֶיךָ לוֹ:

Therefore, Levi does not have a portion and an inheritance with his brothers. YHWH is his inheritance, as YHWH your God said to him.
Deut 10:9

That Dtr is the one highlighting matters important both to the Levites and Judahite throne seems clear when we consider that the notice concerning the Calebites' inheritance (". . . until this day because he followed fully after YHWH"; Josh 14:14) is the next in sequence to another notice concerning the Levites' inheritance (". . . until this day. Only to the tribe of Levi he did not give an inheritance. The offerings to YHWH the God of Israel are his inheritance, as he said to him"; Josh 13:13b-14a).[48] Moreover, both of these notices reflect central concerns for Dtr: wholehearted devo-

---

45. There are no "kings of Judah" during the time of Samuel, as this is the period of the United Monarchy. This is, in fact, the only such reference to the "kings of Judah" in Samuel, which has suggested to many that it has been added by a later hand. See, e.g., the comments of Abravanel and R. Simon discussed in chapter 1, as well as McCarter (*1 Samuel*) on this verse.

46. Several manuscripts read עַל־כֵּן as opposed to לָכֵן in 1 Sam 27:6, making the above connections more explicit.

47. The only other occurrence of עַל־כֵּן הָיָה in the DH is, in my opinion, also from Dtr, even carrying with it an implied "until this day" element: "Therefore, it has become a proverb: 'Is Saul also among the prophets?'" (1 Sam 10:12).

48. The connection between Caleb's inheritance and the Judahite throne would likely have been understood by Dtr's audience, especially given the traditions associating Caleb with Judah (Num 34:19; Josh 14:6) and Hebron with David's first capital (2 Sam 2:11; 5:5). These connections would be all the more apparent if, as some have argued, it was believed David became the *rōš bêt 'āb* or *nāśî* of the Calebite clan following Nabal's death. See J. D. Levenson, "1 Samuel 25 as Literature and as History," *CBQ* 40 (1978) 11–28; Levenson and B. Halpern, "The Political Import of David's Marriages," *JBL* 99 (1980) 507–18.

tion to YHWH (Josh 14:14; cf. Deut 1:36; 1 Kgs 11:6) and the rights and responsibilities of the Levites (Josh 13:13–14; cf. Deut 10:9; Deut 18:1–2).

## 8. Judahite-Edomite Interaction

Further confirming that Dtr has the interests of the Judean monarchy in view is the repeated use of "until this day" in connection with Edom, Judah's southern neighbor. In Deuteronomy, "until this day" occurs in the context of Edom's initial settlement of Seir (Deut 2:22). Then three times in 2 Kings "until this day" gives witness to continuing Judahite-Edomite interaction:

> וַיִּפְשַׁע אֱדוֹם מִתַּחַת יַד־יְהוּדָה עַד הַיּוֹם הַזֶּה אָז תִּפְשַׁע
> לִבְנָה בָּעֵת הַהִיא

And Edom rebelled from under the hand of Judah until this day. Then Libnah rebelled at that time.

2 Kgs 8:22

> הוּא־הִכָּה אֶת־אֱדוֹם בְּגֵיא־מֶלַח עֲשֶׂרֶת אֲלָפִים וְתָפַשׂ אֶת־
> הַסֶּלַע בַּמִּלְחָמָה וַיִּקְרָא אֶת־שְׁמָהּ יָקְתְאֵל עַד הַיּוֹם הַזֶּה

And [Amaziah] struck ten thousand Edomites in the Valley of Salt and he seized Sela in battle, and he named it Joktheel until this day.

2 Kgs 14:7

> בָּעֵת הַהִיא הֵשִׁיב רְצִין מֶלֶךְ־אֲרָם אֶת־אֵילַת לַאֲרָם
> וַיְנַשֵּׁל אֶת־הַיְהוּדִים מֵאֵילוֹת וַאֲדוֹמִים בָּאוּ אֵילַת
> וַיֵּשְׁבוּ שָׁם עַד הַיּוֹם הַזֶּה

At that time, Rezin, king of Aram, recovered Elath for Aram and he drove the Judahites from Elath, and the Edomites entered Elath and live there until this day.

2 Kgs 16:6

Cogan and Tadmor's comments on these last three uses of "until this day" corroborate our findings for the whole of the DH:

> ... in all three instances, the subject [of "until this day"] is Judah-Edomite relations. The editor, Dtr[1], gave expression by use of *until this day* to his special interest in the question of territorial claims in the Negev and the Red Sea coast, at the time of renewed Judahite expansion under Josiah.[49]

---

49. Cogan and Tadmor, *2 Kings*, 96. For a survey of Judahite-Edomite interaction during this period, see P. J. King, *Jeremiah: An Archaeological Companion* (Louisville, KY: Westminster/John Knox Press, 1993) 45–63.

Cogan and Tadmor come to a similar conclusion for 2 Kings 17, where "until this day" appears three times (2 Kgs 17:23, 34 and 41) and sets apart two lengthy Deuteronomistic descriptions of the north's (alleged) syncretistic cultic practices:[50]

> Both units should be seen against the background of Josiah's cultic reforms and his expansion into the former territory of the northern kingdom. Josiah moved into Samaria to destroy the altar in Bethel and purge the other cities of their *bāmôt*-shrines (2 Kgs 23:15–19).

Cogan and Tadmor's determination that "until this day" in 2 Kings derives from a Deuteronomistic redactor active during the time of Josiah, when combined with our own findings that "until this day" across the DH reflects a preexilic, Deuteronomistic perspective—including a concern for territorial claims and centralized worship—provides further evidence for connecting "until this day" to the latter part of the seventh century B.C.E. Moreover, if we are correct in our interpretation of 2 Kgs 8:22 (Libnah's past rebellion) and in assigning to Dtr the related phrases "until the day of the exile of the land (i.e., the north)" and "until those days" in connection with the fall of the north and Hezekiah's destruction of the bronze serpent, respectively, then a period for "this day" that falls somewhere between the exile of the North and the destruction of the South finds further support.[51]

Yet, there is one last body of evidence confirming that "until this day" should be connected to the late seventh century B.C.E. in general, and the reforms of Josiah in particular, only it requires that we return to the book of Joshua.

---

50. Cogan and Tadmor, *2 Kings*, 214. As noted in chapter 2, the redactional history of 2 Kings 17 is admittedly complicated, which has resulted in varying interpretations of this material. Even so, regarding the preexilic provenance of the units set apart by "until this day," Cogan and Tadmor seem correct in their observation that it is "highly unlikely that any postexilic writer would speak of foreigners [i.e., the non-Israelite inhabitants of the North] as 'sons of Jacob,' bound by the covenant obligations of the *torah*." Cf. the remarks of Mayes, "References to the exile of Judah within this work, as in 2 Kgs 17:19f., give the impression of being exilic additions to an already existing work which did not know of Judah's destruction" (*Deuteronomy*, 89). For a treatment of scholarship on 2 Kings 17, see Brettler, *The Creation of History*, 112–34.

51. We could add to these observations the evidence of the phrase's last etiological uses in the DH (2 Kgs 17:34, 41). M. Sweeney (*King Josiah of Judah: The Lost Messiah of Israel* [New York: Oxford University Press, 2001] 78–88) has rightly observed that these notices are unique in their use of the participle to describe actions contemporary with the historian. With this in view, the enumeration of generations in v. 41 is noteworthy: כַּאֲשֶׁר עָשׂוּ אֲבֹתָם [גַּם־בְּנֵיהֶם וּבְנֵי בְנֵיהֶם] עֹשִׂים עַד הַיּוֹם הַזֶּה "just as their ancestors did, so [their children and their children's children] are doing until this day"). While this enumeration may simply be a way of describing an activity of longstanding, when we consider the other lines of evidence pointing to a period for "this day" that falls near the reign of Josiah, then this enumeration, in conjunction with the use of the participle to describe an activity contemporaneous with the historian and two generations removed from Hezekiah, is, at minimum, suggestive.

## 9. "Until This Day," Joshua, and the Reforms of Josiah

A number of scholars have noted that Deuteronomistic insertions within the book of Joshua indicate that Dtr has the reforms of Josiah in mind.[52] Some of the evidence for this hypothesis includes:

1. Joshua is commanded to meditate on the book of the law day and night (Josh 1:7–8), which is the responsibility of the king in Deuteronomy's law of the king (Deut 17:18–19), and which finds its fulfillment in Josiah (2 Kgs 22:16; 23:2, 24–25).

2. Joshua is commanded to turn "neither to the right nor to the left" (Josh 1:7) in his obedience to the law of Moses, which is also the obligation of the king in Deuteronomy (Deut 17:20), and which only Josiah is said to have carried out perfectly (2 Kgs 22:2).

3. Joshua conducts a ceremony of covenant renewal where the law is read to the whole congregation (Josh 8:30–35). This not only fulfills Moses' command in Deut 27:2–8, but foreshadows Josiah's covenant renewal where he gathers "all the people" and reads the book of the covenant (2 Kgs 23:1–3).[53]

4. Joshua observes the Passover (Josh 5:10–12), which is not mentioned again until Josiah, who observes it in his eighteenth year (2 Kgs 23:21–23).

Aside from the first two examples, which, significantly, occur in Dtr's own prologue to the book of Joshua, the remaining two "Josianic" passages occur immediately after "until this day."

In Josh 8:29 a pile of stones is erected over the king of Ai "until this day," which is then followed by the description of Joshua reading the law, a description already seen to derive from Dtr. Regarding this narrative, Nelson writes,

---

52. For a discussion of the literature, see R. Nelson, "Josiah in the Book of Joshua," *JBL* 100 (1981) 531–40. For Joshua as royal figure, see J. R. Porter, "The Succession of Joshua," in *Proclamation and Presence: Old Testament Essays in Honour of Gwynne Henton Davies*, ed. J. I. Durham and J. R. Porter (London: SCM/Richmond: John Knox, 1970) 102–32; Weinfeld, *Deuteronomic School*, 170–71; G. E. Gerbrandt, *Kingship according to the Deuteronomistic History* (SBLDS 87; Atlanta: Scholars Press, 1986) 116–23.

53. For the parallels between Josiah's covenant ceremony and Deuteronomy more generally, see N. Lohfink, "2 Kön 23,3 und Dtn 6,17," *Biblica* 71 (1990) 34–42; idem, "Die Ältesten Israels und der Bund: Zum Zusammenhang von Dtn 5,23; 26,17–19; 27,1.9f und 31,9," *BN* 67 (1993) 26–42.

> Scholars have generally been puzzled by the inclusion of these verses in such an awkward place in the sequence of events, *but Dtr clearly went to some effort to break into the sequence of his source (cf. the reference of 9:1 to 8:29) to include them* . . . The emphasis on Joshua as covenant maker and the additional details concerning Joshua's personal copy of the law (Josh 8:32), the reading from a law book (v 34), and the attendance of absolutely everyone (v 35) . . . *point forward in time directly to the royal covenant mediator Josiah.*[54]

This phenomenon occurs again in Josh 5:9, where the place of Israel's circumcision is called Gilgal "until this day," which is then followed by the account of the Israelites' Passover observance:

⁹וַיִּקְרָא שֵׁם הַמָּקוֹם הַהוּא גִּלְגָּל עַד הַיּוֹם הַזֶּה׃
¹⁰וַיַּחֲנוּ בְנֵי־יִשְׂרָאֵל בַּגִּלְגָּל וַיַּעֲשׂוּ אֶת־הַפֶּסַח בְּאַרְבָּעָה עָשָׂר יוֹם
לַחֹדֶשׁ בָּעֶרֶב בְּעַרְבוֹת יְרִיחוֹ׃

> And he called the name of that place Gilgal until this day. And the children of Israel camped at Gilgal and observed the Passover on the fourteenth day of the month in the evening on the plains of Jericho.
>
> Josh 5:9b–10

Dtr's inclusion of his own material immediately following "until this day" fits the editorial pattern observed numerous times above. And again, the material Dtr includes reflects his own particular historical circumstances and interests. As Nelson observes,

> Dtr's editorial activity is more subtle in the case of Josh 5:10–12 than with Josh 1:7, 23:6 or Josh 8:30–35, but once again Joshua serves him as a forerunner of Josiah, providing an explicit historical precedent for Josiah's revolutionary reforming passover.[55]

That Cogan and Tadmor would conclude that "until this day" in 2 Kings reflects the specific political and religious circumstances of Josiah's reign, and that Nelson would *inadvertently* conclude (Nelson does not seem aware that his examples immediately follow "until this day") that Dtr insertions after "until this day" in Joshua reflect this same period, seems beyond coincidence. When we combine their findings with our determination that "until this day" across the DH reflects a preexilic, Deuteronomistic perspective and, when greater precision is granted, points to this very same period, then the conclusion seems inevitable: "until this day" is Dtr's day,

---

54. Nelson, "Josiah in the Book of Joshua," 535 (emphasis mine). For the textual issues related to Josh 8:30–35, see chapter 2.
55. Nelson, "Josiah in the Book of Joshua," 537.

when the temple still stood, the poles of the Ark still protruded beyond the Holy of Holies, and the nation itself had recently undertaken (or, perhaps, was still undergoing[56]) significant cultic reforms under Josiah.[57] The implications of these findings for Deuteronomistic studies are considerable and will be explored after considering the present state of the field.

---

56. While the evidence of "until this day" points to the preexilic period in general, and the reign and reforms of Josiah in particular, this does not require a Josianic date for this history. The culmination of the DH in Josiah may have served another purpose in the preexilic period. See the discussion of these matters in chapter 5 and the conclusion.

57. The Josianic interests reflected in "until this day" agree with recent treatments of two important Deuteronomistic texts: the promise to David (see N. Lohfink, "Welches Orakel gab den Davididen Dauer? Ein Textproblem in 2 Kön 8,19 und das Funktionieren der dynastischen Orakel im deuteronomistischen Geschichtswerk," in *Lingering over Words: Studies in Ancient Near Eastern Literature in Honor of William L. Moran*, ed. T. Abusch, J. Huehnergard, and P. Steinkeller [HSS 37; Atlanta: Scholars Press, 1990] 349–70) and the prayer of Solomon (see G. N. Knoppers, "Prayer and Propaganda: Solomon's Dedication of the Temple and the Deuteronomist's Program," *CBQ* 57 [1995] 229–54).

# 4

# Deuteronomistic Scholarship in Our Day

> The developments which have taken place indicate the very existence of the [Deuteronomistic History] and its status as a new and unique piece of literature in Israelite tradition needs (*sic*) to be reexamined.[1]
>
> —Mark A. O'Brien, *The Deuteronomistic History Hypothesis: A Reassessment*

Prior to Martin Noth's *Überlieferungsgeschichtliche Studien* (*ÜgS*),[2] the books of Joshua through Kings were treated either as the continuation of Pentateuchal sources or as individual literary units brought together through a series of redactions.[3] In truth, these views are not mutually exclusive. No less a scholar than Julius Wellhausen believed that J and E extended into the Former Prophets and that the books of Kings underwent preexilic and exilic redactions.[4] It was left to Noth, however, to argue for the overall unity of what is now referred to as the Deuteronomistic History.

---

1. M. A. O'Brien, *The Deuteronomistic History Hypothesis: A Reassessment* (OBO 92; Freiburg, Switzerland: Universitätsverlag; Göttingen: Vandenhoeck & Ruprecht, 1989) 15.

2. For a survey of scholarship leading up to Noth's theory, as well as the present state of research, see T. Römer and A. de Pury, "Deuteronomistic Historiography (Deuteronomistic History): History of Research and Debated Issues" in *Israel Constructs Its History*, 24–141. For surveys of Deuteronomistic scholarship in general, see L. V. Alexander, *The Origin and Development of the Deuteronomistic History Theory and Its Significance for Biblical Interpretation* (Ann Arbor: University of Michigan, 1993); S. L. McKenzie, "Deuteronomistic History," *ABD* 2.160–68; L. Laberge, "Le Deutéronomiste" in *'De Bien des Manières.' La Recherché Bibliqué aux abords du XXIe Siècle: Actes du Cinquantenaire de l'ACEBAC*, ed. L. Laberge and M. Gourgues (LD 163; Paris: Cerf, 1995) 47–77. The summary presented here highlights those issues most relevant to the present study and includes recent trends not represented in many earlier surveys.

3. See, e.g., S. R. Driver, *Introduction*, 103–203; O. Eissfeldt, *The Old Testament: An Introduction* (New York: Harper, 1965; German original; Tübingen: Mohr, 1934) 241–48; R. H. Pfeiffer, *Introduction to the Old Testament* (New York: Harper, 1948) 293–412.

4. Wellhausen, *Die Composition des Hexateuchs*, 238.

## A SURVEY OF DEUTERONOMISTIC SCHOLARSHIP

## 1. Martin Noth's Original Hypothesis

While acknowledging the diverse traditions preserved in the DH, Noth argued that the history's unity is evidenced in its overarching structure and theological outlook. Structurally, the DH is organized by era, each demarcated by a Deuteronomistic evaluation of Israel's covenant fidelity. These evaluations sometimes appear as the historian's own commentary on a particular period, but more often they are placed as speeches in the mouths of pivotal figures from Israel's past.[5] Thus, the Mosaic era is embodied in the book of Deuteronomy and presented as the last speeches of Moses, speeches that establish the criteria by which Israel will be judged during its tenure in the land (i.e., the Deuteronomic law code of chaps. 12–26). The period of the conquest is initiated and concluded by the first and last speeches of Joshua (Josh 1:11–15; 23), which similarly enjoin the people to covenant fidelity and, at the same time, hint of Israel's failure in this regard. The period of the judges begins with the Deuteronomist's own summary of Israel's disobedience (Judg 2:10–23), setting forth the pattern of apostasy-oppression-repentance-deliverance that gives shape to the book, and ends with Samuel's farewell speech (1 Sam 12:6–25), which reminds the people of God's past deliverance and of their need to uphold their covenant obligations under monarchy. Solomon's temple dedication speech (1 Kgs 8:12–51) reiterates the importance of covenant loyalty, while anticipating the nation's disobedience and need for repentance. The period of the divided monarchy is initiated by the prophet Ahijah of Shiloh (1 Kings 9 and 11), who similarly foresees Israel's disobedience and the destruction of the northern kingdom, and this period finds its denouement in the Deuteronomist's own condemnation of Israel's apostasy in the wake of the north's deportation by Assyria (2 Kgs 17:7–41). In view of these well-placed Deuteronomistic speeches, Noth writes,

> This practice of inserting general retrospective and anticipatory reflections at certain important points in the history . . . strongly supports the thesis that Dtr was conceived as a unified and self-contained whole.[6]

In addition to these "retrospective and anticipatory reflections," Noth discerned an internal chronological structure that gave the DH its coherence.[7] The book of Deuteronomy and the conquest of Canaan under Joshua

---

5. Noth, *The Deuteronomistic History*, 6.
6. Noth, *The Deuteronomistic History*, 6.
7. Noth, *The Deuteronomistic History*, 18. For similar observations about the use of summary speeches and prayers in Chronicles, see O. Plöger, "Reden und Gebete im deuterono-

required little chronological tampering. However, the literary units making up the rest of the DH—especially the (artificial) chronology of the judges and the synchronization of the reigns of the kings of Israel and Judah—demanded significant editorial energy.[8] While the historian's basic treatment of his sources was conservative, Dtr selected and arranged his sources, as well as added his own material, to fit his own purpose in writing this history.[9] This purpose, according to Noth, was to demonstrate to Israel that its demise was due to its continual disobedience to God:

> Dtr did not write his history to provide entertainment in hours of leisure or to satisfy a curiosity about national history, but intended to teach the true meaning of the history of Israel from the occupation to the destruction of the old order. The meaning which he discovered was that God was recognizably at work in this history, continuously meeting the accelerating moral decline with warnings and punishments and, finally, when these proved fruitless, with total annihilation.[10]

For Noth, therefore, the unity of the DH derives from a single historian writing shortly after the last notice in this work; namely, the release of Jehoiachin in 562 B.C.E. (2 Kgs 25:30). The purpose of the DH, moreover, was didactic, even condemnatory, underscoring that Israel's present crisis was due not to God's abandonment of the nation, but rather the nation's abandonment of God by repeatedly violating the covenant established at Sinai.

It has been suggested that Noth's own circumstances at the time of his writing—during World War II and in relative academic isolation at Königsberg—influenced his conclusions about the circumstances of Dtr at the time of his writing. Perhaps. Even so, the evidence marshaled by Noth in defense of his theory has made it one of the most enduring fixtures of biblical scholarship.

## 2. Early Reactions to Noth's Theory of a Deuteronomistic History

Although the impact of Noth's study was at first minimal due to its publication during the war and in limited number, by the end of the 1950s his

---

mistichen und chronistischen Geschichtswerk," in *Festschrift für Günther Dehn zum 75. Geburtstag*, ed. W. Schneemelcher (Neukirchen-Vluyn: Neukirchener Verlag, 1957) 35–49. Reprinted in O. Plöger, *Aus der Spätzeit des Alten Testaments* (Göttingen: Vandenhoeck & Ruprecht, 1975) 50–66.

8. Noth, *The Deuteronomistic History*, 9–10.
9. Noth, *The Deuteronomistic History*, 84–88.
10. Noth, *The Deuteronomistic History*, 89.

theory had gained wide acceptance.[11] This acceptance was due, in part, to the independent confirmation of his thesis from a study that actually predated Noth's work, but which was not published until after the war.

## Alfred Jepsen

A. Jepsen, in his *Die Quellen des Königsbuches*, proposed that the books from Joshua to 2 Kings were largely the product of two exilic redactors.[12] According to him, the first of these ($R^I$) combined an account of Solomon's reign and a synchronistic chronology of the kings of Judah and Israel with a work describing the history of Jerusalem's cult. For Jepsen, this redactor had priestly concerns and wrote this "royal history" shortly after the destruction of Jerusalem (ca. 580 B.C.E.).[13]

Jepsen's second redactor ($R^{II}$) was responsible for the bulk of the prophetic material in the DH, as well as the other narratives of a non-annalistic nature—particularly the "Succession Narrative," the conquest, and the period of the judges. According to Jepsen, $R^{II}$ had an outlook similar to Hosea and Jeremiah, and was heavily influenced by the teaching of Deuteronomy, which served as the prologue to $R^{II}$'s revised history. Jepsen concluded, therefore, that this second redactor came from prophetic circles.[14]

Although Jepsen and Noth differed regarding the number of redactors responsible for the DH, the similarities between Noth's single exilic redactor and Jepsen's $R^{II}$, as well as their common determination of the unity of the DH, provided important support for Noth's theory.[15] Jepsen also agreed with Noth that the historian was located in Judah, where access to sources would be more feasible.

It was not long, however, before scholars began to voice disagreements over the details of Noth's analysis—in particular with his proposal that the primary purpose of this history was to serve as a diatribe against those in exile.

---

11. There were, to be sure, those who argued against Noth's hypothesis. See, e.g., O. Eissfeldt, *Geschichtschreibung im Alten Testament: Ein kritischer Bericht* (Berlin: Evangelische Verlagsanstalt, 1948); G. Fohrer, *Einleitung in das Alte Testament* (Heidelberg: Quelle & Meyer, 1969).

12. A. Jepsen, *Die Quellen des Königsbuches* (2nd ed.; Halle: Niemeyer, 1956). The first edition was published in 1953, though the manuscript was already complete by 1939.

13. Jepsen, *Die Quellen des Königsbuches*, 10, 22–23, 54–60.

14. Jepsen, *Die Quellen des Königsbuches*, 76–101.

15. Jepsen himself equated $R^{II}$ with Noth's Dtr. Two additional studies provided independent confirmation of Noth's hypothesis: Y. Kaufmann, *The Religion of Israel*, trans. M. Greenberg (Chicago: University of Chicago Press, 1960. Hebrew; Tel Aviv, 1937–47) 205–11; I. Engnell, *A Rigid Scrutiny: Critical Essays on the Old Testament*, trans. and ed. J. T. Willis and H. Ringgren (Nashville: Abingdon, 1969) 58–67.

## Gerhard von Rad

One such scholar was G. von Rad.[16] While von Rad agreed that this history was the work of an exilic author, he believed that the theme of divine grace, especially as embodied in the promise to David of an enduring fiefdom (2 Sam 7:4–16), was too prevalent simply to be subsumed under Noth's theme of judgment and inevitable disaster. In order to account for the tension between the dual themes of promise and exile, von Rad postulated a messianic sentiment among the exiles who believed that the Davidic promises would be fulfilled in the future. For von Rad, the mention of Jehoiachin's release from prison was not merely an antiquarian notice about the fate of the last living king of Judah, but was a harbinger of the restoration of the Davidic throne.[17]

Soon other scholars followed suit, arguing for a more positive purpose behind the DH.[18] While their individual analyses differed from von Rad's on various points, their overall conclusions were the same: Noth's hypothesis, while correct in dating the DH to the exile, did not take sufficient account of its thematic and theological diversity.

## 3. Numerous Exilic Redactions of the Deuteronomistic History

### Rudolf Smend and the "Göttingen School"

As a further attempt to account for the DH's thematic and theological diversity, R. Smend and those following his lead (the so-called Göttingen school) have postulated that the DH underwent at least three stages of development, each representing different interests in the exilic period.[19]

---

16. G. von Rad, *Studies in Deuteronomy* (SBT 9; London: SCM, 1953; German original; Göttingen: Vandenhoeck & Ruprecht, 1947) 74–91. See also his "The Deuteronomic Theology of History in I and II Kings," in *The Problem of the Hexateuch and Other Essays* (Edinburgh: Oliver & Boyd; New York: McGraw-Hill, 1966) 205–21; idem, *Theology of the Old Testament* (New York: Harper & Row, 1962), vol. 1, esp. 343–44.

17. Von Rad writes: "At all events, [Jehoichin's release] must be interpreted by every reader as an indication that the line of David has not yet come to an irrevocable end" (*Studies*, 90–91).

18. See, e.g., H. W. Wolff, "Das Kerygma des deuteronomischen Geschichtswerk," *ZAW* 73 (1961) 171–86; and W. Brueggemann, "The Kerygma of the Deuteronomistic Historian," *Int* 22 (1968) 387–402.

19. The main works of this school include: R. Smend, "Das Gesetz und die Völker: Ein Beitrag zur deuteronomistischen Redaktionsgeschichte," in *Probleme biblischer Theologie*, ed. H. W. Wolff (Munich: Kaiser, 1971) 494–509; idem, *Die Entstehung des Alten Testaments*

Similar to Jepsen, the Göttingen school proposes the existence of an initial Deuteronomistic History (DtrH; later DtrG), which was written shortly after the exile (ca. 580 B.C.E., according to Dietrich).[20] This history portrayed, among other things, the conquest as complete and the monarchy as divinely favored (cf. Jepsen's R$^I$).[21] The second redactional level (which Dietrich places between 580 and 560 B.C.E.) accounts for much of the prophetic material in the DH, and is therefore given the siglum DtrP.[22] To this stage of development belongs the negative view of monarchy, since those responsible for this redaction represented prophetic (specifically "Jeremianic") interests and perceived kingship as a threat to their authority (cf. Jepsen's R$^{II}$).[23] The third redactional level (which Dietrich dates to ca. 560 B.C.E.) reflects an interest in law, and is therefore designated DtrN (for *nomistic*). DtrN's view of kingship attempts to strike a balance between the contradictory opinions expressed in DtrG and DtrP. While the monarchy is, in principle, a rejection of YHWH's rule, the monarchy could succeed if it remained faithful to YHWH, just as David had done.[24]

---

(Stuttgart: W. Kohlhammer, 1978); W. Dietrich, *Prophetie und Geschichte* (FRLANT 108; Göttingen: Vandenhoeck & Ruprecht, 1972); idem, "David in Überlieferung und Geschichte," *VF* 22 (1977) 44–64; idem, "Josia und das Gesetzbuch (2 Reg. XXII)," *VT* 27 (1977) 13–35; T. Veijola, *Die ewige Dynastie: David und die Entstehung seiner Dynastie nach der deuteronomistischen Darstellung* (AASF, B 193; Helsinki: Suomalainen Tiedeakatemia, 1975); idem, *Das Königtum in der Beurteilung der deuteronomistischen Historiographie: Eine redaktionsgeschichtliche Untersuchung* (AASF, B 198; Helsinki: Suomalainen Tiedeakatemia, 1977). Presented here is a synthesis of these works, though one should keep in mind that differences exist among their individual treatments.

20. Dietrich, *Prophetie und Geschichte*, 143–44. Smend has since placed DtrH after 560 B.C.E., pushing the subsequent redactional levels (DtrP and DtrN) even later. See Smend, *Die Enstehung*, 123–25; idem, "Der Ort des Staates im Alten Testament," *ZTK* 80 (1983) 245–61.

21. Veijola, *Die ewige Dynastie*, 127–42. In this regard, Veijola makes an adjustment to Dietrich's and Smend's models by assigning the pro-Davidic material to the original history (DtrH), and not to DtrN.

22. Dietrich, *Prophetie und Geschichte*, 133–34.

23. Dietrich, *Prophetie und Geschichte*, 104.

24. The influence of the Göttingen school on subsequent scholarship has been sizable. See, e.g., W. Roth, "The Deuteronomic Rest-Theology: A Redaction-Critical Study," *BR* 21 (1976) 5–14; E. Würthwein, *Die Bücher der Könige: 1 Kön 1–16* (ATD 11.1; Göttingen: Vandenhoeck & Ruprecht, 1977); idem, *1 Kön 17–2 Kön 25* (ATD 11.2; Göttingen: Vandenhoeck & Ruprecht, 1984); A. G. Auld, *Joshua, Moses and the Land: Tetrateuch-Pentateuch-Hexateuch in a Generation since 1938* (Edinburgh: T & T Clark, 1980); L. J. Hoppe, "The Meaning of Deuteronomy," *BTB* 10 (1980) 111–17; J. A. Soggin, *Judges: A Commentary* (OTL; London: SCM, 1981); G. H. Jones, *1 and 2 Kings* (NCB; Grand Rapids: Eerdmans, 1984); U. Becker, *Richterzeit und Königtum: Redaktionsgeschichtliche Studien zum Richterbuch* (BZAW 192; Berlin: de Gruyter, 1990); E. Ben-Zvi, "The Account of the Reign of Manasseh in II Reg 21, 1–18 and the Redactional Unity of the Book of Kings," *ZAW* 102 (1991) 335–74; O. Kaiser, *Grundriss der Einleitung in die kanonischen und deuterokanonischen Schriften des Alten Testaments* I (3 vols.; Gütersloh: Gerd Mohn, 1992).

## 4. A Josianic Edition of the Deuteronomistic History

### Frank Moore Cross

While the theory of a dual redaction of the DH finds its antecedents in the work of Kuenen and Wellhausen, F. M. Cross has provided both the thematic evidence and the historical moment for a preexilic composition of the DH.[25] Combining the insights of these earlier scholars with Noth's observations about the unity of the DH, Cross argues that the contradictory messages of eternal kingship and imminent exile are best understood as the result of two distinct editions of the DH: one preexilic, the other exilic. As for the provenance of the preexilic edition, Cross locates the answer in the two dominant themes of the books of Kings: the unconditional promise to David and the sin of Jeroboam.[26] While these themes find expression throughout these books, both culminate in the reign of Josiah. In relation to the unconditional promise to David, Josiah is presented as the ideal Davidide; no other king receives so positive a review from Dtr: "[Josiah] did what was right in the eyes of YHWH and walked in all the ways of David his father; and he did not turn to the right or to the left" (2 Kgs 22:2). In relation to the sin of Jeroboam, it is Josiah who brings an end to his apostasy by destroying the altar at Bethel, an event that is even predicted at the altar's construction (1 Kgs 13:2–5). Cross sees in this unusual case of *vaticinium post eventum* important confirmation for a history that originally culminated in this king's reign. For Cross,

> ... the juxtaposition of the two themes, of threat and promise, provide the platform of the Josianic reform. The Deuteronomistic history, insofar as these themes reflect its central concerns, may be described as a propaganda work of the Josianic reformation and imperial program.[27]

The idyllic period of Josiah was cut short, however, with his unexpected death at Megiddo, and within a relatively short period Judah found itself in exile. It was while in exile, according to Cross, that a second edition of the DH was produced, which left much of the original work unchanged, but brought this history up to date by inserting several passages throughout making the promise to David conditional and speaking of the inevitability of Judah's fall.

Cross's theory of a dual redaction of the DH, in general, and his proposal of a Josianic edition, in particular, have had a significant impact on

---

25. Cross, *CMHE*, 274–89. As noted in chapter 1, Cross's treatment originally appeared as "The Structure of the Deuteronomistic History" in *Perspectives in Jewish Learning*, 9–24.
26. Cross, *CMHE*, 278–85.
27. Cross, *CMHE*, 284.

Deuteronomistic studies.[28] Contributing to its early impact was the work of two scholars, who, though working independent of one another, provided additional support for Cross's theory, while at the same time refining several of his original arguments.

### Richard Elliott Friedman

In his *The Exile and Biblical Narrative*, R. E. Friedman identifies a number of parallels between the descriptions of Moses in Deuteronomy and Josiah in Kings.[29] For example, the phrase "none arose like him" occurs only in connection with these two figures (Deut 34:10; 2 Kgs 23:25). In addition, only Moses and Josiah crush objects of worship "thin as dust": Moses destroys Aaron's golden calf (Deut 9:21) and Josiah destroys the *bāmāh* of Bethel (2 Kgs 23:15), the location of Jeroboam's golden calf. Moreover, Moses' admonitions to love God "with all your heart and with all your soul and with all your strength" (Deut 6:5) and to read the book of the Law "in the ears" of all the people (Deut 31:11) are fulfilled only by Josiah (2 Kgs 23:2, 25).

For Friedman, the number and character of these parallels indicate that the DH originally culminated in the reign of Josiah (Cross's Dtr¹).[30] As further evidence for this conclusion, Friedman points out that after Josiah's death David is no longer used as a measure of a king's greatness, nor is a

---

28. See, e.g., R. G. Boling, *Judges* (AB 6a; 1975); M. Cogan, "Israel in Exile—The View of a Josianic Historian," *JBL* 97 (1978) 40–44; J. Rosenbaum, "Hezekiah's Reform and the Deuteronomistic Tradition," *HTR* 72 (1979) 23–44; Boling and G. E. Wright, *Joshua* (AB 6; 1982); P. K. McCarter, *1 Samuel* (AB 8; 1980); idem, *1 Samuel* (AB 9; 1984); G. Vanoni, "Beobachtungen zur deuteronomistischen Terminologie in 2 Kön 23,25–25,30," in *Das Deuteronomium: Entstehung, Gestalt und Botschaft*, ed. N. Lohfink (BETL 68; Leuven: Leuven University Press, 1985) 357–62; Cogan and Tadmor, *2 Kings* (AB 11; 1988); A. Moenikes, "Zur Redaktionsgeschichte des sogenannten deuteronomistischen Geschichtswerks," *ZAW* 104 (1992) 333–48; H.-J. Stipp, *Jeremia im Parteienstreit: Studien zur Textentwicklung von Jer 26, 36–43 und 45 als Beitrag zur Geschichte Jeremias, seines Buches und judäischer Parteien im 6. Jahrhundert* (BBB 82; Frankfurt: Hain, 1992); G. N. Knoppers, *Two Nations under God: The Deuteronomistic History of Solomon and the Dual Monarchies* (HSM 52–53; Atlanta: Scholars Press, 1994); M. Cogan, *1 Kings* (AB 11; 2000); S. McKenzie, *The Chronicler's Use of the Deuteronomistic History* (HSM 33; Atlanta: Scholars, 1984); idem, *The Trouble with Kings: The Composition of the Books of Kings in the Deuteronomistic History* (VTSup 42; Leiden: E. J. Brill, 1991); though, cf. McKenzie's "The Trouble with Kingship," in *Israel Constructs Its History*, 286–314, where he favors an early exilic date for the original Deuteronomistic History.

29. Friedman, *The Exile and Biblical Narrative*, 7–10.

30. Friedman, *The Exile and Biblical Narrative*, esp. 9–10. See also his "From Egypt to Egypt: Dtr¹ and Dtr²," in *Traditions in Transformation: Turning Points in Biblical Faith*, Frank Moore Cross Festschrift, ed. B. Halpern and J. D. Levenson (Winona Lake: Eisenbrauns, 1981) 167–92.

king's response to the high places used as a criterion for determining his covenant faithfulness. Quite the contrary, after Josiah's reign, the promises to David are never again mentioned. According to Friedman, "These matters constitute more than arguments from silence. This is a full-fledged change of perspective and manner of presentation of history."[31] Based on Friedman's analysis of the secondary material within this corpus, these changes in perspective, though still Deuteronomistic, reflect the historical circumstances of the exile and represent a second edition of the DH (Cross's Dtr²).[32] Although this updated version derives from a slightly later period, the consistency of theological outlook, literary forms and redactional procedures suggests to Friedman that both come from the same hand; namely, Baruch ben Neriah, who, in cooperation with Jeremiah, also wrote much of the book bearing this prophet's name.

## *Richard D. Nelson*

Although the details of Nelson's analysis differ from Friedman's, he similarly argues that changes in regnal formulae after Josiah point to an edition of the DH ending in this king's reign (Cross's Dtr¹).[33] In particular, Nelson observes that prior to Josiah the regnal formulae, although characterized by free variation, all fall within a unity of expression and outlook that suggests a single redactional hand. After Josiah, the regnal formulae, though still Deuteronomistic in perspective, no longer show the creativity of the earlier redactor, having become terse and rigid. In addition, the basis for comparison for the last kings of Judah are now simply "the fathers"—an inappropriate grouping in light of the positive appraisals of a number of Judah's kings by the earlier redactor. According to Nelson, "The most likely explanation for this stylistic shift is that we have here the woodenly imitative work of some supplementary editor, not the creative and free variation of the original author."[34]

In addition to this shift in regnal formulae, Nelson's analysis of passages generally regarded as secondary to the DH reveals their unified thematic and linguistic character, a character that is best understood as deriving from a redactor who shared many of the same views as the preexilic redactor, but who is clearly writing after the fall of Jerusalem (Cross's Dtr²).[35]

---

31. Friedman, *The Exile and Biblical Narrative*, 7.
32. Friedman, *The Exile and Biblical Narrative*, 10–43.
33. Nelson, *Double Redaction*, 29–42.
34. Nelson, *Double Redaction*, 31.
35. Nelson, *Double Redaction*, 43–98.

## 5. A Hezekian Edition of the Deuteronomistic History

As a modification of Cross's theory, a number of scholars have proposed the existence of an even earlier, perhaps Hezekian, edition of the DH.

### Helga Weippert

One such scholar is H. Weippert, who has argued that changes in regnal formulae point to at least three stages of development for the DH.[36] The first of these ($R^I$), which Weippert dates to just after the fall of the north, is discernible by the stock phrases used to characterize the reigns from Jehoshaphat to Ahaz in the south ("he did good in the eyes of the LORD" and "only the high places were not removed, and the people continued to sacrifice and burn incense at the high places") and from Jehoram to Pekah in the north ("he did evil in the eyes of the LORD," "only he clung to the sin(s) of Jeroboam ben Nebat which he caused Israel to sin," and "he/they did not turn away from them").[37] Other changes in regnal formulae allow Weippert to identify a second redactional level ($R^{II}$), which saw the addition of the reigns of Rehoboam to Asa in the south, and Jeroboam to Ahaziah in the north. As part of this same stage of development, an account of the reigns from Hezekiah to Josiah was added, suggesting to Weippert that this stage dates to Josiah's reign. The third level ($R^{III}$) completes the regnal notices, and is of exilic provenance.[38]

### Baruch Halpern

B. Halpern has contributed a number of additional arguments for a Hezekian history, while at the same time refining Weippert's analysis.[39]

---

36. H. Weippert, "Die 'deuteronomistischen' Beurteilungen der Könige von Israel und Juda und das Problem der Redacktion der Königsbücher," *Bib* 53 (1972) 301–39; see also, idem, "Die Ätiologie des Nordreiches und seines Königshauses (I Reg 11,29–40)" *ZAW* 95 (1983) 344–75; idem, "Ahab el campeador? Redaktionsgeschichtliche Undersuchungen zu 1 Kön 22" *Bibl* 69 (1988) 457–79.

37. Weippert, "Die 'deuteronomistischen' Beurteilungen," 319–23.

38. Others following the general analysis of Weippert (though with variations), include W. B. Barrick, "On the 'Removal of the High Places' in 1–2 Kings," *Bib* 55 (1974) 257–59; G. C. Heider, *The Cult of Molek: A Reassessment* (JSOTSup 43; Sheffield: JSOT, 1985); A. Lemaire, "Vers L'histoire de la Redaction des Livres des Rois," *ZAW* 98 (1986) 221–36. M. Sweeney (*King Josiah*, esp. 170–77) has similarly suggested, based on his analysis of several key passages in the DH, that the Josianic edition likely was preceded by a Hezekian history.

39. B. Halpern, "Sacred History and Ideology: Chronicles' Thematic Structure—Indica-

Halpern takes seriously the notice that during Hezekiah's reign an enrollment took place (1 Chr 4:41). He finds confirmation for this report in the number of descendants listed in the genealogies of David and Saul. In particular, the Saulide list given in 1 Chronicles 9 contains the same number of generations (thirteen) as David's, whose genealogy ends with Hezekiah, suggesting that both lists were compiled during this king's reign. Moreover, the term for enrolling populations is used for the last time in connection with Hezekiah (2 Chr 31:16, 17, 19). Halpern identifies further evidence for a Hezekian history based on changes in the royal burial notices in Kings and Chronicles. Up to the time of Hezekiah, nearly every notice specifies burial "in the city of David," while after Hezekiah there is no mention of such a stipulation (2 Kgs 21:18, 26; 23:30; 2 Chr 33:20, 24; 35:24). In addition, Halpern argues that the notice that no king ever arose like Hezekiah, either before him or *after him* (2 Kgs 18:5), is best understood as coming from a Hezekian history, since Josiah later receives a similar accolade (2 Kgs 23:25).[40] For Halpern, this history "exalted Solomon, rejected northern independence, and looked forward to a period of expansion, wealth, or of reconstitution."

Building on this earlier work and an updated analysis of regnal formulae by I. Provan,[41] Halpern and Vanderhooft have marshaled additional evidence for a Hezekian history, including noting further changes in regnal death and burial notices, regnal evaluations, source citations, the placement of supplementary notes in regnal formulae, and the practice of identifying queen mothers by name, patronym, and birthplace—all of which point to a history culminating in Hezekiah's reign.[42] When combined with the evidence for a Josianic history, Halpern and Vanderhooft argue for the development of the DH in three stages: Hezekian, Josianic, and exilic.[43]

---

tions of an Earlier Source," in *The Creation of Sacred Literature: Composition and Redaction of the Biblical Text*, ed. R.E. Friedman (NES 22; Berkeley and Los Angeles: UC Press, 1981) 35–54.

40. For a different interpretation of the incomparability notice applied to Hezekiah, see G. N. Knoppers, "'There was None like Him': Incomparability in the Books of Kings," *CBQ* 54 (1992) 411–31). Knoppers argues that all three incomparability statements in the DH (Solomon, Hezekiah, and Josiah) are the Deuteronomist's way of highlighting different characteristics of ideal leaders.

41. I. Provan, *Hezekiah and the Books of Kings: A Contribution to the Debate about the Deuteronomistic History* (BZAW 172; Berlin and New York: Walter de Gruyter, 1988). Provan's conclusions differ from those of Weippert and Halpern in that his "Hezekian" Deuteronomistic History (that is, the DH ending with Hezekiah's reign) was actually produced during the reign of Josiah.

42. B. Halpern and D. S. Vanderhooft, "The Editions of Kings in the 7th–6th Centuries B.C.E." *HUCA* 62 (1991) 179–244.

43. For a more recent examination of regnal formulae, see E. Eynikel (*The Reform of King Josiah and the Composition of the Deuteronomistic History* [OTS 33; Leiden: E. J. Brill, 1996]). Eynikel similarly concludes, based on regnal formulae and his own redactional analysis of

## Andrew D. H. Mayes

The last scholar to be considered under this multi-tiered development of the DH is A. D. H. Mayes.[44] Mayes, whose analysis is among the most detailed in identifying the redactional layers of the DH, similarly argues that this history was compiled by a Deuteronomist, who himself had access to earlier materials, including traditions about the conquest of the land and the period of the judges, various prophetic tales, and a limited royal history dating to the reign of Hezekiah.[45] This historian, who had a positive view of the monarchy, wrote around the time of Josiah's reforms. The DH was subsequently edited by an exilic Deuteronomist, whose contribution to the various parts of the DH is uneven, but whose insistence on the importance of obedience to the Mosaic covenant is consistent throughout. This Deuteronomist had a negative view of the monarchy but an optimistic view of Israel's future should it repent of its wrongdoing and renew its commitment to follow the Mosaic Law.

Although Mayes's conclusions are not that different from others who argue for a pre-Josianic royal history, what makes Mayes's analysis of the DH of particular interest is his attempt to reckon with the skeleton that has lurked in the closet of biblical studies ever since Noth's original study; namely, the problem of the so-called Tetrateuch.[46] The idea that Dtr lopped off the end of his Pentateuchal sources in favor of his own conclusion is, in Mayes's estimation, inconsistent with this historian's treatment of his sources elsewhere.[47] Mayes's remedy for this problem is to posit that the DH is actually the earlier of the two works, and that the Tetrateuch is a subsequent "introduction" to the DH.[48] For Mayes, this solution preserves the unity of the DH while providing an explanation for the abrupt ending

---

2 Kings 22–23, that there existed a Hezekian (though dating post-Hezekiah), Josianic and exilic redactions of the material now making up the DH, though the earliest phases of redaction (Hezekian and Josianic) were limited largely to the books of Kings. Eynikel's analysis makes him skeptical of a unified DH prior to the work of Dtr², whom he places in the exilic period. Against the view that changes in regnal formulae, and especially burial formulae, indicate the existence of an earlier history, see N. Na'aman, "Death Formulae and the Burial Place of the Kings of the House of David," *Bib* 85 (2004) 245–54.

44. A. D. H. Mayes, *The Story of Israel between Settlement and Exile: A Redactional Study of the Deuteronomistic History* (London: SCM, 1983).

45. Mayes, *The Story of Israel*, 133–36.

46. Mayes is not the first to raise this problem resulting from the so-called Tetrateuch. See already G. von Rad, *Studies in Deuteronomy*; idem, "Hexateuch oder Pentateuch," *VF* 1 (1947–48) 52–56; A. Bentzen, *Introduction to the Old Testament*, II (2 vols.; Copenhagen: G. E. C. Gad, 1948) 75.

47. Mayes, *The Story of Israel*, 139.

48. Mayes, *The Story of Israel*, 141, 149.

of the Tetrateuchal sources. Ideologically, the prefacing of the DH with the Tetrateuch, along with the subsequent appropriation of Deuteronomy to form the Pentateuch, represents the postexilic community's effort to shift the focus of its traditions from temple and monarchy to ethical and social demands, thus adapting Israel's traditions to meet their changing circumstances.[49]

## 6. The Gradual Formation of the Deuteronomistic History in Deuteronomistic "Circles" or "Schools"

Related to the theory of a two- or three-tiered redaction of the DH is the proposal that the DH developed as a gradual process within Deuteronomic circles or schools.

### Ernest W. Nicholson

E. W. Nicholson has argued that many of the traditions making up the DH were originally preserved by northern prophetic circles. Nicholson writes, "Beginning with Samuel there arose a series of prophetic personalities and groups who cherished the old traditions from generation to generation."[50] With the fall of the north, these groups were forced south, where there existed a deep-rooted belief in YHWH's unique covenant with the Davidic throne. These former northerners joined with Hezekiah in enacting various reforms, most notably the centralization of the cult in Jerusalem and the promotion of the exclusive worship of YHWH.

The reign of Manasseh proved an inauspicious time for these reformers, but it did provide them with an opportunity to prepare for future reforms. Consequently, during this period they drafted a document that sought to revive the old Mosaic covenant, but in a way that reconciled it with the covenant ideology surrounding the Davidic dynasty and the centralization of the cult at Jerusalem.[51] This document—an early edition of the book of Deuteronomy—became the basis for Josiah's religious reforms. Eventually these prophetic circles produced the DH, which was probably begun in the late-preexilic period, but was largely the product of the exilic period, being completed shortly after 561 B.C.E. (the release of Jehoiachin).[52]

---

49. For a more recent formulation of this position, see Mayes, "Deuteronomistic Ideology and the Theology of the Old Testament" in *Israel Constructs Its History*, 456–80.

50. E. W. Nicholson, *Deuteronomy and Tradition* (Philadelphia: Fortress, 1967) 122. Nicholson is not the first to propose the existence of Dtr "circles." See already H. W. Hertzberg, *Die Bücher Josua, Richter, Ruth* (ATD 9; Göttingen: Vandenhoeck & Ruprecht, 1956) 9.

51. Nicholson, *Deuteronomy and Tradition*, 123.

52. Nicholson, *Deuteronomy and Tradition*, 123–24.

## Moshe Weinfeld

M. Weinfeld has similarly postulated that the DH was the result of several stages of composition/redaction within Deuteronomic circles. The main differences between Weinfeld's and Nicholson's models, however, are the dates assigned to these stages and the ideology informing them. For Weinfeld, the Deuteronomic literature (which includes the book of Jeremiah) developed in three general stages.[53] The first saw the production of the book of Deuteronomy, which Weinfeld dates sometime in the latter half of the seventh century B.C.E. (just before Josiah's reign). This stage was followed by the composition of a Deuteronomic edition of the books of Joshua to 2 Kings, which was completed in the first half of the sixth century. The third stage saw the composition of the prose sermons in Jeremiah, which Weinfeld dates to the latter half of the sixth century.

Despite the seeming rigidity of these stages, Weinfeld admits that the book of Deuteronomy consists of more than one editorial strand and that the DH shows signs of varying literary strata. That is, Weinfeld is not concerned primarily with delineating the exact parameters of each stage of development, nor with locating the precise dates of their composition. Rather, he is most concerned with outlining the overall development of the Deuteronom(ist)ic literature, a development Weinfeld summarizes as follows:

> The thesis of the present study is that deuteronomic composition is the creation of scribal circles which began their literary project some time prior to the reign of Josiah and were still at work after the fall of Judah.[54]

Based on the similarities in language and interests between the DH and biblical wisdom literature, Weinfeld places this circle of scribes within the wisdom tradition of ancient Israel.[55]

## 7. Prophetic Precursors to the Deuteronomistic History

### P. Kyle McCarter

In his commentaries on the books of Samuel, P. K. McCarter proposes a slightly different model for the development of the DH, which represents

---

53. M. Weinfeld, *Deuteronomic School*, 7–9.
54. Weinfeld, *Deuteronomic School*, 9.
55. For a similar notion of "schools" gradually producing the Deuteronomistic literature, though in the exilic and postexilic periods, see R. F. Person, Jr., *The Deuteronomic School: History, Social Setting, and Literature* (SBLSBL 2; Boston: Brill, 2002).

in some ways a compromise between Cross's theory of Josianic DH and the Göttingen school's theory of a prophetic stratum.

McCarter contends that a number of the major literary units found in the DH underwent a preDtr redaction by someone with prophetic interests. The texts making up this preDtr redaction in the book of 1 Samuel include the Ark Narrative, the stories about Saul's early career, and the so-called "History of David's Rise." In the words of McCarter:

> The prophetic writer who incorporated [these sources] into his history amplified them and reworked parts of them, sometimes with considerable license, to reflect his particular *Tendenz*. Everywhere he introduced the dominant figure of the prophet Samuel, whose activity became the organizing feature of his work. The result was a systematic narrative in three sections, each structurally complete within itself but pointedly interconnected with the others.[56]

McCarter argues that a similar development occurred in 2 Samuel, where the primary source for the preDtr redaction was the Succession Narrative. According to McCarter, when these sources came into the hands of a Deuteronomistic redactor (during the time of Josiah) they were already relatively organized and of considerable length. McCarter argues that the negative—or, at minimum, "reserved"—view of kingship and its subjection to prophetic authority is to be traced to this preDtr level of redaction, the positive view being a part of both this redactor's sources (especially in the "History of David's Rise" and "Succession Narrative") and Dtr's own contributions. These contributions sought to promote the Davidic dynasty, in general, and the Josianic reforms, in particular. McCarter dates this preDtr redaction shortly after the fall of Samaria, when northern prophetic traditions merged with southern sources. Thus, while McCarter agrees in general with the Göttingen school's notion of a prophetic stratum in the DH, he disagrees with their determination that this layer was secondarily added to this corpus and was of exilic provenance. For McCarter, the prophetic stratum "is an organic part of the whole" and "does not sit awkwardly atop the Deuteronomistic organization . . . but seems rather to underlie it."[57]

## Antony Campbell

A. Campbell has similarly argued for a preDtr work underlying the DH,[58] and, like McCarter, he believes this material reflects a northern prophetic

---

56. McCarter, *1 Samuel*, 18.
57. McCarter, *2 Samuel*, 8.
58. A. Campbell, *Of Prophets and Kings: A Late Ninth-Century Document (1 Samuel 1–2 Kings 10)* (CBQMS 17; Washington: Catholic Biblical Association of America, 1986).

perspective. However, unlike McCarter, Campbell assigns individual narratives within this work to different prophetic groups. Therefore, while McCarter describes this corpus as deriving from a "Prophetic Historian," Campbell prefers to refer to this material as a "Prophetic Record" in recognition of its diverse origins, though he argues that these traditions were eventually joined into a coherent pre-Dtr narrative.[59] Another point of departure for these two scholars is the dating of this prophetic record. McCarter places its composition in the eighth century, since, for him, it represents most closely the prophetic interests of this period. Campbell, however, locates its origins in the ninth century—in particular, during the reign of Jehu—arguing that the goal of this work was to legitimize Jehu's prophetic anointing and royal ascension.[60] Thus, while McCarter argues that the prophetic history presented a negative view of the monarchy, Campbell believes that it promoted the monarchy as divinely favored when serving as a vehicle for religious reform.

## 8. A Singular Exilic or Postexilic Composition

A number of scholars have returned to Noth's original hypothesis of a single exilic or even postexilic Deuteronomistic Historian. These models usually deviate from Noth's hypothesis, however, by emphasizing the Deuteronomist's role as creative *author* of a largely original work over against his role as conservative *editor* of preexisting materials.

### Hans-Detlef Hoffmann

Based on the application of traditio-historical analysis, H.-D. Hoffmann has argued that the books of Kings are structured according to a pattern of positive and negative reforms that climax in the person of Josiah.[61] This

---

59. According to Campbell, this "prophetic record" consisted largely of the Samuel material, the Elijah and Elisha material, and culminated in the revolt of Jehu.

60. For similar views on the importance of Jehu's reign in giving rise to an early prophetic history or record, see M. O'Brien, *The Deuteronomistic Hypothesis: A Reassessment* (OBO 92; Freiburg, Switzerland: Universitätsverlag, 1989); and M. White, *The Elijah Legends and Jehu's Coup* (BJS 311; Atlanta: Scholars Press, 1997); idem, "'The History of Saul's Rise': Saulide State Propaganda in 1 Samuel 1–14," in *"A Wise and Discerning Mind": Essays in Honor of Burke O. Long*, ed. S. M. Olyan and R. C. Culley (BJS 325; Providence, RI: Brown University, 2000) 271–92. Cf. A. Rofé ("Ephraimite versus Deuteronomistic History" in *Storia e Tradizioni di Israele: Scritti in Onore di J. Alberto Soggin*, ed. D. Garrone and F. Israel [Brescia: Paideia, 1991] 221–35), who argues for an Ephraimite history (northern, anti-monarchic) that was subsequently incorporated into the DH.

61. H.-D. Hoffmann, *Reform und Reformen: Untersuchungen zu einen Grundthema der deuteronomistischen Geschichtsschreibung* (ATANT 66; Zürich: Theologischer Verlag, 1980).

patterning, along with the overall unity of the DH, suggests to Hoffmann that it is the product of a single author living after the fall of Jerusalem. Also similar to Noth, Hoffmann argues that the original aim of this work was to underscore Israel's covenant/cultic unfaithfulness, which was the reason for the nation's earlier disasters. The culmination of this history in Josiah's reforms, therefore, is not an indication of its preexilic provenance (*contra* Cross) but more a reflection of its purpose: to promote cultic reform in the postexilic period. According to Hoffmann, however, Noth's conception of a historian who is both author *and* editor is fundamentally flawed, as it goes against the conventions of ancient historiography.[62] While earlier traditions may inform some narratives, the DH is largely the work of a creative author working from very few sources in the exilic or postexilic period.

## *John Van Seters*

J. Van Seters's comparison of historiographic genres in the ancient Near East and Mediterranean Basin leads him to the conclusion that Dtr is "the first known historian in Western civilization truly to deserve this designation."[63] Van Seters bases this assessment on what he understands to be Dtr's methods of researching, combining, and arranging his sources for the purpose of rendering to Israel an account of its past. For Van Seters, however, the sources at Dtr's disposal were far fewer than is usually thought. For example, Van Seters contends that the so-called Court History, which most scholars believe was part of Dtr's original work, is actually a post-Dtr addition.[64] Regarding the other sources making up Dtr's account of the early monarchy, Van Seters contends they never had a separate existence outside of their use in this history, nor were they ever combined into collections (*Sammelwerken*) prior to Dtr's historical enterprise (*contra* McCarter). Van Seters ascribes the diversity of views in the DH both to Dtr's willingness to tolerate inconsistencies in his text as well as to later additions to the DH which sought to correct the Deuteronomistic presentation of Israel's past. Beyond the Court History, these later additions consisted of parts of the Elisha cycle and all of "the Yahwist, who supplemented Dtr by extending the history back in time to the beginning of the

---

62. Hoffmann, *Reform und Reformen*, 16–17. For a recent critique of Hoffmann's argument, see H. N. Rösel, "Does a Comprehensive 'Leitmotiv' Exist in the Deuteronomistic History?" in *The Future of the Deuteronomistic History*, 195–211.

63. Van Seters, *In Search of History*, 362.

64. Van Seters, *In Search of History*, 277–91. See also his "The Deuteronomistic History: Can It Avoid Death by Redaction?" in *The Future of the Deuteronomistic History*, 213–22.

world."⁶⁵ According to Van Seters, P was added to this work as an attempt to, among other things, establish a "cultic identity" for the postexilic community in Jerusalem. Thus, similar to Mayes, Van Seters views Genesis through Numbers as secondary to the DH, providing a "prologue" to this work and a corrective to Dtr's particular view of Israel's past.⁶⁶

Similar to Noth, Van Seters argues, "It was Dtr himself who collected his material and put it into the sequence and chronological scheme in which it now appears from Deuteronomy to 2 Kings."⁶⁷ Yet, contrary to Noth, the purpose of the DH was not to emphasize Israel's covenant infidelity to those in exile but to give those returning from exile a renewed sense of national identity. The promise to David, therefore, is to be understood not as a preexilic conviction in the inviolability of the Judean state but rather as a postexilic expectation in the imminent restoration of the Davidic throne.⁶⁸ Concerning Dtr's perspective, Van Seters argues that he is prophetic in orientation, being influenced by Deuteronomy, which in turn was influenced by northern prophetic traditions, such as those reflected in the book of Hosea.

## Brian Peckham

Although B. Peckham holds to the preexilic provenance of the original DH, he argues that this work was later edited and incorporated into a larger history by a single historian working in the postexilic period.⁶⁹ Thus, like Van Seters, Peckham attributes the final form of Israel's history to an author living after the exile. However, unlike Van Seters, Peckham argues that the author of the DH (his Dtr²) had at his disposal several of the works Van Seters contends were not available to him, including J and the Court History.⁷⁰ In fact, in this way Peckham's theory of the composition of the DH may be thought of as a reversal of Van Seters's. Specifically, Peckham contends that Dtr² not only possessed J, but used this source as the foundation

---

65. Van Seters, *In Search of History*, 361.
66. See also Van Seters, "The Deuteronomistic Redaction of the Pentateuch. The Case Against It" in *Deuteronomy and Deuteronomic Literature: Festschrift C. H. W. Brekelmans*, ed. M. Vervenne and J. Lust (BETL 133; Leuven: University Press, 1997) 301–19. The proposal that Genesis through Numbers may be secondary is prior to the work of Van Seters and Mayes. See, e.g., M. Rose, *Deuteronomist und Jahwist: Untersuchungen zu den Berührungspunkten beider Literaturwerke* (ATANT 67; Zürich: Theologischer Verlag, 1981).
67. Van Seters, *In Search of History*, 356.
68. Van Seters, *In Search of History*, 290.
69. B. Peckham, *The Composition of the Deuteronomistic History* (HSM 35; Atlanta: Scholars, 1985).
70. Peckham, *The Composition of the Deuteronomistic History*, 1.

for reconstructing Israel's early history. Another source available to this historian was Dtr¹, which was a continuation of J probably composed during the time of Josiah. This source recounted the history of Israel from Deuteronomy to the reign of Hezekiah. Two other works used by Dtr² were P, which was originally written as an alternative to J, and E, which was a supplement to J and P and provided a different view of Israel's past.[71]

According to Peckham, Dtr² reworked these sources to produce the history now found in Genesis to 2 Kings (D. N. Freedman's "Primary History"[72]). This historian "had access to libraries, administrative records, detailed scholarly information, informal sources, ribald stories, and the relative wisdom of the ages."[73] Moreover, Dtr²'s editorial/authorial contributions are everywhere present, including Leviticus, where he is responsible for the "priestly and ritual precepts" found in Leviticus 8:1–11:45.[74] Although Peckham is not the first to see the hand of Dtr in the Tetrateuchal sources, his reconstruction makes Dtr's influence among the most pervasive.[75]

## 9. A Return to Pre-Nothian Models

Just as some scholars have called for a return to Noth's original hypothesis, so others have called for a return to pre-Nothian models for understanding the development of Israel's traditions.

### *Claus Westermann*

One such scholar is C. Westermann, who has argued that the Former Prophets should no longer be viewed as a unified historical work, brought

---

71. Peckham, *The Composition of the Deuteronomistic History*, 3–15.
72. D. N. Freedman, "The Deuteronomic History," *IDBSup*, 226–28.
73. Peckham, *History and Prophecy: The Development of Late Judean Literary Traditions* (New York: Doubleday, 1993) 518.
74. Peckham, *History and Prophecy*, 612.
75. For a discussion of the literature, see M. Vervenne, "The Question of 'Deuteronomic' Elements in Genesis to Numbers" in *Studies in Deuteronomy. Festschrift C. J. Labuschange*, ed. F. García Martínez et al. (VTSup 53; Leiden: E. J. Brill, 1994) 243–68. For the identification of Deuteron(ist)ic elements in the Tetrateuch with varying explanations, see C. H. W. Brekelmans, "Die sogenannten deuteronomistischen Elemente in Genesis bis Numeri. Ein Beitrag zur Vorgeschichte des Deuteronomiums," *Volume du Congrès Genève 1965*, VTSup 15 (1966) 90–96; P. Weimar, *Untersuchungen zur Redaktionsgeschichte des Pentateuch* (BZAW 146; Berlin: de Gruyter, 1977); H. Ausloos, "Les extrêmes se touchent . . . Proto-Deuteronomic and Simili-Deuteronomistic Elements in Genesis-Numbers" in *Deuteronomy and Deuteronomic Literature. Festschrift C. H. W. Brekelmans*, ed. M. Vervenne and J. Lust (BETL 133; Leuven: University Press, 1997) 341–66.

together as part of the same Deuteronomistic redaction, but rather as individual works, each with its own distinct compositional history and purpose.[76] In making such a proposal, Westermann does not deny the presence of Deuteronomistic material within these works. Rather, he contends that this material is too diverse in perspective and redactional procedure to be subsumed under Noths' model of a single Deuteronomistic redactor. In addition, Westermann takes issue with Noth's view that Deuteronomy provides an adequate introduction for a discrete history, since both this book and the books that follow assume the traditions found in the earlier works. Moreover, Westermann disagrees with Noth's contention that a historian could countenance the number of diverging views now found in the historical books. Rather, these inconsistencies are best accounted for by hypothesizing discrete compositional histories for each of these works. Only later were these individual units brought together, but this redaction had more to do with arranging these works in chronological order, not with imposing a theological unity over the whole.

## Reinhard G. Kratz

R. G. Kratz is another scholar who has argued against Noth's theory of a unified DH, calling it—in ironic reversal of Noth's own pronouncement about the hypothesis of a Hexateuch—"an error of scholarship."[77] For Kratz, Noth's contention that Dtr truncated the Patriarchal traditions in preference for his own material "is not only unsatisfactory but also quite improbable."[78] Not only does such a model go against Noth's own view of the historian's approach toward his sources (i.e., "conservative") but it also ignores the evidence for "an old narrative of settlement in Joshua which continues the narrative of Genesis-Numbers seamlessly." Kratz's own analysis leads him to return to the dominant model prior to Noth's *ÜgS*; namely, that of a Hexateuch, which was only later joined to the traditions

---

76. C. Westermann, *Die Geschichtsbücher des Alten Testaments: Gab es ein deuteronomistisches Geschichtswerk?* (TB AT 87; Gütersloh: Kaiser, 1994). Westermann's work is in many ways an extension of earlier arguments against Noth's theory of a unified Deuteronomistic redaction. See, e.g., A. Weiser, *Einleitung in das Alte Testament* (Göttingen: Vandenhoeck & Ruprecht, 1963) 117–66.

77. R. G. Kratz, *The Composition of the Narrative Books of the Old Testament* (London and New York: T & T Clark, 2005; German original; Göttingen: Vandenhoeck & Ruprecht, 2000) 217.

78. Kratz, *The Composition of the Narrative Books*, 126. Concerning Deuteronomy in particular Kratz argues that it originally "neither closed the Pentateuch nor opened the Deuteronomistic history but . . . was inserted into the basic text which runs from Num. 25.1a through Deut 34.5f (without the additions) to Josh. 2.1."

now making up Judges through Kings, forming what Kratz refers to as the Enneateuch. Although this process of compiling Israel's traditions included Deuteronomistic redactors, these redactions "grew up in blocks over a lengthy period."[79]

The first redaction (Dtr$^G$ = DtrH), which Kratz dates to ca. 560 B.C.E., saw the combination of traditions related to David and Solomon (1 Samuel 1–1 Kings 2) with the synchronized reigns of the kings of Israel and Judah. The second stage of compilation (Dtr$^R$) witnessed the joining of this royal history with the Hexateuch by means of the period of the judges, which was constructed for this purpose from separate local traditions or, perhaps, a loose collection of heroic tales. Other Deuteronomistic redactions followed (e.g., Dtr$^S$ = DtrP, DtrN), both prior to and following the inclusion of P, which had its own literary history beginning in the Persian period.[80] The final step was the separation of the Enneateuch into the Torah and Former Prophets, which reflected the centrality of the Mosaic law for the postexilic community.

## 10. So-Called "Minimalist" Views of Ancient Israelite Historiography

While most of the scholars discussed above ascribe authentic historical impulses or, at minimum, antiquarian interests to those responsible for compiling Israel's history, several recent treatments of Israelite historiography deny such principles ever governed the recounting of Israel's past.

### *Philip R. Davies*

Due in large part to the dearth of inscriptional and archaeological evidence for an "ancient Israel," P. R. Davies has argued that the biblical account of

---

79. Kratz, *The Composition of the Narrative Books*, 209.
80. For others arguing against Noth's theory of a unified DH, see the recent treatments of E. Würthwein, *Studien zum deuteronomistischen Geschichtswerk* (BZAW 227; Berlin: W. de Gruyter, 1994) esp. 1–11; A. G. Auld, *Joshua Retold: Synoptic Perspectives* (Edinburgh: T & T Clark, 1998) 120–26; E. A. Knauf, "Does 'Deuteronomistic Historiography' (DtrH) Exist?" in *Israel Constructs Its History*, 388–98; H. Rösel, "Does A Comprehensive 'Leitmotiv' Exist in the Deuteronomistic History?" in *The Future of the Deuteronomistic History*, 195–211; idem, *Von Josua bis Jojachin: Untersuchungen zu den deuteronomistischen Geschichtsbüchern des Alten Testaments* (VTSup 75; Leiden: E. J. Brill, 1999); K. Schmid, *Erzväter und Exodus: Untersuchungen zur doppelten Begründung der Ursprünge Israels innerhalb der Geschichtsbücher des Alten Testaments* (WMANT 81; Neukirchen-Vluyn: Neukirchener, 1999), esp. 162–65; idem, "Das Deuteronomium innerhalb der 'deuteronomistischen Geschichtswerke' in Gen–2 Kön" in *Das Deuteronomium zwischen Pentateuch und deuteronomistischem Geschichtswerk*, ed. R. Achenbach and E. Otto (FRLANT; Göttingen: Vandenhoeck & Ruprecht, 2004) 193–211.

Israel is not based upon authentic preexilic sources, but rather was fabricated by postexilic scribes in order to justify territorial claims and political power in Persian-period Yehud.[81] Certainly there were political entities known as "Israel" and "Judah" in the central highlands of Palestine, as Assyrian and Babylonian records attest, but there is little connection between these entities and the ideological constructs found in the Bible. Davies argues, therefore, that the literary creation of "Biblical Israel" must be distinguished from the actual history of those occupying Iron Age Palestine, or what he calls "Historical Israel."

Davies attributes the literary unevenness and differences of perspective that many scholars cite as evidence for the long and variegated history of the biblical text to differences of opinion among the scribal schools active during the Persian period.[82] During the Hasmonean period these texts formed the basis of a national archive that was promoted as authoritative within the Jewish community in order to further Maccabean dynastic ambitions. Davies concludes, "Once the practitioners of traditional biblical scholarship . . . relinquish their anguished hold on a real 'ancient Israel' and cease to practise a theologically-dictated form of historical criticism, the disciplines of both theology and history may be the better for it."[83]

## Niels P. Lemche

N. P. Lemche is another scholar who has argued that the biblical account of Israel's past is the creation of Jewish scribes living in the late-Persian and early-Hellenistic periods.[84] Similar to Davies, Lemche bases his claims largely upon the lack of evidence for an ancient Israel in the archaeological and inscriptional record. Lemche points out, for example, that the traditional means for identifying something as "Israelite" (e.g., four-roomed houses, collared-rim pottery, etc.) are also found in non-Israelite contexts. In addition, the archaeological record does not support the biblical claims of a united monarchy in the tenth century B.C.E., but rather point to the emergence of a rather modest Israelite state not much before the ninth century B.C.E., and a Judahite one not much earlier than the eighth century

---

81. Davies, *In Search of 'Ancient Israel,'* 95. Davies's assessment of the archaeological and inscriptional evidence is based largely upon T. L. Thompson's *The Early History of the Israelite People: From the Written and Archaeological Sources* (Leiden: E. J. Brill, 1992).

82. Davies, *In Search of 'Ancient Israel,'* esp. 113–33. For a contrary view on the diversity of perspectives reflected in the DH, see, e.g., N. K. Gottwald, *The Politics of Ancient Israel* (Louisville: Westminster John Knox, 2001) 160.

83. Davies, *In Search of 'Ancient Israel,'* 161.

84. N. P. Lemche, *The Israelites in History and Tradition*, 165. See also his "The Old Testament—A Hellenistic Book?," 163–93.

B.C.E. The inscriptional record suffers from similar deficiencies, with references to biblical personalities and entities in Mesopotamian, Egyptian, and Syro-Palestinian sources being too sketchy to provide any concrete information for reconstructing Israel's past.

In light of the lack of evidence for Israel's preexilic history, Lemche argues that "ancient Israel" is little more than the invention of postexilic scribes who sought "to legitimize their own religious community and its religio-political claims on land and religious exclusivity." He concludes by asserting, "The Israel found on the pages of the Old Testament is an artificial creation which has little more than one thing in common with the Israel that existed once upon a time in Palestine, that is, the name."[85]

## SUMMARY

Deuteronomistic scholarship stands at a crossroads, with paths leading in very different directions than first marked out by Noth. Even among the majority of scholars who still find Noth's original course trustworthy, there are considerable differences over how to interpret various landmarks along the way (e.g., the promise to David, the critiques of monarchy, etc.). These debates are not merely haggling over details, but reflect deep differences of opinion about who produced Israel's history, when and why. The answers to these questions, as most scholars agree, have significant implications for interpreting the biblical text, as well as for tracing the development of Israelite history and religion. Although a single phrase cannot address all the issues being raised, "until this day" does allow us to answer many of the questions engaging Deuteronomistic studies, providing a necessary corrective to several of the views presented above and marking out a fairly reliable course for future inquiries.

---

85. For similar views of Israelite history, see G. Garbini, *History and Ideology in Ancient Israel* (London: SCM Press Ltd., 1988); K. W. Whitelam, *The Invention of Ancient Israel: The Silencing of Palestinian History* (London: Routledge, 1996); T. L. Thompson, "Martin Noth and the History of Israel" in *The History of Israel's Traditions: The Heritage of Martin Noth*, ed. S. L. McKenzie and M. P. Graham (JSOTSup 182; Sheffield: JSOT, 1994) 81–90; idem, *The Mythic Past*. For recent critiques, see I. W. Provan, "Ideologies, Literary and Critical: Reflections on Recent Writing on the History of Israel," *JBL* 114/4 (1995) 585–606; G. N. Knoppers, "The Vanishing Solomon: The Disappearance of the United Monarchy from Recent Histories of Ancient Israel," *JBL* 116 (1997) 19–44; A. Hurvitz, "The Historical Quest for 'Ancient Israel' and the Linguistic Evidence of the Hebrew Bible: Some Methodological Observations," *VT* 47 (1997) 301–15; B. Halpern, "The State of Israelite History," in *Reconsidering Israel and Judah: Recent Studies in Deuteronomistic History*, ed. G. N. Knoppers and J. G. McConville (SBTS 8; Winona Lake, IN: Eisenbrauns, 2000); M. Brettler, "The Copenhagen School: The Historiographical Issues," *AJS Review* 27/1 (2003) 1–22.

# 5

# "Until This Day" and Deuteronomistic Studies

> If ["until this day"] could be assigned definitely to the hand of the Deuteronomistic Historian himself and not to the wording of the historian's sources, we could then establish a sure core of preexilic redactional material over against the exilic material presupposing an inevitable disaster.[1]
>
> —Richard D. Nelson,
> *The Double Redaction of the Deuteronomistic History*

The field of Deuteronomistic studies can no longer be characterized as *refining* Noth's original hypothesis, but rather as *reconsidering* or, in some cases, *rejecting* the whole. The questions being asked are fundamental: Is the DH the result of a single exilic redactor (Noth, Hoffmann, Van Seters), several exilic redactional levels (the Göttingen School) or a growing body of traditions among Deuteronomistic schools or circles (Nicholson, Weinfeld)? Did there exist an earlier Josianic edition of the DH (Cross, Friedman, Nelson), and if so, was this in turn based upon an earlier Hezekian (Weippert, Provan, Halpern and Vanderhooft) or even prophetic history (McCarter, Nicholson, Campbell)? Are the tensions within the DH best explained as deriving from the compilation of disparate sources by a single historian (Noth, Cross), successive redactions by those with distinct interests and concerns (the Göttingen School), or differences of opinion among contemporaneous scribal schools in the postexilic period (Davies)? Can we still speak of a unified DH, or has the identification of distinct redactional procedures in the individual books made such a theory untenable (Westermann, Kratz)? Finally, what is the purpose of the DH? Is it meant to serve as an object lesson to those in exile (Noth, Hoffmann), as propaganda for the reform efforts of Hezekiah, Josiah or even Jehu (Halpern and Vanderhooft, Cross and Campbell, respectively), as a source

---

1. R. Nelson, *The Double Redaction*, 23.

120  *The Time, Place, and Purpose of the Deuteronomistic History*

of national identity and messianic expectation for the exilic or postexilic communities (Von Rad, Van Seters), or as a fabrication to justify territorial claims and political power in the Persian or Hellenistic periods (Davies, Lemche)?

Fortunately, the evidence of "until this day" allows us to address, even answer, many of these questions.

## THE PROVENANCE AND SCOPE OF THE DEUTERONOMISTIC HISTORY

One significant finding from our study is that there existed a preexilic, likely Josianic, edition of the DH. Although any single piece of evidence could be considered inconclusive, it is the convergence of numerous pieces of evidence that makes such a determination possible.

First, "until this day" reflects a unified geographical perspective across the DH. Of its forty-three appearances, thirty-eight refer explicitly to southern entities or interests. Indeed, the phrase reflects a detailed knowledge of the south, making reference to individual locations (Josh 5:9; 7:26; Judg 10:4; 18:12; 2 Sam 6:8; etc.), piles of stone (Josh 4:9; 7:26; 8:29; 10:27), springs (Judg 15:19; 2 Kgs 2:2) and monuments (1 Sam 6:18; 2 Sam 18:18). By way of contrast, three of the five northern entities said to persist "until this day" are vast geographical areas in the far north consisting of numerous cities: Havvoth Jair, with upward to sixty cities (Deut 3:14; Judg 10:4) and the Cabul with twenty (1 Kgs 9:13). Yet, even here we noted that the use of the phrase in reference to these regions relates to Dtr's interest in Levitical inheritance rights in the north (Josh 13:13–14; cf. Deut 10:8–9; 18:1–2). In addition, the only individual objects said to persist "until this day" in the north mark former sites of Baal worship (Judg 6:24; 2 Kgs 10:27), both of which were destroyed in Deuteronomic fashion (נָתַץ; see Deut 7:5) and reflect Dtr's interest in centralized worship—an interest that shows up elsewhere in connection with our phrase (see, e.g., Josh 9:27: עַד־הַיּוֹם הַזֶּה אֶל־הַמָּקוֹם אֲשֶׁר יִבְחָר, "until this day at the place he will choose").

Second, "until this day" reflects a unified temporal perspective: namely, preexilic. Both Israel and Edom are still in rebellion against the kingdom of Judah "until this day" (1 Kgs 12:19; 2 Kgs 8:22); the "kings of Judah" still possess Ziklag (1 Sam 27:6; cf. Josh 14:14); a law concerning war spoils remains in effect (1 Sam 30:25; cf. Deut 20:14); non-Israelite forced laborers continue to be used at the temple (Josh 9:27; 1 Kgs 9:21); the Levitical priests still have responsibility for carrying "the Ark of the Covenant of YHWH" (Deut 10:8; cf. Josh 4:7–9; 8:29–35); and the poles of the Ark still protrude from the Holy of Holies (1 Kgs 8:8). As noted earlier, most of these entities cannot properly be said to persist after the Babylonian destruction of Jerusalem in 586 B.C.E. Moreover, these notices further attest to the southern perspective of the one(s) employing this phrase, as they concern either the Davidic throne (1 Sam 27:6; 30:25; 1 Kgs 12:19; 2 Kgs 8:22) or the Jerusalem temple (Deut 10:8; Josh 9:27; 1 Kgs 8:8; 9:21).

Third, and as already alluded to, "until this day" consistently appears adjacent to Dtr redactional material, including trademark Dtr phrases, such as אַל־תִּירָא וְאַל־תֵּחָת "do not fear or be dismayed"; Josh 7:26–8:1), אֶל־הַמָּקוֹם אֲשֶׁר יִבְחָר ("at the place he will choose"; Josh 9:27), יַעַן אֲשֶׁר מִלֵּא אַחֲרֵי יְהוָה אֱלֹהֵי יִשְׂרָאֵל ("because he followed fully after YHWH"; Josh 14:14), as well as more substantive Dtr contributions to the text, such as the prologue to Deuteronomy (2:22; 3:14), Joshua's building of an altar on Mount Ebal (Josh 8:29–35; cf. Deut 27:1–26), Dtr's evaluation of various kings (see 2 Kgs 8:22–23; 10:27–29), and Dtr's citation of Deuteronomic law (2 Kgs 14:6–7).

Fourth, "until this day" consistently highlights objects and institutions of central interest to Dtr, such as the continuing presence of non-Israelites in the land (Josh 6:25; 13:13; 15:63; Judg 1:21; cf. Deut 7:1–4), the use of these non-Israelites as "forced laborers" (מַס־עֹבֵד; Josh 16:10; 1 Kgs 9:21; cf. Deut 20:10–11), particularly in connection with the temple (Josh 9:27), the destruction (נָתַץ) of non-Yahwistic cultic sites and objects (Judg 6:24; 2 Kgs 10:27; cf. Deut 7:5), and the rights and responsibilities of the Levites (Deut 10:8–9; Josh 4:9; 8:29–35; 13:14; cf. Deut 18:1–8).

Finally, "until this day"—like the case of *vaticinium post eventum* in 1 Kgs 13:2–5—points specifically to the reign and reforms of Josiah, including his covenant renewal ceremony (Josh 8:29–35; cf. 2 Kgs 23:1–3), his centralization of worship (Josh 9:27; Judg 6:24; 2 Kgs 10:27; cf. 2 Kgs 23:5–20) and his Passover observance (Josh 5:9–10; cf. 2 Kgs 23:21–23).

While it is possible that some of these uses derive from Dtr's sources or subsequent redactions of the text—especially in view of the evidence for Deuteronomistic activity in later, and perhaps earlier, periods[2]—there is no place where this is required or even suggested by the evidence. On the contrary, every use of the phrase in the DH can be shown to be integrally related to other uses within this history. Thus, the first appearance of "until this day" in the DH (Deut 2:22) describes Edom's original settlement in Seir, which finds connections with several uses of the phrase near the end of the DH (2 Kgs 8:22; 14:7; 16:6) and which, as Cogan and Tadmor have noted, reflects Dtr's "special interest in the question of territorial claims in the Negev and the Red Sea coast, at the time of renewed Judahite expansion under Josiah."[3] The second appearance of "until this day" (Deut 3:14)

---

2. See, e.g., B. Levinson, *Deuteronomy and the Hermeneutics of Legal Innovation* (New York: Oxford University Press, 1997); J. A. Dearman, "My Servants the Scribes: Composition and Context in Jeremiah 36" JBL 109 (1990) 418–19; M. A. Sweeney, *King Josiah*, 170–77.

3. Cogan and Tadmor, *2 Kings*, 96.

concerns the region of Havvoth Jair, which similarly receives multiple attestations via our phrase (Judg 10:4; Josh 13:13) and which reflects Dtr's interest in northern territorial claims, particularly as these relate to the inheritance rights of the Levites (Josh 13:13–14; 1 Kgs 9:13; cf. Deut 10:8–9). The third appearance of "until this day" (Deut 10:8) similarly attests to the rights of the Levites, highlighting their role in bearing the Ark of the Covenant, an interest reflected throughout the DH in connection with our phrase (Josh 4:9; 8:29–35; 1 Sam 5:5; 6:18; 2 Sam 6:8; 1 Kgs 8:8). The fourth use of "until this day" (Deut 34:6) refers to the burial place of Moses, the foundational figure of the DH and the mediator of the law that gives Dtr his criteria for evaluating the nation and its leadership. The fifth use of "until this day" (Josh 4:9) marks the place where the "Levitical priests" (Josh 3:3) bear "the Ark of the Covenant of YHWH" (Josh 4:7)—again, central concerns for Dtr (see, e.g., Deut 10:8–9; 18:1–2; Josh 8:30–35; 14:14). The sixth use of the phrase (Josh 5:9) is followed by the description of Joshua's Passover, which, as Nelson rightly observes, points forward to Josiah's reforming Passover (2 Kgs 23:21–23).[4] The seventh use of "until this day" (Josh 6:25) is followed by Joshua's curse upon the one who would rebuild Jericho, a prediction to which Dtr returns in his account of its rebuilding as evidence of the prophecy-fulfillment pattern that runs throughout Israel's history (1 Kgs 16:34), including elsewhere in connection with our phrase (2 Kgs 2:22). The eighth and ninth uses of "until this day" (Josh 7:26) are followed by the Deuteronom(ist)ic injunction, "do not fear or be dismayed," which, as noted earlier, appears in the DH only in material belonging to Dtr (see, e.g., Deut 1:21; 31:8; Josh 10:25). The tenth and eleventh uses of "until this day" (Josh 8:28–29) are followed by Joshua's building of the altar upon Mount Ebal, which fulfills Moses' command in Deuteronomy 27 and during which the "Levitical priests" bear the "Ark of the Covenant of YHWH" (Josh 8:33) while Joshua reads the "torah of Moses"—all central concerns of Dtr (see, e.g., Deut 10:8–9; 18:1–2). The twelfth use of the phrase (Josh 9:27) is immediately followed by the Deuteronomistic phrase "at the place he will choose," which not only highlights Dtr's concern for centralized worship (Judg 6:24; 2 Kgs 10:27) but also reflects his interest in the use of non-Israelite forced labor during his day—an interest that, once again, finds expression throughout the DH by means of "until this day" (Josh 16:10; 1 Kgs 9:21; cf. Josh 15:63; Judg 1:21; 2 Sam 4:3; cf. Deut 20:11). Etc.[5]

These observations lead to another important implication of our study: Dtr's preexilic DH contained most of what we now have before us. The evidence for this is the presence of "until this day" in every major lit-

---

4. Nelson, "Josiah in the Book of Joshua," 537.
5. For the remaining connections among the uses of "until this day," see the analysis in chapter 3 and the discussion below.

erary unit making up the DH, maximally including: the prologue (Deut 2:22; 3:14), Deuteronomic law code (Deut 10:8) and epilogue (Deut 34:6) of Deuteronomy; the conquest narratives (Josh 4:9; 5:9; 6:25; 7:26; 8:28, 29; 9:27; 10:27) *and* inheritance lists (Josh 13:13; 14:14; 15:63; 16:10) of Joshua; the prologue (Judg 1:21, 26), heroic tales (Judg 6:24; 10:4; 15:19) and epilogue (Judg 18:12) of Judges; the "Ark Narrative" (1 Sam 5:5; 6:18; 2 Sam 6:8), "History of David's Rise" (1 Sam 27:6; 30:25; 2 Sam 4:3) and "Succession Narrative" (2 Sam 18:18) of Samuel; and the "Acts of Solomon" (1 Kgs 8:8; 9:13, 21; 10:12), prophetic cycles (1 Kgs 12:19; 2 Kgs 2:2), and "Chronicles of the Kings of Israel/Judah" (2 Kgs 8:22; 14:7; 16:16) of Kings.[6] Certainly there were later additions to this history, as even Noth argued.[7] Moreover, it is evident that many of the sources making up the DH underwent their own redactional histories prior to being incorporated into Dtr's larger work, again as Noth acknowledged.[8] That is, the conclusion that "until this day" reflects a unified perspective across the DH does not discount the evidence for redactional complexity within these texts.[9] Still, this unity argues against excising large narrative strands or blocks from Dtr's original history.

---

6. For the identification of these narrative units, see chapter 3. In truth, it is difficult to determine which narratives derive from priestly/prophetic (e.g., the Samuel or Elijah-Elisha material) and which from royal sources (e.g., the Chronicles of the Kings of Judah). I am inclined to ascribe most narratives to priestly/prophetic sources or to Dtr, perhaps as his own elaboration on annalistic sources (see the discussion below and in the conclusion). The prophetic provenance of most narratives helps to explain the open criticisms of the monarchy, which would hardly be characteristic of royal annals. The prophets, moreover, would have a vested interest in preserving stories about their interactions with, as well as the abuses/sins of, Israel's kings. This understanding finds support in the Chronicler's list of sources for the monarchic period (1 Chr 29:29; 2 Chr 9:29; 12:15; 13:22; 16:11; 20:34; 24:27; 25:26; 26:22; 27:7; 28:26; 32:32; 33:19; 35:26–27; 36:8), much of which are prophetic records. For a recent defense of the authenticity of these citations, see A. F. Rainey, "The Chronicler and His Sources—Historical and Geographical" in *The Chronicler as Historian*, ed. M. P. Graham, K. G. Hoglund, and S. L. McKenzie (JSOTSup 238; Sheffield: England, 1997) 30–72. Even if the Chronicler's attribution of sources to prophets is secondarily derived, that the criticisms of monarchy in the DH find their origins among priestly/prophetic circles is a reasonable hypothesis. For a fuller discussion of the Chronicler's sources, see G. N. Knoppers, *1 Chronicles 1–9: A New Translation with Introduction and Commentary* (AB 12; New York: Doubleday, 2004) 123–26.

7. I am in general agreement with the analyses of Cross (*CMHE*, 285–87), with the refinements of Friedman (*The Exile and Biblical Narrative*), Nelson (*The Double Redaction*) and others, as to the content and character of the additions to Dtr's original history. However, certainty in these matters—as in so many areas related to the redaction of biblical texts—is difficult to attain and, therefore, the determination of what might be primary and secondary to Dtr's original DH merits continual reevaluation.

8. Noth's conclusions in this regard remain sound even if he did not trace this prehistory. See, e.g., the criticisms of D. A. Knight, *Rediscovering the Traditions of Israel: The Development of the Traditio-Historical Research of the Old Testament, with Special Consideration of Scandinavian Contributions* (SBLDS 9; Missoula, MT: Scholars Press, 1975), esp. 162–63.

9. See, e.g., the works of Smend, Dietrich, and Viejola discussed in the previous chapter.

The implications of these findings for the present state of the field cannot be overstated, especially for those studies that assign significant blocks of material in the DH to post-Dtr redactional levels. Van Seters, for example, though admitting that some discrepancies in the DH are due to Dtr's toleration of inconsistencies in his sources, argues that others derive from later additions to his work. One such "addition," as we noted above, is the Court History (2 Sam 2:8–4:12; 9–20 and 1 Kings 1–2).[10] Yet our phrase appears twice within this corpus (2 Sam 4:3; 18:18), suggesting that the Court History was, indeed, originally part of Dtr's work. And, in fact, 2 Sam 4:3 reflects Dtr's interest in the presence of foreigners in Israel (Beerothites in Gittaim; cf. Josh 13:13; 15:63; 16:10; Judg 1:21; 1 Kgs 9:21; etc.), and 2 Sam 18:18 reflects Dtr's interest in stone memorials (Absalom's Pillar; cf. Josh 4:9; 7:26; 8:29; 1 Sam 6:18; etc.). Yet, beyond these more general connections—which, after all, could be attributed to anyone wanting to highlight such matters—there are specific reasons for ascribing "until this day" in these two passages to Dtr.

First, "until this day" in both passages appears in redactional material—a phenomenon observed repeatedly in connection with Dtr's use of the phrase in the DH.[11] Hertzberg, for example, rightly characterizes 2 Sam 4:3 as "a marginal note of a later period in the history of the text inserted into the narrative, whose course [it] interrupt[s]."[12] Similarly, McCarter correctly observes that 2 Sam 18:18 is "a late redactional notice introduced to identify a monument well known in the time of the redactor who added it."[13]

Yet, more than their shared status as redactional comments, these two notices share specific connections with other uses of "until this day" in the DH. For example, the Beerothites of 2 Sam 4:3, who dwell among Israel "until this day," are certainly to be associated with the Beerothites of Josh 9:17, who deceive Joshua into making a covenant and who, as a result, serve as forced laborers "until this day" (Josh 9:27). That "until this day" in Josh 9:27 is followed immediately by another of Dtr's characteristic redactional comments ("at the place he will choose") affirms Dtr's interest in these Beerothites, especially in their service at the temple. Moreover, that this whole pericope fulfills Deuteronomic law (Deut 20:10–15) in how to

---

10. Van Seters, *In Search of History*, 277–91.
11. See, esp., Childs's analysis in chapter 1 and my own analysis in chapter 3 concerning the redactional nature of "until this day."
12. Hertzberg, *Samuel*, 264. The full quotation is: "The one and a half verses are, in fact, a marginal note of a later period in the history of the text inserted into the narrative, whose course they interrupt." Cf. McCarter (*2 Samuel*, 127), who says of this same verse and a half: "This parenthesis may have been inserted by a later hand." See also Caquot and de Robert, *Samuel*, 394.
13. McCarter, *2 Samuel*, 407. See also Caquot and de Robert, *Samuel*, 553.

treat those conquered from distant lands (even if, in this case, it is falsified) further affirms that Dtr has an interest in these Beerothites as forced laborers (וַיִּהְיוּ לְךָ לָמַס וַעֲבָדוּךָ; Deut 20:11; cf. Josh 16:10; 1 Kgs 9:21).

Another indication that Dtr is the source of "until this day" in 2 Sam 4:3 is its presence in the fuller phrase וַיִּהְיוּ־שָׁם גָּרִים עַד הַיּוֹם הַזֶּה. The only other occurrences of וַיִּהְיוּ־שָׁם עַד הַיּוֹם הַזֶּה anywhere in the Bible are Josh 4:9 and 1 Kgs 8:8, both of which relate to "the Ark of the Covenant of YHWH" and belong to Dtr. In the first instance, the stones commemorating the Ark's role in providing dry passage for the Israelites "are there until this day." In the second, the poles of the ark, which protrude from the Holy of Holies, "are there until this day." The only other use of וַיִּהְיוּ־שָׁם to describe a continued state of being is found in Deut 10:5,[14] which, not coincidentally, also refers to the Ark:

וָאֵפֶן וָאֵרֵד מִן־הָהָר וָאָשִׂם אֶת־הַלֻּחֹת בָּאָרוֹן אֲשֶׁר עָשִׂיתִי
וַיִּהְיוּ שָׁם כַּאֲשֶׁר צִוַּנִי יְהוָה

> And I turned and descended from the mountain, and I placed the tablets into the Ark that I had made. And they are there as YHWH commanded me.

That the statement "they are there as YHWH commanded me" belongs to the historian seems clear, for it not only reflects Dtr's interest in the Ark, and more particularly his interest in the Ark as container for the law tablets (cf. Deut 31:24–26 and 1 Kgs 8:9, 21),[15] but it immediately precedes an insertion into Moses' speech (Deut 10:6–9) which itself contains material we have already seen derives from Dtr and reflects his specific concerns; namely, the Levites' role in bearing "the Ark of the Covenant of YHWH" and their inheritance rights. These connections are too specific and many to be coincidental. Rather, they reveal a patterned use of our phrase in the DH, making the assignation of "until this day" in 2 Sam 4:3 to Dtr the most reasonable assessment of the evidence.

Second Sam 18:18, then, by its very association with the Court History, should be considered part of Dtr's preexilic history. Yet, more connects 2 Sam 18:18 to Dtr than just its relationship to 2 Sam 4:3 and the larger Court History. A "heap of stones" (גַּל־אֲבָנִים) is erected only three times in the Hebrew Bible, two of which receive Dtr's affirmation that they persist "until this day": the burial place of Achan (Josh 7:26) and the burial place

---

14. The only other occurrences of וַיִּהְיוּ שָׁם in the Bible refer to historically past moments: "And the three sons of Zeruiah were there" (2 Sam 2:18); "And they were with David three days" (1 Chr 12:40); "And [Naomi and her family] were there (i.e., Moab)" (Ruth 1:2).

15. Nelson, *The Double Redaction*, 123–24.

of the king of Ai (Josh 8:29). The third גַּל־אֲבָנִים is the burial place of Absalom:

> וַיִּקְחוּ אֶת־אַבְשָׁלוֹם וַיַּשְׁלִיכוּ אֹתוֹ בַיַּעַר אֶל־הַפַּחַת הַגָּדוֹל
> וַיַּצִּבוּ עָלָיו גַּל־אֲבָנִים גָּדוֹל מְאֹד
>
> And they took Absalom and cast him into a big pit in the forest. And they piled upon him a very large pile of stones.
>
> 2 Sam 18:17

The affinities between 2 Sam 18:17 and Josh 8:29 are apparent enough:

> וַיֹּרִידוּ אֶת־נִבְלָתוֹ מִן־הָעֵץ וַיַּשְׁלִיכוּ אוֹתָהּ אֶל־פֶּתַח שַׁעַר הָעִיר
> וַיָּקִימוּ עָלָיו גַּל־אֲבָנִים גָּדוֹל עַד הַיּוֹם הַזֶּה
>
> And they brought his corpse down from the tree and cast it into the opening of the gate of the city. And they erected over him a large pile of stones until this day.

However, it is not Absalom's burial place that is said to persist "until this day," but his pillar described in the next verse:

> וְאַבְשָׁלֹם לָקַח וַיַּצֶּב־לוֹ בְחַיָּו אֶת־מַצֶּבֶת אֲשֶׁר בְּעֵמֶק־הַמֶּלֶךְ
> כִּי אָמַר אֵין־לִי בֵן בַּעֲבוּר הַזְכִּיר שְׁמִי וַיִּקְרָא לַמַּצֶּבֶת עַל־שְׁמוֹ
> וַיִּקָּרֵא לָהּ יַד אַבְשָׁלֹם עַד הַיּוֹם הַזֶּה
>
> And during his lifetime Absalom took and erected for himself the pillar that is in the King's Valley, for he said, "I do not have a son to cause my name to be remembered." And he called the pillar by his name. And it is called "Absalom's monument" until this day.
>
> Sam 18:18

The historian, when confronted with more than one account of a memorial to Absalom, chose to verify the better known (and more southern) of the two: the pillar of Absalom in the King's Valley (perhaps just outside of Jerusalem[16]), as opposed to a pile of stones "in the forest of Ephraim"[17] (which, according to the narrative, was located in Gilead east of the Jordan; cf. 17:24, 26; 18:6). This is consistent with Dtr's editorial activity elsewhere: he includes more than one tradition about a matter when he has them,

---

16. On the possible locations of the King's Valley, see chapter 2.

17. The precise location of the forest of Ephraim—whether it is east or west of the Jordan (or both, as suggested by Josh 17:14–18)—is unknown, as is the question of whether or not the "Ephraim" of 2 Sam 13:23 should be understood as "Ophrah" (as suggested by McCarter).

despite the tensions this introduces into his history.[18] As McCarter has characterized this particular case: "The implied connection between 'Abishalom's Monument,' obviously a memorial stela of some kind, and the 'large pile of stones' of v. 17 is spurious—indeed, it is silly." Nevertheless, that a similar historiographic intent and methodology underlies the use of "until this day" in all three cases of גַּל־אֲבָנִים is clear.[19]

In light of the above evidence, it is difficult to follow Van Seters in maintaining that the Court History was secondarily added to the DH by a post-Dtr redactor. This requires us to postulate a development of the text whereby this postexilic redactor (or an even later one) secondarily added to an already secondary Court History redactional comments in which he employed "until this day" in the same manner and reflecting the same interests as Dtr elsewhere in his history. Such a model is too complicated to commend itself.

The same could be said of Van Seters's analysis of other units within the DH. For example, Van Seters ascribes the inheritance lists of Joshua to a post-Dtr redaction of the DH.[20] However, "until this day" appears four times within these lists in ways that connect it specifically to other uses of the phrase within this history. Thus, "until this day" in Josh 13:13 is followed immediately by the notice concerning the inheritance rights of the Levites (". . . until this day. Only to the tribe of Levi he did not give an inheritance. The offerings of YHWH the God of Israel are his inheritance, as he said to him" [Josh 13:13b–14]), which finds expression elsewhere in connection with our phrase (". . . until this day. Therefore, Levi does not have a portion and an inheritance with his brothers. YHWH is his inheritance, as YHWH your God said to him" [Deut 10:8b–9]) and which reflects Dtr's interest in the rights and responsibilities of the Levitical priests (Deut 18:1–2). In Josh 14:14, "until this day" is followed by the Deuteronomistic phrase "because he followed fully after YHWH," which reflects Dtr's concern for wholehearted devotion to the God of Israel (see, e.g., Deut 1:36; Josh 14:8, 9; 1 Kgs 11:6) and mirrors a redactional technique

---

18. See, e.g., the two accounts of Gideon building an altar to YHWH at Ophrah (Judges 6), only one of which receives the notice "until this day" (Judg 6:24).

19. Note, also, Caqout and de Robert's (*Les livres de Samuel*, 554) suggestion that Dtr's explanation of Absalom's pillar reflects the Deuteronomistic polemic against מַצֵּבוֹת. For similar observations, see R. A. Carlson, *David, The Chosen King: A Traditio-Historical Approach to the Second Book of Samuel* (Stockholm: Almqvist & Wiksell, 1964) 138, 187. Such an explanation may apply to many of the stone memorials said to exist "until this day": Dtr makes plain that these structures fulfill a commemorative, not a sacrificial, role. For further discussion, see the conclusion.

20. Van Seters, *In Search of History*, 322–53. Noth, it should be said, did not include these lists as part of Dtr's original work, though he admitted, "the language and attitude of this section are very akin to Dtr" (*The Deuteronomistic History*, 40).

seen elsewhere, where Dtr follows the phrase immediately with his own material (see, e.g., Josh 9:27: "... until this day at the place he will choose"). In Josh 15:63, "until this day" attests to the continuing presence of Jebusites in Jerusalem, which receives mention again by Dtr in the book of Judges (1:21) and which reflects his interest in the use of non-Israelite forced labor during his day, particularly in connection with the temple (Josh 9:27; 1 Kgs 9:21). In Josh 16:10, "until this day" makes explicit mention of this institution (מַס־עֹבֵד), which again finds expression elsewhere in the DH (1 Kgs 9:21) and which borrows its idiom from Deuteronomic law (יִהְיוּ לְךָ לָמַס וַעֲבָדוּךָ; Deut 20:11]). This is not to say that these inheritance lists were not secondarily added to the narratives of which they are now a part. In fact, they no doubt had a separate existence prior to Dtr's inclusion of them into his history. However, that it was Dtr who included them is difficult to deny given the interrelationship among the uses of "until this day" in these lists and other parts of the DH.[21]

Not only does the evidence of "until this day" provide a necessary corrective to studies that date the DH to the late-exilic or postexilic periods and assign large units to post-Dtr redactional levels, it is also useful for refining those studies that, while arguing for the preexilic provenance and overall unity of the DH, determine that various strands within this larger work are secondary to Dtr's original enterprise. A case in point is S. McKenzie's important work on the books of Kings.[22] Although McKenzie agrees that most of what is now in the DH was present in its first edition (which he originally argued belonged to the preexlic period, though he now dates it to the early exilic period[23]), he argues that the Elijah-Elisha material was part of a post-Dtr redaction of the text. As "until this day" appears twice in this material, a closer look at his argument is in order.

One passage that McKenzie assigns to a post-Dtr redactor is 2 Kings 2. This chapter describes, among other things, Elisha's healing of the waters at Jericho, a condition that we are informed persists "until this day." Regarding the Elijah and Elisha narratives in general, McKenzie writes, "the absence of Dtr's remarks within them contrasts with his use of sources elsewhere and is a strong indication that he did not edit them."[24] In addition to an absence of Deuteronomistic redactional material, McKenzie

---

21. See, also, G. J. Wenham ("The Deuteronomic Theology of the Book of Joshua," *JBL* 90 [1971] 140–48), who similarly argues for the inclusion of the inheritance lists as part of Dtr's original work.

22. S. McKenzie, *The Trouble with Kings*.

23. McKenzie previously located this first edition in the time of Josiah, but he has since argued for an exilic date ("The Trouble with Kingship," in *Israel Constructs Its History*, 286–314), though deriving from Judah (specifically, Mizpah) and just after the destruction of Jerusalem (ca. 580 B.C.E.).

24. McKenzie, *The Trouble with Kings*, 148.

argues that these narratives show signs of literary "unevenness" when compared to the surrounding narratives, suggesting that they have been added secondarily to Dtr's history.

First, it should be said that the relative absence of Dtr editing within a work does not mean that it was not part of Dtr's original history. It has long been observed that the books of Samuel show relatively light Dtr editing, but this is not an adequate reason to excise the bulk of this corpus from the original DH.[25]

Second, "unevenness" depends on one's perspective. For while McKenzie believes that both the Elijah and Elisha material has been placed awkwardly into the DH, Van Seters argues that the Elijah material is well integrated and reflects "the Dtr concern about the incursion of the Canaanite cults and the Dtr aversion for the house of Ahab."[26]

Third, and related to the previous point, the "unevenness" of the kind McKenzie describes is to be expected, especially given Dtr's incorporation of disparate sources into his history. Royal annals and prophetic tales—not too unlike royalty and prophets—do not always mix well. Nor, in fact, do royal annals always mix well with each other. Similar unevenness is in evidence throughout the DH as the result of Dtr's attempt to synchronize the lives of northern and southern kings. Thus, at one moment, king PN of Judah "lies down with his fathers," and at the next he is in his Nth year of reign and involved in political intrigues or military exploits.

First Kings 15, which McKenzie assigns to Dtr's original history, is a good case in point: In 1 Kgs 15:24, Asa of Judah "lies down with his fathers." In v. 28, however, Asa is alive again and in his third year of reign. Then, in v. 32, he is at war with Baasha, king of Israel, who, in turn, dies in Asa's twenty-sixth year in 16:8. Of course, such staggering of King's reigns is standard fare in the DH. Therefore, when McKenzie argues that the Elisha material fits awkwardly in its context because "The account in 3:4–27 includes Jehoshaphat, whose reign has already been closed by Dtr (1 Kgs 22:45–50)" and "Elisha's last oracle to Jehoash (13:14–19) and posthumous miracle (vv 20–21) are recounted after Dtr's formulaic report of Jehoash's death and burial (13:13)," one is left unconvinced that these are indications of a post-Dtr redaction.[27]

Finally, based on the present study, "until this day" *is* Dtr's contribution to the passage that McKenzie seeks. As support for this, our phrase is followed by the phrase "according to the word of Elisha which he spoke," כִּדְבַר אֱלִישָׁע אֲשֶׁר דִּבֶּר, which parallels Dtr's characteristic way of high-

---

25. See, e.g., the discussions of McCarter, *1 Samuel*, 15–17; and A. Campbell, *1 Samuel* (FOTL 7; Grand Rapids, MI: Eerdmans, 2003) 331–32.

26. Van Seters, *In Search of History*, 305.

27. McKenzie, *The Trouble with Kings*, 97.

130  *The Time, Place, and Purpose of the Deuteronomistic History*

lighting a fulfilled prophecy and reflects his interest in the efficacy of the prophetic word.[28] This interest, as noted earlier, shows up elsewhere in connection with our phrase—indeed, it appears in connection with this same city (Josh 6:25–26; 1 Kgs 16:34).[29] Given these several lines of converging evidence, it seems best to assign 2 Kgs 2:22, as well as the story to which it refers (at least 2 Kgs 2:19–22), and the story that presupposes it (all of 2 Kings 2), to Dtr's original history.

The second passage McKenzie attributes to a post-Dtr redactor is 2 Kgs 10:18–28, which describes Jehu's destruction of the temple and altar of Baal in Samaria. McKenzie gives two reasons for assigning this material to a post-Dtr redactor. First, Jehu's defeat of the "prophets of Baal" has affinities with Elijah's similar victory at Mount Carmel (1 Kings 18). Since the Mount Carmel episode belongs to a post-Dtr redactor, so must this. Second, the Deuteronomistic summary of Jehu's reign does not mention Jehu's destruction of the temple of Baal. Since Dtr would not fail to mention such an important event, especially in view of his interests in the destruction of such sites, this episode must have been added secondarily to Dtr's original DH.

As we observed in chapter 2, 2 Kgs 10:18–28 is one of only two places where "until this day" is used to testify to *individual* objects in the north.[30] In chapter 3, we observed that this was not coincidence, as both objects said to persist "until this day" in the north mark the locations of former places of Baal worship—a demonstrably Deuteronomistic concern (see, e.g., Deut 7:1–5; 12:1–7; Judg 2:1–5) that is described in characteristically Deuteronomistic language (נָתַץ). Beyond this evidence, there are specific textual reasons for including this passage in Dtr's original historical work.

We have already addressed McKenzie's general argument for assigning the Elijah material to a post-Dtr redactor ("unevenness"). Regarding McKenzie's second argument: the summary of Jehu's reign does, in fact, mention his destruction of the temple of Baal, only in the more general statement immediately following the event: "And (or "Thus") Jehu destroyed Baal worship in Israel" (2 Kgs 10:28). This raises what is the central issue for McKenzie's analysis—where to start Dtr's summary. McKenzie starts it with v. 29, which then leads him to the conclusion that Dtr's summary does not mention Jehu's destruction of Baal's temple. Yet, v. 29 clearly assumes the presence of v. 28, as is demonstrated by the use of רַק

---

28. Cf., e.g., 1 Kgs 14:18; 15:29; 16:12, 34; etc.

29. As noted in chapter 3, Joshua's curse on Jericho not only participates in the pattern of prophecy and fulfillment manifest throughout the DH but it also prepares the ground, quite literally, for Elisha's miracle. For similar observations regarding the importance of Joshua's curse on Jericho and its fulfillment as part of Dtr's emphasis on the credibility of the prophetic word, see M. A. Sweeney, "Hiel's Re-Establishment of Jericho," 104–15.

30. See also Judg 6:24 (Gideon's altar to YHWH at Ophrah).

("only") to introduce v. 29: "*Only* Jehu did not turn away from the sins of Jeroboam son of Nebat, by which he caused Israel to sin: the golden calves at Bethel and Dan." Without v. 28, this contrast is meaningless. In fact, whenever רַק is used by Dtr in regnal formulae, the preceding statement being contrasted belongs to Dtr or, at minimum, is presumed by Dtr. Thus, regarding Jehoash—the only other king besides Jehu to have destroyed a temple of Baal—Dtr reports:

וַיַּעַשׂ יְהוֹאָשׁ הַיָּשָׁר בְּעֵינֵי יְהוָה כָּל־יָמָיו אֲשֶׁר הוֹרָהוּ יְהוֹיָדָע הַכֹּהֵן
רַק הַבָּמוֹת לֹא־סָרוּ עוֹד הָעָם מְזַבְּחִים וּמְקַטְּרִים בַּבָּמוֹת

And Jehoash did right in the eyes of YHWH all the days of his life, as the priest Jehoiada instructed him. Only the high places were not removed; the people still sacrificed and burnt incense at the high places.

2 Kgs 12:3–4

And again, in Dtr's appraisal of Amaziah, we encounter רַק twice:

וַיַּעַשׂ הַיָּשָׁר בְּעֵינֵי יְהוָה רַק לֹא כְּדָוִד אָבִיו כְּכֹל אֲשֶׁר־עָשָׂה
יוֹאָשׁ אָבִיו עָשָׂה: רַק הַבָּמוֹת לֹא־סָרוּ עוֹד הָעָם מְזַבְּחִים
וּמְקַטְּרִים בַּבָּמוֹת

And he did what was right in the eyes of YHWH, only not like his father David; according to all that his father Joash did, he did. Only the high places were not removed; the people still sacrificed and burnt incense at the high places.

2 Kgs 14:3–4

And so on (cf. 2 Kgs 15:3–4, 34–35).[31]

Thus, contrary to McKenzie's analysis, v. 28 belongs to (or is presumed by) Dtr and, by implication, Dtr's summary includes a reference to Jehu ridding Israel of Baal worship. And this should not surprise us, since this provides another example where Dtr follows "until this day" with his own material (cf. Josh 6:26; 8:29; 9:27; 13:13; 14:14; etc.) and where he expresses his own interests: in this case, the destruction of Canaanite cultic sites (see esp. Judg 6:24).[32]

Other studies could be put to similar scrutiny.[33] Again, this is not to

---

31. For this use of רַק as an indication of Dtr's editorial activity, see W. B. Barrick, "On the 'Removal of High Places,'" 257–59; Smend, "Das Gesetz und die Völker," 494, 499.
32. Again, cf. Van Seters's remarks that this material reflects "the Dtr concern about the incursion of the Canaanite cults and the Dtr aversion for the house of Ahab" (*In Search of History*, 305).
33. Consider, e.g., the recent works of S. Frolov (*The Turn of the Cycle: 1 Samuel 1–8 in Synchronic and Diachronic Perspectives* [BZAW 342; Berlin/New York: de Gruyter, 2004]), who proposes that 1 Samuel 1–8 was added secondarily to the DH after the exile, though "until this

deny that these analyses provide important insights into the redactional histories of particular texts. McKenzie's observations concerning the unevenness of the Elijah-Elisha materials in the DH, for example, may, in the end, be accurate, especially if we postulate an earlier royal history or record to which these narratives were secondarily added. However, the view that this unevenness indicates *post*-Dtr additions to the DH needs to be reconsidered in view of the evidence of "until this day," which indicates that these materials, even if they once existed independently, have been integrated by Dtr into his preexilic history for his own particular purposes.

## THE NUMBER OF PREEXILIC REDACTIONS OF THE DEUTERONOMISTIC HISTORY

The above discussion naturally raises the question of whether there existed a history prior to the Josianic edition. Specifically, what do we make of those studies arguing for an earlier royal (Weippert, Halpern and Vanderhooft) or prophetic history or record (Campbell, McCarter)?

One piece of evidence from our study that might be thought to point to a pre-Josianic edition of the DH is the use of "until this day" in 1 Kgs 12:19 to describe the continuing rebellion of the north:[34]

וַיִּפְשְׁעוּ יִשְׂרָאֵל בְּבֵית דָּוִד עַד הַיּוֹם הַזֶּה

And Israel has rebelled against the house of David until this day.

At first glance this notice seems to suggest that the north still exists as a political entity and, therefore, that "this day" refers to a period before the Assyrian conquest. This is possible. However, beyond the evidence already presented for the unified socio-political perspective reflected in the use of

---

day" appears twice in this corpus in connection with "the Ark of the Covenant of YHWH" (1 Sam 5:5; 6:18), a major concern of the preexilic Deuteronomist (see the discussion on the Ark of the Covenant above and in chapter 3); P. Guillaume (*Waiting for Josiah: The Judges* [JSOTSup 385; London/New York: Clark, 2004]), who assigns a number of passages in Judges to postJosianic redactions (some as late as 150 B.C.E.) where "until this day" appears with clear associations to other uses in the DH (e.g., Judg 1:21 [cf. Josh 15:63]; Judg 10:4 [cf. Deut 3:14]); and S. Otto (*Jehu, Elia und Elisa: Die Erzählung von der Jehu-Revolution und die Komposition der Elia-Elisa-Erzählungen* [BWANT 152; Stuttgart: W. Kolhammer, 2001]), who reconstructs seven redactional levels in the Elijah-Elisha material based largely upon the premise that Dtr could not countenance inconsistencies in his history (*contra* the evidence of "until this day") and assigns passages where "until this day" appears to divergent groups in the exilic and postexilic periods, even when its use reflects similar interests elsewhere in the DH (e.g., 2 Kgs 2:22 [cf. Josh 6:25–26); 2 Kgs 10:27 [cf. Judg 6:24]).

34. See, e.g., W. Schniedewind (*How the Bible Became a Book*, 79), who assigns this notice to the reign of Hezekiah, though without taking into account other uses of the phrase in Kings or elsewhere.

"until this day" across the DH, there are several reasons for assigning this particular notice to Dtr.

First, we have already observed that the last uses of our phrase in the DH (2 Kgs 17:23, 34, and 41), though deriving from a time after the fall of Israel, still present the north as the inheritors of the promises (and problems) of the old north.[35] That is, the one employing "until this day" in the DH understands (and, as we will see momentarily, is ideologically committed to defending) that a connection exists between the northerners before and after the Assyrian conquest.

Second, assigning "until this day" in 1 Kgs 12:19 to the time of Hezekiah does not really resolve any problems, since those arguing for a Hezekian edition of the DH place its composition *after the fall of the north*, when northern traditions would have had opportunity to be merged with southern traditions. Therefore, to ascribe "until this day" in this isolated case to the time of Hezekiah does not make the statement any more true than postulating a Josianic date. In either case, the north has fallen.

Third, and related to the previous two points, the only other notice of rebellion against Judah "until this day" is Edom's (2 Kgs 8:22), which Cogan and Tadmor have convincingly argued reflects Dtr[1]'s interest in the Negev and Red Sea coast due to Judahite territorial expansion in this area during the reign of Josiah.[36] The notice concerning the north's continued rebellion should be interpreted in the same way, only in the opposite direction: it reflects Judahite interest in *northern* territorial claims.[37] In the case of the north, however, these claims are motivated not only by political interests but by theological ones (inextricable spheres for Dtr). Specifically, just as Israel's rebellion against the throne of Judah persists "until this day" (1 Kgs 12:19), so Israel's rebellion against YHWH persists "until this day" (2 Kgs 17:34, 41). Both conditions require northern expansion: one to regain the boundaries of the former Davidic state, the other to reinstate centralized worship as dictated in the book of Deuteronomy.[38] Thus, "until this day"

---

35. See the discussion of these verses in chapter 3. See also the one occurrence of עַד־עָתָּה when not in direct speech (2 Kgs 13:23), which likely derives from the historian and which presents the north as still viable, though having experienced significant loss: "And YHWH was gracious to them and had compassion on them. He turned toward them on account of his covenant with Abraham, Isaac and Jacob, and he was unwilling to destroy them, and he has not cast them from his presence even until now."

36. Cogan and Tadmor, *2 Kings*, 96. See the discussion of "Judahite-Edomite Interaction" in chapter 3.

37. Cf. Dtr's interest in other northern sites, such as Havvoth Jair (Deut 3:14; Judg 10:4), Geshur and Maacah (Josh 13:14), and the Cabul (1 Kgs 9:13). This interest in northern expansion during Josiah's reign should not be confused with success in this regard, especially for the far northern regions.

38. It is no accident that these two purposes—both highlighted by "until this day"—align so well with the themes identified by Cross as directing the preexilic Deuteronomistic History.

in 1 Kgs 12:19 not only reconciles with a late seventh-century B.C.E. date for the DH, it further establishes it.

Having said this, I am persuaded by the arguments for (re)new(ed) literary output during the reign of Hezekiah, and the arguments for an initial history ending with this king are also compelling.[39] No doubt this output was due, in part, to the infusion of northern royal and prophetic traditions into the south as a result of the Assyrian conquest of Israel (as will be discussed in more detail below). Moreover, the redactional nature of "until this day" indicates that the Josianic Dtr is working with preexisting written records. However, whether some of these sources had already been combined into a royal (Weippert, Halpern and Vanderhooft) or prophetic (Campbell, McCarter) history when Dtr inherited them is difficult to say based solely on the evidence of "until this day."

Thus, while the evidence provided by our study does not preclude an earlier royal or prophetic history—and may even point in this direction given that "until this day" has been added secondarily to preexisting written traditions—the evidence of "until this day" allows us to speak confidently only of a Josianic edition, which was later updated in the exilic period.[40]

# THE PURPOSE OF THE DEUTERONOMISTIC HISTORY

Once the preexilic provenance and overall scope of the first edition of the DH has been determined, we are in a better position to address the purpose of this work.

---

39. I have in mind especially the work of Weippert, "Die 'deuteronomistischen' Beurteilungen"; Halpern and Vanderhooft, "The Editions of Kings in the 7th–6th Centuries B.C.E."; and Eynikel, *The Reform of King Josiah*, though I am partial to Provan's (*Hezekiah and the Books of Kings*) view that this Hezekian history may have been compiled during the reign of Josiah.

40. See the fuller discussion of these matters in the conclusion. Presently I am leaning toward the view that this updating took place shortly after the fall of Jerusalem, likely in Judea, perhaps at Mizpah (ca. 580 B.C.E.). This was roughly Noth's and Jepsen's view, though they understood this to be the provenance of the original composition of the DH. See, more recently, McKenzie, "The Trouble with Kingship" in *Israel Constructs Its History*, 286–314. Thus, I am in general agreement with McKenzie on the origin of the Mizpah material, only I would argue this material derives from Dtr[2], not Dtr[1]—though I am of the opinion that these redactions derive from the same person or group responsible for the original DH. For the importance of Mizpah following the demise of Jerusalem, see most recently O. Lipschits, *The Fall and Rise of Jerusalem: Judah under Babylonian Rule* (Winona Lake, IN: Eisenbrauns, 2005). See also H. J. Stipp, "Gedalja und die Kolonie von Mizpa," *ZAR* 6 (2000) 155–71. For the Babylonian administration of Judah during this period, see D. S. Vanderhooft, *The Neo-Babylonian Empire and Babylon in the Latter Prophets* (HSM 59; Altanta: Scholars Press, 1999).

## 1. The Deuteronomistic History as "Propaganda"

Since the original version of the DH was written prior to the exile, the optimism surrounding the Davidic dynasty can no longer be ascribed to exilic messianism (*contra* von Rad, Van Seters, etc.) or to political agendas from the Persian or Hellenistic periods (*contra* Davies, Thompson, etc.), but must derive from actual events in preexilic Israel. As has been argued by a number of scholars and confirmed by the present study, the reason for this optimism during Dtr's day is Josiah.[41] Thus, *one* purpose behind this history might be said to be "propaganda" in support of Josiah's reforms. However, an important caveat must be introduced here. If the *primary* purpose underlying the DH is propaganda, then whoever commissioned its writing (Josiah?) hired the wrong person(s).[42] Put another way: If the DH is propaganda, then it is a complicated piece of propaganda with a message that has taken over two thousand years to decipher—and still we debate its meaning. At one moment the monarchy is being condemned as a rejection of YHWH's authority (1 Sam 8:6–9), and at the next David is promised an enduring fiefdom (2 Sam 7:5–17). At another moment the people's waywardness is embodied in the refrain: "There was no king in Israel, the people did what was right in their own eyes" (Judg 17:6; 21:25) and at the next Israel's apostasy—an apostasy that even exceeds the period of the judges—is blamed on Israel's kings (1 Kgs 12:26–33; 2 Kgs 23:26–27). The original audience would have fared little better than we in understanding, let alone being persuaded by, this "propaganda." That is, propaganda is an ill-suited term for the DH. While Dtr certainly supports Josiah and his reforms, he is not beholden to the king or the monarchy in any absolute sense.

Yet, herein lies the answer to what is to my mind one of the main purposes behind the compilation of Israel's traditions.

---

41. This is not to say that the promise to David is Josianic, as this tradition no doubt had its roots in ancient Judean royal ideology. However, the inclusion of this promise in the DH, as well as the use of David as the measure for southern kings, should be traced to Dtr and his enthusiasm for the Josianic reforms.

42. The recent proposal of M. Leuchter (*Josiah's Reform and Jeremiah's Scroll: Historical Calamity and Prophetic Response* [HBM 6; Sheffield: Sheffield Phoenix Press, 2006], esp. 50–86), that the DH represents an attempt to persuade northern priests (specifically, Shilonites) of the merit of Josiah's rule and reforms, would help to account for the inclusion of criticisms of monarchy, even in a work sponsored by monarchy. Moreover, the inclusion of these criticisms might serve the additional purpose of underscoring Josiah's righteousness in comparison to earlier monarchs, making him worthy of such loyalty from these priests, whereas previous kings were not. However, it is also likely that the criticism of monarchy reflected a period shortly after Josiah's reign, and that the culmination of the history in Josiah served the purpose of persuading a later monarch to follow in Josiah's footsteps (see the conclusion.)

## 2. The Deuteronomistic History as "History"

While the *impetus* behind the DH may have been Josiah's reforms, one of the main purposes of the DH was to produce just that—a history.[43] Certainly Dtr framed this account in terms of his own ideology, his own view of how things work and of how things came to be as they are. Still, as scholars working on the problem of historiography have long noted, this is true of any historian—ancient or modern.[44] Concerning the DH in particular, M. Brettler rightly observes, ". . . to the extent that the Deuteronomist honestly believed his ideology and, like all of us, was simply viewing the past from the perspective of his present, he was writing history like all other historians."[45] It may even be argued that Dtr is more forthcoming with his agenda than most historians—ancient or modern. The criteria by which Dtr evaluates kings, for example, leave little doubt about where this historian stands on religious/cultic matters. However, that a historical impulse informs Dtr's writing is manifest both in his citation of sources (e.g., the Acts of Solomon, the Chronicles of the Kings of Israel/Judah, etc.) and in his verification of events by appealing to extant objects and institutions said to derive from these events. This is especially true of the book of Joshua, where we find numerous appeals to stone memorials and ancient ruins in order to substantiate Dtr's received traditions. As noted earlier, similar references can be found in the works of Greek and Roman historians.[46]

There are differences as well, however. Herodotus, for example, will pass judgment on a tradition, even expressing his incredulity despite the presence of confirmatory evidence (e.g., a monument, cultic practice, etc.).[47] Conversely, Dtr does not privilege us with his opinion on these matters. In fact, he avoids first person discourse altogether. Yet, that Dtr was aware of

---

43. It has been argued by some (see, e.g., E. A. Kauf, "From History to Interpretation," in *The Fabric of History: Text, Artifact and Israel's Past*, ed. D. Edelman [JSOTSup 127; Sheffield: JSOT Press, 1991] 26–64) that the genre "history writing" is anachronistic for this period. Even if this is granted (certainly the formal category is later, but this is a separate issue from how to define what Dtr, or Herodotus for that matter, may have been doing), Dtr sought to give Israel "an account of its past" (following Huizinga's definition of history writing)—even if affected by his own perspective (see the discussion below).

44. See, e.g., Van Seters, *In Search of History*, esp. 1–7; Halpern, "The State of Israelite History" in *Considering Israel and Judah*, 540–65; G. N. Knoppers, "Is There a Future for the Deuteronomistic History?" in *The Future of the Deuteronomistic History*, 119–34; I. W. Provan, *1 and 2 Kings* (NIBC; Peabody, MA: Hendrickson, 1995) 6–9.

45. M. Z. Brettler, *The Creation of History in Ancient Israel*, 78. See the similar remarks by Knoppers, "Is There a Future for the Deuteronomistic History?," 129–34.

46. See, e.g., Herodotus, *Histories* 1.181; 2.135.4; 4.10.3; 4.12.1; 7.178.2, etc.; Thucydides, *Peloponnesian War* 1.93.2, 5; 2.15.2, 5; 6.54.7, etc.; Pausanias, *Description of Greece* 3.22.12; 8.15.4; 8.44.1, etc.

47. See, e.g., *Histories* 2.122.2.

these divergent traditions and the problems they introduced into his history is apparent not only on logical grounds (how could he fail to notice them, especially given their number and proximity?) but also by his use of "until this day" to confirm the persistence of the same entities, even when the accounts of their origins differed (e.g., Havvoth Jair, foreign forced labor, Jebusites in Jerusalem; etc.).

Why, though, would Dtr be willing to allow these tensions, these competing accounts and perspectives, in his retelling of Israel's past? Why, for example, does Dtr include two accounts of the naming of Havvoth Jair (Deut 3:14; Judg 10:4), of the origin of non-Israelite forced labor in Jerusalem (Josh 9:27; 1 Kgs 9:21; cf. Josh 16:10), of the reason for Jebusites in Jerusalem (Josh 15:63; Judg 1:21; cf. 1 Kgs 9:21)?[48] And moving outside what is confirmed by "until this day," why would Dtr include two accounts of how David became acquainted with Saul (1 Sam 16:14–23; 17:55–58), two accounts of Saul's rejection by YHWH (1 Sam 13:1–15; 15:1–35), two (or more) perspectives on the institution of monarchy (Judg 17:6; 21:25; 1 Sam 8:6–22; 2 Sam 7:5–17)? And so on.

One reason may be that Dtr was able to reconcile many of these conflicting accounts in his own mind.[49] For example, Dtr likely believed that the notices blaming both Judah and Benjamin for the Jebusite presence in Jerusalem were equally true since Jerusalem lies near the Judahite-Benjaminite border and during Dtr's time Benjamin was considered part of the kingdom of Judah.[50] Thus, Dtr's confirmation of the Jebusite presence in Jerusalem with reference to the culpability of both Judah and Benjamin made perfect sense in light of his own historical circumstances.

Another reason for Dtr's willingness to incorporate competing accounts into his history may have been his unwillingness to discount any received tradition. In this way, Herodotus and Dtr once again come out of the same historical mold.[51] Herodotus similarly provides more than one account for the origin of an object or institution when he has them. Again,

---

48. We could add to this: two accounts of altars at or near the Jordan River (Josh 4:8, 9); two accounts of altars built by Gideon at Ophrah (Judg 6:24, 26); and two accounts of memorials to Absalom (2 Sam 18:17, 18); among others.

49. Knoppers' ("Is There a Future for the Deuteronomistic History," 132) observation that "some of the alleged major discrepancies between various sections of the Deuteronomistic presentation are more apparent than real" should also be kept in mind.

50. It also seems that a significant number of Benjaminites resided in Jerusalem during the latter years of the Judean monarchy (see, e.g., Jer 6:1), including, perhaps, Dtr—if, in fact, he can be connected to the priests at Anathoth. See B. Halpern, "Shiloh," *ABD* 5.1213–15.

51. Childs ("Until This Day," 290–292) provides a brief comparison of the biblical use of "until this day" with similar Greek and Roman formulae. Van Seters's concern that Childs overemphasizes the similarities among the Greco-Roman and biblical uses is well founded (*In Search of History*, 49–50), though Childs himself highlights several important differences, including the Greco-Roman tendency toward first person report (e.g., ἐς ἐμὲ ἔτι, μέχρι ἐμεῦ, etc.).

the difference is that, while Herodotus will express his opinion about the reliability of an account, Dtr does not pass judgment on his sources—at least not directly.[52] Despite these differences, Dtr's use of "until this day" is—to quote Van Seters—"a historiographic convention," and provides further evidence for Dtr's historical aims when compiling Israel's traditions.[53]

There is, however, a more immediate reason why Dtr incorporated differing accounts and perspectives into his history.

## 3. The Deuteronomistic History as "Mediation"

The very term Deuteronomistic implies that Dtr came from or, at minimum, sought to represent the views of those responsible for the book of Deuteronomy—a determination that has been thoroughly born out by the present evaluation of Dtr's use of "until this day."[54] In addition, the obvious affinities between Dtr's outlook and the views expressed in the book of Jeremiah have long been observed by scholars and no doubt helped give rise to the rabbinic tradition that Jeremiah compiled the books of Kings (and, in the opinion of Abravanel, the books of Samuel as well). However, our study of "until this day" has further elucidated the interests of this historian, placing him in a very particular segment (or "circle/school" to use Nicholson's and Weinfeld's terms) of Israelite society.

The evidence presented above strongly suggests that Dtr was a Levite or, at minimum, sought to represent the interests of the Levites. This conclusion seems clear from Dtr's use of "until this day" to confirm the ongoing presence of objects and institutions of concern to this group, including

---

52. Although Dtr does not openly evaluate his sources, by applying "until this day" to the varying traditions within his history, Dtr lets his audience know that he is aware of the discrepancies among his sources and may even be inviting comparison. For a treatment of the narrative techniques in Herodotus's *History* and the Bible, see D. N. Freedman and S. Mandell, *The Relationship between Herodotus' History and Primary History* (SFSHJ 60; Atlanta: Scholars Press, 1993), esp. 153–54.

53. This conclusion holds true regardless of the historian's motives (e.g., whether to confirm a received tradition, to give a sense of authenticity to an account, or to increase the historian's credibility) or the accuracy of his sources. For what is still an insightful discussion of the historical impulse manifest in Israel's traditions, see B. Halpern, *The First Historians: The Hebrew Bible and History* (San Francisco: Harper and Row, 1988).

54. See the discussion above concerning Dtr's repeated use of "until this day" to highlight objects and institutions related to Deuteronomic law. This evidence does not mean that Dtr agreed in every respect with the laws set forth in this corpus. See, e.g., G. Knoppers ("Rethinking the Relationship between Deuteronomy and the Deuteronomistic History: The Case of Kings," *CBQ* 63 [2001] 393–415), who notes the tensions between Deuteronomy's law of the king and Dtr's appraisal of the monarchy in the books of Kings. The laws of Deuteronomy were, by my view, inherited by Dtr and, though he shared their general perspective and, in most cases, their specific teachings, he emphasized those aspects of the law most relevant to his own historical circumstances.

their inheritance rights, their responsibilities in "ministering before YHWH," their rights to the "offerings of YHWH" and their role in bearing "the Ark of the Covenant of YHWH" (see esp., Deut 3:14; 10:8–9; Josh 13:13–14; Judg 10:4; cf. Josh 4:9; 8:30–35; 1 Sam 5:5; 6:18; 2 Sam 6:8; 1 Kgs 8:8). Moreover, the use of our phrase to underscore the efficacy of the prophetic word (see, e.g., Josh 6:25–26; 2 Kgs 2:22; cf. 1 Kgs 16:34), when combined with Dtr's use of the prophecy-fulfillment pattern throughout the DH, strongly suggests that Dtr had a corresponding interest in—and likely a connection to—Israel's prophetic heritage.

When we combine Dtr's priestly/prophetic heritage with his role as a historian writing in support of the Davidic throne, and the reforms of Josiah in particular, then we have accounted for the diverse perspectives preserved in the DH.[55] As a representative of priestly/prophetic circles, with their general antipathy toward the monarchy, Dtr had in his possession narratives recounting the many confrontations between prophets and kings (e.g., Samuel and Saul, Nathan and David, Elijah and Ahab, etc.). As far as his priestly/prophetic sources were concerned—and Dtr clearly agreed[56]—the kings of both north and south, with few exceptions, received failing grades. The very institution was a compromise, a rejection of divine authority (1 Sam 8:7). Dtr, however, like Samuel before him, had become reconciled with the idea of monarchy.[57] According to Dtr, a king, in proper relationship with YHWH and, by implication, in submission to Levitical and prophetic authority (Deuteronomy 17–18), could be a powerful force for cultic reform. This was true of Jehu in the north, of Jehoash and

---

55. R. Albertz's ("In Search of the Deuteronomists: A First Solution to a Historical Riddle" in *The Future of the Deuteronomistic History*, 1–17) proposal of a Dtr coalition of priests, prophets and high-ranking officials would also explain this diversity of perspective, but does not, to my mind, adequately account for the unified use of "until this day" across the DH. That is, even if the DH represents the interests of a coalition, the consistency of perspective and redactional procedure reflected in the use of "until this day" points toward a single hand—or, if involving a group, a single mind. Moreover, Albertz's contention that this coalition of Davidides and Hilkiades produced this history in Babylonian exile, while getting close to the ideological milieu of this work (i.e., royal and priestly), misses its geographical and temporal setting. Cf., also, idem, "Die Intentionen und Träger des deuteronomistischen Geschichtswerks," in *Schöpfung und Befreiung: Für Claus Westermann zum 80. Geburtstag*, ed. R. Albertz, F. W. Golka and J. Kegler (Stuttgart: Calwer Verlag, 1989) 37–53.

56. One need only read Dtr's own appraisal of most kings—"PN did evil in the eyes of YHWH" (1 Kgs 15:26, 34; 16:19, 25, 30; 21:20, 25; 22:52, etc.)—to be convinced of his own general displeasure toward the monarchy.

57. It may even be that Samuel's reconciliation with monarchy reflects Dtr's own (1 Sam 8:4–9). In this way, Dtr's role as mediator between royal and priestly interests is similar to the Göttingen school's perception of DtrN. However, rather than mediating disparate views within an already existing history, as the Göttingen school argues, Dtr is the one mediating between the sources he himself is incorporating into his history. See the recent analysis of M. Leuchter ("A King Like All the Nations," 543–58), who similarly argues that Samuel's speech in 1 Samuel 8 reflects the perspective and redactional procedures of the Josianic Dtr.

Hezekiah in the south, and was perfectly embodied in Josiah, who "turned neither to the right nor to the left" (Deut 17:20; 2 Kgs 22:2) in his obedience to the Mosaic Law.[58]

Thus, when bringing together the traditions of Israel's past, Dtr incorporated both southern royal traditions, with their emphases on Judah and the Davidic throne, and priestly/prophetic traditions, with their emphases on prophetic authority, a zeal for the sanctity of the cult, and a corresponding negative or "reserved" (following McCarter) view of the monarchy. This was no easy undertaking, but Dtr's literary skill, his respect for his sources, and his own priestly/prophetic convictions—convictions that would not allow him to whitewash the reigns of *any* of Israel's kings, including David (*contra* the Chronicler)[59]—has resulted in the rich and eclectic history we now possess.

---

58. For similar remarks on Dtr's view of kingship, see McKenzie, "The Trouble with Kingship," 308.

59. That Dtr is the one incorporating the negative view of David into his history is evidenced by the same literary technique to evaluate David as observed above with Jehu, Jehoash and others: "he did what was right in the eyes of YHWH . . . " followed by a conditional statement introduced by רק. In the case of David, Dtr writes, "For David did what was right in the eyes of YHWH and did not depart from anything that he commanded him all the days of his life, except (רק) in the matter of Uriah the Hittite (1 Kgs 15:5). See Barrick, "Removal of High Places," 257–59. Cf., also, Smend ("Das Gesetz und die Völker," 494, 499), who ascribes the editorial use of רק in Joshua to DtrN, another example where his "nomistic" redactor parallels the activity I am ascribing to the preexilic Dtr (for further discussion, see the conclusion).

# Conclusion

## "Until This Day" and History Writing in Ancient Israel

> It may even be argued that history writing arises at the point when the actions of kings are viewed in the larger context of the people as a whole, so that it is the national history that judges the king and not the king who makes his own account of history.[1]
> —John Van Seters, *In Search of History: Historiography in the Ancient World and the Origins of Biblical History*

The present study has undertaken to address a question that has engaged scholars for nearly two millennia: To whose day does the biblical phrase "until this day" refer?

To early Jewish and Christian commentators this phrase was a conundrum, a difficulty to be addressed while still maintaining the traditional authorial ascriptions. This was no easy task and often resulted in compromises (e.g., "We must certainly understand by 'this day' the time of the composition of the history, whether you prefer the view that Moses was the author of the Pentateuch or that Ezra restored it. In either case I make no objection" [Jerome]) or creative conjectures (e.g., "This is the same Luz that . . . the Angel of Death does not have permission to pass through; rather, when the elderly in it no longer desire to live, they go outside of the walls and die" [Soṭah 46b]).

To the emerging field of critical scholarship "until this day" was a clue, a key that promised to unlock the answers to the questions surrounding the Bible's origins. This was no easy task, but the study of "until this day" helped to establish the inadequacies of the traditional authorial ascriptions (e.g., "The phrase 'until this day' demonstrates by necessity that [the book

---

1. Van Seters, *In Search of History*, 2.

of Joshua] was written long after the affairs it reports" [Abravanel]) and often resulted in insights that played an important role in tracing the development of the biblical text (e.g., "When we put these three considerations together, namely, the unity of the subject of all the books, the connection between them, and the fact that they are compilations made many generations after the events they relate had taken place, we come to the conclusion, as I have just stated, that they are all the work of a single historian" [Spinoza]).

In our own time "until this day" has been little more than an artifact, a remnant of what preoccupied earlier investigations into the Bible, but whose usefulness had since been exhausted. As the present study has argued, however, the phrase had not outlived its usefulness. Quite the contrary: the evidence derived from an analysis of "until this day" addresses some of the most pressing questions engaging biblical scholarship, in general, and Deuteronomistic studies, in particular: When was Israel's history first compiled? Where was it compiled and by whom? What was the original content of this history? How do we explain this history's diversity while still accounting for its overall unity? And, most important, *why* was this history compiled?

The phrase, following Childs, is a redactional comment upon a received tradition.[2] Yet, contrary to Childs, "until this day" does not derive from "many different redactors," but rather from one: Dtr, who employed this phrase as his own personal witness to objects and institutions mentioned in his sources that still existed during *his* day. His day, we have determined, is the late-seventh or early-sixth century B.C.E., during or shortly after the reign of Josiah. The evidence for this conclusion, as the present study has argued, is multifaceted.

The phrase's redactional nature, its unified southern perspective and its consistent preexilic provenance are important starting points, but, in the end, are only suggestive. When we combine this evidence with the data discussed in chapter 3; namely, the phrase's appearance in every source believed to make up the DH (e.g., "The History of David's Rise," "The Acts of Solomon," "The Chronicles of the Kings of Israel/Judah," etc.), its confirmation of the same matters across literary units (e.g., Jebusite presence in Jerusalem, the naming of Havvoth Jair, the policy of non-Israelite forced labor, etc.), its presence immediately adjacent to other trademark Dtr phrases (e.g., "at the place he will choose," "because he followed fully after YHWH," "do not fear or be dismayed," etc.) and larger Dtr editorial contributions (e.g., the curse on Jericho, the building of the altar on Mount

---

2. Childs, "'Until This Day,'" 292. For a fuller treatment of Childs's analysis of the phrase, see chapter 1.

Ebal, the evaluation of kings, etc.), its use in connection with demonstrably Dtr interests (e.g., the removal of high places and Baal worship from Israel, the proper handling of "the Ark of the Covenant of YHWH," the rights and responsibilities of the Levites, etc.), even Josianic policies (e.g., centralized worship, Judahite-Edomite interactions, the Passover, the reading of the Torah of Moses, etc.), then a unified history culminating in Josiah's reign is the most reasonable assessment of the evidence. This unity of use and perspective could not easily derive from "many different redactors." After all, committees seldom produce such unanimity, especially if representing diverse interests or, if representing the same interests, if distanced temporally or geographically. This is not to say that those responsible for the DH did not seek to incorporate diverse perspectives within their account of Israel's past. In fact, as discussed in chapter 5 (and as will be discussed further below), those compiling this history represented a segment of Israelite society with deep roots in the nation's past (i.e., Israel's priestly/prophetic heritage) and sought to represent the interests of an institution with similarly longstanding traditions (i.e., the monarchy). Even so, the consistency of redactional procedure and religio-political perspective reflected in the use of "until this day" across the DH strongly suggests that the compilation of Israel's history fell to an individual or small group working in close association.

If we ask *why* Dtr employed the phrase, several reasons have become apparent from the present study. First, as Childs rightly ascertained, Dtr employed "until this day" much as his Greek and Roman counterparts employed similar formulae: "to validate some aspect of the tradition which can still be verified in his own time." A similar historical impulse is evident in Dtr's appeal to written sources, which is similarly formulaic: "... הֲלֹא־הֵם כְּתוּבִים ("Are these not recorded ... ?")[3] In fact, on more than one occasion Dtr appeals to both extant objects ("until this day") and written sources ("Are these not recorded ... ?") in close proximity (Josh 10:27, 29; 2 Kgs 8:22–23; 10:27, 34; 14:7, 15). Moreover, in at least one case, Dtr uses his method of appeal to written sources to point his audience to an archaeological artifact; namely, the king of Bashan's infamous "iron bedstead" (perhaps a basalt sarcophagus[4]):

כִּי רַק־עוֹג מֶלֶךְ הַבָּשָׁן נִשְׁאַר מִיֶּתֶר הָרְפָאִים הִנֵּה עַרְשׂוֹ עֶרֶשׂ בַּרְזֶל
הֲלֹה[5] הִוא בְּרַבַּת בְּנֵי עַמּוֹן תֵּשַׁע אַמּוֹת אָרְכָּהּ וְאַרְבַּע אַמּוֹת רָחְבָּהּ בְּאַמַּת־אִישׁ

---

3. See, e.g., 1 Kgs 11:41; 14:29; 15:7, 23, 31; 16:5, 14, 20, 27; 22:39, 46; 2 Kgs 1:18; 8:23; 10:34; 12:20; 13:8, 12; 14:15, 18, 28; etc.

4. On the possibility of עֶרֶשׂ בַּרְזֶל meaning "basalt sarcophagus," see A. D. H. Mayes, *Deuteronomy* (NCBC. London: Marshall, Morgan & Scott, 1979; repr., Grand Rapids, MI: Eerdmans/London: Marshall, Morgan & Scott, 1981) 144.

5. Multiple Hebrew mss, the Samaritan Pentateuch, as well as the early translations

> Now only Og, king of Bashan, was left from the remnant of the Rephaim. Behold, his bed is a bed of iron. Is it not in Rabbah of the Ammonites? Its length is nine cubits and its width is four cubits, by the standard cubit.
>
> Deut 3:11

That this notice appears in proximity to Dtr's use of "until this day" (Deut 3:14) and in connection with an interest highlighted elsewhere by our phrase (i.e., the Bashan; Josh 13:13–14; Judg 10:4) further suggests that both means of historical appeal belong to Dtr.[6]

Another reason Dtr employs "until this day" is as a redactional strategy. Specifically, Dtr takes the opportunity afforded him by the interruption of his source to insert additional material reflecting his own historical circumstances and religio-political perspective. Thus, Dtr follows "until this day" in Josh 5:9 with the account of Joshua's passover (v. 10), which, as Nelson rightly observes, "[provides] an explicit historical precedent for Josiah's revolutionary reforming passover."[7] Dtr follows "until this day" in Josh 6:25 with the curse on anyone who would rebuild Jericho (v. 26), a curse to which Dtr returns later in his history as part of his prophecy-fulfillment pattern (1 Kgs 16:34; cf. 2 Kgs 2:22). Dtr follows "until this day" in Josh 8:29 with the account of Joshua's reading the torah of Moses on Mount Ebal (vv. 30–35), which not only fulfills Moses' command in Deuteronomy 11 and 27 to build this altar and read the law in the hearing of all the people but also points forward to Josiah's covenant renewal ceremony, where he similarly gathers all the people and recites the whole law (2 Kgs 23:1–3).[8] Indeed, Nelson's observations on this last example could, with slight modification,[9] be applied to most uses of the phrase in the DH: "Dtr clearly went to some effort to break into the sequence of his source."[10]

Related to this last point, Dtr employs "until this day" to highlight objects or institutions that attest to the importance of following Deuteronomic law. We have already noted this purpose in connection with the Ark of the Covenant, which receives seven uses of our phrase to highlight occa-

---

(LXX, Syriac, Targumim) all render the Hebrew as לא, though the present reading may be preferred on the principle of *lectio difficilior*.

6. Cf. also Deuteronomy 11, where both means of verification occur (vv. 4, 30), though "until this day" in v. 4 appears in direct speech, a subject requiring separate treatment (see below). On the connection between the historical notice in Deut 3:11 and Deut 2:22, where our phrase also appears, see Mayes, *Deuteronomy*, 144–45; Weinfeld, *Deuteronomy 1–11*, 183.

7. Nelson, "Josiah in the Book of Joshua," 537.

8. For a fuller discussion of Dtr's redactional strategy in connection with "until this day," see chapters 3 and 5.

9. The description of Dtr's method as "break[ing] into his source" does not, in my opinion, capture the essence of his editorial technique (as Nelson seems to acknowledge in his comments on Josh 5:1–2).

10. Nelson, "Josiah in the Book of Joshua," 537.

sions when the ark was handled properly (Deut 10:8; Josh 4:9; 8:30–35) or not (1 Sam 5:5; 6:18; 2 Sam 6:8). Other places where Dtr highlights the fulfillment of Deuteronomic law by means of "until this day" include the burial mound of Achan (Josh 7:26), which testifies to the seriousness of violating the law concerning war spoils (Deut 13:18); the ruins of Ai and Jericho, which give testimony to the destruction of cities in keeping with (the same) Deuteronomic law (Deut 13:17); the stones covering the king of Ai (Josh 8:29) and those covering the cave at Makkedah (Josh 10:27), which mark places where corpses were handled according to Deuteronomic procedure (Deut 21:22–23); and, as noted above, the altar on Mount Ebal (Josh 8:30–35), which not only fulfills Moses' command to build such an altar (Deut 27:1–8) but also shows the "Levitical priests" (Josh 8:33) fulfilling their Deuteronomic duty of bearing "the Ark of the Covenant of YHWH" (Deut 10:8) and, fittingly enough, overseeing the recitation and implementation of Deuteronomic law (Deut 17:18–20; 27:9).

Another reason Dtr employs "until this day" relates to the Deuteronom(ist)ic emphasis on remembering the words and deeds of YHWH and passing these on to future generations (Deut 6:4–7; 11:2–7). As noted at the beginning of our study, the number of monuments said to persist "until this day" throughout the land would certainly give testimony to God's past actions on Israel's behalf. With this purpose in view, it seems significant that the first monument erected by the Israelites upon entering Canaan is explicitly tied to the phenomenon of the Kinderfrage:

> Your children will ask in time to come, "What do these stones mean to you?" And you will say to them that the waters of the Jordan were cut off before the Ark of the Covenant of YHWH. When it passed through the Jordan, the waters of the Jordan were cut off! And these stones will be a memorial to the children of Israel forever.
>
> Josh 4:6b-7

This episode, in essence, sets the pattern for how to interpret other monuments soon to be erected, whether the stones in the Valley of Achor (Josh 7:26), which testify to the importance of obeying God's commands, the stones over the mouth of the cave at Makkedah (Josh 10:27), which testify to God's deliverance in battle, or the remains of the city of Ai (Josh 8:28), which testify to both. The presence of these monuments would certainly assist parents in fulfilling the Deuteronomic charge to pass on God's words and deeds "while walking along the way" (Deut 6:7; 11:19).

These observations highlight one final reason why Dtr employs "until this day": his concern for centralized worship. This purpose is transparent where Dtr makes explicit mention of this concern in connection with our phrase (e.g., Josh 9:27; "until this day at the place he will choose") or where he points to places that mark the destruction of alternate sites of worship (e.g., Judg 6:24; 2 Kgs 10:27). Yet, Dtr's interest in centralized worship seems even to be in evidence when he uses the phrase to connect what were no doubt conspicuously human-made memorials/altars to specific events from Israel's past. This concern is given explicit expression by Dtr in his account of the confrontation over the altar built by the Transjordanian tribes (Joshua 22). This altar, which likely existed during Dtr's day and bore a striking resemblance to the altar in Jerusalem ("this replica of the altar of YHWH" [v. 28]), is divested of any sacrificial function (vv. 26, 28). Indeed, the purpose of this altar is communicated expressly by means of the Kinderfrage:

> We did this thing out of concern that in time to come your children might say to our children, "What have you to do with YHWH, the God of Israel? For YHWH has made the Jordan a boundary between us and you, O Reubenites and Gadites. You have no portion in YHWH." Thus your children might make our children to cease worshiping YHWH. So we said, "Let us build an altar, not for burnt offering or for sacrifice, but for a witness between us and you, and between our generations after us, that we may perform the service of YHWH in his presence with our burnt offerings and with our sacrifices and with our offerings of wellbeing, in order that your children may never say to our children in time to come, "You have no portion in YHWH."
>
> Josh 22:24–27

Thus, Dtr's use of "until this day" in connection with other stone memorials, such as the monument of twelve stones near the Jordan (Josh 4:6–9) or the altar on Mount Ebal (Josh 8:30–35), becomes a polemic against interpreting these as alternate sites of worship, giving answer to the implied, if not explicitly stated, question: If centralized worship has been a long-standing institution in Israel, then "What do these stones mean to you?" (Josh 4:6b). The answer, given several times for clarity by the Transjordanian tribes, is that these are "not for burnt offering or sacrifice," rather they are for remembrance (e.g., the altar near the Jordan) and recommitment (e.g., the altar on Mount Ebal).[11]

The present study has also helped to establish the general scope and content of Dtr's preexilic history. In short, the preexilic DH was largely complete. The evidence for this conclusion, as noted in chapter 5, is not

---

11. As noted in chapter 5, Caquot and de Robert (*Les livres de Samuel*, 554) have made a similar proposal for Absalom's pillar, which they suggest reflects the Deuteronomistic polemic against מצבות. See also the comments by R. A. Carlson, *The Chosen King*, 138, 187. Such a motive may even explain Dtr's one negative affirmation: "And no one knows the place of [Moses'] burial until this day" (Deut 34:6), which may be an attempt to dissuade (or discredit) veneration of Moses' tomb. That another object traced to the legendary Moses was so venerated "until those days" (i.e., the days of Hezekiah; 2 Kgs 18:4) further points in this direction.

merely that "until this day" appears in every major source believed to make up this history, including the prologue, law code and epilogue of Deuteronomy, the conquest account and inheritance lists of Joshua, the prologue, heroic tales and epilogue of Judges, the Ark Narrative, History of David's Rise, and Succession Narrative of Samuel, and the Acts of Solomon, prophetic cycles, and Chronicles of the Kings of Israel/Judah of Kings. Rather, it is the unified temporal, geographical and religio-political perspective reflected in its use across the DH that argues against removing large narrative strands or sources from Dtr's original work. For example, we have already taken note of the repeated use of the phrase in connection with the Ark of the Covenant (Deut 10:8; Josh 4:9; 8:30–35; 1 Sam 5:5; 6:18; 2 Sam 6:8; 1 Kgs 8:8). This repetition, we observed in chapter 4, was purposeful, as it served to underscore the sanctity of "the Ark of the Covenant of YHWH" and the right of the "Levitical priests" to bear it—both central concerns of Dtr.[12] Yet, also noteworthy is the distribution of "until this day" in connection with this theme: the laws of Deuteronomy (10:8), the conquest narratives of Joshua (4:9; 8:30–35), the "Ark Narrative" of 1 and 2 Samuel (1 Sam 5:5; 6:18; 2 Sam 6:8), and "the Acts of Solomon" of 1 Kings (1 Kgs 8:8).[13] And this is not the only case where "until this day" provides evidence for the overall unity and scope of Dtr's original history. Consider again Dtr's interest in the persistence of non-Israelites in Israel, which finds its origins and idiom (מַס־עֹבֵד) in Deuteronomic law (יִהְיוּ לְךָ לָמַס וַעֲבָדוּךָ Deut 7:1–3; Deut 20:10–18), and which finds expression throughout the DH, including the conquest narratives (Josh 9:27) *and* inheritance lists (13:13; 15:63; 16:10) of Joshua, the prologue of Judges (1:21), and "the Acts of Solomon" of Kings (1 Kgs 9:21). Recall, too, Dtr's use of "until this day" in connection with the destruction of alternate sites of worship (Judg 6:24; 2 Kgs 10:27), which again finds its origins and idiom (e.g., נָתַץ) in the same(!) Deuteronomic law (Deut 7:4–5) and which highlights Dtr's interest in centralized worship, which also finds explicit expression in connection with our phrase ("until this day at the place he will choose" [Josh 9:27]). Other Deuteronomistic interests highlighted by "until this day"—such as the Levites' inheritance rights (Deut 10:8–9; Josh 13:13–14; cf. Deut 18:1–2), Judahite-Edomite relations (Deut 2:22; 2 Kgs 8:22; 14:7; 16:6), and the effi-

---

12. It should be reemphasized that this focus on the Ark of the Covenant would be peculiar in the exilic or postexilic periods when the Ark is gone (Jer 3:16)—unless we want to postulate that debates about who has the right to bear the Ark became a cipher for debates about the legitimate priesthood at a later period. While this is possible, it is neither the most likely interpretation of the evidence nor does it account for the other uses of "until this day," which similarly point toward the preexilic period. See the discussion in chapter 2.

13. Again, the exact parameters of these sources, even their independent existence, do not affect our overall observations about the distribution of and connections among the uses of "until this day" in the DH. See the discussion in chapter 3.

cacy of the prophetic word (Josh 6:25–26; 2 Kgs 2:22; cf. Deut 18:15–22)—similarly attest to the overall unified use of this phrase throughout the DH and, hence, the overall unity and scope of Dtr's original work. In fact, Dtr's use of "until this day" to testify to the same entities throughout this history, even when the accounts of their origins differ (e.g., the naming of Havvoth Jair, the presence of non-Israelite forced labor in Jerusalem, etc.), as well as Dtr's willingness to incorporate materials from different segments of Israelite society (e.g., royal versus prophetic, southern versus northern) indicates that most of the tensions present within this history do not derive from subsequent redactions of the text but from Dtr himself (as Noth originally argued).[14]

Related to this last point, our study has also allowed us to locate Dtr within a particular segment of Israelite society. The repeated use of "until this day" with reference to the rights and responsibilities of the Levites demonstrates that they were much more than an antiquarian interest for Dtr, or a faction he had to accommodate when compiling his history. Rather, the "Levitical priests," as Dtr makes plain in redactional material accompanying our phrase, played a central role in many of Israel's past successes and held the key—quite literally in the "torah of Moses"—to Israel's future successes. After all, it was the Levites who were called apart by Moses "to carry the Ark of the Covenant of YHWH, to stand before YHWH, to minister to him and to bless his name until this day" (Deut 10:8). It was the "Levitical priests" who, in lieu of a tribal allotment, were given "YHWH as their inheritance," including the "offerings of YHWH" (Josh 13:14; cf. Deut 18:1–2). It was the "Levitical priests" who, in obedience to the Mosaic command, carried "the Ark of the Covenant of YHWH" in front of the Israelites to provide them with dry passage when entering Canaan (Josh 3:3). And it was the "Levitical priests" who bore "the Ark of the Covenant of YHWH" while Joshua read the "torah of Moses" to all the people (Josh 8:30–35). Indeed, it is when a leader submits himself to the torah of Moses, "meditating on it day and night" and refusing to turn "either to the right or to the left" that the nation is promised blessing and longevity in the land (Deut 17:18–20).

These sentiments, which are only realized in Joshua and Josiah, are expressed in the law of the king (Deut 17:14–20), which itself prepares the reader for the emphasis observed in connection with "until this day"—namely, the role of the "Levitical priests" in mediating between YHWH, the king, and the people. Thus, immediately prior to the explication of the law of the king, the people are commanded to go "to the place YHWH will choose" and present their difficult cases before the "Levitical priests" and

---

14. For similar remarks, see G. N. Knoppers, "Is There a Future for the Deuteronomistic History?" in *The Future of the Deuteronomistic History*, 119–34, esp. 129–34.

the judge at that time (vv. 8–9). Following these instructions, the king is commanded "to have a copy of this torah written for him on a scroll by the Levitical priests" (v. 18). The law then turns to the rights of the "Levitical priests," who, though having "no inheritance among their brothers" are guaranteed "the offerings of YHWH as their inheritance" since "YHWH is their inheritance, as he said to them" (Deut 18:1–2). That these concerns, even these exact phrases, show up in editorial material following Dtr's use of "until this day" in the DH is not coincidental. Nor is it coincidence that the laws concerning the central role of the "Levitical priests" in Israel's royal and cultic administration are followed by the criteria for determining a true prophet (vv. 15–22), as the confirmation of the prophetic word is another central interest of Dtr, manifest not only in his use of the prophecy-fulfillment pattern in his history, but also in his use of "until this day" to attest to the efficacy of the prophetic word (see, e.g., Josh 6:25b-26; 1 Kgs 16:34; 2 Kgs 2:22).

Thus, in agreement with many scholars discussed in chapter 4, I trace Dtr's heritage to northern priestly/prophetic circles who had taken up residence in and around Jerusalem following the fall of the north. They would have brought with them many of the traditions now making up part of the DH. As for the antiquity of these traditions, it is difficult to say, as is the role of oral transmission in this process.[15] No doubt these northern Levites believed themselves to be the inheritors of very old traditions, some even extending back to Moses. As for Dtr's other sources, such as the Acts of Solomon, the Chronicles of the Kings of Israel, and the Chronicles of the Kings of Judah, these no doubt represent actual written materials employed by him when reconstructing Israel's past. If Dtr was merely trying to enhance his credibility by such citations, then the paucity of sources cited is puzzling, especially for the earlier periods. We might add that, in view of Dtr's temporal and geographical setting, such citations would, if fabricated, undermine his credibility.[16] Moreover, Dtr's chronological precision for the tenth–seventh centuries—especially for Israel and Judah, but also for Assyria, Egypt and Babylonia—indicates that he had recourse to

---

15. For the role of written and oral transmission in the preservation of Israel's traditions, see esp. S. Niditch, *Oral World and Written Word: Ancient Israelite Literature* (Louisville: Westminster John Knox Press, 1996); W. M. Schniedewind, *The Word of God in Transition: From Prophet to Exegete in the Second Temple Period* (JSOTSup 197; Sheffield: JSOT Press, 1995); D. M. Carr, *Writing on the Tablet of the Heart: Origins of Scripture and Literature* (New York/Oxford: Oxford University Press, 2005).

16. Even Herodotus, the so-called Father of History *and* Lies, does not fabricate when referring to objects or institutions about which his audience is well familiar (e.g., the oracle at Delphi). See D. Fehling, *Herodotus and His 'Sources': Citation, Invention and Narrative Art*, trans. J. G. Howie (Leeds: Great Britain, Francis Cairns Pub. Ltd., 1989; German original; Berlin/New York: W. de Gruyter, 1971) 129.

actual and, in some cases, centuries old sources.[17] Other sources, such as the epic poetry and heroic tales of Judges, whether received in written or oral form, would date back further still.[18]

These northern Levites were also likely the ones responsible for the legislation that eventually became the Deuteronomic law discovered during Josiah's reign and that served as the basis of his reforms.[19] After all, it was to these same "Levitical priests" that Moses entrusted this law shortly before his death (Deut 31:25–26), commanding them to place it next to "the Ark of the Covenant of YHWH"—the other sacred trust of these priests. This historical circumstance might even explain the emergence of the term "Levitical priests" itself. Agreeing with M. Rehm, "Levites" and "Levitical priests" do not necessarily reflect two different groups active at the same time (i.e., priestly ranks), but rather "(essentially) the same group working at two different times."[20] The general title, "Levites," reflects the earlier stage (*contra* Rehm), when Levites were dependent upon local sanctuaries and communities for support (e.g., between the reigns of Jeroboam I and Hezekiah). This period, which may have included also the initial stages of northern settlement in the south following the fall of Israel, accounts for the commands in the Deuteronomic law to care for "the Levites, aliens, orphans and widows" (Deut 14:27–29; 26:12–13). The compound form, "Levitical priests," represents a later stage, when many Levites had become attached to the Jerusalem cult. This fuller title, according to this reconstruc-

---

17. For a recent assessment of the historical data, see B. Halpern, "The State of Israelite History," 540–65. For a recent assessment of the linguistic data, see A. Hurvitz, "The Historical Quest for 'Ancient Israel' and the Linguistic Evidence of the Hebrew Bible: Some Methodological Observations," *VT* 47 (1997) 301–15. For a recent assessment of the archaeological and cultural data, see W. Dever, *What Did the Biblical Writers Know and When Did They Know It?*. Acerbity aside, Dever has made the case for the antiquity of many of Israel's traditions, particularly as these reflect detailed, often incidental, knowledge of archaeological and cultural data that would have been inaccessible to later scribes, except by recourse to written material. For a collection of essays related to the antiquity of Israel's traditions from a variety of methodological approaches, see J. Day, ed., *In Search of Preexilic Israel*.

18. A 12th c. B.C.E. date for the original form of the Song of Deborah remains the scholarly consensus. See, e.g., H. D. Neef, *Deboraerzählung und Deboralied: Studien zu Jdc 4,1–5,31* (BTS 49; Neukirchen-Vluyn: Neukirchener Verlag, 2002). For a contrary view, see C. Levin, "Das Alter des Deboralieds," in *Fortschreibungen: Gesammelte Studien zum Alten Testament* (BZAW 316; Berlin: W. de Gruyter, 2003) 124–41. On the antiquity of the epic poetry in general, see the classic study of F. M. Cross and D. N. Freedman, *Studies in Ancient Yahwistic Poetry* (SBLDS 24; Missoula, MT: Scholars Press, 1975; repr. Grand Rapids, MI/Cambridge U.K.: Eerdmans, 1997).

19. What precisely was found (e.g., the Song of Moses, a version of Deuteronomy 12–28, etc.) and whether this served as the basis or justification for Josiah's reforms are matters of ongoing debate. See J. Lundbom, *Jeremiah 1–20: A New Translation with Introduction and Commentary* (AB 21A; New York, NY: Doubleday, 1999) 105–6.

20. M. Rehm, "Levites and Priests," *ABD* 6:297–310.

tion, served to emphasize that these Levites, even if relative newcomers to Jerusalem, were full and equal members of the temple's establishment. Rehm seems correct in his assessment:

> The trend of upgrading the Levites, begun in Hezekiah's time, was seemingly continued by Josiah. He ordered the centralization of all sacrifice in Jerusalem, but he gave the Levites (of the countryside, including those still in the north) the opportunity to join their fellow Levites who were already in Jerusalem (Deut 18:6–8).

It may even be that Josiah removed or demoted the established priesthood of his father and grandfather as part of his religious reforms, providing the opportunity for the discovery of the Deuteronomic law code and its promulgation.[21]

Regardless of our conclusions on this final matter, Dtr's affiliation with Israel's priestly/prophetic heritage, when combined with his support of Josiah's reforms, provides the explanation for the diversity of traditions now preserved within the DH. Dtr was a mediator of competing ideologies. As a defender of the Josianic reforms, Dtr included material in his history that acknowledged the Davidides' right to rule (2 Sam 7:4–16), particularly when a righteous king (i.e., Josiah) occupied the throne (Deut 18:18–20; 1 Sam 12:14–15). Yet, as a representative of northern priestly/prophetic circles, Dtr included traditions in his history that called the monarchy to account for its misdeeds. Even David, who was Dtr's model for subsequent rulers (1 Kgs 3:14; 14:8), does not escape his prophetic rebuke (1 Kgs 15:5). In fact, it was Dtr's unwillingness to promote the Davidic throne at the expense of his northern priestly/prophetic heritage that compelled him to place their competing claims and traditions side-by-side. Thus, the "objectivity" afforded Dtr by his heritage made him write more than just another piece of royal propaganda, examples of which could be found throughout the ancient Near East and which, as Van Seters has rightly argued, is not true history writing. In this way, the earliest history writing—a history "that judges the king and not the king who makes his own account of history"[22]—was as much the result of Dtr's internal convictions as of his external circumstances.[23]

---

21. It is likely that these Levites felt they had ancient claim to service at YHWH's altar, either due to their pedigree (e.g., descendants of Abiathar) or piety (e.g., Samuel) or both. For one way of understanding the recasting of older laws in support of a Deuteronomic reform, see B. Levinson, *Deuteronomy and the Hermeneutics of Legal Innovation*.

22. Van Seters, *In Search of History*, 2.

23. For the external circumstances allowing for the production of a history in the late-seventh, early sixth centuries B.C.E., see esp. W. M. Schniedewind, "Jerusalem, the Late Judahite Monarchy, and the Composition of Biblical Texts," *Jerusalem in Bible and Archaeology: The First Temple Period*, ed. A. G. Vaughn and A. E. Killebrew (SBLSS 18; Atlanta, GA: Society of Biblical Literature, 2003) 375–93.

Thus, at one moment we hear the report of the royal scribes, whose job it was to hail the king as divinely favored and, more mundanely, to record the business of state; at another we hear the concerns of the priests, whose desire it was to promote singular devotion to YHWH and whose duty it was to preserve the sanctity of the cult; and at still another we hear the voice of the prophets, speaking out against the ills of the monarchy and calling the people back to obedience to YHWH.

And Dtr gave expression to it all. Certainly it was not everything. He tells us that.[24] But he is to be commended for all that he did allow to find voice in his history, despite the cacophony that sometimes results. If Dtr had not given expression to these disparate perspectives, these different "voices," from Israel's past, then we would have lost much of Israel's traditions about itself and, in the process, we would have lost much of Israel's history.

# FINAL OBSERVATIONS AND FUTURE TRAJECTORIES

A number of questions still remain, not the least of which is whether there existed an earlier, perhaps Hezekian, history prior to Dtr's Josianic history. Although a full treatment of this issue cannot be accomplished here, a few observations are in order.

As noted in chapter 5, the redactional nature of "until this day" indicates that Dtr was working with preexisting written materials, and it is possible that some of these materials were joined together prior to Dtr's historical enterprise. Yet, if there did exist an earlier history, then this would help to unite the seemingly diverging analyses of Weippert, Halpern and others, on the one hand, and the Göttingen school, on the other. Both groups, for example, hypothesize an initial history that was focused upon and largely favorable to the monarchy. This history, in turn, was then combined with traditions from someone with prophetic and, if we merge the Göttingen school's second and third redactional stages, "nomistic" interests. If we shift the Göttingen school's earliest stages of redaction into the preexilic period, as the evidence of "until this day" would seem to require, and link their DtrP and DtrN with Dtr, who, as we have seen, has both prophetic and "nomistic" interests, then the seemingly disparate analyses of these two "schools" actually come into close alignment.[25] In short, the

---

24. Note the constant refrain: "As for the rest of the details of King PN's reign, are they not written in the Book of the Chronicles of the Kings of Israel/Judah?" (1 Kgs 14:29; 15:7, 23, 31; 16:5, 14, 20; etc.).

25. As noted in chapter 5, Smend's identification of secondary elements in Joshua cor-

earlier history (DtrH), which was largely favorable toward the monarchy, was subsequently filled out and tempered by Dtr, whose interests were largely priestly and prophetic.[26] Even if one rejects the notion of a preDtr royal history, moving the Göttingen school's earliest redactional level(s) into the preexilic period allows for a more direct comparison with Cross's model.[27]

Another area requiring further attention is the use of "until this day" outside the DH.[28] Most relevant for the present study is its use in the Tetrateuch, especially in view of recent studies that have argued for literary and redactional continuity between these two "works."[29] Does the use of the

---

relate to the present study's identification of secondary elements belonging to the preexilic Dtr, both in terms of thematic interests (e.g., the torah of Moses) and editorial techniques (e.g., the redactional use of רק).

26. That priestly and prophetic interests are not mutually exclusive hardly needs comment, but is, in any case, demonstrated by Deuteronomic law (see, e.g., Deut 18:6–22) and by such notable figures as Moses, Samuel and Jeremiah.

27. For similar observations, see Campbell, "Martin Noth and the Deuteronomistic History," 50, 53.

28. For a complete list of etiological uses, see chapter 2, n. 3. For its use in Genesis, see the discussion below. The Chronicler uses the phrase ten times, five of which repeat material from the DH (1 Chr 10:19 = 1 Kgs 12:19; 1 Chr 13:11 = 2 Sam 6:8; 2 Chr 5:9 = 1 Kgs 8:8; 2 Chr 8:8 = 1 Kgs 9:21; 2 Chr 21:10 = 2 Kgs 8:22). Therefore, the most straightforward explanation for its five unique uses (1 Chr 4:41, 43; 5:26; 2 Chr 20:26; 35:25) is imitation, though we cannot overlook the possibility that some of these "unique" uses derive from the Chronicler's preexilic sources. See, e.g., S. Japhet (*I and II Chronicles* [OTL; Louisville, KY: Westminster John Knox] 126–27) on 1 Chr 4:41, 43 and H. G. M. Williamson (*1 and 2 Chronicles* [NCBC. Grand Rapids, Michigan: Eerdmans; London: Marshall, Morgan & Scott, 1982] 410) on 2 Chr 35;25. The one use in Ezekiel (20:29) is noteworthy, since it appears in a chapter that contains other Deuteronomistic concepts and phrases, which scholars ascribe either to a Deuteronomistic redaction of the book or to the author of Ezekiel himself, who, in this chapter in particular, borrows from Deuteronom(ist)ic terminology for his own didactic purposes. Whatever the precise origins of this material, the use of "until this day" with the Niphal (וַיִּקָּרֵא) and to describe the naming of a category of objects ("Bamah"), as opposed to its use with the Qal and to describe the specific name of an object, does not correspond to its use in the DH. For a discussion of the Deuteronomistic language in Ezekiel 20, see M. Greenberg, *Ezekiel 1–20* (AB 22; Garden City, New York: Doubleday, 1983) 363–88. For those ascribing this particular unit (vv. 27–29) to a redactor (Deuteronomistic or otherwise), see, e.g., W. Eichrodt, *Ezekiel: A Commentary*, trans. C. Quin (OTL; Philadelphia: Westminster, 1970) 361; W. Zimmerli, *Ezekiel 1: A Commentary on the Book of the Prophet Ezekiel, Chapters 1–24*, trans. R. E. Clements (Hermeneia; Philadelphia: Fortress, 1979) 404–12; J. W. Wevers, *Ezekiel* (NCBC; Grand Rapids: Eerdmans, 1982) 156. For those ascribing this material to the author of Ezekiel, see T. Krüger, *Geschichtskonzepte im Ezechielbuch* (BZAW 180; Berlin: de Gruyter, 1989), 210–12; D. I. Block, *The Book of Ezekiel, Chapters 1–24* (NICOT; Grand Rapids, MI/Cambridge, U.K.: Eerdmans, 1997) 641–45; R. Levitt Kohn, *A New Heart and A New Soul: Ezekiel, the Exile and the Torah* (JSOTSup 160; Sheffield: Sheffield Academic Press, 2002).

29. Consider, e.g., the comments of Rendtorff (*The Old Testament*, 186) regarding the redactional techniques evident in Num 33:50–56: "Here numerous 'Deuteronomistic' formulations are striking . . . these show clearly that here *the same redaction* was at work as in the

phrase in the Tetrateuch shed any light on the theory of a unified history spanning from Genesis to Kings (the so-called Primary History)? I have argued elsewhere that it does, that the use of the phrase in the Tetrateuch reflects similar editorial techniques and religio-political interests as in the DH and may, in the end, derive from the same redactional hand (i.e., Dtr).[30]

For example, "until this day" in both works highlights institutions or policies involving priests. Compare, for example, Gen 47:26 and Josh 13:13b–14:

וַיָּשֶׂם אֹתָהּ יוֹסֵף לְחֹק עַד־הַיּוֹם הַזֶּה עַל־אַדְמַת מִצְרַיִם לְפַרְעֹה לַחֹמֶשׁ
רַק אַדְמַת הַכֹּהֲנִים לְבַדָּם לֹא הָיְתָה לְפַרְעֹה:

And Joseph made it a statute until this day in the land of Egypt that to Pharaoh should go the fifth. Only the land of the priests alone did not become Pharaoh's.

Gen 47:26

וַיֵּשֶׁב גְּשׁוּר וּמַעֲכָת בְּקֶרֶב יִשְׂרָאֵל עַד הַיּוֹם הַזֶּה
רַק לְשֵׁבֶט הַלֵּוִי לֹא נָתַן נַחֲלָה אִשֵּׁי יְהוָה אֱלֹהֵי יִשְׂרָאֵל
הוּא נַחֲלָתוֹ כַּאֲשֶׁר דִּבֶּר־לוֹ

And Geshur and Maacah settled in the midst of Israel until this day. Only to the tribe of Levi he did not give an inheritance. The offerings to YHWH the God of Israel are his inheritance, as he said to him.

Josh 13:13–14

Both passages relate to priestly land rights: Gen 47:26 protects priests against royal encroachment while Josh 13:13–14 provides support for priests in the absence of guaranteed land holdings. Moreover, both passages introduce priestly exceptions by means of רַק ("only"). Indeed, these mark the only passages in the Primary History where רַק introduces an exclusionary clause specifically involving priests, except one—Gen 47:22, which also occurs in the context of the Joseph narrative:

רַק אַדְמַת הַכֹּהֲנִים לֹא קָנָה כִּי חֹק לַכֹּהֲנִים מֵאֵת פַּרְעֹה וְאָכְלוּ
אֶת־חֻקָּם אֲשֶׁר נָתַן לָהֶם פַּרְעֹה עַל־כֵּן לֹא מָכְרוּ אֶת־אַדְמָתָם:

Only the land of the priests [Joseph] did not purchase, because it was a fixed allowance for the priests from Pharaoh. And they ate their allowance that Pharaoh gave to them. Therefore, they did not sell their land.

---

Deuteronomistic history" (emphasis mine). See also the discussion of Westermann and Kratz in chapter 4.

30. J. C. Geoghegan, "Additional Evidence for a Deuteronomistic Redaction of the 'Tetrateuch,'" *CBQ* 67/3 (2005) 405–21. I wish to thank the Catholic Biblical Association for granting permission to present material here that, in a slightly different form, first appeared in the above noted article.

The use of רַק to introduce exceptions has been identified as a redactional technique of Dtr in the DH, even in the context of "until this day."[31] Moreover, Gen 47:26 marks the only time "until this day" is used to highlight a policy or practice outside of Israel except the rule of the threshold at the temple of Dagon (1 Sam 5:5), which has clear affinities to another use of "until this day" in Genesis:

עַל־כֵּן לֹא־יֹאכְלוּ בְנֵי־יִשְׂרָאֵל אֶת־גִּיד הַנָּשֶׁה אֲשֶׁר עַל־כַּף
הַיָּרֵךְ עַד הַיּוֹם הַזֶּה כִּי נָגַע בְּכַף־יֶרֶךְ יַעֲקֹב בְּגִיד הַנָּשֶׁה׃

Therefore, the Israelites do not eat the thigh muscle that is on the hip socket until this day, because he struck Jacob on the hip socket at the thigh muscle.

Gen 32:33

עַל־כֵּן לֹא־יִדְרְכוּ כֹהֲנֵי דָגוֹן וְכָל־הַבָּאִים בֵּית־דָּגוֹן
עַל־מִפְתַּן דָּגוֹן בְּאַשְׁדּוֹד עַד הַיּוֹם הַזֶּה

Therefore, the priests of Dagon and all those entering the house of Dagon do not step upon the threshold of Dagon in Ashdod until this day.[32]

1 Sam 5:5

Both passages recount how contact with the divine results in a cultic prohibition that persists "until this day." Moreover, these mark the only appearance of the formula עַד הַיּוֹם הַזֶּה + plural verb + עַל־כֵּן לֹא in the Hebrew Bible. The closest linguistic parallel (specifically, עַל־כֵּן + plural verb + עַד הַיּוֹם הַזֶּה) appears only one time in the Bible (Judg 18:12), in a passage where Dtr calls attention to a site that attests to Dan's northern migration and that explains why Gershonite-Levites served at the sanctuary of Dan "until the exile of the land" (Judg 18:30), which itself has connections with other the uses of "until this day" in the DH (i.e., Levitical inheritance rights), including Josh 13:14.

Another point of contact between "until this day" in Genesis and the DH is its use in connection with Israel's neighbors, Moab and Ammon (Gen 19:37, 38), which mirrors Dtr's use of the phrase in connection to Edom in Deut 2:22 (cf. 2 Kgs 8:22; 14:7; 16:6). In fact, the only other mention of Moab and Ammon as "descendants of Lot" occurs in this same chapter of

---

31. See Smend, "Das Gesetz und die Völker," 494, 499; Barrick, "On the 'Removal of the High Places,'" 257–59, for the redactional use of רַק by the Deuteronomist(s). For its use in connection with "until this day" in the DH, see esp. Josh 13:13b-14; 1 Kgs 8:8b-9; 2 Kgs 10:27b-29.

32. LXX of 1 Sam 5:5 adds ὅτι ὑπερβαίνοντες ὑπερβαίνουσιν following "until this day," which, if original, would make the grammatical parallels between these two passages even more explicit (i.e., the presence of a כִּי clause in both). Cf. Josh 6:25.

Deuteronomy (Deut 2:8–9; 17–19), and in a context that presumes a knowledge of the Genesis 19 tradition.

Finally, and related to this last point, "until this day" in Gen 35:20 attests to the persistence of Rachel's tomb, which only receives mention again in the DH (1 Sam 10:12) and, by allusion, in the Deuteronomistically-oriented book of Jeremiah (31:15). Indeed, not only does the phrase in Gen 19:38 and 35:20 testify to matters that are later presumed by Dtr in the DH but "until this day" in both cases is followed by the same itinerary notice וַיִּסַּע ("and he set out"), which serves as a redactional bridge, moving the main character from the location specified in one tradition to that of another.[33]

At minimum, this evidence suggests that Dtr was familiar with the use of the phrase in the Tetrateuch, allowing him to imitate it in his own writing. However, it may be that Dtr, who most scholars agree combined northern and southern sources in the DH, did the same for the earlier period. After all, "until this day" in Genesis consistently appears at the juncture of the main northern and southern sources hypothesized for this corpus.[34] In view of this evidence, H. Holzinger's observations, made over a century ago, are noteworthy:

> The relationship [between R$^{JE}$ and R$^D$] is so marked that it is frequently difficult to decide whether a secondary passage is to be ascribed to R$^{JE}$ or a Deuteronomistic editor ... It must be asked whether, given this evidence, it is not altogether simpler to identify R$^{JE}$ with R$^D$, and thus combine the two redaction stages J + E and JE + D into one single stage J + E + D.[35]

Such a hypothesis is all the more probable if, as a number of scholars have recently argued (in agreement with the scholarly consensus prior to

---

33. According to traditional source analysis, the itinerary notice in Gen 20:1 moves Abraham "from there," which is presumably Mamre (18:1 = J), to Gerar, where he engages in his second wife-sister act (20:2–18 = E). The use of the notice in Gen 35:21 relocates Jacob from near Bethlehem (35:19 = E) to Migdal Eder (35:21 = J). For the identification of sources, see Driver, *Introduction*; M. Noth, *A History of Pentateuchal Traditions*; and R. E. Friedman, *The Bible with Sources Revealed*. The identification, even existence, of a distinct J or E source is a matter of ongoing debate. For a history of the debate, see E. Nicholson, *The Pentateuch in the Twentieth Century: The Legacy of Julius Wellhausen* (Oxford: Clarendon, 1998).

34. Gen 19:37, 38 = J → E; Gen 26:33 = J → P (or, more likely, R$^{JE}$); Gen 32:33 = E → J; Gen 35:20 = E → J; Gen 47:26 = E → J. The precise source change between Gen 47:26–27 is a matter of disagreement. Driver (*Introduction*, 16) and Noth (*A History of Pentateuchal Traditions*, 267) indicate that the change is between J and P. Friedman, however, argues for a change between E and J. In either case, they all agree that a change takes place. Even if one rejects the notion of a distinct J and E source, that "until this day" is redactional in Genesis seems relatively secure.

35. H. Holzinger, *Einleitung in den Hexateuch* (Freiburg: Mohr, 1893) 490, as cited in Nicholson, *The Pentateuch in the Twentieth Century*, 242–43.

Noth), the Tetrateuchal sources extend beyond Numbers.³⁶ As D. N. Freedman has observed:

> If J and E actually carried the story down into the period of the monarchy, then [the Deuteronomistic Historian] must have used them, as he used the court history, D, and other sources. And if he made use of JE for the post-Mosaic period, he could hardly have dismissed or ignored it in the pre-Mosaic and Mosaic eras. It is likely, therefore, that [the Deuteronomistic Historian] compiled his history along the same lines as J and E (or JE, which is presumably all that was available to him)—i.e., he began with Genesis and carried the story down to the reign and reformation of Josiah.³⁷

While "until this day" cannot, by itself, demonstrate that the same redactional hand is involved in both the Tetrateuch and DH,³⁸ the similarities in its use in both "works" provides additional evidence for this possibility.³⁹

---

36. For a recent defense of at least one Pentateuchal source (i.e., J) continuing into the DH (to 1 Kings 2), see R. E. Friedman, *The Hidden Book in the Bible* (San Francisco: HarperSanFrancisco, 1998). For the literary relationship between the Patriarchal narratives and the Court History more generally, see, e.g., J. A. Emerton, "Judah and Tamar," *VT* 29 (1979) 403–15; G. Rendsburg, "David and His Circle in Genesis XXXVIII," *VT* 36/4 (1986) 438–46; idem, "Biblical Literature as Politics: The Case of Genesis," in *Religion and Politics in the Ancient Near East*, ed. A. Berlin (Bethesda, MD: University of Maryland Press, 1996) 47–70; R. B. Coote and D. R. Ord, *The Bible's First History: From Eden to the Court of David with the Yahwist* (Philadelphia: Fortress, 1989); D. N. Freedman, "Dinah and Shechem, Tamar and Amnon," in *God's Steadfast Love: Essays in Honor of Prescott Harrison Williams, Jr.*, Austin Seminary Bulletin 105.2 (1990) 51–63. Republished in *Divine Commitment and Human Obligation* (Grand Rapids, MI: Eerdmans, 1997) 485–95; C. Ho, "The Stories of the Family Troubles of Judah and David: A Study of their Literary Links," *VT* 49/4 (1999) 514–31; R. de Hoop, "The Use of the Past to Address the Present: The Wife-Sister Incidents (Gen 12,10–20; 20,1–18; 26,1–16)" in *Studies in the Book of Genesis: Literature, Redaction, and History*, ed. A. Wénin (BETL 155; Leuven: Leuven University Press, 2001) 359–69; J. C. Geoghegan, "Israelite Sheepshearing and David's Rise to Power," *Biblica* 87/1 (2006) 55–63.

37. Freedman, "Pentateuch," *IDB* 3:716–17.

38. Peckham's proposal—namely, that a subsequent Deuteronomistic redactor (his Dtr²) joined the DH with the Tetrateuch traditions—provides another possible way of reconstructing this process. For a summary of Peckham's argument, see chapter 4.

39. Even in view of this evidence, I consider the possibility that Dtr is the source of "until this day" in Genesis considerably less certain than for the DH, where there is significantly more material for analysis (six versus forty-three uses) and where the phrase consistently appears in connection with other Dtr redactional material, which is comparatively lacking in the case of Genesis (though this cannot be said of the Tetrateuch more generally). For the identification of Deuteronom(ist)ic elements in the Tetrateuch, with varying explanations, see C. H. W. Brekelmans, "Die sogenannten deuteronomistischen Elemente in Genesis bis Numeri. Ein Beitrag zur Vorgeschichte des Deuteronomiums," *Volume du Congrès Genève 1965* (VTSup 15; 1966) 90–96; P. Weimar, *Untersuchungen zur Redaktionsgeschichte des Pentateuch* (BZAW 146; Berlin: de Gruyter, 1977); H. Ausloos, "Les extrêmes se touchent . . . Proto-Deuteronomic and Simili-Deuteronomistic Elements in Genesis-Numbers" in *Deuteronomy*

158   *The Time, Place, and Purpose of the Deuteronomistic History*

Another use of the phrase that bears even more directly on the present study and, therefore, deserves brief attention, is "until this day" in direct speech.[40] A cursory appraisal of its use in direct speech in the DH reveals that the phrase is found precisely in those units assigned by Noth and others to Dtr (or, in its last uses in Deuteronomy and Kings, to Dtr²) as a means of structuring his history: (1) Moses' final speech (Deut 29:4); (2) Joshua's penultimate speech (Josh 23:8–9); (3) YHWH's acquiescence to monarchy (1 Sam 8:8); (4) Samuel's final speech (1 Sam 12:2); (5) the promise to David (2 Sam 7:6); and (6) the prophetic predictions of impending disaster for Jerusalem (2 Kgs 20:17; 21:15).[41] That is, what was determined to be a predominantly Deuteronomistic phrase in etiological contexts seems also to have been one in direct speech.[42] Weinfeld observed this for the fuller

---

*and Deuteronomic Literature: Festschrift C. H. W. Brekelmans*, ed. M. Vervenne and J. Lust (BETL 133; Leuven: University Press, 1997) 341–66. R. Rendtorff, *The Old Testament: An Introduction* (Philadelphia: Fortress, 1986. German original; Neukirchen-Vluyn: Neukirchener Verlag, 1983); Rendtorff, *The Problem of the Process of Transmission in the Pentateuch* (JSOTSup 89; Sheffield: JSOT, 1990. German original; Berlin: de Gruyter, 1977); N. Lohfink, "Deutéronome et Pentateuque: État de la recherche," in *Le Pentateuque: Débats et recherches* (Lectio Divina 151; Paris: du Cerf, 1992) 35–64; W. H. C. Propp, *Exodus 1–18: A New Translation with Commentary* (AB 2; New York: Doubleday, 1998) 376–78. As Propp observes concerning the D-like material in Exodus, "However we explain it, the phenomenon is undeniable" (*Exodus*, 377).

40. Of the thirty-two uses of "until this day" in direct speech, three appear in the "Tetrateuch" (Gen 48:15; Exod 10:6; Num 22:30), fifteen in the DH (Deut 11:4; 29:3; Josh 22:3, 17; 23:8, 9; Judg 19:30; 1 Sam 8:8; 12:2; 29:3, 6, 8; 2 Sam 7:6; 2 Kgs 20:17; 21:15); one in Isaiah (39:6, which repeats 2 Kgs 20:17), nine in Jeremiah (3:25; 7:25; 11:7; 25:3; 32:20, 31; 35:14; 36:2; 44:10), and one each in Ezekiel (20:31; though cf. 2:3), Ezra (9:7), Nehemiah (9:32) and 1 Chronicles (17:5, which repeats 2 Sam 7:6).

41. Cogan and Tadmor (*2 Kings*, 262–63) are correct, in my opinion, that 2 Kgs 20:17 does not point to the ultimate destruction of the nation, but rather to the events of 598/7 B.C.E. There is no mention, for example, of the final destruction of Jerusalem and the temple, only that "what is in your palace" will be carried away. Moreover, the prophet speaks only of "some" of the king's sons going into exile to serve in the Babylonian royal court. The same may be true of 2 Kgs 21:15, though it's tone is certainly more foreboding. Again, see Cogan and Tadmor (*2 Kings* 270–71), who rightly observe that the threat of exile "can in no way be evidence ipso facto for an exilic date." As for the reconstruction offered below, I agree with those ascribing this unit to a subsequent Deuteronomistic redaction, though I attribute this redaction to the same hand(s) responsible for the first edition of the DH. For similar observations, see Friedman, "From Egypt to Egypt: Dtr¹ to Dtr²," 176–78.

42. A similar argument could be made for the phrase כַּיּוֹם הַזֶּה ("as at this day") which occurs only in direct speech and predominantly in the DH and Jeremiah, even appearing in close proximity with "until this day" in both works. See Weinfeld, *Deuteronomic School*, 174–75. The statistics for כַּיּוֹם הַזֶּה are as follows: one in Genesis (50:20); twelve in the DH (Deut 2:30; 4:20, 38; 6:24; 8:18; 10:15; 29:27; 1 Sam 22:8, 13; 1 Kgs 3:6; 8:24, 61), six in Jeremiah (Jer 11:5; 25:18; 32:20; 44:6, 22, 23); two each in Daniel (9:7, 15), Ezra (9:7, 15) and Chronicles (1 Chron 28:7; 2 Chron 6:15=1 Kgs 8:24), and one in Nehemiah (Neh 9:10). The uses in Daniel, Ezra and Nehemiah all show familiarity with its use in Jeremiah, and the one unique use in Chronicles (1 Chron 28:7) shows familiarity with its use in the DH (1 Kgs 3:6).

phrase מִן־הַיּוֹם אֲשֶׁר יָצְאוּ מִמִּצְרַיִם וְעַד הַיּוֹם הַזֶּה ("from the day that they came out of Egypt and until this day"),[43] and the hypothesis that Dtr constructed many of the speeches in the DH has long been suggested by scholars and fits well with what we know about the methods of other ancient historians.[44] It is noteworthy, in light of this evidence, that the phrase appears nine times in the book of Jeremiah, especially in view of recent studies that have argued for a more direct relationship between the redactions of the DH (Dtr[1] and Dtr[2]) and this book.[45] After all, "this day" *is* Jeremiah's day, and the relationship between the DH and this prophetic book has long been observed.[46] Whether Jeremiah—a northern prophet/priest with access to scribal resources and the repository of Israel's traditions during the reigns of Josiah and subsequent kings[47]—was involved directly in the compilation of the DH or whether we ascribe such activity to "Jeremianic" or "Deuteronomistic" circles (e.g., the Shaphanides), will likely always be a matter of debate.[48] Even so, that "until this day" was a Jeremi-

---

43. Weinfeld, *Deuteronomy and the Deuteronomic School*, 341.

44. See, e.g., Thucydides, *History* 1.22. See, too, Weinfeld's comments on oration in the DH (*Deuteronomy and the Deuteronomic School*, 51–53).

45. Although coming to different conclusions regarding the purpose and provenance of these redactions, see, e.g., R. E. Friedman, "From Egypt to Egypt: Dtr[1] to Dtr[2]"; idem, "The Deuteronomistic School" in *Fortunate the Eyes That See: David Noel Freedman Festschrift*, ed. A. Beck, A. Bartlet, P. Raabe and C. Franke (Grand Rapids, MI: Eerdmans, 1995) 70–80. T. Römer, "Is There a Deuteronomistic Redaction in the Book of Jeremiah?" in *Israel Constructs Its History*, 399–421; B. Gosse, "Trois étapes de la rédaction du livre de Jérémie: La venue du Malheur contre ce lieu (Jérusalem) puis contre tout chair (Judah et les nations) et enfin de noveau contre ce lieu, mais identifié cette fois en Babylon," *ZAW* 111 (1999) 508–29; W. L. Holladay, "Elusive Deuteronomists, Jeremiah, and Proto-Deuteronomy," *CBQ* 66/1 (2004) 55–77; M. Leuchter, *Josiah's Reform and Jeremiah's Scroll*.

46. As noted in chapter 1, Jewish tradition held that Jeremiah was responsible for the compilation of Kings, a determination based in large part upon the parallels in language and perspective between these two books. The most influential studies on the Deuteronomistic redaction of Jeremiah remain those of W. Thiel: *Die deuteronomistische Redaktion von Jeremia 1–25* (WMANT 41; Neukirchen-Vluyn: Neukirchener Verlag, 1973); *Die deuteronomistische Redaktion von Jeremia 26–45* (WMANT 52; Neukirchen-Vluyn: Neukirchener Verlag, 1981). For a recent analysis of the parallel phraseology between the DH and Jeremiah, see G. H. Parke-Taylor, *The Formation of the Book of Jeremiah: Doublets and Recurring Phrases* (SBLMS 51; Atlanta, GA: Society of Biblical Literature, 2000) esp. 267–92. Parke-Taylor concludes: "the preponderance of Deuteronomistic phrases in large sections of the book of Jeremiah leads on (*sic*) to the strong probability that such a redaction took place" (292).

47. Not to mention Jeremiah's close association with those involved in the discovery of the law connected with Josiah's reforms. See, e.g., Jer 26:24; 29:3; 36:10–12; 39:14; 43:6.

48. Surveys of Jeremianic scholarship are too numerous to list here, though a sense of the diversity of the field can be gained by comparing the views of R. P. Carroll (*Jeremiah: A Commentary* [OTL; London: SCM Press, 1986]), who feels that little if anything can be ascribed to the actual prophet and that Baruch is likely a fictional character (49), with those of J. Muilenburg ("Baruch the Scribe," in *Proclamation and Presence: Essays in Honour of G. Henton Davies,*

anic idiom is certain, and that the phrase even formed part of the actual prophet's own linguistic repertoire is difficult to deny given its presence in passages usually connected with the prophet or his close associates (e.g., Baruch ben Neriah). With this in mind, the words recorded for the prophet in Jer 25:3 bear repeating:

> For twenty-three years, from the thirteenth year of King Josiah son of Amon of Judah *until this day*, the word of YHWH has come to me, and I have spoken to you repeatedly, but you have not listened.[49]

Jer 36:1–2 similarly makes reference to "this day":

> In the fourth year of Jehoiakim, son of Josiah, king of Judah, this word came to Jeremiah from YHWH: "Take a scroll and write on it all the words that I have spoken to you against Israel and Judah and all the nations from the day I spoke to you, from the days of Josiah *until this day*."[50]

Though reckoned differently, "this day" is, importantly, the same day: 605 B.C.E., when Babylon, under its new king, Nebuchadnezzar, defeated Egypt at Carchemish and the future of Judah was very much in doubt. This circumstance, and the events that followed, certainly qualify as "a period of crisis" that some scholars deem necessary for the production of a national history (i.e., when the future of the nation is in doubt). Of course, certainty in identifying what belongs to the prophet and what belongs to later tradents is notoriously difficult. We need only recall that John Bright's lament, with which this study began, was penned while working on his commentary on Jeremiah: "scarcely a single statement can be made about the state of the field that would not be subject to qualification."[51] Be this as it may, if recent studies arguing for a shared redactional history for the DH and Jeremiah are correct, then the evidence of "until this day" in both works suggests that, while the preservation of the past was certainly a

---

ed. H. T. Frank and W. L. Reed [Nashville/New York: Abingdon Press, 1970] 42–63), who attributes considerable material to the historical Jeremiah and argues that Baruch played a significant role in the compilation of the book up to Jer 45:5. For a recent assessment of the field, see Lundbom, *Jeremiah 1–20*, 57–101. For a survey of scholarship on the possible Deuteronomistic editing of Jeremiah, see Holladay, "Elusive Deuteronomists," 55–77. I am in general agreement with Holladay that the Deuteronomistic elements in Jeremiah are not due to subsequent Deuteronomistic redactions but derive from the prophet himself, who was "profoundly shaped by Proto-Deuteronomy" (76).

49. For the proximity of these words to the prophet, see J. Lundbom, *Jeremiah 21–36: A New Translation with Introduction and Commentary* (AB 21B; New York: Doubleday, 2004) 242–44.

50. For the association of these words to the prophet, see Lundbom, *Jeremiah 21–36*, 585–86.

51. J. Bright, "Modern Study of Old Testament Literature," in *The Bible and the Ancient Near East*, 2.

motivating factor in compiling Israel's history, it was not the ultimate reason for its production (or, if it was first compiled during the reign of Josiah, its reissue during the reign of Jehoiakim or a subsequent monarch).[52]

As Noth rightly ascertained, the DH was a sermon to a disobedient nation. Only, it was not addressed to a nation languishing in exile to explain its demise, as "until this day" attests. Rather, the DH was written to a nation on the brink of destruction, especially if it continued on its present course. As Jeremiah warns in his Temple Sermon (where, it should be noted, "until this day" [v. 25] also appears as the idiom of the prophet and in a manner paralleling its use elsewhere in Jeremiah and in the DH):

> Will you steal and murder and commit adultery and swear falsely and sacrifice to Baal and go after other gods that you have not known, and then come and stand before me in this house, which is called by my name, and say, "We are safe!" To do all these abominations?! Has this house, which is called by my name, become a den of thieves to you? . . . Therefore, I will do to the house that is called by my name, in which you trust, and to the place that I gave to you and to your ancestors, what I did to Shiloh. And I will cast you out of my sight, just as I cast out your kindred, all the offspring of Ephraim.
>
> Jer 7:9–11a, 14–15

Thus, similar to Jeremiah's Temple Sermon delivered "near the beginning of Jehoiakim's reign" (Jer 26:1) and the scroll given to Jehoiakim "in

---

52. It may be that the first edition of the DH was begun during Josiah's reign and culminated with Hezekiah (see, e.g., Provan). This history was then updated during the reign of Jehoiakim or a subsequent monarch (e.g., Zedekiah; see below) as part of the prophet's attempt to persuade Judah's leadership to follow in Josiah's footsteps (see, e.g., Jer 22:15–17). Perhaps it is to this same redactional stage that the incorporation of prophetic and "nomistic" elements should be ascribed (see, e.g., Smend, Dietrich, Viejola, McKenzie). The final edition (or penultimate edition, if we ascribe 2 Kgs 25:27–30 to an even later hand) saw the addition of the reigns of kings following Josiah, the destruction of Jerusalem, and the predictions of exile to Babylon and a return to Egypt. It may be, however, that the original compilation of the DH was, from the start, intended to persuade Jehoiakim or a subsequent Judahite king of the need to continue in Josiah's Deuteronomic reforms and to maintain (or reinstate?) the Levitical priests (i.e., the Hilkiades?) in their role as the rightful administers of the law and administrators of the temple. This scenario would help to explain the preexilic provenance of the phrase in most of its occurrences along with the open criticism of the monarchy and nation when not following Deuteronomic law. In either case, the redaction of the DH should, as several scholars have noted, be ascribed to the same "circles" (in my view, largely consisting of Jeremiah and Baruch) responsible for the book of Jeremiah. The evidence of "until this day" indicates that both works were begun in the late preexilic period (most uses of "until this day") and were largely complete by the early exilic period (the final uses of "until this day" in direct speech; e.g., Deut 29:3; 2 Kgs 21:15; cf. Jer 44:10). See, e.g., the remarks of Mayes, who, in agreement with earlier analyses of Kings, concludes that it is "very probable that this preexilic work was composed during the reign of Jehoiakim" (*Deuteronomy*, 89).

[his] fourth year" (Jer 36:1), the DH was a written appeal to the nation, and particularly to its royal and temple elite, to change its ways before it was too late.[53] The north had failed in this regard and, as a result, it remained in exile "until this day" (2 Kgs 17:23). But it was not too late for Judah. As Jeremiah declares after his arrest in connection with the Temple Sermon, "It was YHWH who sent me to prophesy against this house and against this city all the words you have heard. Therefore, mend your ways and your deeds and listen to YHWH your God, so that YHWH may renounce the punishment he has decreed for you" (Jer 26:12–13). Such a mending of ways, while primarily involving obedience to the torah of Moses, had political implications as well. After all, Moses had long ago condemned dependence on Egypt as a tragic reversal of the liberation accomplished by YHWH during the exodus (Deut 17:16; 28:68). If the nation wanted to survive, it had to cease looking to Egypt for military aid and submit to Babylonian hegemony (see, e.g., Jer 2:18, 36–37; 27:1–8). The recurrent use of "until this day" in direct speech in relation to the exodus experience—both in the DH (Deut 11:4; 1 Sam 8:8; 2 Kgs 21:15) and in Jeremiah (Jer 7:25; 11:7; 32:20)—would further underscore this point.

Yet, according to the prophet, the most pressing issue facing the nation was not its geo-political posturing but its posture toward YHWH. As Jeremiah reminds Jehoiakim concerning his father, Josiah:

> Did not your father eat and drink and do justice and righteousness? Then it was well with him. He administered justice for the poor and needy. Then it was well. Is this not what it means to know me? declares YHWH. But your eyes and heart are set only on your dishonest gain, on shedding innocent blood, and on committing oppression and violence.
> 
> Jer 22:15b-17

The book of Jeremiah, like that of Kings, ends tragically, with the nation in ruins and many of its inhabitants dispersed or dead. That Moses would

---

53. Such a reconstruction makes sense of Dtr's appeal to written sources, which would have been accessible, both physically and intellectually, to royal and temple officials. I would date this version of the DH (which, as noted above, may have been preceded by an earlier, Josianic, history culminating in Hezekiah) sometime after Jehoiakim's rejection of Jeremiah's scroll. The literary contrast between Josiah's positive response to the Mosaic scroll (2 Kings 22) and Jehoiakim's negative response to the Jeremianic scroll (Jeremiah 36), then, would serve as a rebuke of Jehoiakim (see in this regard, Jer 22:15–17) or, perhaps, as an object lesson for a subsequent Judahite king (e.g., Zedekiah, who did, according to the book of Jeremiah, show moments of contrition and who even instituted a Deuteronomic reform [Jer 34:8–11], however short lived). For the parallels between 2 Kings 22 and Jeremiah 36, see esp. C. D. Isbell, "2 Kings 22–23: A Stylistic Comparison," *JSOT* 8 (1978) 33–45; G. Minette de Tillesse, "Joiaqim, repoussoir du 'Pieux' Josias: Parallélismes entre II Reg 22 et Jer 36," *ZAW* 105 (1993) 352–76.

see the nation's eventual demise and final descent into Egypt with such perspicuity (Deut 28:68) and that Jeremiah, "a prophet like Moses" (Deut 18:15–19), would be a part of this reverse exodus, suggests that this history, which likely had its beginnings in the reforms of Josiah, remained among the prophet's retinue until the end.[54] Indeed, the book of Jeremiah places the prophet's last use of our phrase in Egypt:

> You have not shown contrition until this day, and you have not shown reverence. You have not followed the torah and the laws that I have set before you and your ancestors.
>
> Jer 44:10

This would not be the nation's ultimate fate, however. In a vision ascribed to the prophet during the Babylonian siege of Jerusalem and in a context where our phrase twice appears (Jer 32:20, 31), YHWH declares,

> Behold, I will gather them from all the lands where I banished them in my anger and wrath and great fury, and I will bring them back to this place and let them dwell in safety. They will be my people, and I will be their God. I will give them singleness of heart and character to revere me for all time, so that it will be well with them and their children after them. And I will make an everlasting covenant with them that I will not cease from doing good to them and I will put it in their hearts to revere me so that they will not turn away from me. And I will rejoice in doing good to them and I will plant them in this land in faithfulness, with all my heart and with all my soul.
>
> Jer 32:37–41

---

54. For similar conclusions, see Friedman, "From Egypt to Egypt," 167–92. The absence of Jeremiah from the DH can be explained in several ways. First, much of the history was composed during his lifetime and, therefore, reference to him was unnecessary. Second, following the initial compilation of the DH the compositional attention seems to have shifted to material now found in the book of Jeremiah, where the prophet's role in Judah's national life is well chronicled. Third, we should not overlook Deut 18:18, which, though certainly finding expression in several prophetic figures throughout Israel's history, is particularly apropos to Jeremiah. That is, just as 1 Kgs 13:2 points forward to Josiah, so Deut 18:18 points forward to Jeremiah. For the parallels between the Deuteronomic description of the "prophet like Moses" and Jeremiah, see, e.g., Holladay, "Elusive Deuteronomists," 67–77; Lundbom, *Jeremiah 1–20*, 233–34. Another possible objection to Jeremiah's involvement in compiling or redacting the DH is the apparent dismissive attitude toward "the Ark of the Covenant of YHWH" expressed in Jer 3:16. However, this attitude toward the Ark parallels the prophet's attitude toward the temple: both objects played an important part in Israel's past, the Ark as the throne of God (Jer 3:17) and the temple as the place for God's name to dwell (Jer 7:10, 11, 14, etc.). Yet, neither the Ark nor the temple has any enduring efficacy apart from the people's obedience to the covenant (Jer 7:4). For the general agreement between the DH and the book of Jeremiah, see Römer, "Deuteronomistic Redaction," 399–421.

In view of the present study's emphasis on consulting the works of earlier scholars, it seems fitting to conclude with the comments of Abravanel, who, though certainly influenced by rabbinic tradition in his analysis of the biblical books, may have been very close to the reality when describing the compilation of Israel's history:

> The prophet Jeremiah gathered together and combined these writings and set the books in order based on their accounts. . . . It is [Jeremiah] who says "until this day" and he was the one who wrote "previously in Israel," "for the prophet of today was previously called a seer," and the rest of the phrases that I have demonstrated indicate a later time—all of them are from the activity of the arranger and compiler.

# Bibliography

Aharoni, Y. *The Land of the Bible: A Historical Geography*. Philadelphia: Westminster, 1979. Hebrew original, Jerusalem: Mosad Bialik, 1962.
Ahituv, S., and E. D. Oren, eds. *The Origin of Early Israel—Current Debate*. Beer-sheva: Ben-Gurion University of the Negev Press, 1998.
Ahlström, G. *The History of Ancient Palestine*. Sheffield: JSOT Press, 1993.
———. "The Travels of the Ark: A Religio-Political Composition." *JNES* 43 (1984) 141–49.
Albertz, R. "Die Intentionen und Träger des deuteronomistischen Geschichtswerks." Pages 37–53 in *Schöpfung und Befreiung: Für Claus Westermann zum 80. Geburtstag*. Edited by R. Albertz, F. W. Golka, and J. Kegler. Stuttgart: Calwer Verlag, 1989.
———. "In Search of the Deuteronomists: A First Solution to a Historical Riddle." Pages 1–17 in *The Future of the Deuteronomistic History*. Edited by T. Römer. BETL 147. Leuven: Leuven University Press, 2000.
Alexander, L. V. *The Origin and Development of the Deuteronomistic History Theory and Its Significance for Biblical Interpretation*. Ann Arbor: University of Michigan, 1993.
Astour, M. C. "Shaveh, Valley of." *ABD* 5:1168.
Athas, G. *The Tel Dan Inscription: A Reappraisal and a New Interpretation*. JSOTSup 360. Sheffield: Sheffield Academic Press, 2003.
Auld, A. G. *Joshua, Moses and the Land: Tetrateuch-Pentateuch-Hexateuch in a Generation since 1938*. Edinburgh: T & T Clark, 1980.
Ausloos, H. "Les extrêmes se touchent . . . Proto-Deuteronomic and Simili-Deuteronomistic Elements in Genesis-Numbers." Pages 341–66 in *Deuteronomy and Deuteronomic Literature: Festschrift C. H. W. Brekelmans*. Edited by M. Vervenne and J. Lust. BETL 133. Leuven: Leuven University Press, 1997.
Ayling, S. E. *John Wesley*. London: Collins, 1979.
Barrick, W. B. "On the 'Removal of the High Places' in 1–2 Kings." *Bib* 55 (1974) 257–59.
Barstad, H. M., and B. Becking. "Does the Stele from Tel-Dan Refer to a Deity Dôd." *BN* 77 (1995) 5–12.
Becker, U. *Richterzeit und Königtum: Redaktionsgeschichtliche Studien zum Richterbuch*. BZAW 192. Berlin: Walter de Gruyter, 1990.
Bennett, B. M., Jr. "The Search for Israelite Gilgal." *PEQ* 104 (1972) 111–22.
Bentzen, A. *Introduction to the Old Testament*. 2 vols. Copenhagen: G. E. C. Gad, 1948.

Ben-Zvi, E. "The Account of the Reign of Manasseh in II Reg 21, 1–18 and the Redactional Unity of the Book of Kings." *ZAW* 102 (1991) 335–74.
———. "On the Reading *bytdwd* in the Aramaic Stele from Tel Dan." *JSOT* 64 (1994) 25–32.
Biran, A., and J. Naveh. "An Aramaic Stele Fragment from Tel Dan." *IEJ* 43 (1993) 81–98.
———. "The Tel Dan Inscription: A New Fragment." *IEJ* 45/1 (1995) 1–18.
Blenkinsopp, J. *Gibeon and Israel: The Role of Gibeon and the Gibeonites in the Political and Religious History of Early Israel.* SOTS 2. Cambridge: University Press, 1972.
Block, D. I. *The Book of Ezekiel: Chapters 1–24.* NICOT. Grand Rapids, MI/Cambridge, U.K.: Eerdmans, 1997.
Blum, E. *Studien zur Komposition des Pentateuch.* BZAW 189. Berlin: Walter de Gruyter, 1990.
Boling, R. G. *Judges: A New Translation with Notes and Commentary.* AB 6A. Garden City, NY: Doubleday, 1975.
———. *Joshua: A New Translation with Notes and Commentary.* AB 6. Garden City, NY: Doubleday, 1982.
Brecht, M. *Martin Luther.* Translated by J. L. Schaaf. 3 vols. Philadelphia: Fortress, 1985–1993.
Brekelmans, C. H. W. "Die sogenannten deuteronomistischen Elemente in Genesis bis Numeri. Ein Beitrag zur Vorgeschichte des Deuteronomiums." Pages 90–96 in *Volume du Congrès Genève 1965.* VTSup 15. 1966.
Brett, M. G. "Genocide in Deuteronomy: Postcolonial Variations on Mimetic Desire." Pages 75–89 in *Seeing Signals, Reading Signs: The Art of Exegesis. Studies in Honor of Anthony F. Campbell, SJ for his Seventieth Birthday.* Edited by M. A. O'Brien and H. N. Wallace. JSOTSup 415. London/New York: T&T Clark, 2004.
Brettler, M. Z. *The Creation of History in Ancient Israel.* London/New York: Routledge, 1995.
———. "The Copenhagen School: The Historiographical Issues." *AJS Rev* 27/1 (2003) 1–22.
Briend, J. "The Sources of the Deuteronomistic History." Pages 360–86 in *Israel Constructs Its History: Deuteronomistic Historiography in Recent Research.* Edited by A. de Pury, T. Römer, and J.-D. Macchi. JSOTSup 306. Sheffield: Sheffield Academic Press, 2000. French original, Geneva: Labor et Fides, 1996.
Bright, J. "Modern Study of Old Testament Literature." Pages 13–31 in *The Bible and the Ancient Near East: Essays in Honor of William Foxwell Albright.* Edited by G. E. Wright. Garden City, NY: Doubleday, 1961.
Brodsky, H. "Bethel." *ABD* 1:710–11.
Brueggemann, W. "The Kerygma of the Deuteronomistic Historian." *Int* 22 (1968) 387–402.
Burke, G. T. "Celsus and the Old Testament." *VT* 36 (1986) 241–45.
Burney, C. F. *Notes on the Hebrew Text of the Books of Kings.* Oxford: Clarendon, 1903.
Callaway, J. A. *The Early Bronze Age Citadel and Lower City at Ai et-Tell.* Cambridge: ASOR, 1980.
Campbell, A. F. *The Ark Narrative 1 Sam 4–6; 2 Sam 6: A Form-Critical and Traditio-Historical Study.* SBLDS 16. Missoula, MT: Scholars Press, 1975.

———. *Of Prophets and Kings: A Late Ninth-Century Document 1 Samuel 1–2 Kings 10*. CBQMS 17. Washington, DC: Catholic Biblical Association of America, 1986.

———. "Martin Noth and the Deuteronomistic History." Pages 31–62 in *The History of Israel's Traditions: The Heritage of Martin Noth*. Edited by S. L. McKenzie and M. P. Graham. JSOTSup 182. Sheffield: JSOT, 1994.

———. *1 Samuel*. FOTL 7. Grand Rapids, MI: Eerdmans, 2003.

———, and M. A. O'Brien. *Unfolding the Deuteronomistic History: Origins, Upgrades, Present Text*. Minneapolis: Fortress, 2000.

Caquot A., and P. de Robert. *Les Livres de Samuel*. CAT 6. Geneva: Labor et Fides, 1994.

Carlson, R. A. *David, the Chosen King: A Traditio-Historical Approach to the Second Book of Samuel*. Stockholm: Almqvist & Wiksell, 1964.

Carr, D. M. *Writing on the Tablet of the Heart: Origins of Scripture and Literature*. New York/Oxford: Oxford University Press, 2005.

Chadwick, H. *Augustine*. Past Masters Series. Oxford: Oxford University Press, 1986.

Cheyne, T. K. *Founders of Old Testament Criticism*. London: Methuen, 1893.

Childs, B. S. "A Study of the Formula 'Until This Day.'" *JBL* 82 (1963) 279–92.

Clark, M. T. *Augustine*. Washington, DC: Georgetown University Press, 1994.

Cogan, M. "Israel in Exile—The View of a Josianic Historian." *JBL* 97 (1978) 40–44.

———, and H. Tadmor. *2 Kings: A New Translation with Introduction and Commentary*. AB 11. Garden City, NY: Doubleday, 1988.

Coote, R. B. *Early Israel: A New Horizon*. Minneapolis: Fortress, 1990.

———, and D. R. Ord, *The Bible's First History: From Eden to the Court of David with the Yahwist*. Philadelphia: Fortress, 1989.

———, and K. W. Whitelam, *The Emergence of Israel in Historical Perspective*. SWBA 5. Sheffield: Almond Press, 1987.

Cross, F. M. "The Structure of the Deuteronomistic History." Pages 9–24 in *Perspectives in Jewish Learning*. ACJS 3. Chicago: College of Jewish Studies, 1968.

———. *Canaanite Myth and Hebrew Epic: Essays in the History of the Religion of Israel*. Cambridge/London: Harvard University Press, 1973.

———, and D. N. Freedman. *Studies in Ancient Yahwistic Poetry*. SBLDS 24. Missoula, MT: Scholars Press, 1975. Repr. Grand Rapids, MI/Cambridge U.K.: Eerdmans, 1997.

———, and J. T. Milik, "Explorations in the Judean Buqê'ah." *BASOR* 142 (1956) 5–17.

Crouzel, H. *Origen: The Life and Thought of the First Great Theologian*. San Francisco: HarperCollins, 1989.

Cryer, F. H. "On the Recently Discovered 'House of David' Inscription." *SJOT* 8 (1994) 1–19.

Daley, B. E. "Origen's '*De principiis*': A Guide to the 'Principles' of Christian Scriptural Interpretation." Pages 3–21 in *Nova et Vetera: Patristic Studies in Honor of Thomas Patrick Halton*. Edited by J. F. Petruccione. Washington, DC: Catholic University of America Press, 1998.

Davies, P. R. *In Search of 'Ancient Israel.'* JSOTSup 148. Sheffield: JSOT, 1992.

Day, J., ed. *In Search of Pre-Exilic Israel*. JSOTSup 406. Sheffield: JSOT, 2004.

Dearman, J. A. "My Servants the Scribes: Composition and Context in Jeremiah 36" *JBL* 109 (1990) 403–21.

Derow, P., and R. Parker, eds. *Herodotus and His World*. New York: Oxford, 2003.
Dever, W. G. *Who Were the Early Israelites and Where Did They Come From?* Grand Rapids, MI: Eerdmans, 2003.
———. *What Did the Biblical Writers Know and When Did They Know It?: What Archaeology Can Tell Us about the Reality of Ancient Israel*. Grand Rapids, MI: Eerdmans, 2002.
———, H. D. Lance, and G. E. Wright. *Gezer I: Preliminary Report of the 1964–66 Seasons*. Hebrew Union College/Nelson Glueck School of Biblical Archaeology Annual 1. Jerusalem: Hebrew Union College Biblical and Archaeological School, 1970.
Dietrich, W. "David in Überlieferung und Geschichte." *VF* 22 (1977) 44–64.
———. "Josia und das Gesetzbuch 2 Reg. XXII." *VT* 27 (1977) 13–35.
———. *Prophetie und Geschichte*. FRLANT 108. Göttingen: Vandenhoeck & Ruprecht, 1972.
Dietrich, W., and T. Naumann. *Die Samuelbücher*. Erträge der Forschung 281. Darmstadt: Wissenschaftliche Buchgesellschaft, 1995.
Driver, S. R. *Introduction to the Literature of the Old Testament*. New York: Charles Scribner's Sons, 1892.
———. *A Critical and Exegetical Commentary on Deuteronomy*. 3rd ed. ICC. Edinburgh: T & T Clark, 1902. Repr. 1951.
Edelman, D. V., ed. *The Fabric of History: Text, Artifact and Israel's Past*. JSOTSup 127. Sheffield: Sheffield Academic Press, 1991.
Eichrodt, W. *Ezekiel: A Commentary*. Translated by C. Quin. OTL. Philadelphia: Westminster, 1970.
Eissfeldt, O. *The Old Testament: An Introduction*. New York: Harper, 1965. German original,Tübingen: Mohr, 1934.
———. *Geschichtschreibung im Alten Testament: Ein kritischer Bericht*. Berlin: Evangelische Verlagsanstalt, 1948.
Emerton, J. A. "Judah and Tamar." *VT* 29 (1979) 403–15.
Engnell, I. *A Rigid Scrutiny: Critical Essays on the Old Testament*. Translated and edited by J. T. Willis and H. Ringgren. Nashville: Abingdon, 1969.
Eynikel, E. *The Reform of King Josiah and the Composition of the Deuteronomistic History*. OTS 33. Leiden, New York, Cologne: E. J. Brill, 1996.
Fanwar, W. M. "Sela." *ABD* 5:1073–74.
Fehling, D. *Herodotus and His 'Sources': Citation, Invention and Narrative Art*. Great Britain: Francis Cairns Pub. Ltd., 1989. German original, Berlin/New York: Walter de Gruyter, 1971.
Feldman, S. *Philosophy in a Time of Crisis: Don Isaac Abravanel, Defender of the Faith*. New York: Routledge, 2002.
Fogarty, G. "Scriptural Authority: Biblical Authority in Roman Catholicism." *ABD* 5.1024.
Fohrer, G. *Einleitung in das Alte Testament*. Heidelberg: Quelle & Meyer, 1969.
Fornara, C. W. *The Nature of History in Ancient Greece and Rome*. Berkeley: University of California, 1983
Freedman, D. N. "Pentateuch." *IDB* 3:716–17.
———. "The Deuteronomic History." *IDBSup*, 226–28.
———. "Dinah and Shechem, Tamar and Amnon." Pages 485–95 in *God's Steadfast Love: Essays in Honor of Prescott Harrison Williams, Jr.* Austin Seminary Bulletin

105.2 (1990) 51–63. Republished in *Divine Commitment and Human Obligation*. Grand Rapids, MI: Eerdmans, 1997.
———, and S. Mandell. *The Relationship between Herodotus' History and Primary History*. South Florida Studies in the History of Judaism 60. Atlanta: Scholars Press, 1993.
———, and J. C. Geoghegan. "Martin Noth: Retrospect and Prospect." Pages 128–52 in *The History of Israel's Traditions: The Heritage of Martin Noth*. Edited by S. L. McKenzie and M. P. Graham. JSOTSup 182. Sheffield: JSOT, 1994.
Friedman, R. E. *The Exile and Biblical Narrative: The Formation of the Deuteronomistic and Priestly Works*. HSM 22. Chico: Scholars Press, 1981.
———. "From Egypt to Egypt: Dtr$^1$ and Dtr$^2$." Pages 167–92 in *Traditions in Transformation: Turning Points in Biblical Faith*. Frank Moore Cross Festschrift. Edited by B. Halpern and J. D. Levenson. Winona Lake, IN: Eisenbrauns, 1981.
———. *Who Wrote the Bible?* New York: Summit Books, 1987.
———. "Torah (Pentateuch)." *ABD* 6:612.
———. "The Deuteronomistic School." Pages 70–80 in *Fortunate the Eyes That See. David Noel Freedman Festschrift*. Edited by A. Beck, A. Bartelt, P. Raabe, and C. Franke. Grand Rapids, MI: Eerdmans, 1995.
———. *The Hidden Book in the Bible: The Discovery of the First Prose Masterpiece*. San Francisco: HarperCollins, 1998.
———. *The Bible with Sources Revealed: A New View into the Five Books of Moses*. San Francisco: HarperSanFrancisco, 2003.
Fritz, V., and P. R. Davies, eds. *The Origins of the Ancient Israelite States*. JSOTSup 228. Sheffield: Sheffield Academic Press, 1996.
Frolov, S. "Succession Narrative: A 'Document' or a Phantom?" *JBL* 121/1 (2002) 81–104.
———. *The Turn of the Cycle: 1 Samuel 1–8 in Synchronic and Diachronic Perspectives*. BZAW 342. Berlin/New York: Walter de Gruyter, 2004.
Gal, Z. "Cabul, Jiphtah-El and the Boundary between Asher and Zebulun in the Light of Archaeological Evidence." *ZDPV* 101 (1985) 114–27.
Galil, G., and M. Weinfeld, eds. Studies in Historical Geography and Biblical Historiography. Leiden: Brill, 2000.
Garbini, G. *History and Ideology in Ancient Israel*. London: SCM Press Ltd., 1988.
Geoghegan, J. C. "'Until This Day' and the Preexilic Redaction of the Deuteronomistic History." *JBL* 122/2 (2003) 201–27.
———. "The Abrahamic Passover." Pages 47–62 in *Le-David Maskil: A Birthday Tribute for David Noel Freedman*. Biblical and Judaic Studies 9. Edited by R. E. Friedman and W. H. C. Propp. Winona Lake, IN: Eisenbrauns, 2004.
———. "Additional Evidence for a Deuteronomistic Redaction of the 'Tetrateuch,'" *CBQ* 67/3 (2005) 405–21.
———. "Israelite Sheepshearing and David's Rise to Power." *Bib* 87/1 (2006) 55–63.
Gerbrandt, G. E. *Kingship according to the Deuteronomistic History*. SBLDS 87. Atlanta: Scholars Press, 1986.
Gilbert, P. *Petite histoire de l'exégèse biblique*. Lire la Bible 94. Paris: Cerf, 1992.
Goetschel, R. *Isaac Abravanel: Conseiller des Princes et Philosophe, 1437–1508*. Paris: Albin Michel, 1996.

Goodblatt, D. "The Babylonian Talmud." Pages 257–336 in *Aufstieg und Niedergang der Römischen Welt II Principat*. 19.2. Edited by H. Temporini and W. Haase. Berlin/New York: Walter de Gruyter, 1979.

Gosse, B. "Trois étapes de la rédaction du livre de Jérémie: La venue du Malheur contre ce lieu (Jérusalem) puis contre tout chair (Judah et les nations) et enfin de noveau contre ce lieu, mais identifié cette fois en Babylon." *ZAW* 111 (1999) 508–29.

Gottwald, N. K. *The Tribes of Yahweh: A Sociology of the Religion of Liberated Israel, 1250–1050 B.C.E.* Maryknoll, NY: Orbis, 1979.

———. *The Politics of Ancient Israel*. Louisville: Westminster John Knox, 2001.

Grabbe, L. L., ed. *Can a "History of Israel" Be Written?* JSOTSup 245. Sheffield: Sheffield Academic Press, 1997.

———, ed. *Did Moses Speak Attic? Jewish Historiography and Scripture in the Hellenistic Period*. JSOTSup 317. Sheffield: Sheffield Academic Press, 2001.

Graham, M. P., K. G. Hoglund, and S. L. McKenzie, eds. *The Chronicler as Historian*. JSOTSup 238. Sheffield: JSOT, 1997.

Grant, R. M., and D. Tracy. *A Short History of the Interpretation of the Bible*. New York: Macmillan, 1963.

Gray, E. M. *Old Testament Criticism: Its Rise and Progress*. New York and London: Harpers, 1923.

Gray, J. *1 & 2 Kings*. OTL. Philadelphia: Westminster, 1970.

Greenberg, M. *Ezekiel 1–20: A New Translation with Introduction and Commentary*. AB 22. Garden City, NY: Doubleday, 1983.

Guillaume, P. *Waiting for Josiah: The Judges*. JSOTSup 385. London/New York: Clark, 2004.

Halpern, B. "Sectionalism and the Schism." *JBL* 93 (1974) 519–32.

———. "Levitic Participation in the Reform Cult of Jeroboam I." *JBL* 95 (1976) 33–40.

———. *The Constitution of the Monarchy in Israel*. HSM 25. Chico: Scholars Press, 1981.

———. "Sacred History and Ideology: Chronicles' Thematic Structure—Indications of an Earlier Source." Pages 35–54 in *The Creation of Sacred Literature: Composition and Redaction of the Biblical Text*. Edited by R. E. Friedman. University of California Publications: Near Eastern Studies 22. Berkeley/Los Angeles: University of California Press, 1981.

———. *The First Historians—The Hebrew Bible and History*. Harper & Row, 1988.

———. "Shiloh." *ABD* 5:1213–15.

———. "Erasing History: The Minimalist Assault on Ancient Israel." *Bible Review* 11/6 (1995) 26–35, 47.

———. "The State of Israelite History." Pages 540–65 in *Reconsidering Israel and Judah. Recent Studies in Deuteronomistic History*. Edited by G. N. Knoppers and J. G. McConville. SBTS 8. Winona Lake, IN: Eisenbrauns, 2000.

———, and D. S. Vanderhooft. "The Editions of Kings in the 7th–6th Centuries B.C.E." *HUCA* 62 (1991) 179–244.

Handy, L. K., ed. *The "Age of Solomon": Scholarship at the Turn of the Millennium*. Leiden: Brill, 1997.

Hanson, R. P. C. *Allegory and Event: A Study of the Sources and Significance of Origen's Interpretation of Scripture*. Richmond, VA: John Knox Press, 1959.

Heider, G. C. *The Cult of Molek: A Reassessment*. JSOTSup 43. Sheffield: JSOT, 1985.
Herrmann, S. *Der Prophet Jeremia und das Buch*. EF 271. Darmstadt: Wissenschaftliche Buchgesellschaft, 1990.
Hertzberg, H. W. *Die Bücher Josua, Richter, Ruth*. ATD 9. Göttingen: Vandenhoeck & Ruprecht, 1956.
Ho, C. "The Stories of the Family Troubles of Judah and David: A Study of their Literary Links." *VT* 49/4 (1999) 514–31.
Hobbes, T. *Leviathan, or The Matter, Form, and Power of a Commonwealth Ecclesiastical and Civil* (1651). Oxford/New York: Oxford Press, 1996.
Hoffmann, H.-D. *Reform und Reformen: Untersuchungen zu einen Grundthema der deuteronomistischen Geschichtsschreibung*. ATANT 66. Zurich: Theologischer Verlag, 1980.
Holladay, J. S., Jr. "The Kingdoms of Israel and Judah: Political and Economic Centralization in the Iron IIA-B (ca. 1000–750 B.C.E.)." Pages 368–98 in *The Archaeology of Society in the Holy Land*. Edited by T. E. Levy. New York: Facts on File, 1995.
Holladay, W. L. "Elusive Deuteronomists, Jeremiah, and Proto-Deuteronomy." *CBQ* 66/1 (2004) 55–77.
Holland, T. A., and E. Netzer. "Jericho." *ABD* 3:723–40.
Holzinger, H. *Einleitung in den Hexateuch*. Freiburg: Mohr, 1893.
Hood, F. C. *The Divine Politics of Thomas Hobbes*. Oxford: Clarendon Press, 1964.
de Hoop, R. "The Use of the Past to Address the Present: The Wife-Sister Incidents (Gen 12,10–20; 20,1–18; 26,1–16)." Pages 359–69 in *Studies in the Book of Genesis: Literature, Redaction, and History*. Edited by A. Wénin. BETL 155. Leuven: Leuven University Press, 2001.
Hoppe, L. J. "The Meaning of Deuteronomy." *BTB* 10 (1980) 111–17.
Hornblower, S., ed. *Greek Historiography*. Oxford: Clarendon, 1994.
Huizinga, J. "A Definition of the Concept of History." Pages 1–10 in *Philosophy and History: Essays Presented to Ernst Cassirer*. Edited by R. Klibansky and H. J. Paton. New York: Peter Smith, 1963.
Hunter, A. G., and P. R. Davies, eds. *Sense and Sensitivity: Essays on Reading the Bible in Memory of Robert Carroll*. JSOTSup 348. London: Sheffield Academic Press, 2002.
Hurvitz, A. "The Historical Quest for 'Ancient Israel' and the Linguistic Evidence of the Hebrew Bible: Some Methodological Observations." *VT* 47 (1997) 301–15.
Isbell, C. D. "2 Kings 22–23: A Stylistic Comparison." *JSOT* 8 (1978) 33–45.
Japhet, S. *I and II Chronicles*. OTL. Louisville, KY.: Westminster John Knox.
Jepsen, A. *Die Quellen des Königsbuches*. 2nd ed. Halle: Niemeyer, 1956.
Jones, G. H. *1 and 2 Kings*. NCB. Grand Rapids: Eerdmans, 1984.
Kahle, P. "The Greek Bible Manuscripts Used by Origen" *JBL* 79 (1960) 111–18.
Kaiser, O. *Grundriss der Einleitung in die kanonischen und deuterokanonischen Schriften des Alten Testaments* I. 3 vols.; Gütersloh: Gerd Mohn, 1992.
Kamesar, A. *Jerome, Greek Scholarship, and the Hebrew Bible*. Oxford: Oxford University Press, 1993.
Kannengiesser, C., and W. L. Petersen, eds. *Origen of Alexandria*. Notre Dame, IN: Notre Dame Press, 1988.

Kaufmann, Y. *The Religion of Israel*. Translated by M. Greenberg. Chicago: University of Chicago Press, 1960. Hebrew original, Tel Aviv: Mosad Bialik, 1937–47.
Kelly, J. N. D. *Jerome: His Life, Writings, and Controversies*. New York: Harper & Row, 1975. Repr. Grand Rapids, MI: Hendrickson, 1998.
King, P. J. *Jeremiah: An Archaeological Companion*. Louisville, KY: Westminster/John Knox Press, 1993.
Knauf, E. A. "From History to Interpretation." Pages 26–64 in *The Fabric of History: Text, Artifact and Israel's Past*. Edited by D. Edelman. JSOTSup 127. Sheffield: JSOT Press, 1991.
———. "Does 'Deuteronomistic Historiography' (DtrH) Exist?" Pages 388–98 in *Israel Constructs Its History: Deuteronomistic Historiography in Recent Research*. Edited by A. de Pury, T. Römer, and J.-D. Macchi. JSOTSup 306. Sheffield: Sheffield Academic Press, 2000. French original, Geneva: Labor et Fides, 1996.
———, et al. "BaytDawīd ou BaytDōd? Une relecture de la nouvelle inscription de Tel Dan." *BN* 72 (1994) 60–69.
Knight, D. A. *Rediscovering the Traditions of Israel: The Development of the Traditio-Historical Research of the Old Testament, with Special Consideration of Scandinavian Contributions*. SBLDS 9. Missoula, MT: Scholars Press, 1975.
Knoppers, G. N. "'There Was None like Him': Incomparability in the Books of Kings." *CBQ* 54 (1992) 411–31.
———. *Two Nations under God: The Deuteronomistic History of Solomon and the Dual Monarchies*. HSM 52–53. Atlanta: Scholars Press, 1994.
———. "Prayer and Propaganda: Solomon's Dedication of the Temple and the Deuteronomist's Program." *CBQ* 57 (1995) 229–54.
———. "The Vanishing Solomon: The Disappearance of the United Monarchy from Recent Histories of Ancient Israel." *JBL* 116 (1997) 19–44.
———. "Is There a Future for the Deuteronomistic History?" Pages 119–34 in *The Future of the Deuteronomistic History*. Edited by T. Römer. BETL 147. Leuven: Leuven University Press, 2000.
———. "Rethinking the Relationship between Deuteronomy and the Deuteronomistic History: The Case of Kings." *CBQ* 63 (2001) 393–415.
———, and J. G. McConville, eds. *Reconsidering Israel and Judah. Recent Studies in Deuteronomistic History*. SBTS 8. Winona Lake, IN: Eisenbrauns, 2000.
Kofoed, J. B. *Text and History: Historiography and the Study of the Biblical Text*. Winona Lake, IN: Eisenbrauns, 2005.
Kratz, R. G. *The Composition of the Narrative Books of the Old Testament*. London and New York, NY: T & T Clark, 2005. German original, Göttingen: Vandenhoeck & Ruprecht, 2000.
Kraus, H.-J. *Geschichte der historisch-kritischen Erforschung des Alten Testaments*. 3rd edition. Neukirchen-Vluyn: Neukirchener Verlag, 1982.
Krüger, T. *Geschichtskonzepte im Ezechielbuch*. BZAW 180. Berlin: Walter de Gruyter, 1989.
Kuenen, A. *Historisch-kritische Einleitung in die Bücher des alten Testaments*. Translated by Th. Weber. Leipzig: Otto Schulze, 1887–89. Dutch original, Leiden: Akademische Boekhandel van P. Engels, 1861–65. French translation, Paris: Michel Levy, 1866.
Laberge, L. "Le Deutéronomiste." Pages 47–77 in *'De Bien des Manières.' La Recherche*

*Biblique aux abords du XXIe Siècle: Actes du Cinquantenaire de l'ACEBAC*. Edited by L. Laberge and M. Gourgues. LD 163. Paris: Cerf, 1995.
Lawee, E. *Isaac Abarbanel's Stance toward Tradition: Defense, Dissent, and Dialogue*. Albany, NY: State University of New York Press, 2001.
Lemaire, A. "Vers L'histoire de la Rédaction des Livres des Rois." *ZAW* 98 (1986) 221–36.
———, and M. Saebø, eds. *Congress Volume Oslo 1998*. VTSup 80. Leiden: Brill, 2000.
Lemche, N. P. "David's Rise." *JSOT* 10 (1978) 2–25.
———. *Ancient Israel: A New History of Israelite Society*. Sheffield: JSOT, 1988.
———. "The Old Testament—A Hellenistic Book?" *SJOT* 7 (1993) 163–93.
———. *The Israelites in History and Tradition*. Louisville, KY: Westminster John Knox, 1998.
———, and T. L. Thompson, "Did Biran Kill David? The Bible in the Light of Archaeology." *JSOT* 64 (1994) 3–22.
Leuchter, M. "A King Like All the Nations: The Composition of 1 Sam 8,11–18." *ZAW* 117 (2005) 543–58.
———. *Josiah's Reform and Jeremiah's Scroll: Historical Calamity and Prophetic Response*. HBM 6. Sheffield: Sheffield Phoenix Press, 2006.
Levenson, J. D. "1 Samuel 25 as Literature and as History." *CBQ* 40 (1978) 11–28.
———, and B. Halpern, "The Political Import of David's Marriages." *JBL* 99 (1980) 507–18.
Levin, C. "Das Alter des Deboraliedes." Pages 124–41 in *Fortschreibungen: Gesammelte Studien zum Alten Testament*. BZAW 316. Berlin/New York: Walter de Gruyter, 2003.
Levinson, B. M. *Deuteronomy and the Hermeneutics of Legal Innovation*. New York/Oxford: Oxford University Press, 1997.
Levitt Kohn, R. *A New Heart and a New Soul: Ezekiel, the Exile and the Torah*. JSOTSup 160. Sheffield: Sheffield Academic Press, 2002.
———. "A Prophet Like Moses? Rethinking Ezekiel's Relationship to the Torah." *ZAW* 114 (2002) 236–54.
Levy, T. E., ed. *The Archaeology of Society in the Holy Land*. New York: Facts on File, 1995.
Lipschits, O. *The Fall and Rise of Jerusalem: Judah under Babylonian Rule*. Winona Lake, IN: Eisenbrauns, 2005.
Lohfink, N. "Kerygmata des Deuteronomistischen Geschichtswerks." Pages 87–100 in *Die Botschaft und die Boten*. H. W. Wolff Festschrift. Edited by J. Jeremias and L. Perlitt. Neukirchen-Vluyn: Deukirchener Verlag, 1981.
———. "Welches Orakel gab den Davididen Dauer? Ein Textproblem in 2 Kön 8,19 und das Funktionieren der dynastischen Orakel im deuteronomistischen Geschichtswerk." Pages 349–70 in *Lingering over Words: Studies in Ancient Near Eastern Literature in Honor of William L. Moran*. Edited by T. Abusch, J. Huehnergard, and P. Steinkeller. HSS 37. Atlanta: Scholars Press, 1990.
———. "2 Kön 23,3 und Dtn 6,17." *Bib* 71 (1990) 34–42.
———. "Deutéronome et Pentateuque: État de la recherche." Pages 35–64 in *Le Pentateuque: Débats et recherches*. Lectio Divina 151. Paris: du Cerf, 1992.
———. "Die ältesten Israels und der Bund: Zum Zusammenhang von Dtn 5,23; 26,17–19; 27,1.9f und 31,9." *BN* 67 (1993) 26–42.

———. "Gab es eine deuteronomistische Bewegung?" Pages 313–82 in *Jeremia und die "deuteronomistische Bewegung."* Weinheim: Beltz Athenäum, 1995.

Long, B. O. *The Problem of Etiological Narrative in the Old Testament.* BZAW 108. Berlin: Walter de Gruyter, 1968.

———. "Etymological Etiology in the Dt Historian." *CBQ* 31 (1969) 35–41.

Long, V. P., ed. *Israel's Past in Present Research: Essays on Ancient Israelite Historiography.* Winona Lake, IN: Eisenbrauns, 1999.

———, D. W. Baker, G. J. Wenham, eds. *Windows into Old Testament History: Evidence, Argument and the Crisis of Biblical Israel.* Grand Rapids, MI: Eerdmans, 2002.

Lundbom, J. R. "Jeremiah, Book of." *ABD* 3:706–21.

———. "Jeremiah (Prophet)." *ABD* 3:686–90.

———. *Jeremiah 1–20: A New Translation with Introduction and Commentary.* AB 21A. New York, NY: Doubleday, 1999.

———. *Jeremiah 21–36: A New Translation with Introduction and Commentary.* AB 21B. New York, NY: Doubleday, 2004.

———. *Jeremiah 37–52: A New Translation with Introduction and Commentary.* AB 21C. New York, NY: Doubleday, 2004.

Malamat, A. *History of Biblical Israel: Major Problems and Minor Issues.* Leiden: Brill, 2001.

Masius, A. *Josuae imperatoris historia illustrata et explicata* (1574).

Mayes, A. D. H. *Deuteronomy.* NCBC. London: Marshall, Morgan & Scott, 1979. Repr., Grand Rapids, MI: Eerdmans/London: Marshall, Morgan & Scott, 1981.

———. *The Story of Israel between Settlement and Exile: A Redactional Study of the Deuteronomistic History.* London: SCM, 1983.

———. "Deuteronomistic Ideology and the Theology of the Old Testament." Pages 456–80 in *Israel Constructs Its History: Deuteronomistic Historiography in Recent Research.* Edited by A. de Pury, T. Römer, and J.-D. Macchi. JSOTSup 306. Sheffield: Sheffield Academic Press, 2000. French original, Geneva: Labor et Fides, 1996.

Mazor, L. "The Origin and Evolution of the Curse upon the Rebuilder of Jericho: A Contribution of Textual Criticism to Biblical Historiography." *Textus* 14 (1988) 1–26.

McCarter, P. K. Jr. "The Apology of David." *JBL* 99 (1980) 489–504.

———. *I Samuel: A New Translation with Introduction, Notes and Commentary.* AB 8. Garden City, NY: Doubleday, 1980.

———. *II Samuel: A New Translation with Introduction, Notes and Commentary.* AB 9. Garden City, NY: Doubleday, 1984.

———. "The Books of Samuel." Pages 260–80 in *The History of Israel's Traditions: The Heritage of Martin Noth.* Edited by S. L. McKenzie and M. P. Graham. JSOTSup 182. Sheffield: JSOT, 1994.

McKenzie, S. L. *The Chronicler's Use of the Deuteronomistic History.* HSM 33. Atlanta: Scholars Press, 1984.

———. "The Prophetic History in Kings." *HAR* 9 1985 203–23.

———. *The Trouble with Kings: The Composition of the Books of Kings in the Deuteronomistic History.* VTSup 42. Leiden: E. J. Brill, 1991.

———. "Deuteronomistic History." *ABD* 2:160–68.
———. "The Book of Kings in the Deuteronomistic History." Pages 281–307 in *The History of Israel's Traditions: The Heritage of Martin Noth*. Edited by S. L. McKenzie and M. P. Graham. JSOTSup 182. Sheffield: JSOT, 1994.
———. "The Trouble with Kingship." Pages 286–314 in *Israel Constructs Its History: Deuteronomistic Historiography in Recent Research*. Edited by A. de Pury, T. Römer, and J.-D. Macchi. JSOTSup 306. Sheffield: Sheffield Academic Press, 2000. French original, Geneva: Labor et Fides, 1996.
———. "The Divided Kingdom in the Deuteronomistic History." Pages 135–45 in *The Future of the Deuteronomistic History*. Edited by T. Römer. BETL 147. Leuven: Leuven University Press, 2000.
———, and M. P. Graham, eds. *The History of Israel's Traditions: The Heritage of Martin Noth*. JSOTSup 182. Sheffield: JSOT, 1994.
McNally, R. E. *The Bible in the Early Middle Ages*. Westminster, MD: Newman, 1959.
Millard, A. R., J. K. Hoffmeier, and D. W. Baker, eds. *Faith, Tradition, and History: Old Testament Historiography in Its Near Eastern Context*. Winona Lake, IN: Eisenbrauns, 1994.
Miller, P. D., and J. J. M. Roberts. *The Hand of the Lord: A Reassessment of the "Ark Narrative" of 1 Samuel*. The Johns Hopkins Near Eastern Studies. Baltimore: Johns Hopkins, 1977.
Minette de Tillesse, G. "Joiaqim, repoussoir du 'Pieux' Josias: Parallélismes entre II Reg 22 et Jér 36." *ZAW* 105 (1993) 352–76.
Moenikes, A. "Zur Redaktionsgeschichte des sogenannten deuteronomistischen Geschichtswerks." *ZAW* 104 (1992) 333–48.
Momigliano, A. *The Classical Foundations of Modern Historiography*. Berkeley: University of California Press, 1990.
Montgomery, J. A. "Archival Data in the Book of Kings." *JBL* 53 (1934) 46–52.
Moore, G. F. *A Critical and Exegetical Commentary on Judges*. ICC. New York: Charles Scribner's Sons, 1906.
Muilenburg, J. "The Site of Ancient Gilgal." *BASOR* 140 (1955) 11–27.
———. "Baruch the Scribe." Pages 42–63 in *Proclamation and Presence: Essays in Honour of G. Henton Davies*. Edited by H. T. Frank and W. L. Reed. Nashville/New York: Abingdon Press, 1970. Repr. pages 229–45 in *A Prophet to the Nations: Essays in Jeremiah Studies*. Edited by L. G. Perdue and B. W. Kovacs. Winona Lake, IN: Eisenbrauns, 1984.
Na'aman, N. "Beth-David in the Aramaic Stela from Tel Dan." *BN* 79 (1995) 17–24.
———. "Death Formulae and the Burial Place of the Kings of the House of David." *Bib* 85 (2004) 245–54.
Nelson, R. D. *The Double Redaction of the Deuteronomistic History*. JSOTSup 18. Sheffield: JSOT, 1981.
———. "Josiah in the Book of Joshua." *JBL* 100 (1981) 531–40.
———. *Joshua: A Commentary*. OTL. Louisville: Westminster John Knox, 1997.
Netanyahu, B. *Don Isaac Abravanel: Statesman and Philosopher*. Philadelphia: Jewish Publication Society of America, 1953.
Nicholson, E. W. *Deuteronomy and Tradition*. Philadelphia: Fortress, 1967.
———. *The Pentateuch in the Twentieth Century: The Legacy of Julius Wellhausen*. Oxford: Oxford University Press, 1998.

Noth, M. "Die fünf Könige in der Höhle von Makkeda." *PJ* 33 (1937) 22–36.
———. *The Deuteronomistic History*. JSOTSup 15. Sheffield: JSOT, 1981. German original, Halle: Niemeyer, 1943.
———. *A History of Pentateuchal Traditions*. Chico, CA: Scholars Press, 1981. German original, Stuttgart, 1948.
———. *Numbers: A Commentary*. OTL. Philadelphia: Westminster, 1968. German original, Göttingen: Vandenhoeck & Ruprecht, 1966.
Neef, H. D. *Deboraerzählung und Deboralied: Studien zu Jdc 4,1–5,31*. BTS 49. Neukirchen-Vluyn: Neukirchener Verlag, 2002.
Neusner, J. *The Formation of the Babylonian Talmud: Studies on the Achievements of Late Nineteenth and Twentieth Century Historical and Literary-Critical Research*. Leiden: E. J. Brill, 1970.
Niditch, S. *Oral World and Written Word: Ancient Israelite Literature*. Louisville: Westminster John Knox Press, 1996.
O'Brien, M. A. *The Deuteronomistic History Hypothesis: A Reassessment*. OBO 92. Freiburg, Schweiz: Universitätsverlag; Göttingen: Vandenhoeck & Ruprecht, 1989.
O'Donnell, J. J. *Augustine: A New Biography*. New York: HarperCollins, 2005.
Oeming, M., and A. Graupner, eds. *Altes Testament und christliche Verkündigung: Festschrift für A. H. J. Gunneweg zum 65. Geburtstag.*; Stuttgart: W. Kohlhammer, 1987.
O'Keefe, J. J., and R. R. Reno. *Sanctified Vision: An Introduction to Early Christian Interpretation of the Bible*. Baltimore: Johns Hopkins University Press, 2005.
Olyan, S. "Zadok's Origins and the Tribal Politics of David." *JBL* 101 (1982) 177–93.
Oren, E. D. "'Esh-Shari'a, Tel Sera,'" *EAEHL* 4 (1978) 1059–69.
———. "Ziklag: A Biblical City on the Edge of the Negev." *BA* 45 (1982) 155–66.
Orlinsky, H. M. "Jewish Influences on Christian Translations of the Bible." in *Essays in Biblical Culture and Bible Translation*. New York: Ktav, 1974.
Otto, S. *Jehu, Elia und Elisa. Die Erzählung von der Jehu-Revolution und die Komposition der Elia-Elisa-Erzählungen*. BWANT 152. Stuttgart: W. Kolhammer, 2001.
Parke-Taylor, G. H. *The Formation of the Book of Jeremiah: Doublets and Recurring Phrases*. SBLMS 51. Atlanta, GA: Society of Biblical Literature, 2000.
Peckham, B. *The Composition of the Deuteronomistic History*. HSM 35. Atlanta: Scholars Press, 1985.
———. *History and Prophecy History: The Development of Late Judean Literary Traditions*. New York, NY: Doubleday, 1993.
Person, R. F. *The Deuteronomic School: History, Social Setting, and Literature*. SBLSBL 2. Boston: Brill, 2002.
de la Peyrere, I. *The Theological Systeme upon that Presupposition, that Men were before Adam*. London, 1655.
Pfeiffer, R. H. *Introduction to the Old Testament*. New York: Harper, 1948.
Plöger, O. "Reden und Gebete im deuteronomistichen und chronistischen Geschichtswerk." Pages 50–66 in *Festschrift für Günther Dehn zum 75. Geburtstag*. Edited by W. Schneemelcher. Neukirchen-Vluyn: Neukirchener Verlag, 1957, 35–49. Reprinted in O. Plöger, *Aus der Spätzeit des Alten Testaments*. Göttingen: Vandenhoeck & Ruprecht, 1975.
Porter, J. R. "The Succession of Joshua." Pages 102–32 in *Proclamation and Presence: Old Testament Essays in Honour of Gwynne Henton Davies*. Edited by J. I. Durham and J. R. Porter. London: SCM/Richmond: John Knox, 1970.

Preus, J. S. *From Shadow to Promise: Old Testament Interpretation from Augustine to the Young Luther*. Cambridge, MA: Belknap Press/Harvard University Press, 1969.

Propp, W. H. C. "Gershon." *ABD* 2:994–95.

———. *Exodus 1–18: A New Translation with Introduction and Commentary*. AB 2. New York, NY: Doubleday, 1999.

Provan, I. W. *Hezekiah and the Books of Kings: A Contribution to the Debate about the Composition of the Deuteronomistic History*. BZAW 172. Berlin: Walter de Gruyter, 1988.

———. *1 and 2 Kings*. NIBC. Peabody, MA: Hendrickson, 1995.

———. "Ideologies, Literary and Critical: Reflections on Recent Writing on the History of Israel." *JBL* 114/4 (1995) 585–606.

Puech, E. "La stele araméenne de Dan: Bar Hadad II et la coalition des Omrides et de la maison de David." *RB* 101 (1994) 215–41.

de Pury, A., T. Römer, and J.-D. Macchi, eds. *Israel Constructs Its History: Deuteronomistic Historiography in Recent Research*. JSOTSup 306. Sheffield: Sheffield Academic Press, 2000. French original, Geneva: Labor et Fides, 1996.

von Rad, G. *Studies in Deuteronomy*. SBT 9. London: SCM, 1953. German original, Göttingen: Vandenhoeck & Ruprecht, 1947.

———. "Hexateuch oder Pentateuch." *VF* 1 (1947–48) 52–56.

———. "Die deuteronomistische Geschichtstheologie in den Königsbüchern." *Gesammelte Studien zum Alten Testament*. TB AT 8. Munich: Kaiser, 1958, 189–204.

———. *Theology of the Old Testament*. Vol. I. New York: Harper & Row, 1962.

———. *The Problem of the Hexateuch and Other Essays*. Edinburgh: Oliver & Boyd; New York: McGraw-Hill, 1966.

Rainey, A. F. "The Chronicler and His Sources—Historical and Geographical." Pages 30–72 in *The Chronicler as Historian*. Edited by M. P. Graham, K. G. Hoglund, and S. L. McKenzie. JSOTSup 238. Sheffield: JSOT, 1997.

Rebenich, S. *Jerome: The Early Church Fathers*. NY: Routledge, 2002.

Rehm, M. "Levites and Priests." *ABD* 6:297–310.

Rendsburg, G. "David and His Circle in Genesis XXXVIII." *VT* 36/4 (1986) 438–46.

———. "On the Writing *bytdwd* in the Aramaic Inscription from Tel Dan." *IEJ* 45/1 (1995) 22–25.

———. "Biblical Literature as Politics: The Case of Genesis." Pages 47–70 in *Religion and Politics in the Ancient Near East*. Studies and Texts in Jewish History and Culture. Edited by A. Berlin. Bethesda, MD: University Press of Maryland, 1996.

Rendtorff, R. *The Old Testament: An Introduction*. Philadelphia: Fortress, 1986. German original, Neukirchen-Vluyn: Neukirchener Verlag, 1983.

———. *The Problem of the Process of Transmission in the Pentateuch*. Translated by J. Scullion. JSOTSup 89. Sheffield: JSOT, 1990. German original, Berlin: Walter de Gruyter, 1977.

Richter, S. L. *The Deuteronomistic History and the Name Theology. lĕšakkēn šĕmô šām in the Bible and the Ancient Near East*. BZAW 318. Berlin/New York: Walter de Gruyter, 2002.

Rofé, A. "Ephraimite versus Deuteronomistic History." Pages 221–35 in *Storia e Tradizioni di Israele: Scritti in Onore di J. Alberto Soggin*. Edited by D. Garrone and F. Israel. Brescia: Paideia, 1991.

Rogerson, J. W. *Old Testament Criticism in the Nineteenth Century.* Philadelphia: Fortress, 1985.

———. *W. M. L. de Wette, Founder of Modern Biblical Criticism: An Intellectual Biography.* JSOTSup 126. Sheffield: JSOT Press, 1992.

Römer, T. C., ed. *The Future of the Deuteronomistic History.* BETL 147. Leuven: Leuven University Press, 2000.

———. "Is There a Deuteronomistic Redaction in the Book of Jeremiah?" Pages 399–421 in *Israel Constructs Its History: Deuteronomistic Historiography in Recent Research.* Edited by A. de Pury, T. Römer, and J.-D. Macchi. JSOTSup 306. Sheffield: Sheffield Academic Press, 2000. French original, Geneva: Labor et Fides, 1996.

———, and A. de Pury. "Deuteronomistic Historiography (DH): History of Research and Debated Issues." Pages 24–141 in *Israel Constructs Its History: Deuteronomistic Historiography in Recent Research.* Edited by A. de Pury, T. Römer, and J.-D. Macchi. JSOTSup 306. Sheffield: Sheffield Academic Press, 2000. French original, Geneva: Labor et Fides, 1996.

———, and M. Z. Brettler. "Deuteronomy 34 and the Case for a Persian Hexateuch." *JBL* 119/3 (2000) 401–19.

Rose, M. *Deuteronomist und Jahwist: Untersuchungen zu den Berührungspunkten beider Literaturwerke.* ATANT 67. Zürich: Theologischer Verlag, 1981.

———. "Deuteronomistic Ideology and Theology of the Old Testament." Pages 424–55 in *Israel Constructs Its History: Deuteronomistic Historiography in Recent Research.* Edited by A. de Pury, T. Römer, and J.-D. Macchi. JSOTSup 306. Sheffield: Sheffield Academic Press, 2000. French original, Geneva: Labor et Fides, 1996.

Rösel, H. N. *Von Josua bis Jojachin: Untersuchungen zu den deuteronomistischen Geschichtsbüchern des Alten Testaments.* VTSup 75. Leiden: E. J. Brill, 1999.

———. "Does a Comprehensive 'Leitmotiv' Exist in the Deuteronomistic History?" Pages 195–211 in *The Future of the Deuteronomistic History.* Edited by T. Römer, BETL 147. Leuven: Leuven University Press, 2000.

Rosenbaum, J. "Hezekiah's Reform and the Deuteronomistic Tradition." *HTR* 72 (1979) 23–44.

Rost, L. *The Succession to the Throne of David.* HTIBS 1. Sheffield: Almond Press, 1982. German original, BWANT 3/6. Stuttgart: W. Kohlhammer, 1926.

Roth, W. "The Deuteronomic Rest-Theology: A Redaction-Critical Study." *BR* 21 (1976) 5–14.

———. "Deuteronomistisches Geschichtswerk/Deuteronomistische Schule." *TRE* 8 (1981) 543–52.

Rudolph, W. *Chronikbücher.* HAT 21. Tübingen: Mohr, 1955.

Schearing, L. S., and S. L. McKenzie, eds. *Those Elusive Deuteronomists: The Phenomenon of Pan-Deuteronomism.* JSOTSup 268. Sheffield: Sheffield Academic Press, 1999.

Schmid, K. *Erzväter und Exodus: Untersuchungen zur doppelten Begründung der Ursprünge Israels innerhalb der Geschichtsbücher des Alten Testaments.* WMANT 81. Neukirchen-Vluyn: Neukirchener, 1999.

———. "Das Deuteronomium innerhalb der 'deuteronomistischen Geschichtswerke' in Gen–2 Kön." Pages 193–211 in *Das Deuteronomium zwischen Penta-*

*teuch und deuteronomistischem Geschichtswerk*. Edited by R. Achenbach and E. Otto. FRLANT. Göttingen: Vandenhoeck & Ruprecht, 2004.
Schneider, T. J. *Judges*. Berit Olam. Studies in Hebrew Narrative and Poetry. Collegeville, MN: Liturgical Press, 2000.
Schniedewind, W. M. *The Word of God in Transition: From Prophet to Exegete in the Second Temple Period*. JSOTSup 197. Sheffield: JSOT Press, 1995.
———. "Tel Dan Stela: New Light on Aramaic and Jehu's Revolt." *BASOR* 302 (1996) 75–90.
———. *Society and the Promise to David: The Reception History of 2 Samuel 7:1–17*. New York/Oxford: Oxford University Press, 1999.
———. "Jerusalem, the Late Judahite Monarchy, and the Composition of Biblical Texts." Pages 375–93 in *Jerusalem in Bible and Archaeology: The First Temple Period*. Edited by A. G. Vaughn and A. E. Killebrew. SBLSup 18. Atlanta, GA: Society of Biblical Literature, 2003.
———. *How the Bible Became a Book: The Textualization of Ancient Israel*. New York/Cambridge, UK: Cambridge University Press, 2004.
Seeligmann, I. L. "Etiological Elements in Biblical Historiography." *Zion* 26 (1961) 141–69.
———. "Die Auffassung der Prophetie in der deuteronomistischen und chronistischen Geschichtsschreibung." Pages 254–84 in *Congress Volume: Göttingen, 1977*. VTSup 29. Leiden: Brill, 1978.
Seger, J. D. "The Location of Biblical Ziklag according to Tel Halif Excavations." In *Man and Environment in the Southern Shephelah*. Edited by E. Stern and D. Urman. Jerusalem: Masadah, 1988.
Seow, C. L. "Ark of the Covenant." *ABD* 1:387.
Smalley, B. *The Study of the Bible in the Middle Ages*. Notre Dame, IN: Notre Dame Press, 1964.
Smend, R. "Das Gesetz und die Völker: Ein Beitrag zur deuteronomistischen Redaktionsgeschichte." Pages 494–509 in *Probleme biblischer Theologie*. Edited by H. W. Wolff. Munich: Kaiser, 1971.
———. *Die Enstehung des Alten Testaments*. Stuttgart: W. Kohlhammer, 1978.
———. "Der Ort des Staates im Alten Testament." *ZTK* 80 (1983) 245–61.
———. *Deutsche Alttestamentler in drei Jahrhunderten*. Gottingen: Vandenhoeck & Ruprecht, 1989.
Soggin, A. *Judges: A Commentary*. OTL. London: SCM, 1981.
Spinoza, B. *The Chief Works of Benedict de Spinoza*. Translated by R. H. M. Elwes. New York: Dover, 1951. Latin, Hamburg: Apud Henricum Kunraht, 1670.
Stipp, H.-J. *Jeremia im Parteienstreit: Studien zur Textentwicklung von Jer 26, 36–43 und 45 als Beitrag zur Geschichte Jeremias, seines Buches und judäischer Parteien im 6. Jahrhundert*. BBB 82. Frankfurt: Hain, 1992.
———. "Gedalja und die Kolonie von Mizpa." *ZAR* 6 (2000) 155–71.
Strack, H. L., and G. Stemberger. *Introduction to Talmud and Midrash*. Minneapolis, MN: Fortress, 1992.
Stump, E., and N. Kretzmann, eds. *The Cambridge Companion to Augustine*. Cambridge: Cambridge University Press, 2001.
Sweeney, M. A. *King Josiah of Judah. The Lost Messiah of Israel*. New York: Oxford University Press, 2001.

———. "On the Literary Function of the Notice Concerning Hiel's Re-Establishment of Jericho in 1 Kings 16.34." Pages 104–15 in *Seing Signals, Reading Signs: The Art of Exegesis. Studies in Honor of Anthony F. Campbell, SJ for his Seventieth Birthday*. Edited by M. A. O'Brien and H. N. Wallace. JSOTSup 415. London/New York: T&T Clark, 2004.

Taylor, T., ed. *Arguments of Celsus, Porphyry and the Emperor Julian against the Christians*. London: Thomas Rodd, 1830.

Thiel, W. *Die deuteronomistische Redaktion von Jeremia 1–25*. WMANT 41. Neukirchen-Vluyn: Neukirchener Verlag, 1973.

———. *Die deuteronomistische Redaktion von Jeremia 26–45*. WMANT 52. Neukirchen-Vluyn: Neukirchener Verlag, 1981.

Thompson, T. L. *The Early History of the Israelite People: From the Written and Archaeological Sources*. Leiden: E. J. Brill, 1992.

———. "Dissonance and Disconnections: Notes on the *bytdwd* and *hmlk.hdd* Fragments from Tel Dan." *SJOT* 9/2 (1995) 236–40.

———. "Martin Noth and the History of Israel." Pages 81–90 in *The History of Israel's Traditions: The Heritage of Martin Noth*. Edited by S. L. McKenzie and M. P. Graham. JSOTSup 182. Sheffield: JSOT, 1994.

———. *The Mythic Past: Biblical Archaeology and the Myth of Israel*. New York: Basic Books, 1999.

Torjesen, K. *Hermeneutical Procedure and Theological Method in Origen's Exegesis*. Berlin: Walter de Gruyter, 1985.

Tov, E. *Textual Criticism of the Hebrew Bible*. Minneapolis: Fortress, 1992.

Trigg, J. W. *Origen: Bible and Philosophy in the 3rd Century*. Atlanta: John Knox, 1983.

Tuttle, R. G., Jr. *John Wesley: His Life and Theology*. Grand Rapids: Zondervan, 1978.

Van Seters, J. *In Search of History. Historiography in the Ancient World and the Origins of Biblical History*. New Haven: Yale University, 1983.

———. *The Life of Moses: The Yahwist as Historian in Exodus-Numbers*. Louisville: Westminster John Knox, 1994.

———. "The Deuteronomistic Redaction of the Pentateuch. The Case Against It." Pages 301–19 in *Deuteronomy and Deuteronomic Literature. Festschrift C. H. W. Brekelmans*. Edited by M. Vervenne and J. Lust. BETL 133. Leuven: Leuven University Press, 1997.

———. "The Deuteronomistic History: Can It Avoid Death by Redaction?" Pages 213–22 in *The Future of the Deuteronomistic History*. Edited by T. Römer. BETL 147. Leuven: Leuven University Press, 2000.

Vanderhooft, D. S. *The Neo-Babylonian Empire and Babylon in the Latter Prophets*. HSM 59. Altanta: Scholars Press, 1999.

Vanoni, G. "Beobachtungen zur deuteronomistischen Terminologie in 2 Kön 23,25–25,30." Pages 357–62 in *Das Deuteronomium: Entstehung, Gestalt und Botschaft*. Edited by N. Lohfink. BETL 68. Leuven: Leuven University Press, 1985.

Vatke, W. *Die biblische Theologie wissenschaftlich dargestellt. Teil 1. Die Religion des Alten Testamentes nach den kanonischen Büchern entwickelt*. Berlin: G. Bethge, 1835.

———. *Historisch-Kritische Einleitung*. Bonn: E. Strauss, 1886.

Veijola, T. *Die ewige Dynastie: David und die Entstehung seiner Dynastie nach der deuteronomistischen Darstellung*. Annales Academiae scientiarum fennicae, B 193. Helsinki: Suomalainen Tiedeakatemia, 1975.

———. *Das Königtum in der Beurteilung der deuteronomistischen Historiographie: Eine redaktionsgeschichtliche Untersuchung*. Annales Academiae scientiarum fennicae, B 198. Helsinki: Suomalainen Tiedeakatemia, 1977.
Vervenne, M. "The Question of 'Deuteronomic' Elements in Genesis to Numbers." Pages 243–68 in *Studies in Deuteronomy: Festschrift C. J. Labuschange*. Edited by F. García Martínez et al. VTSup 53. Leiden: E. J. Brill, 1994.
Weimar, P. *Untersuchungen zur Redaktionsgeschichte des Pentateuch*. BZAW 146. Berlin: Walter de Gruyter, 1977.
Weinfeld, M. *Deuteronomy 1–11: A New Translation with Introduction and Commentary*. AB 5. Garden City, NY: Doubleday, 1991.
Weippert, H. "Die 'deuteronomistischen' Beurteilungen der Könige von Israel und Juda und das Problem der Redacktion der Königsbücher." *Bib* 53 (1972) 301–39.
———. "Die Ätiologie des Nordreiches und seines Königshauses (I Reg 11,29–40)." *ZAW* 95 (1983) 344–75.
———. "Ahab el campeador? Redaktionsgeschichtliche Undersuchungen zu 1 Kön 22." *Bib* 69 (1988) 457–79.
———. "Geschichten und Geschichte: Verheissung und Erfüllung im deuteronomistischen Geschichtswerk." Pages 116–31 in *Congress Volume: Leuven, 1989*. Edited by J. A. Emerton. VTSup 43. Leiden: Brill, 1991.
Weiser, A. *Einleitung in das Alte Testament*. Göttingen: Vandenhoeck & Ruprecht, 1963.
Wellhausen, J. *Die Composition des Hexateuchs und der historischen Bücher des alten Testaments*. Berlin: Reimer, 1889.
Wenham, G. J. "The Deuteronomic Theology of the Book of Joshua." *JBL* 90 (1971) 140–48.
Westermann, C. *Die Geschichtsbücher des Alten Testaments: Gab es ein deuteronomistisches Geschichtswerk?* TB AT 87. Gütersloh: Kaiser, 1994.
de Wette, W. M. L. *Lehrbuch der historisch kritischen Einleitung in die kanonischen und apokryphischen Bücher des Alten Testaments*. 5th ed. Berlin: Reimer, 1840.
Wevers, J. W. *Ezekiel*. NCBC. Repr. Grand Rapids: Eerdmans, 1982.
White, M. "'The History of Saul's Rise': Saulide State Propaganda in 1 Samuel 1–14." Pages 271–92 in *"A Wise and Discerning Mind": Essays in Honor of Burke O. Long*. Edited by S. M. Olyan and R. C. Culley. BJS 325. Providence, RI: Brown University, 2000.
———. *The Elijah Legends and Jehu's Coup*. BJS 311. Atlanta: Scholars Press, 1997.
Whitelam, K. W. "Between History and Literature: The Social Production of Israel's Traditions of Origin." *SJOT* 2 (1991) 60–74.
———. *The Invention of Ancient Israel: The Silencing of Palestinian History*. London: Routledge, 1996.
Whybray, R. N. *The Succession Narrative: A Study of 2 Samuel 9–20 and 1 Kings 1 and 2*. SBT 2/9. Naperville, IL: Allenson, 1968.
Williamson, H. G. M. *Israel in the Books of Chronicles*. Cambridge: Cambridge Press, 1977.
———. *1 and 2 Chronicles*. NCBC. Grand Rapids, Michigan: Eerdmans; London: Marshall, Morgan & Scott, 1982.
Wolff, H. W. "Die Ebene Achor." *ZDPV* 70 (1954) 76–81.

———. "Das Kerygma des deuteronomischen Geschichtswerk." *ZAW* 73 (1961) 171–86.

Wright, G. E. "The Literary and Historical Problem of Joshua 10 and Judges 1." *JNES* 5 (1946) 105–14.

Würthwein, E. *Die Bücher der Könige: 1 Kön 1–16*. ATD 11.1. Göttingen: Vandenhoeck & Ruprecht, 1977.

———. *Die Bücher der Könige: 1 Kön 17–2 Kön 25*. ATD 11.2. Göttingen: Vandenhoeck & Ruprecht, 1984.

———. "Prophetisches Wort und Geschichte in den Königsbüchern: Zu einer These Gerhard von Rads." Pages 399–411 in *Altes Testament und christliche Verkündigung: Festschrift für A. H. J. Gunneweg zum 65. Geburtstag*. Edited by M. Oeming and A. Graupner. Stuttgart: W. Kohlhammer, 1987.

———. *Studien zum deuteronomistischen Geschichtswerk*. BZAW 227. Berlin: Walter de Gruyter, 1994.

Zimmerli, W. *Ezekiel 1: A Commentary on the Book of the Prophet Ezekiel, Chapters 1–24*. Translated by R. E. Clements. Hermeneia. Philadelphia: Fortress, 1979.

# Index of Biblical Passages and Ancient Sources

*Biblical Passages*

**Genesis**
| | |
|---|---:|
| 12:8 | 49 |
| 14:17–18 | 49 |
| 18:1 | 156 |
| 19 | 156 |
| 19:37 | 14, 42, 155, 156 |
| 19:38 | 42, 155, 156 |
| 20:1 | 156 |
| 20:2-18 | 156 |
| 22:14 | 13 |
| 26:33 | 42, 156 |
| 28:19 | 45 |
| 32:33 | 42, 155, 156 |
| 35:6 | 45 |
| 35:19 | 156 |
| 35:20 | 24, 42, 156 |
| 35:21 | 156 |
| 47:22 | 154 |
| 47:26 | 24, 42, 154, 155, 156 |
| 47:27 | 156 |
| 48:3 | 45 |
| 48:15 | 158 |
| 50:20 | 158 |

**Exodus**
| | |
|---|---:|
| 10:6 | 158 |
| 25:15 | 11 |

**Leviticus**
| | |
|---|---:|
| 2:3, 10 | 79 |
| 4:35 | 79 |
| 5:12 | 79 |
| 6:11 | 79 |
| 7:30 | 79 |
| 8:1-11:45 | 114 |
| 10:12-13 | 79 |
| 21:6 | 79 |
| 21:21 | 79 |
| 24:9 | 79 |

**Numbers**
| | |
|---|---:|
| 14:24 | 72 |
| 22:30 | 158 |
| 32:11 | 72 |
| 32:12 | 72 |
| 32:41 | 44 |
| 33:50-56 | 153 |
| 34:19 | 90 |

**Deuteronomy**
| | |
|---|---:|
| 1:21 | 36, 76, 122 |
| 1:36 | 72, 91, 127 |
| 2:8-9 | 156 |
| 2:17-19 | 156 |
| 2:20-23 | 52 |
| 2:21 | 52 |
| 2:22 | 9, 52, 60, 91, 121, 123, 144, 147, 155 |
| 2:30 | 158 |
| 2:34-35 | 75 |
| 3:6-7 | 75 |
| 3:11 | 144 |
| 3:14 | 25, 29, 34, 43, 44, 50, 59, 64, 77, 78, 84, 85, 120, 121, 123, 131, 133, 137, 139, 144 |
| 4:20 | 38, 158 |
| 6:4-7 | 145 |
| 6:5 | 103 |
| 6:7 | 145 |
| 6:24 | 158 |
| 7:1-3 | 147 |
| 7:1-4 | 83, 121 |
| 7:1-5 | 130 |
| 7:2 | 75, 76 |
| 7:4-5 | 147 |
| 7:5 | 83, 120, 121 |
| 7:21 | 76 |
| 8:18 | 158 |
| 9:21 | 103 |
| 10:1-5 | 89 |
| 10:5 | 11, 125 |
| 10:6-9 | 125 |
| 10:8 | 60, 62, 64, 80, 82, 88, 120, 121, 122, 123, 139, 145, 147, 148 |
| 10:8-9 | 82, 88, 120, 121, 122, 127, 139, 147 |
| 10:9 | 90, 91 |
| 10:15 | 158 |
| 11 | 144 |
| 11:2-7 | 145 |
| 11:4 | 144, 158, 162 |
| 11:19 | 145 |
| 11:30 | 144 |
| 12-26 | 97 |
| 12:1-7 | 130 |
| 12:5-26 | 72 |
| 13:16-17 | 75 |
| 13:16-18 | 58, 76 |
| 13:17 | 36, 75, 145 |

## 184  Index of Passages

| | | | | | | | |
|---|---|---|---|---|---|---|---|
| Deuteronomy (*cont.*) | | 29:4 | 158 | | | | 121, 122, 123, 144, 155 |
| 13:18 | 145 | 29:10 | 81 | | | | |
| 14:23-25 | 72 | 29:27 | 158 | 6:25-26 | | | 72, 74, 130, 132, 139, 148, 149 |
| 14:27-29 | 150 | 31:7 | 23, 76 | | | | |
| 15:20 | 72 | 31:8 | 76, 122 | | | | |
| 16:2-16 | 72 | 31:11 | 72, 103 | 6:26 | | | 33, 45, 131 |
| 17-18 | 139 | 31:24-26 | 13, 89, 125 | 7:26 | | | 5, 16, 25, 28, 36, 37, 40, 43, 45, 48, 50, 62, 75, 76, 120, 121, 122, 123, 124, 125, 145 |
| 17:8-9 | 149 | 31:25-26 | 150 | | | | |
| 17:8-10 | 72 | 34 | 23 | | | | |
| 17:9 | 88 | 34:5 | 14 | | | | |
| 17:14-20 | 148 | 34:6 | 13, 14, 28, 34, 46, 122, 123, 146 | | | | |
| 17:16 | 162 | | | | | | |
| 17:18 | 93, 145, 148, 149 | | | 7:26-8:1 | | | 121 |
| | | 34:10 | 103 | 8:1 | | | 36, 76 |
| 17:18-19 | 93 | | | 8:28 | | | 4, 25, 36, 49, 50, 62, 75, 145 |
| 17:18-20 | 145, 148 | **Joshua** | | | | | |
| 17:20 | 93, 140 | 1:6 | 76 | 8:28-29 | | | 40, 48, 122, 123 |
| 18:1 | 79, 82, 88 | 1:7 | 76, 93, 94 | | | | |
| 18:1-2 | 79, 88, 91, 120, 122, 127, 147, 148, 149 | 1:7-8 | 93 | 8:29 | | | 4, 25, 28, 36, 43, 48, 50, 62, 76, 88, 93, 94, 120, 121, 122, 124, 126, 144, 145 |
| | | 1:9 | 76 | | | | |
| | | 1:11-15 | 97 | | | | |
| 18:1-8 | 121 | 1:18 | 76 | | | | |
| 18:6 | 72 | 3-4 | 4, 88 | | | | |
| 18:6-8 | 151 | 3:3 | 88, 122, 148 | | | | |
| 18:6-22 | 153 | 4:6b | 4, 145, 146 | 8:29b | | | 35, 76 |
| 18:15-19 | 163 | 4:6b-7 | 4, 145 | 8:29b-30 | | | 35 |
| 18:15-22 | 148, 149 | 4:6-9 | 146 | 8:29-35 | | | 120, 121, 122 |
| 18:18 | 151, 163 | 4:7 | 11, 88, 120, 122 | 8:30 | | | 77, 79, 88 |
| 18:18-20 | 151 | 4:7-9 | 11, 120 | 8:30-35 | | | 77, 88, 93, 94, 122, 139, 144, 145, 146, 148 |
| 18:20-21 | 73 | 4:8 | 137 | | | | |
| 20 | 80 | 4:9 | 4, 16, 21, 25, 26, 28, 31, 40, 43, 48, 49, 50, 62, 76, 77, 88, 120, 121, 122, 123, 124, 125, 137, 139, 145, 147 | | | | |
| 20:10 | 80 | | | 8:32 | | | 94 |
| 20:10-11 | 121 | | | 8:33 | | | 88, 122, 145 |
| 20:10-15 | 124 | | | 8:34 | | | 94 |
| 20:10-18 | 147 | | | 8:35 | | | 94 |
| 20:11 | 80, 82, 122, 125, 128 | | | 9 | | | 59, 81 |
| | | | | 9:1 | | | 94 |
| 20:14 | 58, 120 | | | 9:2 | | | 77 |
| 20:14-17 | 75 | | | 9:17 | | | 124 |
| 21:22-23 | 145 | 4:19 | 45 | 9:27 | | | 5, 16, 25, 34, 35, 58, 59, 64, 65, 71, 81, 83, 86, 87, 120, 121, 122, 123, 124, 128, 131, 137, 145, 147 |
| 23:17 | 72 | 5:1 | 77 | | | | |
| 24:8 | 88 | 5:1-2 | 144 | | | | |
| 26:2 | 72 | 5:9 | 16, 25, 28, 31, 40, 45, 50, 94, 120, 121, 122, 123, 144 | | | | |
| 26:12-13 | 150 | | | | | | |
| 27 | 122, 144 | | | | | | |
| 27:1-8 | 36, 77, 145 | | | | | | |
| 27:1-26 | 121 | 5:9-10 | 121 | 9:27b | | | 35 |
| 27:2-8 | 93 | 5:10 | 45, 93, 94, 144 | 10:25 | | | 76, 122 |
| 27:9 | 145 | 5:10-12 | 93, 94 | 10:27 | | | 25, 35, 40, 43, 48, 50, 62, 70, 75, 76, 120, 123, 143, 145 |
| 28:68 | 162, 163 | 6 | 72, 74, 75 | | | | |
| 29 | 81 | 6:25 | 22, 25, 26, 37, 54, 72, 78, | | | | |
| 29:3 | 13, 158, 161 | | | | | | |

*Index of Passages* 185

| | | | | | |
|---|---|---|---|---|---|
| 10:28a | 75 | **Judges** | | **1 Samuel** | |
| 10:28-43 | 75 | 1 | 12, 48 | 1-8 | 131 |
| 10:29 | 143 | 1:1-2:5 | 35 | 4–6 | 70 |
| 13:8-12 | 86 | 1:16 | 46 | 5:5 | 16, 25, 40, 60, |
| 13:11 | 54 | 1:21 | 11, 12, 14, 15, | | 62, 77, 89, 122, |
| 13:13 | 25, 28, 54, 57, | | 54, 55, 59, 65, | | 123, 131, 139, |
| | 64, 78, 81, 82, | | 82, 83, 121, | | 145, 147, 155 |
| | 85, 88, 91, | | 122, 123, 124, | 6:18 | 5, 16, 40, 50, |
| | 120, 121, 122, | | 128, 131, 137 | | 52, 62, 64, 86, |
| | 123, 124, 127 | 1:23 | 45 | | 89, 120, 122, |
| 13:13-14 | 78, 88, 91, | 1:26 | 12, 45 | | 123, 124, 131, |
| | 120, 122, 127, | 1:28 | 80 | | 139 |
| | 139, 144, 147, | 1:30 | 80 | 8 | 139 |
| | 154, 155 | 1:33 | 80 | 8:4-9 | 139 |
| 13:14 | 79, 121, | 1:35 | 80 | 8:6-9 | 135 |
| | 133, 148, 155 | 2:1-2 | 84 | 8:6-22 | 137 |
| 13:30 | 44, 78 | 2:1-5 | 130 | 8:7 | 139 |
| 14:6 | 90 | 2:6-3:6 | 35 | 8:8 | 158, 162 |
| 14:8 | 72, 127 | 2:10-23 | 97 | 10:12 | 90, 156 |
| 14:9 | 72, 127 | 3:7 | 35 | 12:2 | 158 |
| 14:14 | 16, 25, 28, 35, | 6 | 84, 127 | 12:6-25 | 97 |
| | 55, 72, 79, 82, | 6:24 | 5, 40, 49, 61, | 12:14-15 | 151 |
| | 86, 88, 89, 90, | | 64, 85, 87, | 15:1-35 | 137 |
| | 120, 121, 122, | | 120, 121, 122, | 15:35 | 86 |
| | 123, 127 | | 123, 127, 130, | 16:14-23 | 137 |
| 15:7 | 45 | | 131, 132, 137, | 17:55-58 | 137 |
| 15:9 | 46 | | 146, 147 | 22:8 | 158 |
| 15:10 | 48 | 6:26 | 137 | 22:13 | 158 |
| 15:41 | 48 | 6:28 | 84 | 25 | 90 |
| 15:63 | 14, 15, 16, 25, | 6:30 | 84 | 26:20 | 50 |
| | 28, 33, 34, 38, | 6:31 | 84 | 27:6 | 16, 31, 40, 55, |
| | 54, 55, 59, 65, | 6:32 | 84 | | 64, 89, 120, 123 |
| | 81, 82, 83, 121, | 6:35 | 61 | 29:3 | 158 |
| | 122, 123, 124, | 10 | 78 | 29:6 | 158 |
| | 128, 131, 137 | 10:4 | 40, 43, 44, 50, | 29:8 | 158 |
| 16:10 | 16, 25, 33, 34, | | 59, 64, 77, 78, | 30:25 | 40, 58, 120, |
| | 35, 38, 54, 55, | | 84, 120, 122, | | 123 |
| | 58, 59, 80, 81, | | 123, 131, 133, | | |
| | 82, 86, 121, | | 137, 139, 144 | **2 Samuel** | |
| | 122, 123, 124, | 15:19 | 40, 49, 50, | 2:8-4:12 | 124 |
| | 125, 128, 137 | | 64, 120, 123 | 2:11 | 90 |
| 17:13 | 80 | 16:31 | 35 | 2:18 | 125 |
| 17:14-18 | 126 | 17-21 | 35 | 4:2b-3 | 124 |
| 21 | 85 | 17:6 | 135, 137 | 4:3 | 40, 52, 54, 122, |
| 21:27 | 86 | 18 | 18, 45, 87 | | 123, 124, 125 |
| 22 | 146 | 18:1 | 43, 87 | 5:5 | 90 |
| 22:3, 17 | 158 | 18:12 | 45, 50, 88, | 6:8 | 5, 40, 42, 46, |
| 22:24-27 | 146 | | 123, 155 | | 50, 62, 89, 120, |
| 22:28 | 146 | 18:30 | 17, 86, 87, 155 | | 122, 123, 139, |
| 23 | 97 | 19-21 | 35 | | 145, 147, 153 |
| 23:6 | 94 | 19:30 | 158 | 6:23 | 86 |
| 23:8-9 | 158 | 21:25 | 135, 137 | 7 | 3 |

## 186  Index of Passages

| 2 Samuel (cont.) | | 9:20-21 | 15, 83 | 2 Kings | |
|---|---|---|---|---|---|
| 7:1-17 | 3 | 9:21 | 5, 35, 38, 42, | 1:18 | 70, 143 |
| 7:4-16 | 100, 151 | | 58, 64, 65, 80, | 2 | 128, 130 |
| 7:5-17 | 135, 137 | | 82, 85, 120, | 2:2 | 38, 120, 123 |
| 7:6 | 158 | | 121, 122, 124, | 2:19-22 | 130 |
| 9-20 | 70, 124 | | 125, 128, 137, | 2:22 | 40, 50, 73, 122, |
| 13:23 | 126 | | 147, 153 | | 130, 132, 139, |
| 17:24 | 126 | 10:11 | 61 | | 144, 148, 149 |
| 18:6 | 126 | 10:12 | 5, 61, 64, 123 | 2:23 | 74 |
| 18:17 | 49, 126 | 11:6 | 72, 91, 127 | 3:4-27 | 129 |
| 18:17-18 | 49, 137 | 11:41 | 38, 70, 143 | 8:16-24 | 35 |
| 18:18 | 5, 40, 48, 50, | 12:18 | 80 | 8:22 | 27, 33, 38, 39, |
| | 64, 120, 123, | 12:19 | 27, 42, 59, 60, | | 42, 59, 60, 64, |
| | 124, 125, 126 | | 64, 120, 123, | | 66, 74, 86, 91, |
| 19:25 | 86 | | 132, 133, 153 | | 92, 120, 121, |
| 20:3 | 86 | 12:26-33 | 135 | | 123, 133, 147, |
| 20:24 | 80 | 13:2-5 | 102, 121 | | 153, 155 |
| 21:2 | 34 | 13:26 | 73 | 8:22-23 | 121, 143 |
| 24:16 | 26, 33 | 14:8 | 151 | 8:23 | 38, 70, 143 |
| 24:23 | 15 | 14:15 | 33 | 10:18-28 | 130 |
| | | 14:18 | 73, 130 | 10:27 | 5, 38, 43, 61, |
| **1 Kings** | | 14:19 | 70 | | 64, 70, 84, 85, |
| 1-2 | 124 | 14:29 | 70, 143, 152 | | 87, 120, 121, |
| 2 | 116, 157 | 15 | 129 | | 122, 132, 146, |
| 3:2 | 43, 87 | 15:5 | 140, 151 | | 147 |
| 3:6 | 158 | 15:7 | 70, 143, 152 | 10:27 | 143 |
| 3:14 | 151 | 15:23 | 143, 152 | 10:27-29 | 121 |
| 4:6 | 80 | 15:31 | 143, 152 | 10:27b-29 | 155 |
| 4:13 | 44 | 15:24 | 129 | 10:28 | 130, 131 |
| 5:27 | 80 | 15:28 | 129 | 10:29 | 130 |
| 5:28 | 80 | 15:29 | 73, 130 | 10:34 | 70, 143 |
| 8:1 | 89 | 15:31 | 70 | 11:17-18 | 84 |
| 8:6 | 89 | 15:32 | 129 | 12:3-4 | 131 |
| 8:8 | 5, 11, 27, 28, | 16:5 | 70, 143, 152 | 12:20 | 70, 143 |
| | 38, 42, 50, 61, | 16:8 | 129 | 13:8 | 70 |
| | 62, 64, 85, 89, | 16:12 | 73, 130 | 13:8, 12 | 143 |
| | 120, 122, 123, | 16:14 | 70, 143 | 13:13 | 129 |
| | 125, 139, 147, | 16:19 | 139 | 13:14-19 | 129 |
| | 153 | 16:20 | 70, 143 | 13:20-21 | 129 |
| 8:8b-9 | 155 | 16:25 | 139 | 13:23 | 133 |
| 8:9 | 89, 125 | 16:27 | 70, 143 | 14:1-7 | 35 |
| 8:12-51 | 97 | 16:30 | 139 | 14:3-4 | 131 |
| 8:21 | 89, 125 | 16:34 | 33, 72, 73, | 14:6-7 | 121 |
| 8:24 | 158 | | 122, 130, 139, | 14:7 | 33, 46, 50, 60, |
| 8:47 | 33 | | 144, 149 | | 66, 91, 121, 123 |
| 8:61 | 158 | 17:16 | 73 | 14:7 | 143 |
| 9 | 55, 59 | 18 | 130 | 14:15 | 143 |
| 9:7-8 | 33 | 21:20, 25 | 139 | 14:18 | 70, 143 |
| 9:13 | 21, 44, 85, 120, | 22:39 | 70, 143 | 14:28 | 143 |
| | 122, 123, 133 | 22:45-50 | 129 | 15:3-4 | 131 |
| 9:15 | 59, 80 | 22:46 | 70, 143 | 15:5 | 86 |
| 9:16 | 33, 38, 55 | 22:52 | 139 | 15:6 | 70 |

| | | | | | | |
|---|---|---|---|---|---|---|
| 15:34-35 | 131 | 2:36-37 | 162 | 9:15 | 158 |
| 16:1-9 | 35 | 3:16 | 147, 163 | | |
| 16:6 | 33, 39, 54, 60, 66, 91, 121 | 3:17 | 163 | **Ezra** | |
| | | 3:25 | 158 | 9:7 | 158 |
| 16:16 | 123 | 6:1 | 137 | 9:15 | 158 |
| 17 | 57, 92 | 7:4 | 163 | | |
| 17:7-41 | 97 | 7:9-11a | 161 | **Nehemiah** | |
| 17:23 | 38, 55, 57, 92, 162 | 7:10 | 163 | 9:10 | 158 |
| | | 7:11 | 163 | 9:32 | 158 |
| 17:24-41 | 57 | 7:14 | 163 | 11:33 | 54 |
| 17:34 | 38, 57, 92, 133 | 7:14-15 | 161 | | |
| | | 7:25 | 158, 161, 162 | **1 Chronicles** | |
| 17:34-40 | 57 | 11:5 | 158 | 2:23 | 44 |
| 17:41 | 57, 92 | 11:7 | 158, 162 | 4:41 | 42, 106, 153 |
| 18:4 | 43, 48, 87, 146 | 17:11 | 50 | 4:43 | 12, 42, 153 |
| | | 22:15-17 | 161, 162 | 5:26 | 42, 153 |
| 18:5 | 106 | 25:3 | 158, 160 | 7:21 | 54 |
| 19:8 | 74 | 25:18 | 158 | 8:13 | 54 |
| 19:35-36 | 42 | 26:1 | 161 | 9 | 106 |
| 20:17 | 33, 158 | 26:12-13 | 162 | 10:19 | 42, 153 |
| 21:15 | 158, 161, 162 | 26:24 | 159 | 12:40 | 125 |
| 21:18 | 106 | 27:1-8 | 162 | 13:6 | 46 |
| 21:26 | 106 | 29:3 | 159 | 13:11 | 42, 153 |
| 22-23 | 107, 162 | 31:15 | 156 | 17:5 | 158 |
| 22:2 | 93, 102, 140 | 32:20 | 158, 162, 163 | 28:7 | 158 |
| 22:4 | 60 | 32:31 | 158, 163 | 29:29 | 17, 22, 123 |
| 22:16 | 93 | 34:8-11 | 162 | | |
| 23:1-3 | 93, 121, 144 | 35:4 | 60 | **2 Chronicles** | |
| 23:2 | 93, 103 | 35:14 | 158 | 2:7 | 61 |
| 23:4 | 60 | 36 | 121, 162 | 5:9 | 42, 61, 89, 153 |
| 23:5-20 | 121 | 36:1 | 160, 162 | 6:15 | 158 |
| 23:12-15 | 84 | 36:1-2 | 160 | 8:8 | 42, 153 |
| 23:15 | 76, 92, 103 | 36:2 | 158 | 9:10 | 61 |
| 23:15-19 | 92 | 36:10-12 | 159 | 9:29 | 123 |
| 23:15-20 | 76 | 39:14 | 159 | 12:15 | 123 |
| 23:21-23 | 93, 121, 122 | 43:6 | 159 | 13:22 | 123 |
| 23:24-25 | 93, 103 | 44:6 | 158 | 16:11 | 123 |
| 23:25 | 103, 106 | 44:10 | 158, 161, 163 | 20:26 | 42, 153 |
| 23:26-27 | 135 | 44:22 | 158 | 20:34 | 123 |
| 23:30 | 106 | 44:23 | 158 | 21:10 | 42, 153 |
| 23:31 | 74 | 45:5 | 160 | 24:27 | 123 |
| 24:18 | 74 | | | 25:26 | 123 |
| 25 | 33 | **Ezekiel** | | 26:22 | 123 |
| 25:18 | 60 | 2:3 | 158 | 27:7 | 123 |
| 25:27-30 | 4, 161 | 20:29 | 42, 153 | 28:26 | 123 |
| 25:30 | 98 | 20:31 | 158 | 31:16 | 106 |
| | | | | 31:17 | 106 |
| **Isaiah** | | **Ruth** | | 31:19 | 106 |
| 39:6 | 11, 158 | 1:2 | 125 | 32:32 | 123 |
| | | | | 33:19 | 123 |
| **Jeremiah** | | **Daniel** | | 33:20 | 106 |
| 2:18 | 162 | 9:7 | 158 | 33:24 | 106 |

| 2 Chronicles (cont.) | |
|---|---|
| 35:24 | 106 |
| 35:25 | 153 |
| 35:26-27 | 123 |
| 36:8 | 123 |
| 36:10 | 10 |

## Ancient Sources

**Herodotus**
*Histories*

| | |
|---|---|
| 2.122.2 | 136 |
| 2.135.4 | 42, 136 |
| 2.141.6 | 42 |
| 4.10.3 | 42, 136 |
| 4.12.1 | 42, 136 |
| 7.178.2 | 42, 136 |

**Thucydides**
*Peloponnesian War*

| | |
|---|---|
| 1.22.1 | 159 |
| 1.93.2, 5 | 42, 136 |
| 2.15.2, 5 | 42, 136 |
| 6.54.7 | 42, 136 |

**Pausanias**
*Description of Greece*

| | |
|---|---|
| 3.22.12 | 42, 136 |
| 8.15.4 | 42, 136 |
| 8.44.1 | 42, 136 |

**Babylonian Talmud**

| | |
|---|---|
| B. Bat. 14b-15a | 17 |
| B. Bat. 15a | 13, 14 |
| B. Šabb. 54a | 44 |
| Soṭah 46b | 11, 12, 141 |
| Yoma 53b-54a | 10 |
| Yoma 54a | 11 |

**Josephus**
*Antiquities*

| | |
|---|---|
| 5.8.9 §300 | 50 |
| 7.10.3 §243 | 49 |
| 8.5.3 §142 | 44 |

**Origen**
*Contra Celsum* 2.54   19

**Jerome**
*Adv. Helvidium* 1.7   20

**Augustine**
*Luc. de Jesu Nave* 6.25   5

# Index of Authors

Abelard, 20, 22, 23, 26, 40
Abraham ben Moses ben Maimon, 10
Abravanel, 5, 14, 15, 16, 17, 18, 25, 26, 31, 40, 90, 138, 142, 164
Aharoni, Y., 46, 61
Ahituv, S., 1
Ahlström, G., 2, 70
Albertz, R., 139
Alexander, L. V., 96
Andrew of Saint Victor, 9
Astour, M. C., 49
Augustine, 5, 14, 20, 21, 22, 26, 27
Auld, A. G., 101, 116
Ausloos, H., 114, 157
Ayling, S. E., 25

Baker, D. W., 1, 2, 61
Barrick, W. B., 105, 131, 140, 155
Barstad, H. M., 3
Bartlet, A., 159
Beck, A., 159
Becker, U., 101
Becking, B., 3
Bennett, B. M., Jr., 45
Bentzen, A., 107
Ben-Zvi, E., 2, 101
Berlin, A., 157
Biran, A., 2
Blenkinsopp, J., 52
Block, D. I., 153
Boling, R. G., 38, 49, 78, 103
Brecht, M., 23
Brett, M. G., 76
Brettler, M. Z., 57, 92, 118, 136
Briend, J., 71, 76

Bright, J., 1, 6, 160
Brueggemann, W., 100
Burke, G. T., 19

Callaway, J. A., 49
Calvin, J., 24, 25, 28
Campbell, A. F., 39, 70, 73, 110, 111, 119, 129, 132, 134, 153
Caquot, A., 38, 124, 127, 146
Carlson, R. A., 127, 146
Carr, D. M., 149
Carroll, R. P., 159
Chadwick, H. 20
Cheyne, T. K., 32
Childs, B. S., 9, 37, 38, 39, 40, 41, 43, 65, 67, 70, 72, 124, 137, 142, 143
Clark, M. T., 20
Cogan, M., 39, 42, 54, 57, 61, 64, 72, 74, 91, 92, 94, 103, 121, 133, 158
Coote, R. B., 157
Cross, F. M., 3, 38, 39, 45, 102, 103, 119, 123, 133, 150, 153
Crouzel, H., 18
Cryer, F. H., 2

Daley, B. E., 18
Davies, P. R., 1, 4, 116, 117, 119, 135
Day, J., 2, 150
Dearman, J. A., 121
Dever, W. G., 3, 55, 150
Dietrich, W., 70, 101, 123, 161
Driver, S. R., 35, 44, 71, 77, 79, 96, 156

Edelman, D. V., 1, 136
Eichrodt, W., 153

## Index of Authors

Eissfeldt, O., 96, 99
Eliezer ben Hyrcanus, 10
Emerton, J. A., 73, 157
Engnell, I., 99
Eynikel, E., 106, 134

Fanwar, W. M., 46
Fehling, D., 149
Feldman, S., 15
Fogarty, G., 21
Fohrer, G., 99
Frank, H. T., 160
Franke, C., 159
Freedman, D. N., 114, 138, 150, 157, 159
Friedman, R. E., 39, 79, 103, 104, 106, 119, 123, 156, 157, 158, 159, 163
Fritz, V., 1
Frolov, S., 70, 131

Gal, Z., 44
Garbini, G., 118
García Martínez, F., 114
Garrone, D., 111
Geoghegan, J. C., 154, 157
Gerbrandt, G. E., 93
Gilbert, P., 32
Goetschel, R., 15
Golka, F. W., 139
Goodblatt, D., 10
Gosse, B., 159
Gottwald, N. K., 45, 117
Gourgues, M., 96
Grabbe, L. L., 1, 2
Graham, M. P., 39, 118, 123
Grant, R. M., 32
Gray, E. M., 20, 26, 32
Gray, J., 72
Greenberg, M., 99, 153
Guillaume, P., 131

Hallo, W. W., 88
Halpern, B., 59, 85, 86, 90, 103, 105, 106, 118, 119, 132, 134, 136, 137, 138, 150, 152
Handy, L. K., 1
Hanson, R. P. C., 18
Heider, G. C., 105

Hertzberg, H. W., 108, 124
Ho, C., 157
Hobbes, T., 5, 14, 27, 28, 29, 30, 31, 40
Hoffmann, H.-D., 111, 112, 119
Hoffmeier, J. K., 1
Hoglund, K. G., 123
Holladay, J. S., 59
Holladay, W. L., 159, 160, 163
Holland, T. A., 50
Holzinger, H. 156
Hood, F. C., 27
Hoop, R. de, 157
Hoppe, L. J., 101
Hurvitz, A., 118, 150

Ibn Ezra, 14, 23, 25, 40
Isbell, C. D., 162
Israel, F., 111

Japhet, S., 153
Jepsen, A., 99, 101, 134
Jerome, 19, 20, 23, 40, 141
Jones, G. H., 101
Josephus, 44, 49, 50

Kahle, P., 18
Kaiser, O., 101
Kamesar, A., 19
Kannengiesser, C., 18
Kauf, E. A., 136
Kaufmann, Y., 99
Kegler, J., 139
Kelly, J. N. D., 19
King, P. J., 91
Knauf, E. A., 2, 116
Knight, D. A., 123
Knoppers, G. N., 95, 103, 106, 118, 123, 136, 137, 138, 148
Kofoed, J. B., 2
Kratz, R., 115, 116, 119, 154
Kraus, H.-J., 27, 28, 32
Kretzmann, N., 20
Krüger, T., 153
Kuenen, A., 9, 14, 33, 34, 35, 36, 38, 40, 41, 59, 64, 66, 67, 71, 102

Laberge, L., 96
Lance, H. D., 55

## Index of Authors

Lawee, E., 15
Le Clerc, J. 27
Lemaire, A., 1, 105
Lemche, N., P., 2, 4, 70, 117, 118, 120
Leuchter, M., 88, 135, 139, 159
Levenson, J. D., 90, 103
Levin, C., 150
Levinson, B. M., 121, 151
Levitt Kohn, R., 153
Levy, T. E., 59
Lipschits, O., 134
Livy, 28
Lohfink, N., 93, 95, 103, 158
Long, B. O., 1, 38, 43
Lundbom, J. R., 150, 160, 163
Lust, J., 113, 114, 158
Luther, M., 21, 23, 24, 25, 40

Macchi, J-D., 71
Maimonides, 10
Malamat, A., 2
Mandell, S., 138
Masius, A., 26, 27, 28
Maurus, R., 22
Mayes, A. D. H., 92, 107, 108, 113, 143, 144, 161
Mazar, B., 46
McCarter, P. K., 46, 50, 70, 90, 103, 109, 110, 112, 119, 124, 126, 127, 129, 132, 134, 140
McConville, J. G., 118
McKenzie, S. L., 38, 39, 70, 96, 103, 118, 123, 128, 129, 130, 131, 132, 134, 140, 161
McNally, R. E., 21
Milik, J. T., 45
Millard, A. R., 1
Miller, P. D., 70
Minette de Tillesse, G.,162
Moenikes, A., 103
Montgomery, J. A., 9, 74
Moore, G. F., 17, 38, 78, 84
Muilenburg, J., 45, 159

Na'aman, N., 2, 107
Naumann, T., 70
Naveh, J., 2

Neef, H. D., 150
Nelson, R. D., 38, 39, 40, 41, 45, 55, 89, 93, 94, 104, 119, 122, 123, 125, 144
Netanyahu, B., 15
Netzer, E., 50
Neusner, J., 10
Nicholas of Lyra, 23
Nicholson, E. W., 36, 108, 109, 119, 138, 156
Niditch, S., 149
Noth, M., 6, 39, 48, 71, 77, 79, 89, 96, 97, 98, 99, 100, 102, 107, 111, 112, 113, 114, 115, 116, 118, 119, 123, 127, 134, 148, 156, 157, 158, 161

O'Brien, M. A., 73, 96, 111
O'Donnell, J. J., 20
O'Keefe, J. J., 22
Olyan, S., 111
Ord, D. R., 157
Oren, E. D., 1, 55
Origen, 18, 19, 40, 61
Orlinsky, H. M., 23
Otto, E., 116
Otto, S., 131

Parke-Taylor, G. H., 159
Pausanias, 42, 136
Peckham, B., 87, 113, 114, 157
Person, R. F., 109
Peyrère, I. de la, 29
Pfeiffer, R. H., 96
Plöger, O., 97, 98
Porter, J. R., 93
Preus, J. S., 21
Propp, W. H. C., 60, 86, 158
Provan, I., 106, 118, 119, 134, 136, 161
Puech, E., 2
Pury, A. de, 71, 96

Raabe, P., 159
Rad, G. von, 4, 73, 100, 107, 135
Radak, 14, 15, 23, 40, 41, 59, 65
Rainey, A., 123
Rashbam, 14, 40
Rashi, 11, 13, 14, 23, 40
Rebenich, S., 19

Reed, W. L. 160
Rehm, M., 150
Rendsburg, G., 2, 157
Rendtorff, R., 153, 158
Reno, R. R., 22
Robert, P. de, 38, 124, 127, 146
Roberts, J. J. M., 70
Rofé, A., 111
Rogerson, J. W., 32
Römer, T., 71, 96, 159, 163
Rose, M., 113
Rosenbaum, J., 103
Rost, L., 70
Roth, W., 101

Saebø, M., 1
Schiffman, L. H., 88
Schmid, K., 116
Schneider, T. J., 17
Schniedewind, W. M., 3, 132, 149, 151
Seeligmann, I. L., 37, 73
Seger, J. D., 55
Semler, J. S., 32
Seow, C. L., 88
Simon, R., 31, 32, 90
Smalley, B., 9, 22
Smend, R., 32, 100, 101, 123, 131, 140, 152, 155, 161
Soggin, A., 101, 111
Spinoza, B., 5, 14, 30, 31, 40, 142
Stemberger, G., 10
Stipp, H.-J., 103, 134
Strack, H. L., 10
Stump, E., 20
Sweeney, M. A., 73, 92, 105, 121, 130
Symmachus, 18, 50

Tadmor, H., 39, 42, 54, 57, 64, 74, 91, 92, 94, 103, 121, 133, 158
Theodotion, 18
Thiel, W., 159

Thompson, T. L., 2, 4, 117, 118, 135
Thucydides, 42, 136, 159
Torjesen, K., 18
Tov, E., 54
Tracy, D., 32
Tuttle, R. G., Jr., 25

Van Seters, J., 7, 70, 112, 113, 119, 124, 127, 129, 131, 135, 136, 137, 138, 141, 151
Vanderhooft, D. S., 106, 119, 132, 134
Vanoni, G., 103
Vatke, W., 9, 36, 40, 41, 66, 67, 71
Vaughn, A. G., 151
Veijola, T., 101, 123, 161
Vervenne, M., 113, 114, 158

Wallace, H. N., 73
Weimar, P., 114, 157
Weinfeld, M., 2, 30, 44, 71, 72, 75, 76, 77, 78, 93, 109, 119, 138, 144, 158, 159
Weippert, H., 73, 105, 106, 119, 132, 134, 152
Weiser, A., 115
Wellhausen, J., 5, 32, 35, 36, 64, 66, 96, 102, 156
Wenham, G. J., 2, 128
Wesley, J., 14, 25
Westermann, K., 114, 115, 119, 139, 154
Wette, W. M. L. de, 14, 32, 33, 34, 36, 40
Wevers, J. W., 153
White, M. 111
Whitelam, K. W., 4, 118
Whybray, R. N., 70
Williamson, H. G. M., 153
Wolff, H. W., 45, 100
Wright, G. E., 1, 48, 55, 103
Würthwein, E., 73, 101, 116

Zimmerli, W., 153

# Index of Foreign Terms and Phrases

**Hebrew**

אָבֵל, 50
אֲדוֹמִים, 54
אָז, 74, 91
אֶל־הַמָּקוֹם אֲשֶׁר יִבְחַר, 71
אַל־תִּירָא, 76, 121
אַל־תַּעַרץ וְאַל־תֵּחָת, 76
אַלְמֻגִּים, 61
אֲרַמִּים, 54
אֶרֶץ כָּבוּל, 44
אִשֵּׁי יהוה, 79

בַּיּוֹם הַהוּא, 71, 75, 80, 88
בָּעֵת הַהִוא, 74, 91

גַּל־אֲבָנִים, 125, 127
גַּל־אֲבָנִים גָּדוֹל, 48, 76, 126

וַיְהִיוּ שָׁם, 125

חַוֹּת, 44, 77, 78
חֲזַק וֶאֱמָץ, 76

יהוה אֱלֹהֵי יִשְׂרָאֵל, 79

כַּאֲשֶׁר דִּבֶּר, 57, 79, 90, 154
כָּבוּל, 44
כִּדְבַר אֱלִישָׁע, 73

כִּדְבַר יהוה, 73
כַּיּוֹם הַזֶּה, 158

מִלֵּא אַחֲרֵי, 55, 72, 79, 121
מַס וַעֲבָדוּךְ, 80, 125, 128, 147
מַס־עֹבֵד, 55, 58, 59, 80, 81, 82, 121, 128, 147
מצבות, 61, 127, 146
מַצֶּבֶת, 49, 126

נַחֲלָה, 72, 79, 86, 88, 89, 90, 154
נָתַן, 84, 120, 121, 130, 147

עַד הַיּוֹם הַזֶּה, 37, 43, 59, 66, 73, 74, 75, 76, 77, 78, 79, 82, 86, 88, 89, 90, 91, 92, 94, 125, 126, 132, 154, 155, 159
עַד־הַיּוֹם הַהוּא, 43, 86
עַד הַיָּמִים הָהֵם, 43, 87
עַד־הֵנָּה, 43
עַד־יוֹם גְּלוֹת הָאָרֶץ, 86
עַד־עֶצֶם הַיּוֹם הַזֶּה, 43, 48
עַד־עָתָּה, 43, 133
עֵין הַקּוֹרֵא, 50
עֲיָרִים, 44
עֵמֶק עָכוֹר, 45
עָרִים, 44
עֶרֶשׂ בַּרְזֶל, 143

## Index of Foreign Terms and Phrases

פֶּרֶץ, 46

פתח שער העיר, 48

רַק, 79, 87, 130, 131, 140, 143, 153, 154, 155

תֵּל עוֹלָם, 75

### Akkadian

*elammukku*, 61
*ina tarṣi*, 74
*ina umišuma*, 74

### Arabic

eṣ-Ṣiyyāgh, 50
*ḥiwā*, 44

### Greek

ἄλλους δώδεκα λίθους, 49
ἐς ἐμὲ ἔτι, 137
ἐκάλεσεν, 49
ἕως τῆς ἡμέρας ταύτης, 52, 55
εἰς τὸν βόθρον, 48
λίθου, 50
μέγαν, 48
μέχρι ἐμεῦ, 137
ὅριον, 44
πόλεις, 44

### Latin

*alios quoque duodecim lapides*, 49
*civitatum*, 44
*lectio difficilior*, 58, 144
*lectio brevior*, 58
*nihil innovetur nisi quod traditum est*, 21
*sola scriptura*, 23
*vaticinium post eventum*, 102, 121

### Phoenician

*ke bal*, 44

# Index of Subjects

Abdon, 85, 86
Abelard, 20, 22, 23, 26, 40
Abiathar, 151
Abiezerites, 61
Abraham ben Moses ben Maimon, 10
Abraham ben Rambam, 10
Abraham, 133, 156
Abravanel, 5, 14, 15, 16, 17, 18, 25, 26, 31, 40, 90, 138, 142, 164
Absalom's Pillar, 5, 48, 49, 52, 64, 124, 126, 127, 137, 146
Acco, 44
Achan, 4, 16, 28, 45, 48, 75, 76, 125, 145
Achish, 55
Acts of Solomon, 38, 70, 123, 136, 142, 147, 149
Ahab, 33, 73, 105, 129, 131, 139
Ahaz, 54, 105
Ahaziah, 105
Ahijah, 97
Ai (king of), 52, 62, 76, 93, 145
Ai, 4, 48, 49, 50, 52, 55, 62, 75, 76, 126, 145
Alexander the Great, 28
allegorical interpretation, 21, 23
almug wood, 5, 61, 64
altar (of Baal), 62, 84, 130
altar (of YHWH), 58, 61, 64, 71, 81, 84, 127, 130
altars, 83, 84
alternate sites of worship, 76, 145, 146, 147
Amalekites, 12
Amaziah, 46, 91, 131
Ammon/Ammonite, 52, 144, 155
*amoraic*, 11, 12

Amorites, 48, 58, 82
Anathoth, 137
Andrew of Saint Victor, 9
Angel of Death, 12, 141
Aquila, 18, 50
Arabia, 61
Aram/Aramean, 54, 85, 91
Araunah, 15
Argob, 29, 43, 78
Ark (poles of), 5, 11, 27, 61, 62, 64, 89, 95, 120, 125
Ark Narrative, 70, 110, 147
Ark of the Covenant, 4, 5, 10, 11, 12, 13, 16, 17, 18, 27, 28, 31, 40, 46, 50, 52, 60, 61, 62, 65, 67, 79, 85, 88, 89, 90, 95, 120, 122, 123, 125, 131, 139, 143, 144, 145, 147, 148, 150, 163
Asa, 105, 129
Ashdod, 16, 89, 155
Asher, 44, 85
*asherah/asherim*, 83, 87
Assyria, 12, 42, 57, 74, 97, 117, 132, 134, 149
"at that time," 26, 29, 72, 74, 91, 149
"at the place he (YHWH) will choose," 59, 71, 81, 83, 120, 121, 122, 124, 128, 142, 145, 147, 148
Augustine, 5, 14, 20, 21, 22, 26, 27
authorial ascriptions, 5, 14, 15, 20, 22, 24, 30, 40, 41, 141
Azariah, 86
Azekah, 48

Baal (altar of), 62, 84, 130
Baal (pillar of), 61, 64
Baal (temple of), 5, 61, 85, 86, 130

Baal (worship of), 62, 64, 86, 120, 130, 131, 143, 161
Baale-Judah, 46
Baasha, 129
Babylon/Babylonians, 10, 11, 12, 20, 40, 64, 74, 117, 120, 134, 139, 149, 158, 160, 161, 162
Babylonian conquest, 10, 11, 20, 40, 74
Babylonian exile, 11, 57, 99, 102, 113, 119, 139, 161, 162
Babylonian Talmud, 10
*bāmāh/bāmôt*, 92, 103
ban (see also "*ḥerem*"), 5, 45, 48, 75, 76
Baruch ben Neriah, 104, 159, 160
Bashan (king of), 143
Bashan (place), 77, 78, 85, 86, 144
Bathsheba, 2
Beeroth/Beerothites, 33, 52, 124
Beer-Sheba, 55
Benjaminites, 11, 15, 52, 54, 55, 82, 137
Bethel (Beitin), 10, 12, 45, 49, 73, 76, 84, 92, 102, 103, 131
Bethlehem, 156
Beth-Peor, 13, 20, 46
Beth-Shemesh, 5, 16, 31, 50, 52, 62, 64, 86, 89
Bozrah, 46
bronze serpent, 48, 87, 92
burial notices, 106
burial place of Moses, 122
burnt offerings, 146
*bytdwd*, 2

Cabul, 44, 50, 57, 85, 86, 120, 133
Caleb/Calebites, 16, 55, 57, 72, 89, 90
calves (golden), 84, 131
Canaan, 4, 24, 45, 46, 97, 145, 148
Canaanites, 3, 16, 33, 38, 39, 54, 55, 81, 129, 131
Carchemish, 160
Celsus, 19
centralized worship, 72, 83, 87, 92, 108, 120, 121, 122, 133, 143, 145, 146, 147, 151
Christianity, 19
Chronicler, 89, 103, 123, 140, 153
Chronicles of the Kings of Israel, 70, 123, 136, 142, 147, 149, 152

Chronicles of the Kings of Judah, 38, 70, 74, 123, 136, 142, 147, 149, 152
Chronicles (books of), 28, 106
Church Fathers, 18, 19, 21
city of David, 106
collared-rim pottery, 117
conquest narratives, 26, 30, 33, 48, 54, 97, 99, 101, 107, 123, 132, 134, 147
Court History, 112, 113, 124, 125, 127, 157
Covenant (book of), 93
covenant ceremony, 93
covenant renewal, 81, 93, 121, 144
curse (on Jericho), 72, 73, 130, 144
Cyrus, 40

Dagon (image of), 60, 62, 89
Dagon (temple of), 60, 62, 89, 155
Dagon (priests of), 60, 155
*daleth/resh* confusion, 54
Damascene forces, 85
Dan (place), 2, 17, 84, 86, 87, 88, 131, 155
Dan (tribe of), 17
Daniel (book of), 15
Danites, 45, 88
David, 2, 3, 4, 5, 14, 15, 17, 22, 26, 29, 33, 34, 38, 46, 55, 58, 70, 86, 89, 90, 95, 100, 101, 102, 103, 106, 107, 110, 116, 118, 125, 127, 131, 132, 135, 137, 139, 140, 151, 157, 158
Davidic covenant, 3, 4, 102, 104, 113, 108
Davidic dynasty, 2, 3, 4, 55, 59, 108, 110, 135
Davidic state, 27, 89, 100, 108, 113, 121, 133, 139, 140, 151
Deir el-'Azar, 46
Delphi, 149
Deuteronomic law, 75, 97, 121, 123, 125, 128, 138, 144, 147, 150, 151, 153
Deuteronomistic Historian (Dtr), 18, 35, 36, 38, 39, 66, 67, 70, 71, 72, 73, 74, 75, 76, 77, 78, 79, 80, 81, 82, 83, 84, 85, 86, 87, 88, 89, 90, 91, 92, 93, 94, 95, 97, 98, 99, 100, 102, 106, 107, 108, 110, 111, 112, 113, 114, 115, 119,

*Index of Subjects* 197

120, 121, 122, 123, 124, 125, 126, 127, 128, 129, 130, 131, 132, 133, 134, 135, 136, 137, 138, 139, 140, 142, 143, 144, 145, 146, 148, 149, 151, 152, 153, 154, 155, 156, 157, 158, 162
Deuteronomistic History (DH), 3, 6, 7, 38, 39, 41, 42, 43, 49, 58, 62, 64, 65, 67, 70, 71, 72, 73, 76, 77, 80, 86, 87, 89, 90, 91, 92, 93, 94, 95, 96, 97, 98, 99, 100, 101, 102, 103, 104, 105, 106, 107, 108, 109, 110, 111, 112, 113, 114, 115, 116, 117, 118, 119, 120, 121, 122, 123, 124, 125, 127, 128, 129, 130, 131, 132, 133, 134, 135, 136, 139, 142, 144, 146, 147, 149, 151, 153, 154, 155, 156, 157, 158, 159, 160, 161, 162, 163
Deuteronomistic History (unity of), 99, 102, 107, 112, 128
Deuteronomistic interests/perspective, 35, 39, 67, 77, 81, 84, 92, 94, 104, 130, 143
Deuteronomistic language, 39, 71, 75, 77, 84, 88, 122, 130, 153
Deuteronomistic redaction, 36, 67, 71, 72, 84, 88, 93, 97, 115, 121, 128, 153, 158, 159
Deuteronomistic redactor(s), 35, 38, 39, 41, 66, 67, 72, 92, 110, 115, 116, 157
Deuteronomistic studies/scholarship, 6, 64, 95, 96, 103, 118, 119, 142
Deuteronomistic schools/circles, 78, 108, 109, 159
Deuteronomistic speeches, 97, 158
Deuteronomy (book of), 19, 20, 32, 44, 75, 76, 77, 80, 91, 93, 97, 99, 103, 108, 109, 113, 114, 115, 123, 133, 147
Deuteronomy (epilogue of), 123, 147
Deuteronomy (law code of), 123, 147
Deuteronomy (prologue of), 123, 147
"did what was right in the eyes of," 102, 105, 131, 140
dispossession, 16, 54, 55, 58, 60, 78, 81, 82, 83
divided monarchy, 97
"do not fear or be dismayed," 76, 121, 122, 142

Dtr (see "Deuteronomistic Historian")
Dtr$^1$, 39, 91, 103, 104, 114, 133, 134, 158, 159
Dtr$^2$, 103, 104, 107, 113, 114, 134, 157, 158, 159
DtrG, 101, 116
DtrH, 101, 116, 153
DtrN, 101, 116, 139, 140, 152
DtrP, 101, 116, 152
Dtr$^R$, 116
Dtr$^S$, 116
dual redaction (of the DH), 33, 39, 102

editorial technique (of Dtr), 72, 144
Edom/Edomites, 27, 29, 30, 46, 52, 54, 57, 59, 60, 64, 65, 67, 74, 84, 87, 89, 91, 120, 121, 133, 155
Egypt, 24, 28, 42, 45, 55, 83, 103, 118, 149, 154, 158, 159, 160, 161, 162, 163
El Buqê'ah, 45
Elath, 54, 57, 60, 91
Eleazer, 24, 40
Eliezer ben Hyrcanus, 10
Elijah, 50, 128, 130, 139
Elijah material, 129, 130,
Elijah-Elisha material, 70, 111, 123, 128, 129, 132
Elisha, 50, 70, 73, 111, 112, 123, 128, 129, 130, 132
Elisha material, 40, 112, 129
Elohist, 34, 96, 114, 156
Emek Achor (see "Valley of Achor")
Enlightenment, 26, 27
Enneateuch, 116
Ephraim/Ephraimites, 16, 54, 55, 81, 126, 161
epic poetry, 150
Esau, 52
es-Sela', 46
eternal kingship, 102
Eusebius, 46, 48
"evil in the eyes of YHWH," 105
exile, 11, 17, 18, 23, 28, 33, 35, 36, 40, 86, 92, 100, 101, 104, 113, 131, 135
exilic period, 100, 107, 108, 128, 134, 161
exodus from Egypt, 24, 162

## Index of Subjects

Ezekiel (book of), 19, 153
Ezra (person), 20, 23, 26, 40, 141
Ezra tradition, 20, 23, 26

fiefdom, 3, 100, 135
"follow fully after YHWH," 55, 72, 79, 82, 90, 121, 127, 142
forced labor(ers), 5, 16, 35, 55, 58, 59, 64, 65, 71, 80, 81, 82, 83, 85, 120, 121, 122, 124, 128, 137, 142, 147, 148
Former Prophets, 15, 18, 26, 33, 114, 116
four-roomed houses, 117

Gad (the seer), 17, 22
Gad (tribe of), 146
Gath, 54, 55
*gemara*, 12
genealogy, 106
Genesis (book of), 20, 30, 34, 114, 115, 154, 156, 157
Gerar, 156
Gershonites, 85, 86, 88, 155
Gersonides, 14, 40
Geshur/Geshurites, 44, 54, 57, 78, 81, 84, 85, 133, 154
Gezer/Gezerites, 33, 34, 38, 55, 59, 81, 86
Gibeon/Gibeonites, 16, 34, 52, 58, 80, 81, 83, 86
Gideon, 5, 49, 61, 84, 127, 130, 137
Gilead, 44, 77, 78, 126
Gilgal, 16, 28, 31, 45, 49, 50, 94
Girgashites, 58
Gittaim, 52, 124
Golan, 86
golden calf, 103
Göttingen school, 100, 101, 110, 119, 139, 152
Greek historians, 136, 143

Hamutal, 74
*haplography*, 45, 52, 58, 61
Hasmonean period, 117
Havvoth Jair, 43, 44, 50, 57, 59, 77, 78, 80, 82, 84, 85, 86, 120, 122, 133, 137, 142, 148

Hazor, 59
Hebron, 16, 55, 57, 72, 86, 89, 90
Helkath, 85, 86
Hellenistic period, 4, 117, 120
Hephaestus, 42
*ḥerem* (see also "ban"), 5, 76
heretic, 18
Herodotus, 42, 136, 137, 138, 149
heroic tales (of Judges), 150
"hewers of wood and drawers of water," 16, 58, 71, 81, 83
Hexapla, 18
Hexateuch, 34, 100, 101, 107, 115, 116
Hezekiah, 74, 87, 92, 105, 106, 107, 108, 114, 119, 132, 133, 134, 140, 146, 150, 151, 152, 161, 162
Hiel, 73, 130
high places, 87, 104, 105, 131, 143
Hilkiades, 139, 161
Hiram of Tyre, 44, 85
historical books, 4, 30, 31, 32, 114, 115
History of David's Rise, 70, 110, 123, 142, 147
Hittites, 12, 45, 58, 82, 140
Hivites, 58, 82, 83
Holy of Holies, 5, 11, 27, 61, 62, 64, 89, 95, 120, 125
Horites, 29, 52, 60
Horvat Rosh-Zayit, 44
Hosea (book of), 99, 113

Ibn Ezra, 14, 23, 25, 40
"in those days," 87
*ina tarṣi*, 74
*ina umišuma*, 74
inheritance lists, 85, 123, 127, 128, 147
inheritance rights, 90, 127, 147
inheritance, 16, 55, 72, 78, 79, 80, 82, 85, 86, 87, 88, 89, 90, 120, 122, 125, 128, 139, 149, 154, 155
Iron Age, 44, 117
iron bedstead (King of Bashan's), 143
Isaiah (person), 11
Israel, 1, 2, 3, 4, 5, 6, 7, 17, 18, 21, 22, 26, 27, 29, 32, 37, 39, 43, 44, 45, 49, 52, 54, 55, 57, 58, 59, 61, 62, 64, 65, 71, 72, 74, 76, 78, 79, 80, 81, 82, 83, 84,

## Index of Subjects    199

85, 87, 88, 90, 92, 94, 96, 97, 98, 99, 103, 105, 107, 108, 109, 112, 113, 116, 117, 118, 120, 122, 123, 124, 127, 129, 130, 131, 132, 133, 134, 135, 136, 137, 138, 139, 140, 142, 145, 146, 148, 149, 150, 151, 152, 154, 155, 159, 160, 161, 163, 164
Israel (fall of), 2, 65, 87, 92, 105, 108, 118, 133, 149, 150
Israel (history of), 3, 65, 118, 143, 152
Israelite historiography, 1, 6, 116
Israelites, 2, 3, 4, 12, 15, 26, 29, 34, 45, 48, 49, 54, 58, 62, 65, 78, 80, 81, 94, 117, 121, 125, 145, 147, 148, 155

Jacob, 20, 92, 133, 155, 156
Jahwist (source), 34, 96, 113, 156
Jair (the Gileadite), 44, 77, 78
Jair (son of Manasseh), 29, 43, 77, 78
Jebusites, 11, 14, 15, 16, 25, 26, 33, 34, 38, 54, 58, 59, 81, 82, 83, 128, 137, 142
Jehoahaz, 74
Jehoash, 84, 129, 131, 139
Jehoiachin, 4, 10, 98, 100, 108
Jehoiada, 131
Jehoiakim, 160, 161, 162
Jehoram, 59, 60, 74, 105
Jehoshaphat, 105, 129
Jehu, 3, 5, 61, 84, 111, 119, 130, 131, 139, 140
Jephunneh, 16, 72, 89
Jeremiah (book of), 19, 99, 109, 138, 156, 158, 159, 160, 161, 162, 163
Jeremiah (person), 17, 18, 22, 104, 138, 153, 159, 160, 161, 162, 163, 164
Jeremiah (scroll of), 162
Jericho, 33, 45, 48, 50, 54, 72, 73, 75, 94, 122, 128, 130, 142, 144, 145
Jeroboam, 57, 84, 86, 102, 103, 105, 131, 150
Jerome, 19, 20, 23, 40, 141
Jerusalem (fall of), 104, 112
Jerusalem, 3, 5, 11, 12, 14, 15, 16, 25, 26, 27, 33, 34, 38, 40, 44, 46, 49, 54, 55, 59, 60, 61, 64, 65, 81, 82, 83, 89, 99, 108, 113, 121, 126, 128, 134, 137, 142, 146, 148, 149, 150, 151, 158, 161

Jerusalem Talmud, 11
Jesus, 19
Jezreel, 61
Joash, 131
Jokneam, 86
Joktheel, 46, 50, 91
Jonathan (son of Gershom), 17
Jordan River, 4, 49, 50, 52, 62, 76, 88, 126, 137
Josephus, 44, 49, 50
Joshua (book of), 5, 16, 17, 18, 20, 24, 26, 27, 28, 30, 31, 34, 35, 36, 38, 66, 67, 71, 75, 76, 77, 78, 83, 92, 93, 94, 96, 109, 122, 128, 136, 142
Joshua (field of), 16, 31, 50
Joshua (person), 4, 5, 14, 15, 16, 22, 24, 25, 27, 28, 31, 34, 40, 58, 59, 71, 73, 74, 75, 76, 88, 93, 94, 98, 148
Joshua's curse, 33, 73, 122, 130
Joshua's reading of the Law, 36
Josiah, 32, 74, 76, 84, 88, 89, 91, 92, 93, 94, 95, 102, 103, 104, 105, 106, 107, 108, 109, 110, 111, 114, 119, 121, 122, 128, 131, 133, 134, 135, 136, 139, 142, 143, 144, 148, 150, 151, 157, 159, 160, 161, 162, 163
Josianic edition of the DH, 102, 105, 106, 119, 120, 132, 134, 152
Josianic reforms, 36, 102, 110, 135, 151
Judah (bar Ilai), 11, 14
Judah (ben Lakish), 11
Judah (kings of), 16, 31, 55, 64, 89, 90, 98, 99, 104, 116
Judah (kingdom of), 27, 58, 59, 60, 64, 87, 89, 90, 91, 92, 98, 99, 102, 104, 109, 117, 120, 121, 133, 137, 140, 160, 161, 162, 163
Judahite-Edomite relations, 91, 143, 147
Judges (book of), 14, 17, 18, 22, 28, 35, 61, 77, 78, 123, 128, 147
Judges (epilogue of), 123, 147
Judges (heroic tales of), 123, 147
judges (period of), 45, 97, 98, 99, 107, 116, 135
Judges (prologue of), 147
Justinian, 18

## Index of Subjects

Kabul, 44
Kedesh, 86
Kenizzite, 16, 72, 89
*Ketib*, 54
Khirbet 'Ayun Musa, 48
Khirbet el-Mefjir, 45
Khirbet el-Meḥaṭṭa, 48
Khirbet esh-Sheikh Jayil, 48
Khirbet es -Ṣiyyāgh, 50
Khirbet Ras ez-Zeitun, 44
Kidron Valley, 49
*Kinderfrage*, 4, 145, 146
King's Valley, 49, 50, 64, 126
Kings (books of), 17, 18, 22, 27, 28, 30, 33, 35, 36, 38, 64, 66, 67, 70, 71, 77, 83, 84, 91, 92, 94, 96, 99, 102, 103, 106, 107, 109, 111, 113, 116, 123, 128, 138, 147, 154, 158, 162
Kiriath-Jearim, 46, 88
Königsberg, 98

Lachish, 48
latrine, 5, 61, 62, 84
law (book of), 103
law (of Moses), 93, 107, 116, 140
law (of the king), 93, 138, 148
law (Dtr's interest in), 101
Lebanon, 45
*lectio difficilior*, 58, 144
*lectio brevior*, 58
Lehi, 49, 50, 64
Levi (tribe of), 79, 80, 85, 90, 127, 154
Levi, (inheritance of), 79, 80, 90, 127, 154
Levites, 60, 62, 64, 78, 79, 80, 82, 84, 85, 86, 88, 90, 121, 122, 125, 127, 138, 143, 147, 148, 149, 150, 151, 155
Levitical authority, 139
Levitical cities, 85, 86
Levitical priests, 13, 67, 79, 85, 86, 88, 120, 122, 127, 145, 147, 148, 150, 161
Leviticus (book of), 114
Libnah, 74, 86, 87, 91, 92
Lot, 155
Luz, 12, 45, 141
LXX, 18, 43, 44, 46, 48, 49, 50, 52, 54, 55, 57, 58, 61, 62, 77, 144, 155

Maacah/Maacathites, 44, 54, 57, 78, 81, 85, 133, 154
Maccabean, 117
Mahaneh Dan, 45, 46, 50, 88
Maimonides, 10
Makkedah, 48, 50, 52, 62, 75, 145
Mamre, 156
Manasseh (tribe of), 44, 54
maximalists, 3
Megiddo, 59, 102
Mesopotamia, 57
Michal, 86
Migdal Eder, 156
minimalists, 3, 116
Mizpah, 128, 134
Moab, 13, 19, 20, 46, 125, 155
monarchy, 2, 3, 91, 97, 101, 107, 108, 111, 112, 118, 123, 135, 137, 138, 139, 140, 143, 151, 152, 157, 158, 161
Mosaic covenant, 107, 108
Moses, 2, 5, 10, 13, 14, 17, 19, 20, 22, 23, 24, 25, 26, 27, 28, 29, 30, 31, 34, 36, 40, 46, 60, 77, 79, 81, 86, 87, 93, 97, 101, 103, 125, 141, 143, 144, 145, 146, 148, 149, 150, 153, 158, 162, 163
Moses (death of), 10, 13, 14, 24
Moses (law of), 93, 107, 116, 140
Moses (tomb of), 48, 146
Mount Carmel, 130
Mount Ebal, 77, 79, 121, 122, 142, 144, 145, 146
Mount Nebo, 46, 48
Mount Seir, 29
Mushaqqar ridge, 48
Mushite, 85

name theology, 87
Nathan, 17, 22, 139
Nebath, 84
Nebuchadnezzar, 10, 12, 160
Negev, 1, 55, 91, 121, 133
Nehushtan, 87
Nicholas of Lyra, 23
*nomistic*, 101, 140, 152, 161
northern kingdom, 55, 57, 59, 84, 92, 97
Numbers (book of), 115

## Index of Subjects    201

offerings of YHWH, 79, 139, 148, 149
Ophir, 61
Ophrah, 5, 61, 62, 64, 84, 85, 126, 127, 130, 137
oral transmission, 149
Origen, 18, 19, 40, 61
Oxford, 28, 29

Palestine, 2, 4, 117, 118
Passover, 93, 94, 121, 122, 143, 144
Pausanias, 42, 136
Pekah, 105
Pentateuch, 20, 22, 27, 29, 30, 34, 36, 101, 107, 108, 113, 114, 115, 116, 141, 156, 157
Pentateuchal traditions, 72, 96, 107
Perez-Uzzah, 5, 46, 50, 62, 89
Perizzites, 58, 82
Persian period, 3, 4, 116, 117, 120
Petra, 46
Pharaoh, 33, 38, 55, 154
Philistia/Philistines, 5, 16, 17, 31, 49, 50, 52, 55, 62
Phogor (Beth-Peor), 19, 20
pile of stones, 4, 48, 62, 76, 93, 120, 126
Pillar of Absalom, 5, 48, 49, 52, 64, 124, 126, 127, 137, 146
pillars, 61, 83, 84, 87
Pope Stephen I, 21
postDtr redaction, 112, 124, 127, 128, 129, 130, 132
postexilic period, 2, 3, 112, 113, 119, 132
postexilic scribes, 117, 118
preDtr redaction, 110, 153
preexilic edition of DH, 3, 38, 39, 89, 102
preexilic period, 33, 89, 95, 108, 147, 152, 161
preexilic redactor, 104
preexilic sources, 3, 117
pre-Nothian models, 114
Priestly source, 34, 36, 79, 113, 114, 116
priestly/prophetic, 123, 139, 140, 143, 149, 151
priests (of Baal), 61
priests (of Dagon), 16, 31, 60, 155

Primary History, 114, 138, 154
propaganda (DH as), 95, 102, 111, 119, 135, 151
prophecy-fulfillment, 73, 122, 130, 139, 144, 149
prophetic authority, 110, 139, 140
prophetic circles, 64, 99, 108, 123, 139, 149, 151
prophetic history/record, 110, 111, 119, 123, 132, 134
prophetic interests, 110, 111, 153
prophetic word, 73, 130, 139, 148, 149
prophets, 17, 55, 90, 123, 129, 139, 152
prophets (of Baal), 130

*Qere*, 54

Rabanus Maurus, 22
Rabbah bar Nahamani, 11, 12
Rachel's tomb, 24, 156
Radak, 14, 15, 23, 40, 41, 59, 65
Rahab, 21, 22, 26, 37, 54, 72, 74, 78
Rahabites, 54
Ramoth-Gilead, 86
Rashbam, 14, 40
Rashi, 11, 13, 14, 23, 40
$R^I$, 99, 101, 105, 111
$R^{II}$, 99, 101, 105
$R^{III}$, 105
$R^D$, 156
$Rd^1$, 35, 66
$R^{JE}$, 156
Red Sea, 91, 121, 133
redactional technique, 74, 75, 127, 155
Reformation, 23
reforms, 32, 84, 92, 93, 95, 107, 108, 111, 121, 135, 136, 139, 150, 151, 159, 161, 163
regnal formulae, 104, 105, 106, 131
Rehob, 85, 86
Rehoboam, 59, 105
Rephaim, 144
Reubenites, 146
Rezin, 54, 91
Richard Simon, 31, 32
Rise of David, 40
Roman historians, 136, 143

## Index of Subjects

royal annals, 70, 123, 129
royal history, 99, 107, 116, 132, 153
Ruth (book of), 22, 27
Ruth (person), 28

sacrifice, 61, 105, 146, 151, 161
Samaria, 5, 62, 64, 84, 85, 92, 110, 130
Samaritan Pentateuch, 143
Samson, 49
Samuel (books of), 17, 18, 22, 28, 31, 35, 90, 96, 123, 138, 147
Samuel (person), 16, 17, 18, 22, 25, 31, 86, 97, 110, 139, 151, 153
Saul, 33, 34, 54, 90, 106, 110, 111, 137, 139
scribal circles/schools, 109, 117, 119
Sea of Galilee, 44
seer, 17, 164
Segub, 73
Seir, 52, 57, 60, 91, 121
Sela, 46, 60, 91
Sennacherib, 12, 42
Sethos, 42
Shaphanides, 159
Shechem, 20, 157
Shephelah, 48, 55
Shiloh, 97, 137, 161
Shilonites, 135
Shimon (ben Lakish), 11
Simeon (bar Yohai), 10, 13, 40
Simeonites, 12
Sinai, 98
*sola scriptura*, 23
Solomon, 1, 5, 15, 33, 34, 44, 55, 58, 59, 61, 80, 82, 83, 85, 95, 97, 99, 106, 116
sources, 3, 18, 19, 33, 34, 36, 38, 39, 40, 42, 64, 65, 66, 67, 70, 74, 87, 98, 99, 107, 110, 112, 114, 115, 118, 119, 121, 123, 124, 128, 129, 134, 136, 138, 139, 140, 142, 143, 147, 149, 153, 156, 157, 162
Spinoza, 5, 14, 30, 31, 40, 142
spiritual meaning, 22
Spring of the Caller, 50, 64
springs, 49, 50, 64
Succession Narrative, 40, 70, 99, 110, 123, 147

Symmachus, 18, 50
Syria, 45, 57, 85
Syro-Palestinian, 118

Talmud, 10, 11, 12, 13, 14, 31
*tannaim*, 10
Targumim, 43, 54, 62, 144
Tel Dan, 2
tel of perpetual ruin, 75
Tell el-Jazari, 55
Tell el-Khuweilfeh, 55
Tell en-Nitla, 45
Tell esh-Shari'a, 55
Tell es-Sultan, 50
temple of Baal, 5, 61, 62, 84, 130, 131
temple of Dagon, 16, 62, 155
Temple Sermon, 161
temple, 5, 11, 12, 31, 34, 42, 44, 59, 61, 62, 64, 71, 81, 83, 84, 85, 87, 89, 95, 97, 108, 120, 121, 124, 128, 130, 151, 158, 161, 162, 163
Ten Commandments, 11
Tetrateuch, 101, 107, 114, 153, 154, 156, 157, 158
Tetrateuchal sources, 108, 114
Theodotion, 18
threshold, 16, 31, 60, 62, 155
threshold (of Dagon), 16, 62, 155
Thucydides, 42, 136, 159
Timnah, 50
"to the right or to the left," 93, 102, 140, 148
tomb of Rachel, 24
Torah, 10, 13, 15, 19, 20, 24, 26, 31, 92, 116, 122, 143, 144, 148, 149, 153, 162, 163
Tosefta, 11
Transjordan, 44, 54
Transjordanian tribes, 146
tribal allotments, 85
twelve stones, 4, 21, 28, 31, 49, 50, 52, 76, 146
twelve tribes, 49
two-and-a-half tribes, 54

Ugaritic, 61
'Ulla, 11, 12, 14

Umm el-Bayyârah, 46
unevenness (as indication of redactional layers), 117, 129, 130, 132
united monarchy, 90, 117, 118
"until that day," 87, 92
"until the day of the exile of the land," 86, 87
"until this day," 1, 4, 5, 6, 7, 9, 10, 11, 12, 13, 14, 15, 16, 17, 18, 19, 20, 21, 22, 23, 24, 25, 26, 27, 28, 29, 30, 32, 33, 34, 35, 36, 37, 38, 39, 40, 41, 42, 43, 44, 45, 46, 47, 48, 49, 50, 51, 52, 53, 54, 55, 56, 57, 58, 59, 60, 61, 62, 63, 64, 65, 66, 67, 70, 71, 72, 73, 74, 75, 76, 77, 78, 79, 80, 81, 82, 83, 84, 85, 86, 87, 88, 89, 90, 91, 92, 93, 94, 95, 118, 119, 120, 121, 122, 124, 125, 126, 127, 128, 129, 130, 131, 132, 133, 134, 137, 138, 139, 141, 142, 143, 144, 145, 146, 147, 148, 152, 153, 154, 155, 156, 157, 158, 160, 161, 162, 163, 164
"until those days," 87, 146
Uriah, 140
Uzzah (person), 5, 46, 62, 89

Valley of Achor (Emek Achor), 4, 16, 28, 37, 45, 48, 50, 62, 145
Valley of Salt, 46, 60, 91
Valley of Trouble (see "Valley of Achor")

*vaticinium post eventum*, 102, 121
Vulgate, 43, 44, 49, 54, 58, 62

Wâdī Dabr, 45
Wâdī en-Naj l, 50
Wâdī en-Nár, 45
Wâdī en-Nuwē'ime, 45
war spoils, 58, 120, 145
Wellhausen, 5, 32, 35, 36, 64, 66, 96, 102, 156
Wesley, 14, 25
wisdom literature, 109
wisdom tradition, 109
word of YHWH, 73
World War II, 98
worship (centralization of) 83, 108, 121, 151

Yahwist, 112, 157
Yehud, 4, 117
YHWH, 5, 10, 13, 34, 42, 45, 46, 49, 52, 55, 57, 58, 59, 60, 61, 62, 72, 73, 75, 76, 79, 82, 83, 84, 87, 88, 89, 90, 101, 102, 108, 121, 125, 127, 131, 133, 135, 137, 139, 140, 142, 145, 146, 148, 152, 154, 158, 160, 162, 163
YHWH Shalom (altar of), 5, 61

Zedekiah, 74, 161, 162, 163
Ziklag, 55, 57, 64, 89, 90, 120

www.ingramcontent.com/pod-product-compliance
Lightning Source LLC
Chambersburg PA
CBHW021856230426
43671CB00006B/412